*Home Away from Home*

THE BASQUE SERIES

# Home Away from Home

## A HISTORY OF BASQUE BOARDINGHOUSES

Jeronima Echeverria

UNIVERSITY OF NEVADA PRESS, RENO & LAS VEGAS

Basque Series Editor: William A. Douglass

University of Nevada Press, Reno, Nevada 89557 USA

Manufactured in the United States of America
Design by Kristina Kachele

Library of Congress Cataloging-in-Publication Data
Echeverria, Jeronima, 1946–
Home away from home : a history of Basque boardinghouses / by Jeronima Echeverria.
p. cm. — (Basque Series)
Includes bibliographical references.
ISBN 0-87417-329-9 (hardcover : alk. paper)
1. Hotels—West (U.S.)—History. 2. Boardinghouses—West (U.S.)—History.
3. Basque Americans—West (U.S.)—History. I. Title. II. Series.
TX909.E28 1999
647.9478'03'0899992—dc21 99-20593
CIP

The paper used in this book meets the requirements of American National Standard for Information Sciences—Permanence of Paper for Printed Library Materials, ANSI Z39.48-1984. Binding materials were selected for strength and durability.

*This book has been reproduced as a digital reprint.*

ISBN 978-1-948908-52-8 (paper : alk. paper)

*for my parents, Sofia and David*

*and for my friend Lentxo*

Winnemucca
Hotel & Bar
BASQUE &
AMERICAN
FAMILY
COOKING
Coors
BEER
HOTE
BASQUE FOOD

# Contents

## ILLUSTRATIONS

MAPS

## TABLES

# *Preface*

For the past century and a half, Basque immigrants have relied upon the *ostatua Amerikanuak* (hotels and boardinghouses of the American Basques) to help them find their way in the American West. At the Basque hotels, they found a familiar language, cuisine, and culture to ease their way in their new homeland. In later decades, generation after generation of their offspring returned to the *ostatuak* to discover and maintain their Basque identity.

Despite the fact that this ethnic institution was critical to Basques' adaptation to the New World and that the *ostatuak* were the major ethnic institution of Basques before the arrival of their families, next to nothing has been written about them. *Home Away From Home* records the emergence of Basque boardinghouses and describes their critical role in Basque-American communities.

This work on the *ostatu Amerikanuak* is the result of several treasured personal and professional experiences. When I was younger, my parents David and Sofia took me, my brother, and sister to Robidart's Centro Vasco Hotel, to La Puente's Valley Hotel, and to Bakersfield's Noriega and Amestoy Hotels. With them, in these settings, we learned about the *ostatuak* firsthand.

Years later, under the tutelage of generous and patient mentors William A. Douglass, Richard W. Etulain, and Gus Seligmann, this work developed into a scholarly pursuit. Without Seligmann's encouragement, Douglass's vision, and Etulain's editorial guidance, the project would not have materialized. Librarians, research assistants, and colleagues at the Basque Studies Library in Reno, at the Idaho Historical in Boise, at the Bancroft in Berkeley, and at the Henry Madden Library at California State University, Fresno, have provided invaluable assistance and encouragement. Robert Boyd of Oregon's High Desert Museum shared his photographs for this book and deserves special thanks. Professor Thomas Carter and his students from the University of Utah's School of Architecture contributed their field drawings of existing *ostatuak*. Some, like graduate assitant Dominique Comeyne, copy editor Maggie Carr, and Sara Vélez Mallea of the Basque Book Series have given an extra measure to improve the quality of the manuscript. Perhaps most importantly, hundreds of Amerikanuak—like Lentxo Echanis, Lyda Esain, and Elena Celayeta Talbott, Lucia Osa, Jay Hormaechea, and Maria Echanis—gave me the heart and soul of this work by allowing me the privilege of sharing their stories here.

Most scholars dealing with Basque topics have to wrestle with the highly dialectical Basque language, Euskara. That is, should one use the modern unified version of Basque, *batua*, throughout the narrative? If so, should *batua* replace the native speaker's voice if he or she is speaking in Bizkaian, for example? If the speaker is a Basque who has long since dropped his native Euskara and has adopted Spanish as his primary language, what should be done? I have chosen the speaker's voice when possible, employing Basque and non-Basque terms when they were used consistently by the people I interviewed. Thus *batua*, Gipuzkoan, French, or broken English may appear in direct quotations. When linguistic variations among Amerikanuak have appeared, I have attempted to select terms mostly closely associated with the speakers or regions under study.

Additional methodological questions arise when one is considering the *ostatuak*. In several locations, for example, boardinghouses were known by the operator's surname, but the business either had no name or if there was one it was unattainable. Occasionally only a mention of an *ostatu* exists. That is, a few people have reported that they remembered hearing of the place, but documentation was not available. Also census takers, public recorders, and local authors have frequently misspelled Basque surnames. In these cases, the spelling appears as it was discovered in the historical record, with likely errors noted for accuracy in the endnotes.

This book began over ten years ago when I started visiting Basque picnics throughout the eleven Western states and asking for information on the *ostatuak*. At each Basque picnic, I identified the community elders, asked them about the local *ostatuak*, and asked them who could tell me more. This process, repeated several times over, resulted in a remarkable journey. Interviewing led me into *hoteleros'* homes, into their lives, into county and statewide historical collections, into private holdings of letters, memorabilia, and artifacts, out on the range and into the mountains. Although the *ostatuak* presented herein were often located first within the memory span of the people I spoke with or whose interviews I consulted, historical documentation, scholarly and popular literature, and local directories corroborated their existence. And although this study has generated more *ostatuak* than have been previously collected, several Basque boardinghouses lie beyond human memory and will remain unrecorded. For them, and for those I remember fondly, I offer this history of the Basuqe *ostatu* in the full knowledge that several may remain unrecorded.

# Prologue

## Lentxo: Coming to Amerika, Basque-Style

Like so many sons and daughters of Euskadi, as a sixteen-year-old Lentxo Echanis braved the Atlantic in the first decades of the twentieth century to come to America. And, like so many of his countrymen, over the course of his eighty years in the United States he relied upon Basque boardinghouses. In exchange for the promise of loyal patronage and friendship, Basque *hoteleros* provided food and shelter, arranged jobs, encouraged recreation, and served as translators for Lentxo and other newly arrived Basques.[1] Unlike the hotels and *pensiones* of Euskadi, however, the *ostatu* was a New World institution, appearing first in Buenos Aires and Montevideo, Uruguay, and later in California immediately following the gold rush.[2]

In the early decades of the twentieth century, Basque boardinghouses spread throughout the American West, and eventually they sprung up on the eastern seaboard once transcontinental travel via railway was established in the 1870s. Thus the network of *ostatuak* crisscrossing the United States and the influential *hoteleros* who operated them were critical to the immigration story of the Basques, especially during their peak years of immigration, 1890–1930. The Basques' immigration experience is reflected in Lentxo Enchanis's sojourn "to Amerika," his rail trip crossing the Great Plains, his settlement in the Boise and Steens Mountain area, and his eventual resettlement in southern California.

In 1914, at the age of sixteen, Lentxo decided to leave his birthplace and "go to work in Amerika." He had received a letter from his older brothers Joe and Jack who reported that work in the Crowley, Crane, and Steen's Mountain area of southeastern Oregon was plentiful and rewarding. The elder Echanises encouraged him to leave Mutriku, Gipuzkoa, and join them quickly, because they had expanded their herd and desperately needed an additional herder. When the letter arrived, Lentxo was earning seventy *centavos* a day working at a rifle and munitions factory in the neighboring village of Eibar.[3] He was putting in a minimum of six ten-hour days per week, paying his employers for room and board on the premises, sharing a healthy portion of his take-home pay with his parents, and dreaming of a more comfortable future.

Lentxo's parents, Benita and Joxemari, were saddened by their youngest son's decision to leave, but they were not surprised. Because his parents rented their small *baserri* overlooking Mutriku, neither Lentxo nor his older siblings could inherit the Echanis *baserri*, *mendi beltza*, meaning "black" or "dark mountain." Later in life Lentxo described his options as a young man: "Back there, I had no future. But here I had brothers in sheep. You know, it's a sad thing, thinking of my mother and father, that all of their children came here. But there were no chances for us in Mutriku."[4]

Lentxo's final days at the factory passed quickly as he dreamt of his future in America. After his last week at the factory, on Sunday morning he walked through Eibar heading for the bus that would take him to Mutriku's central plaza, just as he had always done on his usual Sunday visits home. He anticipated his climb up the steep hills overlooking Mutriku to *mendi beltza*. Lentxo envisioned the family's meager kitchen and remembered scenes from his childhood. Over the years he, his brothers and parents had sat around that table, each holding a hand-carved spoon and eating from the family's only wooden bowl, placed at the center of the table so that all could reach it. The bowl usually contained warm cornmeal and milk at dawn or a hearty garlic-laced soup at sunset. As he approached *mendi beltza* he mused to himself that it seemed odd that although the family now had more dishes, "only two of us will remain to use them." He wondered whether he or his brothers would ever return, thinking, "Will I be the last Echanis to talk with *Ama* and *Aita*? Will this be my final time at *mendi beltza*?" He had a feeling he would never see his parents or the family home ever again. In both regards his suspicions were borne out in later years.

During that final stay in the *baserri* of his childhood, Lentxo spent a few weeks helping his father clear land and work the crops. He said his good-byes to neighbors and extended family, arranged his travel plans, and raised money for the trip. Of the $150 he thought he would need, Lentxo had saved one third from his work in Eibar. A generous aunt loaned him the balance—and it took him over a decade to repay the loan. Arranging for passports in Gernika, reserving train travel to Hendaia and sea passage by steamship, and buying an $11 travel suit constituted Lentxo's largest pre-trip expenses. The teenager monitored his expenditures carefully. He had to have money on hand upon arrival in the United States, since he knew he would be required to present $30 in gold at the Ellis Island Immigration Center and that the cost of traveling across the United States might be steep.

Lentxo left Europe for the United States just before World War I erupted, as did tens of thousands of other southern Europeans. When the train from his homeland arrived at Hendaia, France, where he would embark on his ocean voyage, he headed for the harbor immediately. Dockside, he spotted an enormous white ship with gray and black smoke billowing from its two smokestacks. It was the largest oceangoing vessel he had ever seen, and certainly the first he had seen close up. Within a few hours the somewhat stunned sixteen-year-old was climbing her gangplanks with about five hundred other anxious travelers.[5] Owing to unseasonably rough weather, the crossing that was anticipated to take six days took fourteen. During the four most violent days of the journey, the seasick, disoriented teenager clung to his bunk, because he found climbing to the main deck and battling the relentless motion of the ship more nauseating than lying still.

On the one calm night during the two-week journey, on the evening after the storm had passed, a Basque bound for Homedale, Idaho, named Toritxu led the small Basque contingent from the steerage compartment up to the main deck. There Toritxu played his concertina while his fellow passengers danced the *aurresku* and *porrusalda*. Lentxo described the scene many decades later: "It was the only peaceful or happy time I remember on the ship. We were happy to have made it through the storm, and I was happy to have a few Gipuzkoans and Bizkaians to talk and dance with."

That same evening, Lentxo danced with a young woman whom he later referred to as Maitia from Lekeitio. In the following days of the journey, they talked frequently, discovering to their mutual delight that they were both destined for work in southern Idaho and southeastern Oregon.

Soon thereafter, Lentxo, Maitia, and a few of their traveling companions vowed to take the transcontinental portion of their journey together, and, thereafter, to stay in contact after they settled in America.

When they arrived at the Ellis Island Immigration Center, however, the ship's Basque contingent was separated into three lines in the Great Reception Hall. After passing through a series of waiting lines and intimidating inspections together, Lentxo and Toritxu exited the building with relief and excitement. Joining some of the other Basques who had collected outside, they learned that Maitia had been detained within. One of the women told them that an inspector had spotted Maitia's slightly deformed left hand, and that Maitia would be sent back to Hendaia on the same ship that had carried them across the Atlantic. Despite the Basques' pleas for leniency on Maitia's behalf, the inspectors stood firm. Much later in life Lentxo remembered how he felt about learning the news that Maitia would not be permitted to enter the United States: "My heart was sick. I didn't even know if I wanted to stay here anymore. Inside there [Ellis] we were treated like a bunch of stupid jackasses in a line. Now they weren't going to let that sweet girl come in. We couldn't say good-bye to her or nothing."

Lentxo and the small band of sojourners had no choice but to recoil from the news and collect themselves, for they had gained admission and could not turn back. Thankfully, their spirits lifted dramatically when they heard a young man shouting, "*Kaixo. Eskualduna zara?*" ("Hello. Are there any Basques here?")[6] After a brief moment of disbelief, the small band joyfully scurried to the man's side. It was Tomas Aguirre. He and his brothers Peter and John used to take turns welcoming transatlantic arrivals from Spain and France and escorting elated patrons to their father's famous boardinghouse on Cherry Street in Greenwich Village.

As others have noted, the boardinghouse of Benita and Valentin Aguirre was legendary among Basque Americans. In addition to greeting newcomers warmly, Valentin had become known for being a master at arranging all the details of traveling in this vast country. He helped fellow Basques book travel to and from New York City, recommended other *ostatuak* along the way, and, with the help of his sons, delivered sojourners to their point of departure on time. In fact, numerous Basque Americans have referred to Aguirre's as "the Basque travel agency" of its time. Consequently, many Basques—including Lentxo—would return to the Aguirres' boardinghouse decades later while en route to Euskadi, or during subsequent trips to the eastern seaboard. They would also strongly encourage their friends and relatives to stop at Valentin's whenever they were traveling through or to New York City.

For two days and one night, Lentxo enjoyed the familiar and warm surroundings of Valentin's boardinghouse on Cherry Street. There he recovered from his seafaring voyage, ate heartily, discussed Idaho and Oregon with newfound friends, and prepared for the long train ride west. When he was ready to depart, one of Valentin's sons took him to the train station, handed him a package of sandwiches, fruit, and wine, and pointed him in the direction of the westward-bound train.

Lentxo showed the train conductor a detailed note, written by Valentin in English, describing the details of his route. As Echanis recalled years later, he showed that slip of paper to everyone he encountered between New York and Boise. At times during the three-thousand-mile trek, Echanis found himself either staring at Valentin's indecipherable handwriting or unconsciously clinging to the one slip of paper that made him and his destination intelligible to strangers.

In 1914 Ogden, Utah, was the end of the line for direct rail travel from New York and the major switching station for westward-bound train travel. As Lentxo stepped onto the train platform in Ogden, he spotted a row of small businesses across the street, among them the small Basque boardinghouse that Valentin Aguirre had described. To Lentxo's delight, it was as easy to find as Valentin had promised. Even though he could neither read nor speak English, Lentxo had successfully negotiated the first leg of his journey across America. At that Ogden boardinghouse, Lentxo ate, bathed, and slept soundly in his sparsely furnished room. The next morning, he had breakfast with some Basque herders from the Intermountain and Great Basin regions. He listened attentively to their stories about herding, about dealing with Americans, and about surviving the long days and nights in the sheep camps. Early that afternoon, after checking to see if he still had Valentin's instructions, the young Gipuzkoan walked back across the street, held up his note and tickets, and boarded a train bound for Boise. On the train, a Pocatello-bound Basque named Domingo called Lentxo over to sit with him. Later they stopped and dined at the small rooming house owned by Domingo's cousin in Pocatello, and Lentxo was tempted to linger a few nights before moving on to Boise. But reluctantly Lentxo moved on. Had he had the time while en route to Boise, Lentxo also could have visited Florencio and Antonia Uriaguerecas' boardinghouse in Gooding or Jose Bengochea's Basque Hotel in Mountain Home.[7] But Lentxo was compelled to follow his brothers' instructions, which were to "go directly to a Basque hotel in Boise and stay there until we come into town for you." By the time Lentxo reached Idaho, he had begun to realize that boardinghouses and the Basques who frequented them were generally easy to locate. Most boardinghouses could be found a block or two from a railroad station, and to make sure he had the right place he had only to stand near the front door of a prospective *ostatu* and listen for the voices of his countrymen speaking Euskara within. With less trepidation than in Ogden, then, he disembarked in Boise and began looking for the town's Basque district.[8]

This time, however, the search proved more difficult. The Boise train station was unique in that it was a little farther from the central *ostatuak* on Idaho, Grove, and Eighth Streets. When Lentxo exited the station, he stared at the Boise River and the bluff that rose up above it. Behind him were the comparatively tall buildings of downtown Boise with the state capitol's dome towering above them. Remembering that Valentin and Peter Aguirre had described numerous boardinghouses as being located in the center of town, Lentxo set off on foot in the direction of what seemed to be downtown.

A few minutes after crossing the tracks of the Oregon Short Line, he entered a busy neighborhood where he heard Euskara being spoken. In very little time he knew he was in the right neighborhood and began inquiring about where he might find a night's lodging.[9] There was a long list of *ostatuak* to choose from in those days: among them Benito Arego's, José Arregui's, the Uberuagas', Anduiza's, the Belausteguis', Barbero's, Antonio Letemendi's, Frank Aguirre's, Jayo's, the Capitol Rooms, and the DeLamar Hotel.[10] Decades later Lentxo confided that he had had two criteria for choosing Barbero's: "Well, first ole' Barbero was from Lekeitio—not far from my Mutriku—and knew some of my people. Second, his place had one of those player pianos, you know. When I heard that music, that's where I had to stay."

Lentxo passed three or four relaxing days before his brother Jack arrived to retrieve him. While waiting, Lentxo discovered that "many of Boise's Bascos were Gipuzkoanos and Bizkainos."[11] Their familiar dialects put him at ease in this new place, where he enjoyed talking with compatriots from Mutriku, Eibar, Gernika, Lekeitio, and other coastal villages that he had only heard a little about in the Old Country. As it happened, it had been a long winter, many herders were in town that spring, since they were staying close to their "home bases" while awaiting summer grazing season.

When Jack Echanis reached town, he began asking after his younger brother. It was only a few hours before the two were united. After talk of home and the voyage, the conversation turned to work in the sheep camps. The next morning the two brothers rose before the sun and rode west out of Boise, hoping to make Ontario before nightfall. In Ontario they were joined by Txomin Patchuaga, another Mutrikan who had worked with Jack and Joe in eastern Oregon. From Ontario the three horsemen started for their Juntura camp, accompanied by two pack mules loaded with supplies for their newest herder.

Within three weeks of saying good-bye to Benita and Joxemari in Mutriku, after a number of new experiences, including an extended and stressful transatlantic crossing and a lengthy transcontinental train ride, Lentxo sat by a campfire in southeastern Oregon, listening to the sheep in the quiet of a High Desert night. All too soon Jack, Joe, and Txomin would leave, and Lentxo would begin his intensive on-the-job training. As he nervously surveyed the thousands of sheep, two sleepy dogs, a tent, pack mule, rifle, cooking gear, and his new leather boots, he marveled at how far he had come and wondered what the future might hold for him.

Although Lentxo Echanis was unaware of it throughout his life, his story of "coming to Amerika" was representative of the experiences of many Basque immigrants coming to the Western United States between 1890 and 1930. At every critical turn in his journey, he placed his fate in the hands of the *ostatuak* and their *hoteleros*. Whether it was Aguirre's well-developed transportation center in New York City or the Ogden boardinghouse, or the tiny house in Pocatello, the network of ethnic boardinghouses made it possible for Lentxo to cross the continent without a personal guide, without knowing English, and without understanding Americans or their customs. Whether en route from Mutriku to a Steen's Mountain sheep camp or, years later, making his way from Boise to Los Angeles, Lentxo relied on services he could find only in the Basque boardinghouses. Although there was no equivalent to the *ostatuak* in his homeland, like other Basques who preceded or succeeded him he learned of America's *ostatuak* out of necessity and often by word of mouth.

After joining his brothers, Lentxo herded sheep on the ranges and mountains of eastern Oregon and southwestern Idaho from 1914 through 1922. During those years, the local Basque boardinghouses became his "home away from home." In addition to providing a roof, a bed, and a bath when he was off the range, they provided entertainment and social contacts in the form of music, card games, and dances.

When he had a free day, Lentxo usually rode down to the railway shipping center in Crane, Oregon, where there was a small boardinghouse owned and operated by Andy Urquidi.[12] If he had more time he might travel farther afield to the larger Star rooming house in Burns, Oregon, and stay there with his friend "Chino" Berdugo.[13] From early 1922 on, Lentxo regularly stopped at Echanis's in Ontario, where his brother Jack and sister-in-law Marie had opened their own boardinghouse on Oregon Street.[14]

On the rare occasions when Lentxo had a few weeks to journey back to Boise's Basque district, he preferred to stay at Barbero's or Anduiza's. At both boardinghouses he appreciated the "home-style" cooking, enjoyed talking with other Basques, and sought out recent arrivals who might carry news of Mutriku. On Grove Street, he could happily play handball, dance on Sunday nights, and bluff his way through many a weak hand of *mus*.

Twice during the eight years he spent herding sheep in Idaho and Oregon Lentxo was told that his bosses had "busted" or "gone broke." After the first incident, he and his brother Joe started their own herd and built it up gradually, but unfortunately three consecutive harsh winters wiped them out. Later, when Lentxo was twenty-four and working for another herder, his brother Joe told him that their boss was claiming to have lost all his profits in a poor banking investment. The younger Echanis was bitterly discouraged. He realized that he had little to show for his eight years of labor, and he was on the verge of making some life-changing decisions. As he described it years later, "Me and my brother were standing on the side of the road there and the sheep weren't ours. We weren't watching our own sheep anymore, and I told my brother, 'What the devil are we doing here?'" For Lentxo, herding for someone else in the hope that he and Joe might someday start on their own again made little sense. Even worse, he feared he might never be able to save enough money to get out of herding. He later remembered, "I didn't have ten cents in my pocket. There, on the side of the road, I nearly went crazy. I threw my shepherd's crook as far as I could. I quit right there. I was so mad I started running the twenty-eight miles to Boise. I didn't know what else to do."

After the disgruntled herder had run-walked about ten miles along the highway, a driver saw him and stopped to offer him a ride. In Boise, at a dry goods store where the owner had been kind to him in the past, Lentxo borrowed supplies, clothing, and a few personal items. He soon discovered that even in Boise it was difficult for herders who spoke only Euskara to find work in other trades. After a few months of picking up odd jobs for Boise *hoteleros* in exchange for room and board and working a few short-term ranch jobs, Lentxo was forced to return to herding. Only six months passed before he quit again. He couldn't get beyond the frustration of working for over eight years and having little to show for it. This time he had a plan for "starting over in Amerika."

Upon making his final break with herding, Lentxo decided to propose marriage to Felicia Madariaga. He had met Felicia at Andy Urquidi's in Crane, Oregon, when he and his brothers drove spring lambs to the rail shipping center there.[15] Felicia had left her home in Gernika, Bizkaia, upon the invitation of her cousins in Crane. When Lentxo met her, Felicia was serving meals, cleaning rooms, and pitching in with kitchen duties at Urquidi's. Lentxo courted her there for two years before asking for her hand in 1922. Thereafter both Lentxo and Felicia worked resolutely to save enough for train fare to Los Angeles where, they had heard, work was plentiful and the climate was inviting.

With his new bride, Lentxo once again counted on the *ostatuak* to help him get by. During their first few months together, Lentxo and Felicia worked and lived in and around the boardinghouses of Boise and Crane. En route to Los Angeles, they stopped in Winnemucca, where they stayed in the boardinghouse of Henri and Augustina Martin. At that time, the Martins operated a small store, a restaurant, the rooms upstairs, and the adjacent Lafayette Hotel and Grill.[16] There were a few other Basque-owned establishments in Winnemucca that the Echanises visited during their two-day stop. They walked a few doors "up the tracks" from the Martin to Etchegoyen's Busch Hotel and also strolled across town to the not too distant Winnemucca Hotel, which featured a beautiful hand-carved oak bar that predated the Civil War.[17] In addition to being the town's oldest and largest hotel in 1922, by that time the Winnemucca had been Basque-owned and operated for decades.

From Winnemucca, the couple embarked upon the final leg of their journey by rail to southern California. Lentxo and Felicia had been told that there was a thriving Basque town not far from the downtown train station in Los Angeles.[18] As they pulled into the somewhat intimidating metropolis, Lentxo feared that the people who had given him advice about coming to this city might have been mistaken. He thought, "How could there be any Basques in this big place?" and "How will I find anyone here who speaks Euskara?" Fearing the worst but compelled to find a place for himself and his bride, he left Felicia waiting in the depot, standing guard over all their worldly possessions.

Free from parcels and baggage, Lentxo set out to find the city's celebrated Basque neighborhood, wandering down unfamiliar and cavernous avenues. About half a mile north of the station he came to the intersection of Alameda and Aliso Streets, where he overheard a group of men shouting at what seemed to be a sporting event. He drew closer and heard them calling out in Euskara. Beyond the crowd were two young *pilotariak* (handball players) playing in a makeshift *cancha* (handball court) along an alleyway.[19] When the pounding of his heart subsided, Lentxo spoke with a few of the men, explained his situation, and asked where he and his wife might be able to stay.

They suggested he speak with a Basque woman named Ines who had a small boardinghouse a few blocks down Aliso Street.[20] After making arrangements with Ines, Lentxo hurried back to retrieve Felicia. The couple stayed at Ines's boardinghouse for a week, again taking odd jobs when possible but primarily relying on Ines's generosity and kindness. Ines, like many other Basque hotelkeepers, extended liberal credit until a future time when boarders would be able to repay their debt.

When a foreman from the Bastanchury Ranch named Valdivino came into town looking for new ranch hands, Lentxo finally found the long-term employment and job security he craved. The Bastanchurys were an Orange County family whose ranch was one of the top citrus producers in California in the 1920s and 1930s. From 1922 through 1942, Lentxo and Felicia lived in a small house on the Bastanchury property in Fullerton. Eventually Lentxo became a foreman at the ranch, and he finally began to speak Spanish and English. As he reported years later, "I worked with so many Mexicans who used to ask me, 'What kind of a Spaniard are you that you can't speak the language?' After a while, I got the hang of it and then learned English pretty good too." Not surprisingly, the ranch hands who worked with Lentxo during those years remembered him fondly. One described Lentxo as "the most hardworking, honest boss I have ever had, . . . the very best."[21]

Even after the Echanises settled in southern California, the *ostatuak* continued to play an important role in their family life. During the 1920s, Lentxo and Felicia occasionally returned to Ines's boardinghouse on Aliso or stayed at the Oyamburu on the corner of Amelia and Turner in Los Angeles's then fading Basque district. During the 1930s many of southern

California's Basques began gathering at Nogues's Valley Hotel and the Puente Hotel in downtown La Puente, California. In fact, some of Lentxo's closest friends formed the La Puente Handball Club, located in the same neighborhood as the hotel. On Sundays Lentxo and his three children enjoyed going over to cheer the *pilota* players on and then joining Felicia and other friends for Sunday dinner at one of the boardinghouses.

In 1940 Jean Baptiste and Grace Robidart built a boardinghouse in nearby Chino, California. At the Robidarts' Centro Vasco, Lentxo and his dearest friends Augustin Mujica, Domingo Segura, and Sam Landa engaged in many competitive rounds of *mus*; caught up with events in one another's lives; enjoyed fine meals accompanied by wine, cigars, and cognac; and brought their families together for the occasional Saturday night dances. For the better part of the past six decades, Lentxo, his children, their children and grandchildren have regularly convened at the Centro Vasco to relive the old days and to celebrate special occasions for the Echanis family.

Furthermore, the boardinghouse that Jack and Marie Echanis opened in 1922 developed into a mainstay for Basques in southeastern Oregon.[22] Over the course of the boardinghouse's five decades of success in Ontario, Lentxo returned for regular extended visits.

Boardinghouses were vital to Lentxo Echanis's successful adaptation to his second homeland, as well as that of the tens of thousands of Basques who immigrated to the United States between the peak years of 1890 and 1930. During those years the *ostatuak* became the most important social and ethnic institution in the lives of new Basque immigrants. Many of Lentxo's countrymen have reported a similar dependence upon boardinghouses during their years in America. The following chapters are dedicated to Lentxo, to his fellow Amerikanuak, and to the boardinghouses they built.

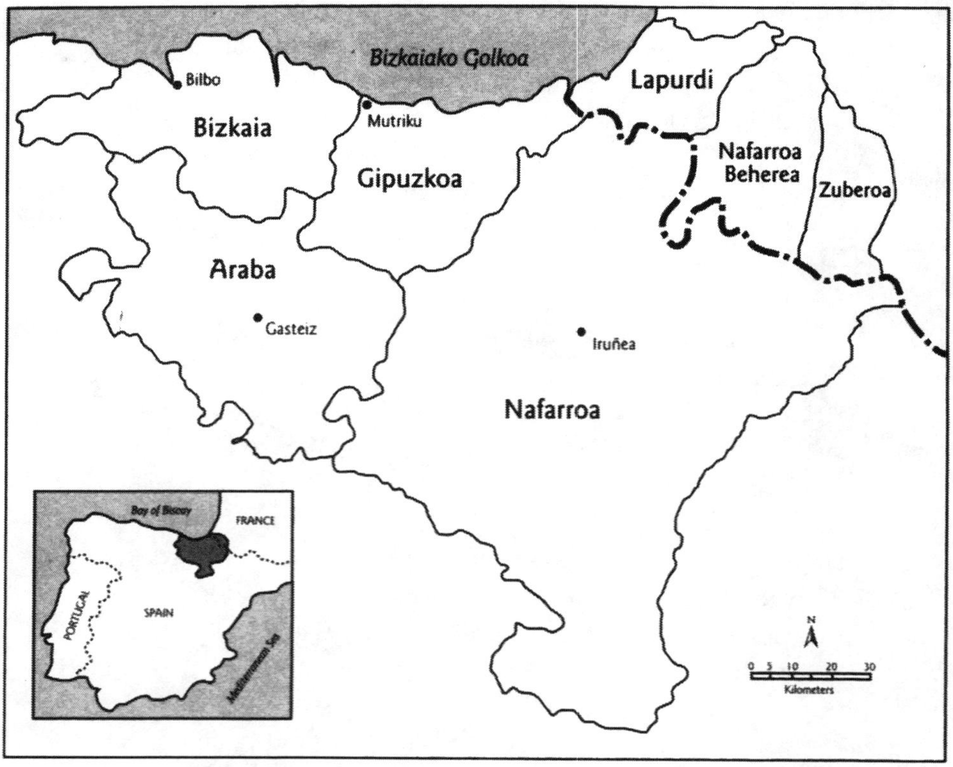


*Fig. 1. A map of Euskal Herria (the Basque Country), showing the seven provinces and the location of Mutriku.* Source: *University of Nevada Press.*

# 1

# From Euskal Herria to the New World

The Basque region occupies portions of north central Spain and southwestern France along the coastal waters of the Bay of Biscay and through the western Pyrenees Mountains. Despite the frustration of not having their own state, the Basque people have tenaciously given their homeland the political name Euskadi (Basque nation) or the less-politicized Euskal Herria (land of Basques). Measuring scarcely one hundred miles in any direction, the Basque homeland is geographically compact. The four Spanish provinces of Navarre, Araba, Gipuzkoa, and Bizkaia constitute six sevenths of the total land mass; the French *départements* of Lapurdi, Nafarroa Beherea, and Zuberoa make up the remainder. Current population estimates for the region are over 3 million, but not all those living in one of the seven Basque provinces are culturally Basque. Nor are they speakers of Euskara. Approximately 670,000 people speak Euskara in Spain and France. Euskaldunak are scattered throughout the world.[1]

## A UNIQUE PEOPLE AND LANGUAGE

In addition to claiming the distinction of being Europe's oldest surviving ethnic group, Basques assert that there is biological evidence that distinguishes them as a people from other European groups. They point to studies that show that European Basques have the highest incidence of O positive blood and the lowest incidence of type B. In addition, the occurrence of the Rhesus negative blood factor is more frequent among Basques than among any of the world's other peoples. Conclusions from recent serological and dermatological research suggest that Old World Basques have maintained a marked preference for endogamy, or marriage within their own group.[2]

Unfortunately there are no thorough studies of endogamous and exogamous behavior in Basque-American communities. In a recent review of the 1990 census of the United States, however, William Douglass noted that the overall growth of the Basque population since 1980 might suggest "that Basques in the United States manifest a greater propensity for endogamy, or marriage within an ethnic group, than most other Americans of European descent."[3] On the other hand, many studies have reported the impression, intuition, or verbal testimony from Basques that "the young ones just aren't marrying our own kind anymore."[4] Few Amerikanuak seem to disagree with this sentiment. Without statistical verification, however, the degree to which second-, third-, and fourth-generation Basques have assimilated and intermingled in the United States cannot be determined.

The Basque language, Euskara, is the only remaining pre-Indo-European language. Beyond factors such as the Basques' long-standing history in the Pyrenees and biological evidence supporting the ethnocentrism of the Basque people, Euskara is the most convincing evidence of the uniqueness of the Basque people. For example, Basques refer to themselves as Euskaldunak, which literally means "holders of the language" or "speakers of Euskara." In the 1960s Morton Levine wrote a series of articles on the relationship between the Basque language and cultural isolationism. In his study of French Basque villages he demonstrated that an internal impulse rather than compelling external factors guided villagers in resisting the outside world. Rejecting the notion that the Pyrenees served as a geographical barrier, Levine asserted that Basques displayed "an unquenchable desire to remain Basque." Calling Basques a "true biological population," Levine suggested that Euskara was a major vehicle both for self-identification and for the exclusion of non-Basques. In fact, Basques enjoy discussing the difficulty of learning Euskara and have numerous folk stories to illustrate their claim. This tendency underscores an important feature of Basque ethnicity found among Basques in Europe and the New

World: they believe themselves to be a unique people, and they use their language and folklore to defend their separateness.[5]

It has been found that the Basque language is less sexist than English or the Romance languages. For example, a recent study comparing male-female gender identification between Euskara and American English serves to elevate the role of Basque women and provoke thought.[6] In this study, coauthor of the *Basque-English Dictionary* Linda White demonstrates that English as spoken in the United States is much more sexist than the Basque language is.[7] For example, Basques use the same third-person pronoun to refer to *he*, *she*, and *it*; depending upon dialect, they use *bera* or *hura*. There is no distinction, no orthographic change to reflect male and female in the third person. In addition, terms such as *postman*, *chairman*, and *milkman* have no direct equivalent in Basque. For example, *chairman* in Euskara is *mahaiburu;* literally this translates to "the head of the table." The Basques completely avoid our American soul-searching over whether a female chair should be called chairwoman, chairperson, or chairman! Nor does the Basque language assign grammatical gender to nouns as in the Romance languages. Those of us studying Euskara do not have to agonize over whether the word for *book* is feminine or masculine, for example; it is simply *liburu*.

Since languages to some extent reflect the culture of the people who employ them, this less sexist approach to labeling among Basques is somewhat encouraging. Such comparisons suggest that Euskara is at least linguistically less sexist than neighboring French and Spanish, as well as American English. Yet this does not mean that Old World society has been or is egalitarian. To paraphrase lexicographers, Euskara can be viewed as a less sexist language in a sexist culture.[8]

There are different theories about what sets Basques apart as a people. One author has suggested that because of collective nobility status Basques developed a strong sense of ethnicity, independence, and self-sufficiency. Others have asserted that serological and linguistic evidence sets Basques apart from other ethnic groups. Yet another group of scholars might argue that it is the Basques' long-standing migratory tradition makes them unique. Whatever the conclusion in these matters, few will argue with a Basque about the uniqueness of his or her culture. Perhaps the most persuasive argument is that for centuries Basques have spoken of themselves as a unique people and believed it fervently.

Many scholars have likewise written about Basques as the "mystery people" of Europe, and this emphasis has tended to inflate their image as a unique ethnic group. In a study of Basques in the New World, especially those who made their way to the *ostatuak*, very little of the "mystery" discussion is relevant.

## EXPLORING THE MIGRATORY TRADITION OF THE BASQUES

The migratory tradition of the Basque people is especially noteworthy when we consider the emergence of the boardinghouses of the New World. William Douglass and Jon Bilbao's history of Basques in the New World, *Amerikanuak*, addresses the Basque migratory tradition from the early whaling and maritime periods through Basque participation in Spain's New World settlement, and into twentieth-century migration.

In the late fifteenth and sixteenth centuries, when the Spanish Crown sought Basque expertise in shipbuilding, navigation, and maritime commerce, the Basques were well positioned to secure for themselves a large role in New World political and economic enterprises. The special role that Basques gained in the Crown's settlement of the New World was an extension of their early economic successes in iron mining, shipbuilding, whaling, and other maritime ventures. It was also rooted in their self-determined political tradition. As early as the thirteenth century, the seven Basque provinces had established political charters known as *fueros* and *fors* in Euskadi and Pays Basque respectively. The *fueros* and *fors* determined the nature of local and regional government, defined the rights of the Basque citizenry, and claimed that Basque regional autonomy superseded the Spanish and French Crowns. This final point was significant because both Crowns negotiated with Basque provinces in recognition of the sovereignty of their *fueros* and *fors*. In several locations, Basque political autonomy under the *fueros/fors* system remained intact until the early nineteenth century.

In addition to the strong regional identity protected by the *fueros* and *fors*, Davydd Greenwood has asserted that understanding the concept of collective nobility for the Basques is essential for understanding Basque history and migration.[9] This is particularly accurate when we consider Spanish Basques who were allowed social and economic status to participate as officials of the Crown and Church during the exploration of the New World. By the fifteenth and sixteenth centuries, the Spanish Crown accepted the collective nobility status that Basque villagers in Gipuzkoa,

Bizkaia, and Araba had granted themselves in earlier centuries.[10] During this period, if a person was able to prove Basque parentage, he would automatically be recognized as noble by virtue of *limpieza de sangre* (purity of blood). Indeed, collective nobility may have contributed to the Basques' strong sense of ethnic identity.[11] But more certainly, collective nobility granted through *limpieza de sangre* gave Basques the social and economic status that made it possible for them to participate as officials of the Crown during the exploration of the New World. By the fifteenth century, Spanish and French Basques retained a degree of official autonomy under the *fuero* and *fors* systems. According to these medieval legal systems, Basques acknowledged that although they were not citizens of Spain or France, they were people of a land that had accepted the Spanish and French monarchs. But more certainly, collective nobility combined with the *fuero* tradition gave Basques a strong political position to negotiate business charters as they joined the Spanish Crown in its New World business and political ventures. Thus, when a twentieth-century student of Basque history reflects on the broad international expanse of the Basque diaspora, he or she should not be surprised. For Basques leaving Spain, and to a lesser degree France, settled in the nations of South America, Central America, the Caribbean, North America, the Philippines, Australia, and parts of Asia.

A high concentration of Basques sailed for the Spanish Crown in the sixteenth century. Whaling and cod fishing had become important economic activities along the Cantabrian coast in the Middle Ages, and, for a time, Basques dominated both industries. Basques also sailed with French fishing fleets to what are now the Atlantic Provinces of Canada. In 1977, after uncovering numerous archival documents referring to a port named "Butus" in Terranova, a large sixteenth-century Basque whaling station that at one time housed hundreds of whalers and a rendering facility, Canadian historian Selma Barkham led archaeologists James Tuck and Robert Grenier to a likely site in Red Bay, Labrador. There, nearly four centuries after the fact, field teams began unearthing the remains of the whaling station. Further work by the Parks Canada Service has revealed that at least a dozen smaller Basque whaling outposts lined the coastal waters of Labrador and Newfoundland and were in operation until the seventeenth century.[12]

As global fishing and whaling efforts expanded, there was an increasing demand for large seaworthy vessels, so shipbuilding developed as an industry in the Spanish Basque provinces during the Middle Ages. Although the famed expedition of Columbus in 1492 was not an immediate economic stimulant to the Trastamara dynasty, it was for the Basque region.[13] In 1498 and again in 1502, for example, Queen Isabella offered generous subsidies to Basque shipbuilders, encouraging the rapid construction of seafaring vessels weighing in excess of six hundred and fifteen hundred tons. Basques enjoyed the benefits of collective nobility that allowed them to enter civil, ecclesiastical, and military orders at home and abroad. Thus on the eve of Spain's imperial dominance in Europe and the New World Basques were in an ideal position to offer their proven skills in service to the Crown.

As Douglass and Bilbao point out in *Amerikanuak*, assessing the numbers of Basque emigrés to the New World between the fifteenth and the nineteenth centuries is nearly impossible. Many ships' records are lost to history, many Basques are likely to have returned to Euskal Herria years after they arrived in America, and a number of Basques probably crossed the Atlantic illegally. Despite the lack of documentation, the Basque exodus to the New World seems to have been sizable over the span of some four hundred years. One scholar, for example, has estimated that 80 percent of the vessels crossing the Atlantic on the American run were staffed and/or owned by Basques in the years between 1520 and 1580.[14]

### Demographic and Economic Factors: Inheritance and the Family Land

Rural farmsteads, like the Echanises' *mendi beltza*, have served as symbols for Basque family lineage because the Basque people have tended to link the family name with the family land. Since the sixteenth century, and perhaps earlier, Basques have taken as their surname the name of their *baserri;* having to sell the family home has been interpreted as a failure, the end of a family's lineage in a particular village.[15] Moreover, rules regarding inheritance of the farmstead vary slightly from village to village: the firstborn child might inherit in one village; whereas the firstborn son might inherit in the next. Occasionally, the child deemed most able to operate the *baserri* will learn sometime in his or her teenage years that he or she has or has not been selected to inherit at some future time.

As William Douglass has demonstrated, decisions regarding primogeniture were often a factor influencing young noninheriting rural Basques to travel to the New World at the turn of the century.[16] In many villages a youth's noninheriting status was the factor that forced him from his (or her) natal village. This was especially true in cases where children knew from an early age that they would not inherit.[17] In more recent decades those who do not stand to inherit might move to a larger town or city in Euskadi.

The majority of Basques who came to America during the peak years of Basque immigration were from the rural *baserriak*. Like Lentxo Echanis and thousands of others, they were frequently the noninheriting rural poor who did not have a promise of a bright future in their home villages. They did not represent a broad cross section of Old World Basque society but rather a very specific demographic group that tended to be less educated and less wealthy than those townspeople and city dwellers who stayed behind.

It should also be remembered that a majority of European Basques have made the village center or urban setting their home. In fact, in her article on the town of Elgeta, Marianne Heiberg divided all the citizens into the *kaletarrak* (people of the *kale*, or street) and the *baserritarrak* (people of the farmstead) and reminded readers that Basque town dwellers were much less likely to emigrate to America than Basques who lived in outlying areas.[18]

Although the Old World inheritance customs among Basques living in the *baserriak* were the major impetus behind the steady flow of young single Basques to the United States between 1890 and 1930, additional factors encouraged migration. Demographic studies indicate that in the last fifty years of the nineteenth century, Europe underwent a population explosion that nearly doubled the number of people on the continent.[19] Dramatic population increases together with the Basques' adherence to primogeniture must have spurred emigration from the rural villages. As Douglass and Bilbao have suggested, however, noninheritance did not necessarily mean a voyage to the Americas. Moving to urban and village centers, marrying into other *baserriak*, or taking religious vows were some of the other available options. Despite such options, leaving Euskal Herria seems to have been greatly preferred in the late nineteenth century. The number of Basques who emigrated from Pays Basque (the French portion of Euskadi) between 1832 and 1907 exceeded 100,000, a substantial number for "an area whose total population for that period fluctuated around one hundred and twenty thousand inhabitants."[20]

## Political Factors

Political and military events in the nineteenth century also provided ample strain on Basque loyalty to France and Spain, and that alienation led to draft evasion. Several engagements of the Napoleonic Wars were fought in the Pyrenees region, and Basques were drawn into the conflict via recruitment and requisitioning on both sides. The French Revolution, which abolished the *fors* system, also introduced the Napoleonic Code of inheritance in the Pays Basque or Iparralde. In 1839 the defeat of the Carlists forces in Spain's First Carlist War brought increased taxation on the Basque provinces, and the relaxation of the *fueros* system under the Treaty of Bergara further reduced Basque privileges in northern Spain. As a result of their defeat in the Second Carlist War in 1876, Spanish Basques lost the remainder of their *fuero* privileges and were conscripted into the military for the first time.

Evasion of military service was widespread among both Spanish and French Basques in the nineteenth century, and the trend later became acute during World War I. For example, official passenger lists from Spain's Consejo de Emigración (Emigration Council) indicate that 18,547 young Spanish Basque men left their homeland between 1911 and 1915.[21] This relatively substantial number does not reflect the number who left illegally or via French ports.

## OLD COUNTRY TRADITIONS AND THE NEW WORLD

The rural Basques, or *baserriak*, brought with them to the New World a high regard for the self-sufficiency they had developed on their farmsteads, and a good deal of ethnic pride. Many, if not most, arrived in America with the intention of working to save enough money so that they could return to Euskal Herria, marry, and retire.

In his famous ethnography of the Basque people, Julio Caro Baroja characterized the Basque community as an intricate network of functions whose origins are closely linked to the geographical contours and Basque adaptations to them. Caro Baroja describes the prototypical Basque farmstead as a self-sufficient unit designed to accommodate a number of needs. In most farmsteads, or *baserriak*, the two- or three-floor dwellings contain a barn area for livestock, a toolshed, and an area to store grains and dry goods.[22] These homes often shelter up to three generations under one roof. The family land often consisted of twenty to thirty acres put to mixed use, yielding vegetables, cereal grains, fruit, timberland for construction, pasture for livestock, and kindling for warming the family. Because of the emphasis on self-sufficiency in the *baserri* system, local transactions as recently as the early decades of this century were on a barter basis rather than a cash basis.[23]

One should also note that the role of the community shepherd in the Old World Basque community was and continues to be quite distinct from that which developed in the American West. At first glance, students of Basque history assume that sheepherding is a traditional Basque occupation in Europe, but actually many Old World communities own collective herds and hire herders from the villages to summer the town's sheep in the mountains. During other seasons small bands of sheep are left to roam the village commons.[24] In many portions of the Basque Country, sheep are altogether absent. Generally speaking, then, sheepherding as a major occupation among Basques is a New World phenomenon.[25]

With good reason, the *baserri* system is commonly portrayed as central to Old World Basque culture. Ethnographers, social historians, and cultural anthropologists tend to describe Basque family dynamics, work distinctions, and social functions as being dependent upon the maintenance and survival of the *baserriak*. And the Basques of agricultural backgrounds who have emigrated to the New World have brought centuries of *baserri* tradition to the New World with them.

### *Lehenbiziko Atia*, the First Neighbor Tradition

One important tradition that Old World Basques carried to the New World from their *baserriak* was the *lehenbiziko atia*, or first neighbor tradition. On the Basque farmsteads, a family relies upon the nearest neighbor for support in family emergencies and for extra hands when necessary. In her study of the French Basque mountain community of Sainte Engrâce, *Circle of Mountains*, for example, Sandra Ott describes the careful rotation of shepherds sharing the responsibility for the village herd.[26] Mutual assistance and cooperation are critical among first neighbors. Neighbors have commonly shared the annual harvests, the slaughter of livestock, the celebration of family holidays, the mourning for a deceased family member, and the larger maintenance work around the *baserriak*.

As Ott notes in *Circle of Mountains*, no two households have the same first neighbors. The asymmetric ordering of first-neighbor relationships tends to reduce competition and encourage mutual assistance. She suggests that the first neighbor system among *baserriak* is distinct from the more generalized mutual support systems found in other rural regions throughout the world.[27] As we shall see in our exploration of the Basque boardinghouses of the American West, Old World Basques carried the *lehenbiziko atia* concept with them to the New World, although in a different form.

A notable instance of this tradition occurred in Bakersfield as recently as November 6, 1979. The staff at Noriega's was awaiting a large funeral party that had been attending the services for Dr. Clerou, a French-American physician who had cared for many Bakersfield Basques. Just before the 150 guests arrived, Louie Elizalde of Noriega's had a fatal heart attack. Word of Louie's death spread rapidly through the neighborhood, and when the news reached Mayie Maitia at the Woolgrower's Restaurant, she left her restaurant and went to Noriega's to manage the large dinner party on behalf of the Elizalde family. When everyone had been served, Mayie slipped unnoticed back to her own restaurant. A more mundane instance of American first neighbor behavior is exemplified by Amelie Sorhondo's kindness toward Catherine Goyenetche. Amelie welcomed Catherine into San Francisco's Basque town with everyday advice for exterminating troublesome roaches. Hotelkeepers transferred the spirit of *lehenbiziko atia* to the New World, whether the help offered was pragmatic or selfless in nature, and they readily helped one another through difficult times.

## Church and *Pilota*

It is also critical to understand the role the village church played in the lives of Old World Basques. Since the sixteenth and seventeenth centuries, Basques have almost universally adopted Catholicism. Even in the most remote village, a small church and *pilota*, or handball, court is likely to dominate the town square.[28] Quite frequently the town cemetery, church, and *pilota* court are all part of the same complex. As Rodney Gallop suggested several decades ago, "These three form a triple symbol of the Basque race. The church stands for faith, the cemetery for tradition and the *pelota* [*pilota*] court for a hard and vigorous outdoor life."[29] One study maintains that the close affiliation between the village clergy and the playing of *pilota* has existed since the Middle Ages.[30] In Euskal Herria, the handball and jai alai courts frequently share a common wall with the village church; whereas in the American West *pilota* courts are most often found adjacent to Basque hotels.

While Old World Basque society is characterized by nearly universal attendance at Mass today, the religious life of American Basques in the West has not followed suit. Irregular church attendance has been explained in part by the occupational specialization of the immigrants (sheepherding) and by their preference for Basque-speaking priests.

Not surprisingly, Basques carried important aspects of their culture with them to the Americas. Ironically, Basques in South and North America created a new social institution to preserve their Old World values and traditions. Basques migrating to the Argentine pampas, the Mexican *altiplano*, the Cuban coast, and the Peruvian highlands in the sixteenth, seventeenth, and eighteenth centuries established way stations and inns to serve their transplanted countrymen in the New World.[31] In the American West, the *ostatuak* were most numerous and widespread in the late nineteenth and early twentieth centuries. The first evidence of Western *ostatuak* in the United States can be found in California, where Basques were drawn in increasing numbers by the lure of gold.

# 2

# From the Mother Lode to the Great Basin

## THE LURE OF CALIFORNIA GOLD

On the morning of January 24, 1848, John Marshall walked out of his cabin toward the tailrace of his sluice and beheld a few glittering particles at the bottom of the box. Neither Marshall nor anyone else could foretell the impact of his discovery on the future of California, or on global migration, for that matter. One result would be an increase in the numbers of immigrants entering the United States in the coming decades. Up through 1847, the annual number of immigrants to California had never exceeded 200,000, but in 1851 the number swelled to 408,000; it peaked in 1854 with 460,000.[1] Not all the new arrivals raced directly to the mines of California, however. Many of them replaced the factory workers in the East who had gone west, others worked in businesses that were booming as a result of the discovery of gold, and still others tried their luck with the sluice boxes and gold pans in other parts of the American frontier.

Nonetheless, in the United States, California's gold rush years were a watershed for immigration in general, and for Basque immigration in particular. Although there are mild disagreements over when the first Basques arrived in the United States, who they were, and where they went after their initial settlement, there is little dispute over the magnetic effect the gold rush had on the Basques. The soundest estimates place the number of Basque immigrants to California at several hundred between 1849 and 1852.[2] These numbers are small when compared with those of larger immigrant groups, such as the Irish, Scots, Germans, and Chinese, but they represent a drastic increase in California's Basque population over a three-year period.

A majority of the Basques striking out for the goldfields of the American West migrated north from Latin America and Mexico. By the 1840s, large colonies of Basques had been established in Buenos Aires and Montevideo. With the news of Marshall's discovery spreading rapidly, the South American Basques with "gold fever" took the most direct route to California via Valparaíso, Chile. Passenger lists of those departing from Valparaíso for San Francisco between January of 1849 and February of 1852 include approximately 170 Basque surnames.[3]

Pedro Altube and Jose Andonaegui are two examples of the Latin American contingent of immigrants to the American West who came to be known as the "Argentine Basques." In 1845 Altube left Oñati, Gipuzkoa, to join his two brothers in Buenos Aires. Four years later he heard the news of the discovery of gold in California and set off on horseback, traveling west to Valparaíso, Chile, where he joined thirty-five other Basques and set sail for San Francisco.[4] Still another young Basque, Jose M. Andonaegui, arrived in Buenos Aires in 1842, and after seven years of working there as a tailor he decided to try his luck in California.[5]

In examining the biographies of fourteen Basques who arrived in California between 1845 and 1860, Douglass and Bilbao noted that eight were from the Río de la Plata area, one was from Mexico, and five had come directly from Europe. Nine of the fourteen entered the mines immediately after arriving, yet none remained in the mining business. Twelve of the fourteen men eventually became involved in livestock ranching.[6]

The direct participation of Basques in gold mining was relatively short-lived. Some may have returned to Euskal Herria in the 1850s, and others took up occupations that served the growing numbers of northern California miners. Gold mining in the Sierra Nevada caused a boom in the state's cattle industry, and California cattlemen were scrambling to keep up with the demand while eyeing the competitive prices offered by their counterparts in Missouri, Texas, and New Mexico.[7] By 1856 the boom in California's cattle industry was over as a result of a combination of droughts, floods, and livestock epidemics. Still, the decline of the cattle industry made way for an increase in the sheep industry.

Since food for hungry miners was often scarce and prices were high, sheep could be sold for as much as $15 to $20 per head in the mining camps. During the 1850s and 1860s, sheep ranching and trailing expanded into cattle lands, gradually surpassing cattle ranching. Other factors contributing to the growth of the sheep industry were the availability of inexpensive land in California, the ability of sheep to survive semiarid pasture better than cattle, sheepherders' access to open grazing on public domain lands, the market for good-quality merino wool, and a ready market for wool products as a consequence of the reduction in cotton production during and after the Civil War.[8]

## THE BURGEONING SHEEP INDUSTRY IN CALIFORNIA

Taken together, the new opportunities in the California sheep industry could scarcely have been better choreographed for "Argentine Basques" once they had become disappointed with their luck in the goldfields. From the pampas these men brought with them a knowledge of open-range herding practices not unlike those that were already being employed in southern and central California. Clearly, the large-scale herding techniques that Basques are credited with bringing with them to the American West were a carryover from Argentina rather than from the Old World. Popular depictions notwithstanding, open-range herding is not found in the Old World, nor is it "instinctively" a Basque innovation.

By the mid-1850s a number of Basque sheepmen were operating in southern California and trailing their sheep north to San Francisco and the mines. Among these Euskaldunak were Domingo Amestoy, Jean Baptiste-Batz, Jean Etchemendy, and Pierre Larronde. In a review of 110 published biographies of Basque men arriving in California between 1845 and 1920, Douglass and Bilbao found that 93 were involved in the sheep business.[9] Seventy-four began as herders, and 52 eventually owned sheep outfits. Another 19 had once owned sheep but evidently had not previously been herders.

From the gold rush years through the close of the century, Basques became increasingly influential in California's sheep industry. The two decades between 1860 and 1880 saw an increase in the number of Basque immigrants to southern and central California.[10] Permits to run sheep in Santa Ana Canyon and Inyo County, for example, reveal that Basques dominated herding in those areas by 1870 and 1897, respectively.[11] By

1890 the dominance of southern California in sheepherding ebbed, and sheep tending developed in central and northern California counties such as Kern, Fresno, San Joaquin, and Mendocino.[12]

Between 1870 and 1900 a new trend in sheep trailing was seen. Bands were trailed east and north from California to the Great Basin area, including northern Nevada, southern Idaho, and southeastern Oregon. In addition to summer pasturing in the mountains, crossing the Sierra Nevada to the east became more desirable once the transcontinental railway was completed in 1869, because the railroads made possible the shipment of wool to eastern markets.

With the growth and geographical expansion of the sheep industry, Basque herders were able to send for their countrymen to join them in the West. Once the railway had been completed, European Basques no longer had to sail the treacherous Tierra del Fuego route to reach the West Coast; they could book passage to New York City, take a passenger train to Ogden, Utah, and then switch trains for points west.

## TRENDS IN BASQUE IMMIGRATION AND MIGRATION IN THE AMERICAN WEST

The completion of the transcontinental railroad and Basque dominance of the expanding sheep industry were two major factors leading to the marked increase of Basque immigrants to the Western United States around the turn of the century. In a recent article, Craig Campbell has demonstrated a close connection between the development of the Western rail system and the migration of Basques (see figure 2).[13] Between 1890 and 1930 a change in the basic migratory pattern of Basques within the United States evolved. Whereas the majority of Basque immigrants first landed in San Francisco and then moved eastward in the gold rush years, in the 1890s most of the Basque immigrants arrived on the East Coast first and then made their way west. Although the peak years of Basque immigration in California probably lasted until the 1930s, there was also an exodus of Basques from California to the Great Basin states from the late nineteenth century through the 1930s.[14]

Because our information regarding larger immigration trends for Basques throughout the twentieth century remains incomplete, our attempts to pinpoint peak years of immigration to date are somewhat intuitive. Although scholars interested in Basque immigration will have to await more

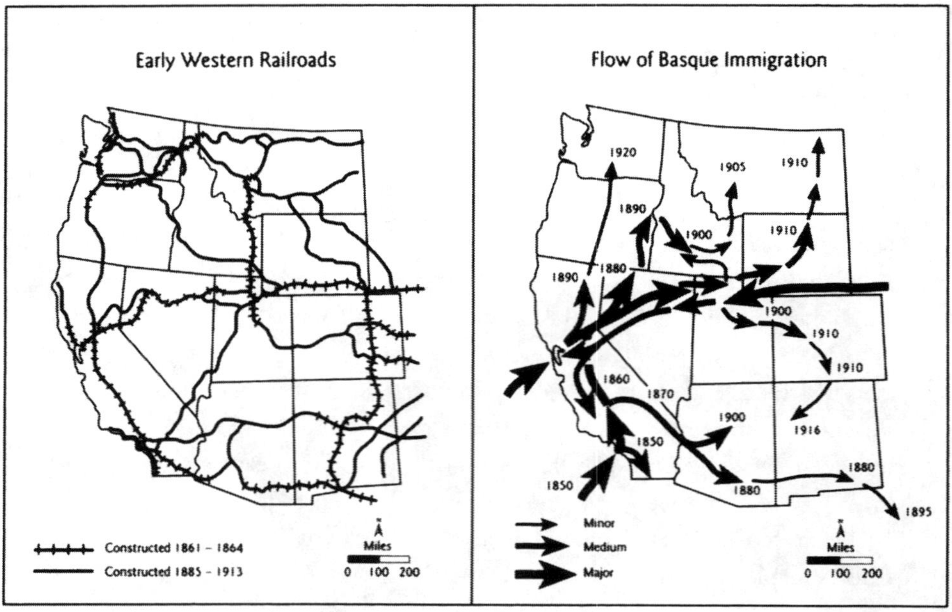


*Fig. 2. Maps showing the parallel development of the rail system and the flow of Basque settlement in the American West.* Source: *Craig Campbell, "Basque American Ethnic Area,"* 83–89.

research on contemporary census materials, the distribution of French Basques, Navarrese, Bizkaians, and Gipuzkoans in the Western United States is well documented.[15] The chain migration of Basques throughout the American West is illustrated in figure 3.

Immigration statistics that have been recently discovered indicate interesting demographic trends among Basques who arrived in New York in the five-year period from 1897 to 1902.[16] Of the 636 names in the records studied, 86 percent were male and 77 percent were single. Although of varying ages, 65 percent of the men ranged in age between sixteen and thirty, and 464 of the 636 were Spanish Basques. A clear pattern emerges: most Basque immigrants during this period were young unmarried males from Spain.

Marie Pierre Arrizabalaga's comparative study of Basques based on the censuses of 1900 and 1910 reveals more insights into Basque immigration to the United States.[17] From her data, one can conclude that Basque Americans have always been and continue to be a relatively small ethnic group. In 1900, when the number of Basques in Euskal Herria was 1,084,616, only 986 Basques were living in California, Nevada, Idaho, and Wyoming.[18] Ten years later, the Old World Basque population was 1,160,023, and Basques living in the four Western states numbered 8,398. Basque Americans in the four Western states represented less than 9 out of every 10,000 Basques in the world; as of 1910 72 out of every 10,000 Basques in the world lived in the four Western states.

Of the 8,398 Basques living in the Western states in 1910, Arrizabalaga found that only 1,212 had emigrated to California before 1900, and that slightly over 14 percent of the group had been in the United States for a decade or longer.[19] Based on Arrizabalaga's findings, only a small number of Basques had been in the United States for ten years or longer as of

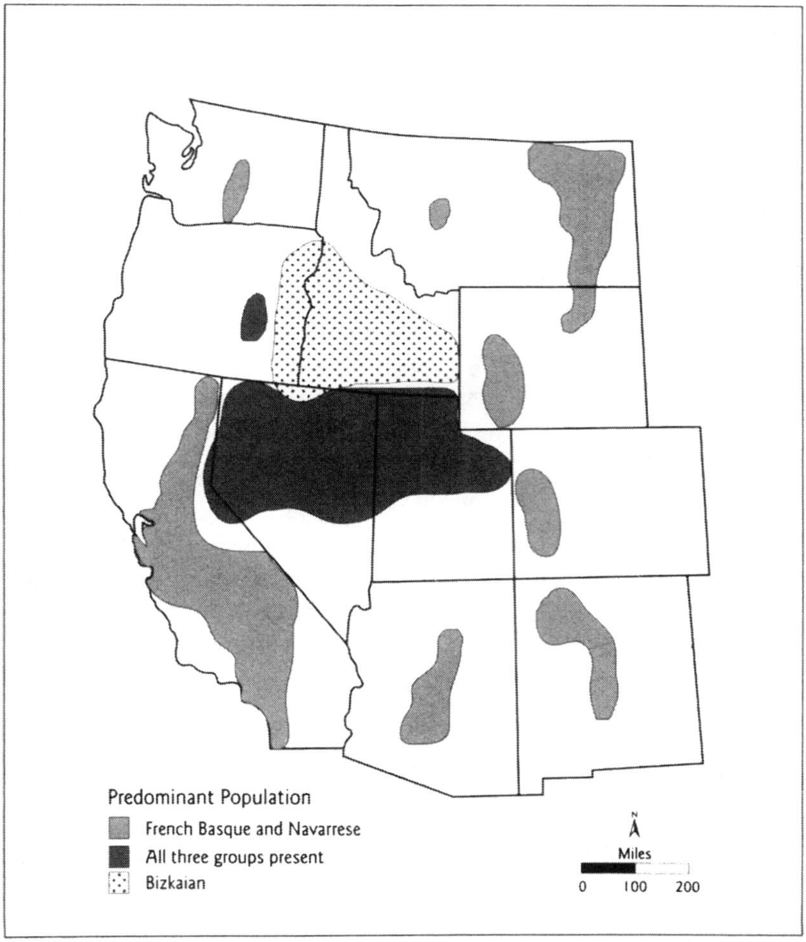


Fig. 3. *Basque-American settlement patterns. This map is based on appendix 7 of Douglass and Bilbao,* Amerikanuak, 431.

Table 2.1 Basque-American Populations in Four Western States, 1900 and 1910

| State | Number in 1900 | Percentage of Total in 1900 | Number in 1910 | Percentage of Total in 1910 |
|---|---|---|---|---|
| California | 745 | 75.5 | 6,267 | 74.6 |
| Idaho | 61 | 6.2 | 999 | 11.9 |
| Nevada | 180 | 18.3 | 971 | 11.6 |
| Wyoming | 2 | — | 161 | 1.9 |
| TOTAL | 988 | 100.0 | 8,398 | 100.0 |

*Source:* Compiled from Arrizabalaga, "Statistical Study," pp. 42, 54, 72, 82, 89, 97, 103, and 110.
*Note:* The total number of Basques listed in the study probably does not include all Basques inhabiting the West in 1900 and 1910. These numbers reflect only those who were recorded in the census records.

1910, and this leads us to the conclusion that the majority of Basques at that time may not have intended to stay for very long or may have been relocating throughout the Western states. Given the relatively low percentage of Basques who had been in the United States for ten years or longer, one could come to the conclusion that there was a high mobility rate among newly arrived Basques at the time. (See table 2.1.) Some of these people may have moved on to other states or returned to Euskal Herria within a few years of arrival.

As we can see in table 2.1, which is based on Arrizabalaga's sample, there was a dramatic increase in Basque migration in the decade between 1900 and 1910. More Basques came to California, Nevada, Idaho, and Wyoming in 1907 than in any other year between 1900 and 1910. One factor partially explaining the Basques' exodus from their homeland in 1907 may have been the widespread crop failure in the Basque Country between 1904 and 1906. The increased number of Basques arriving during these years reached their apogee in 1907.

## THE ADVENT OF THE IMMIGRANT HERDERS

As we saw earlier, Basque immigrants during the early part of the 1900s were most commonly young unmarried Spanish Basque males. They came to join their fellow Basques who were working in the sheep industry, and they usually entered one of two work situations: they worked for another Basque on an established sheep ranch, or they worked for landless sheep owners who depended upon access to open grazing areas. This latter group of "tramp sheep men" have been referred to as "ranchers without ranches."[20] Basque sheepmen sent for brothers, friends, and neighbors from their Old World villages to come over and help them with their herds. Once the newcomers arrived, they were sometimes paid wages in ewes. In this way, a new herder could begin building his own flock within the larger band while grazing the sheep together. Once the newcomer's herd had grown large enough, he could set out on his own, a process now known as "hiving off."

Initially, kinship ties and contacts among Old World compatriots were the key factors in the recruitment of new herders. By the early 1900s, however, Basques were known in several areas of the West as dependable herders, so they had no trouble getting herding work—so much so that from 1900 to 1915 almost every Bizkaian immigrant took a herding job upon arriving in the Great Basin.[21] In her study of Basque immigration into the Western states, Marie Pierre Arrizabalaga found that as of 1900, 87.3 percent of the Basques involved in the sheep and cattle industry were new immigrants, and this percentage increased slightly to 88.1 in 1910.[22] As a result, a surplus of Basque herders developed. By 1920, with the large numbers of incoming herders, the laws of supply and demand came into play and became more influential than kinship ties. Herders were more often recruited from labor pools put together in local Basque hotels than from direct communications made with men back in the Basque Country. At the same time, there was still some correlation between where Basques settled in the Western states and which regional Old World provinces the Basques originally came from. For example, French and Navarrese Basques continued to settle in California, western Nevada, and portions of Wyoming and Montana; while Bizkaian Basques continued their concentrated settlement in the Great Basin (see figure 3).[23]

## CLOSING THE DOOR ON BASQUE IMMIGRANTS THROUGH LEGISLATION

On May 26, 1924, Congress passed a bill, the National Origins Act, that significantly slowed down the flow of Basque immigrants to the American West. The intention of the bill was to limit the number of foreigners entering the United States from certain countries.[24] Also known as the Quota Act, the legislation established quotas for immigrants based on national origin. Because there was a high quota set for French immigrants,

French Basques were relatively unaffected by the bill. Spain's quota, however, was set so small, relatively speaking, that Spanish Basque immigrants suffered by comparison. Concerned with the reduction of incoming Basque herders, representatives from the Woolgrowers Association began putting pressure on their congressmen to initiate legislative reforms, but to little immediate avail.

The Taylor Grazing Act of 1934 was another piece of national legislation that discouraged Basque immigration. Intended as a revision of open-range grazing, the act attempted to conserve the public domain and regulate the livestock industry by limiting the use of public domain lands to landowners.[25] As Senator Edward Taylor of Colorado commented, the bill was written in order to institute systematic control of government-owned lands, "in other words . . . to protect the little fellows" who had been raising livestock before the onslaught of itinerant herders. The senator continued, "At the present time this army of nomadic herds of stock are robbing him [the little fellow] out of his house and home. They [the Basques and other itinerants] pay very little taxes."[26] The Taylor Grazing Act effectively closed the door on open-range herding for nonlandowners—long a mainstay of the Basque itinerant sheepman. As a result of its passage, sheepherding declined as a major vehicle for Basque immigration, and incoming herders were forced to buy or rent grazing land before they could "hive off" with a small band as their predecessors had done before them.

In singling out Basque herders and other itinerants and by labeling them robbers, the senator's commentary reveals a degree of the nativism and antiforeign sentiment present in the public disputes over the Taylor Act. From the newspaper articles and the literature of the times, one can see that Basques suffered from antiforeign sentiment. One account of the gold rush claims that there was fierce prejudice against Latin American miners in California.[27] Perhaps the "Argentine Basques" were also targeted by this brand of nativist sentiment. Near the turn of the century, terms such as "Black Basques," "dirty Bascos," and "garlic snappers" were derogatory references to Basques that were commonly heard in other areas of the West.[28] According to historian Richard Etulain, Basques were "thrice damned" in the Progressive Era: they came to make their money and leave without becoming American citizens; they were clannish and did not speak English; and they took jobs that others did not want.[29] Many Basque Americans believe that the Taylor Grazing Act addressed these differences by reducing the dominant role Basques had played in open-range herding.

In 1937 Basque businessman Felix Urizar leveled his discontent with the Taylor Grazing Act in particular and with anti-Basque sentiment in Harney County in general. In a letter to the editor of the Burns, Oregon, *Times-Herald*, Urizar wrote:

> On today's stage from the Star Hotel Teles Zavala, Joe Zarraoanandia and Thomas Sabala left Burns. Joe Abasolo left last week. They left Harney County seeking a new location to live and run sheep as they have been driven out of Harney County by Mr. Klemme and his unjust administration of the Taylor Grazing Act. Teles Zavala has been in Harney County (since 1904). All this time these men either worked for sheepmen or have themselves, particularly in the last ten years, run from 2,500 to 7,000 of their own sheep.
>
> They are going from Burns, first to Eugene, looking that country over . . . seeking a place to run sheep and invest their money where Mr. Klemme can't run them over because of his racial prejudice and hatred against sheep.[30]

As he decried losing his compatriots in eastern Oregon, Urizar was also acting as a spokesperson for the Basques who felt that the national legislation was unfair.

Years after the act was passed, the conflict between ranchers and sheepmen subsided. By the 1950s the image of the Basque herder had improved dramatically with the appearance of newspaper articles and fiction extolling the virtues of the Basque culture.[31]

National legislation in the 1920s and 1930s brought about a marked decline in the number of Basques who immigrated to this country, and the resulting expansions and contractions in the sheep industry directly affected business at the Basque hotels in the West. The number of Basque hotels operating in Stockton, California, over the course of the past ninety years seems to have reflected general trends in Basque herding and immigration.[32] In the first decade of this century, Stockton had three Basque hotels, and the number jumped to six between 1920 and 1939. In the 1940s the total peaked at eight, reflecting the increase in clientele generated by first- and second-generation Basque Americans. Thereafter these businesses began a steady decline until 1970, when the last Basque hotel in the community closed.[33]

About sixteen years after Senator Taylor's legislation was enacted, Senator Pat McCarran and Representative Walter Baring of Nevada introduced bills before the Eighty-first Congress that would give skilled worker status to incoming herders.[34] In the second session, the McCarran bill was

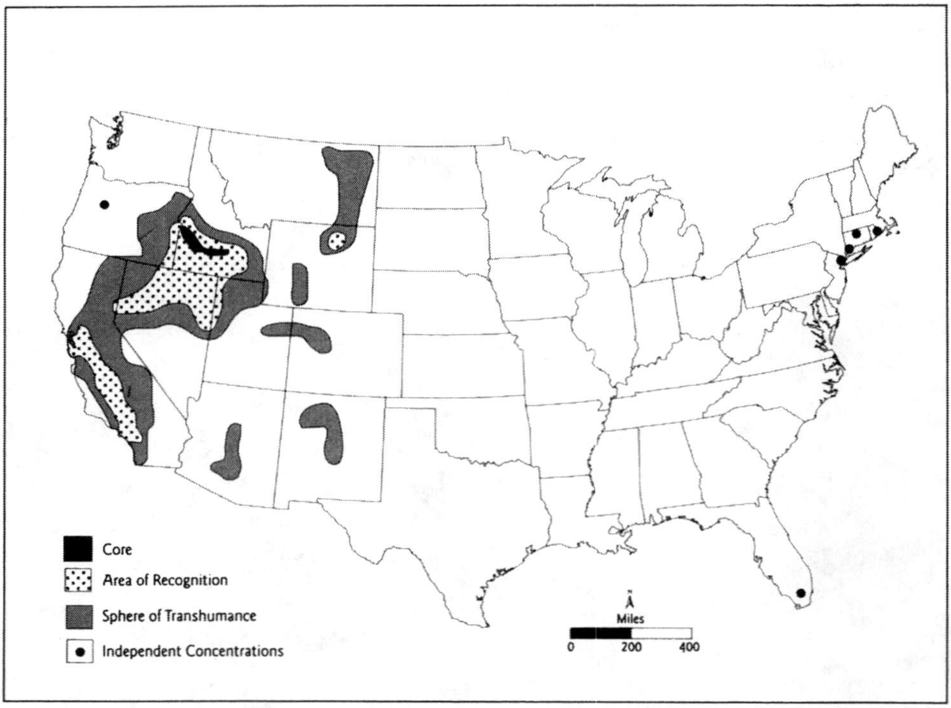


*Fig. 4. The various shadings on this map show areas in the United States where Basques have concentrated, where they have broad recognition among Basques and non-Basques, where they have been known for transhumance, or where they have developed an independent concentration.* Source: *Craig Campbell, "Basque American Ethnic Areas,"* 83–89.

incorporated into another piece of legislation and passed, allowing the admittance of up to 250 sheepherders on an annual basis as of June 30, 1950, in a piece of legislation that was later to be called the Sheepherder's Bill.[35] Then Wyoming's Senator Hunt proposed Senate bill 1217 to provide additional immigrant visas for aliens willing to accept jobs as herders. This bill amended the Sheepherder's Bill of June 30, 1950, and increased the number of sheepherders who would be allowed to enter the country annually from 250 to 550.[36] The passage of these occupation-related bills allowed Basques to continue to enter the United States at restricted levels. These Basques were allowed to stay long enough to be eligible for citizenship, which alleviated some immediate concern. But the new legislation did not diminish the worry within Basque-American communities over the decreasing number of Basques immigrating to the United States.

By the second session of the Eighty-second Congress, pressure was building to revise and codify the maze of immigration and naturalization laws enacted after the National Origins Act. The McCarran-Walter Act, officially known as the Immigration and Nationality Act of 1952, had revised the quota preference structure.[37] Among its many stipulations was one that allowed skilled agricultural workers to enter the country. Notably, the McCarran-Walter Act did not specify Basques as the only nationality able to take advantage of this provision. Nevertheless, many in the sheep industry considered the legislation a "Basque immigration" law. Senator Lehman of New York, for example, objected that admitting more Basque herders was an unfair practice because immigration quotas had not changed for other ethnic groups.[38]

Despite Lehman's objections, the "Sheepherder's Bill" remained part of the McCarran-Walter Act and encouraged the sheep industry, which was in need of revitalization. As author Nason Ruiz stated of the Basques, "No other group in the United States has received so much specific attention and legislation on the basis of occupational specialization."[39] Partly because of these bills, between 1942 and 1961 383 Basque men received permanent residency in the United States.[40] In 1965 the Western Range Association sponsored 1,283 work contracts for Basques, which were sanctioned by Senator Hunt's amendment.[41]

Recent research reveals that Basques have broken from earlier settlement patterns that were closely associated with the sheep industry in the twentieth century. The censuses of 1980 and 1990, for example, show that there are at least a few Basques in each of the fifty states. Of the 47,956 persons in the United States who identified themselves as being of Basque ancestry in 1990, Basque Americans in California outnumbered their counterparts in the state with the second largest population of Basques, Idaho, by a ratio of nearly four to one.[42] Nonetheless, as we can see in geographer Craig Campbell's map of Basque-American ethnic enclaves (figure 4), the area surrounding Boise and southern Idaho contains the most intense concentration of Basques found in the United States today.[43]

As we have seen, several important factors have influenced the settlement and migration patterns of Basques in the United States in the past century and a half. These forces carried them from the California mother lode to the southern and central valleys of California and then east over the Sierra Nevada into the Great Basin region. Throughout their history in this country, wherever they have settled or passed through Basques have established and supported their ethnic boardinghouses. We now turn to a discussion of the nation's earliest *ostatuak* and their *hoteleros*.

# 3

## *Ostatu Amerikanuak*

### The Basque-American Boardinghouse

#### DEFINING THE BASQUE BOARDINGHOUSE

American Basques frequently use the terms ostatuak, *boardinghouses*, and *hotels* interchangeably when describing the establishments that have catered to them over the past one hundred and fifty years. In point of fact, each term is partially accurate, but none describes all such Basque businesses. These places could be called *ostatuak* in that they attempted to maintain Old World Basque ethnicity and identity. Compared to the modern North American hotel, these businesses functioned more as boardinghouses or rooming houses. And yet they were hotels insofar as Basques adapting to the New World have often chosen this term to explain them to their non-Basque friends and associates. Further, the earliest *ostatuak* found in California and Nevada in the 1860s through the 1890s were often small homes stationed along wagon routes, and they would more accurately be labeled Basque outposts. Basque ethnic institutions known as *ostatuak*, boardinghouses, hotels, or outposts share basic elements, however. When the volume of clientele made it possible, they catered exclusively to Basques. In all instances, they were operated by Basques for Basques. They hosted a complex set of social functions that provided Basques with an environment to maintain their ethnicity, and they made Basque transition to and adaptation in the New World possible.

In the over two hundred interviews with *hoteleros* and Basques in general I have conducted or consulted, Basques frequently talked generally rather than specifically about the hotels. They rarely mentioned the names of the hotels they knew without further questioning. For example, when Lentxo Echanis described moving to southern California from Boise in 1922, he could recall the name of the *hotelera* and the hotel's location, but he could not remember the actual name of the boardinghouse or the name of the family that managed it.[1] Thus it could be that the generalized discussion of *ostatuak* in scholarly literature reflects the manner in which Basques themselves have spoken of their hotels, supporting the idea that the *ostatuak* have been and are "invisible institutions."

For consistency, I have generally followed the Basque-American practice of using the terms *hotel*, ostatu, and *boardinghouse* interchangeably. Nonetheless, there are instances in which a few distinctions augment our understanding of the nature of these Basque businesses. There were a number of Basque-owned establishments that were more rooming houses than hotels, boardinghouses, or *ostatuak* in that they offered neither meals nor kitchen privileges to their Basque lodgers.

In Boise during the 1920s, for example, there were a number of Basque-owned establishments that offered neither meals nor kitchen privileges to their Basque lodgers. These were rooming houses rather than hotels, boardinghouses, or *ostatuak*.

A few boardinghouses prepared meals exclusively for their boarders but not for "outsiders." These establishments might have been called either boardinghouses or rooming houses, depending upon the point of view of the person who was describing them. For example, a retired *hotelera* who had owned and operated what would be considered for our purposes a "full-fledged" hotel may have referred to such a place as a rooming house or a "closed" boardinghouse, but certainly not as an *ostatu*. Another Basque, perhaps less acquainted with the hotelkeeper's trade, may have described the same institution as an *ostatu*, a "small hotel," or a "little boardinghouse." Thus distinguishing hotels from other establishments offering lodging has often been a matter of the experiences of the person I spoke with or whose account I read, and often making a determination of how to categorize such an enterprise necessitated lengthy discussion and deliberation.

In American cities and towns that were home to Basques, one might encounter further distinctions between Basque boardinghouses and hotels. Although the terms are still regularly used interchangeably in Basque districts, there were occasionally a few establishments that were com-

*A room at the Star Hotel, Elko, Nevada. Photograph courtesy of the University of Utah Basque Boarding House Project.*

pletely closed to "outsiders," in which the *hoteleros* restricted service to their boarders, possibly a few local Basques, and an occasional invited guest. These were considered boardinghouses, not hotels. The major criterion for distinguishing a boardinghouse from a hotel in this instance was the clientele. Sorhondo's in San Francisco was considered a boardinghouse because it was off-limits to non-Basques. After nearly forty years of service, it closed in 1993. Of the ten Basque-owned establishments that remain today, none can afford to serve Basques exclusively.

To further confuse the discussion, *hotel, boardinghouse,* and ostatu imply different types of businesses in the Old World. Although these terms have been used interchangeably in the United States, in Europe the term *hotelak* refers to those businesses that offer room and board to both "insiders" and "outsiders"; whereas *ostatuak* are inns that rent rooms primarily to known members of the community and do not provide meals. In essence, Basques in the United States seem to have given up the Old World connotations for these terms and adopted a relaxed usage.

In *Living Downtown: A History of Residential Hotels in the United States*, architectural historian Paul Groth discussed a time gone by when living in urban hotels and boardinghouses was more common for Americans than was owning private home dwellings. According to Groth, four types of urban living situations emerged in the American urban landscape between 1880 and 1930: the socially opulent palace hotels, the mid-priced mansions catering to the upper-middle and middle classes, the rooming houses that housed middle- and lower-middle-class workers, and the cheap lodging houses that rented to the lower classes. Further, Groth found that boardinghouse residents "sorted themselves by ethnic, racial, and occupational considerations."[2] In terms of the national typology suggested in *Living Downtown*, the Basque *ostatu* would fall into the fourth category, that of the cheap lodging house, with an ethnic flare. Yet in contrast to Groth's description of lodgers as "people living completely apart from family," the newly arrived Basques often became surrogate children and family members of the *hoteleros*.[3] Groth's work focuses on living situations in large urban centers such as San Francisco and New York, although Basques did not limit themselves to big cities.

## CHARTING THE DEVELOPMENT OF THE BOARDINGHOUSES

Individual Basque boardinghouses can be categorized in terms of certain stages of historical development of the Basque boardinghouses of the West. Some scholars have suggested that five years after the appearance of the first Basque in a critical sheep-raising town an *ostatu* was likely to open, and that within a decade the vicinity might be home to two or more.[4] Where the arrival of that "first Basque" was followed by a rapid growth in the sheep industry, this assertion seems realistic. In towns that were stopovers for Basques traveling by rail, in which the *ostatu* was usually within sight of the station, the five-year theory also seems accurate. And in high-traffic or transition areas, such as Ogden, New York City, and San Francisco, hotels also would have developed rapidly after the arrival of the first Basques.

Even information on the earliest hotels tentatively supports the five-year theory, as in the case of the Plaza Hotel in San Juan Bautista, California. According to the census takers, ten people with Basque surnames were living in and around the town of San Juan Bautista as of 1850.[5] Four years later, Angelo and Maria Zanetta reopened the Plaza Hotel and began entertaining local ranchers and travelers. Among them were Basque ranchers and stockmen from the Mendota and Los Banos areas. The Plaza was a forerunner to later *ostatuak*, and its opening date followed closely after the initial Basque presence in San Juan Bautista, tending to support the five-year claim.

In a few locations where there was a limited Basque presence and relatively slow growth in the Basque population, however, it may have taken longer than five years for a hotel to be established, if one was established at all. This may have been the case in Jordan Valley and Ontario, Oregon, and Ely, Nevada, for example. There was also the experience of Pete Aguerreberry, a Basque miner who wandered through California's Death Valley wilderness searching for mineral wealth in the early twentieth century.[6] Aguerreberry's story includes mention of a few other Basques and a Basque-owned bar in the area, but in the decades he mined the valley, a hotel never appeared. *Ostatuak* may have differed from one another in their patterns of development, just as distinctive types of Basque hotels evolved.

One might also ask how many Basques were needed to support a hotel or group of hotels. For example, Bakersfield in 1900 had a population of 213 Basques and had four hotels.[7] Boise in 1900 had about 250 Basque residents and at least one hotel as well as a number of rooming houses. In 1917 Stockton had "twenty core Basque families and a large floating population of single Basque men" who supported four large *ostatuak* with adjoining handball courts.[8] In these instances, the "floating populations" must have greatly augmented business, since the potential number of "regulars" seems limited. In fact, the hotelkeepers may have relied more on business generated from traveling sheepmen than on local Basque customers.

Although there is little doubt that a lot of *ostatuak* were dependent upon the ebb and flow of bachelor Basque herders, in mining and lumbering communities *ostatuak* were similarly dependent upon the success of those enterprises. In the upper Panoche range in California, Juan Etcheverry's tiny Tres Pinos Hotel was supported by the success of Basque miners at the New Idria mines in the 1870s, just as the boardinghouse in Rupert, Idaho, was supported by Basques working the Minidoka Dam Project. In the northern California towns of Alturas and Susanville, the Beterbide, Goñi, and Arena *ostatuak* relied upon customers who got work in the nearby forests and lumber mills. And in the 1920s and 1930s Mrs. Raymond Uruburu's small boardinghouse in San Pedro counted on the regular arrival of Basque merchant marines to the Port of Los Angeles.[9]

Table 3.1 lists the percentage of the Basque-American population en-

Table 3.1 Occupations of Basques in 1900 and 1910
(IN CALIFORNIA, IDAHO, NEVADA, AND WYOMING)

| Occupations | Number in 1900 | Percentage* in 1900 | Number in 1910 | Percentage* in 1910 |
|---|---|---|---|---|
| Agriculture | 320 | 66.4 | 2,037 | 42.9 |
| Hotel | 32 | 6.6 | 329 | 6.9 |
| Mining | 5 | 1.0 | 380 | 8.0 |
| Laundry | 16 | 3.3 | 269 | 5.7 |
| Unskilled worker | 54 | 11.2 | 971 | 20.4 |
| Railroad | 0 | — | 66 | 1.4 |
| Factory work | 0 | — | 56 | 1.2 |
| Fishing | 1 | .2 | 8 | .2 |
| Office work | 0 | — | 49 | 1.0 |
| Sales | 0 | — | 56 | 1.2 |
| Merchandise | 6 | 1.3 | 55 | 1.1 |
| Bakery | 2 | .4 | 55 | 1.2 |
| Government work | 1 | .2 | 16 | .3 |
| Skilled work | 11 | 2.3 | 194 | 4.1 |
| Professions | 9 | 1.9 | 66 | 1.4 |
| Cloth manufacture | 9 | 1.9 | 28 | .6 |
| Services | 16 | 3.3 | 114 | 2.4 |
| TOTAL | 482 | 100.0 | 4,749 | 100.0 |

*Source:* Arrizabalaga, "Statistical Survey," 126.
An asterisk (*) denotes percentage of the Basque population engaged in this field of work.

gaged in various occupations in California, Nevada, Idaho, and Wyoming as of 1900 and 1910. As we can see, the number of Basques engaged in hotel keeping in the West remained the same or increased slightly from 6.6 to 6.9 percent, but the total number of Basques doing hotel work increased tenfold from 32 in 1900 to 329 in 1910.[10] In Los Angeles County, however, a change in the general pattern occurred. The percentage of Basques employed in hotel-related jobs decreased sharply from 12.3 to 5.4 percent over the same ten-year period, yet that change involved only a net of 10 people. At first glance, the decline in the number of Basques working in hotels in the Los Angeles area seems to contradict the dramatic increase in the Basque population in Los Angeles County during that period.[11] But the drop from 12.3 to 5.4 percent can be partially explained by the small size of the population, especially as compared with the total population of Basques in the four Western states. Another possible explanation is that Los Angeles Basque town hotels were declining in number and importance within the neighborhood as Los Angeles Basques were beginning to move out of the city and into the larger southern California region. Thus although these Basques might still be tallied within the greater Los Angeles County area, they would not be tied to the old downtown boardinghouses.

When we consider the century and a half that has elapsed since the first evidence of Basque boardinghouses in the American West, we note that there were four chronological stages in the history of *ostatuak*. The earliest could be called the formative period, when Basque outposts emerged and boardinghouses gained their first foothold in California and Nevada between approximately 1850 and 1890. The next four decades marked the zenith of Basque hotel keeping, when Basque migration to the United States peaked and *ostatuak* were evident in each of the eleven Western states and in New York City. The 1930s and 1940s constituted a brief hiatus, during which *ostatuak* sustained their success and popularity among Basques, their progeny, and non-Basques, yet the overall number of *ostatuak* declined. The fourth and final period from 1950 to the present has been and continues to be characterized by the dramatic decline and demise of the Basque boardinghouses. Grouping the *ostatuak* into four broad chronological divisions is convenient when we want to study their development over time, but the significance of these chronological divisions should not be overemphasized; each *ostatu* can be placed in one era or another, but some spanned two eras or more and shared the characteristics and trends of those eras.

Throughout this book we will explore specific characteristics of *ostatuak* whose existence we could verify through records, directories, and firsthand accounts. We will not be exploring the earliest hotels, for the most part those that were in business before the 1880s, for a couple of reasons. Unfortunately, firsthand descriptions of these hotels are not available, and our knowledge of this era is diminishing because there are fewer and fewer elderly Basques who can recall the 1890s and early 1900s. The hotels were first found based on verbal accounts, but unfortunately the recollections of hotel owners, customers, and employees, which could bring the *ostatuak* to life again and make the final decade of the nineteenth century part of our historical record, are increasingly difficult to locate. Furthermore, it is not clear that the early hotels served Basques exclusively; whereas by the twentieth century a majority of *ostatuak* were well enough established to cater almost exclusively to Basque boarders. Despite the dangers of "presentism" in history, we are forced to some extent to distinguish between what was and was not a hotel by comparing past establishments to our twentieth-century model of the hotel.

The inner workings of the *ostatuak* operating between 1850 and 1890 are somewhat beyond our reach. How Basques staffed their hotels, who their regular guests were, or how *hoteleros* got along with non-Basques in their communities are questions that remain unanswered. The hotels back then were probably similar to the *ostatuak* of the twentieth century in that they offered simple lodgings, family-style dining, and a shared language and culture. To assume further similarities beyond basic characteristics common to most *ostatuak*, however, would be inappropriate.

Generally, the 1890s seem to be a turning point in the history of Basque hotels. Surges in immigration near the turn of the century and the concomitant growth in the sheep industry certainly led to an increase in the number of Basque hotels in California during that decade. As a result the migration of Basques to other Western states also accelerated in that decade. For example, Richard Etulain has written about the dramatic increase in the number of Basques in Jordan Valley, Oregon; Boise, Idaho; and Yakima, Washington, around 1890 and the decrease in their numbers some thirty years later.[12] As we shall see, the sheer number of *ostatuak* in the eleven Western states increased appreciably in the 1890s.[13] But a word of caution is also warranted: much of our depiction of 1890 as a watershed in the history of the *ostatuak* is based on the limits of our living memory.

## CUSTOMERS AND TYPES OF HOTELS

Basque hotels had a number of potential customer groups; among them were single Basque residents, Basques who lived in the area, Basques who visited from other areas, non-Basque tourists, and local non-Basque residents.[14] Among those taking up residence in the *ostatuak* were newly arrived bachelor herders, Basque herders during off-season, honeymooners, Basque serving girls, and the Basque family who operated the establishment. Non-Basque tourists, out-of-towners, and local residents may have frequented the dining halls and bars of these establishments but were less likely to ask for room and board.

Pleasing such a variety of customer groups has been one of the major challenges Basque hotelkeepers have faced. During peak periods of Basque immigration, from 1890 through 1930, for example, some hotelkeepers could cater exclusively to Basque clientele. Since the 1940s, with the notable decline in the number of Basques immigrating to the United States, hotelkeepers have gradually and then increasingly solicited non-Basque clientele as well as second- and third-generation Basque Americans.

There are further distinctions that can be made among and between

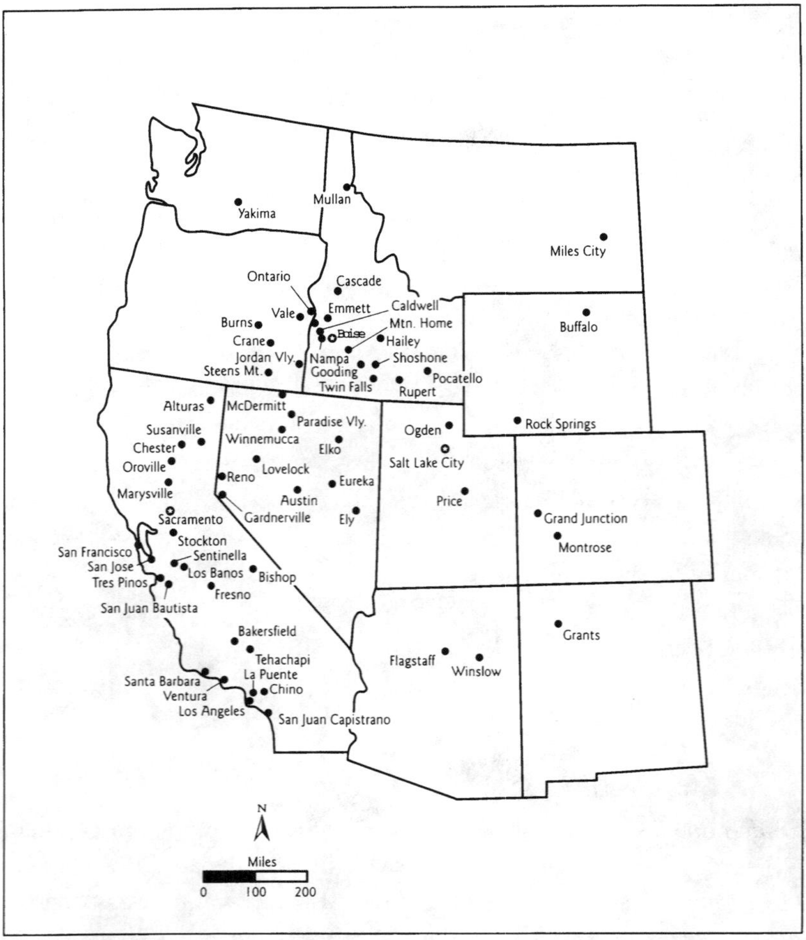


*Fig. 5. Major Basque communities with* ostatuak.

hotels, based on size, location, the *hoteleros'* birthplace, and the number of years an *ostatu* has been in operation. Using location and function as a basis for categorizing *ostatuak*, one can distinguish basic types of hotels: the transit hotel, the spin-off hotel, the regional hotel, the local hotel, the Basque town hotel, and the tourist hotel.

Clearly *ostatuak* throughout the United States often fall into some overlapping categories. For example, Ogden was a regional center for Great Basin Basques, so its Basque hotels were regional hotels, yet they were also transit hotels. Likewise, both regional and local hotels might be found in a Basque town. And a hotel that was once a regional hotel, such as Noriega's in Bakersfield or the Santa Fe in Reno, might today be considered more of a tourist hotel. Although categorizing Basque *ostatuak* can assist us in making useful distinctions, the categories should not be regarded too rigidly.

## The Transit Hotels

Valentin Aguirre's Casa Vizcaína in New York City was a transit hotel whose primary function was to house sojourners for brief periods, help them with their intended travel plans, and send them on their way. In 1914, when Lentxo Echanis arrived in New York City, he stayed at Valentin Aguirre's boardinghouse on Cherry Street. Decades later he remarked at how easy the Aguirres had made his trip, for Valentin's son Tomas had received him at the Ellis Island Immigration Center, Benita had fed and housed him, Valentin had arranged the remainder of his cross-country trip for him, and another son, Peter, had delivered him and his fellow travelers to the train station.

Lentxo's experience at the New York boardinghouse was remarkably similar to that of hundreds, if not thousands, of other Basque immigrants. French Basque Beltran Paris, for example, described his arrival in America to author William Douglass as follows:

> a Spanish Basque guy, Valentin Aguirre, had that [Basque boardinghouse] and it was his son who came to meet the boat. . . . He had a big car waiting to take us to the hotel. We stayed in that place for a day and a half, and then Aguirre sent us to the train station in taxis.[15]

Aguirre's was the consummate transit hotel in that it served more Basques than any other boardinghouse known in the recorded history of these establishments, and in the United States it was the only one that operated a travel agency as part of its business. Among Basques who came to this country before the advent of air travel, it would be difficult to find any who had not stopped at Aguirre's.

In his youth, Valentin Aguirre had been quite a sojourner himself. Born in Monte Sollube, Bizkaia, in 1891, he left his hometown at the age of ten, finding work aboard the *Alceda*, a merchant vessel that sailed from Euskal Herria to ports in South America and Cuba.[16] At the age of twenty-six Valentin gave up life on the open sea and became a tugboat

*New York City* hotelero *Valentin Aguirre*.
*Courtesy of Emilia Doyaga*.

stoker in New York Bay. Four years later he successfully completed the Civil Service exam in English and thus became eligible to work on New York City's boats. During his early New York years, Valentin met his eighteen-year-old bride, Benita Orbe. Although he had been sent to ask the young woman's hand in marriage on behalf of another, when he laid eyes on Benita, he asked for her hand for himself instead. She accepted, and within a few years the two set up their own boardinghouse, which came to be called Casa Vizcaína.

In part because their hotel was located at a significant jumping off point for so many Basque sojourners, Valentin and Benita Aguirre's reputation as boardinghouse owners spread throughout the American West, Latin America, and the Basque Country. Benita's hospitality and good meals attracted numerous New York and East Coast Basques to town on a regular basis. Valentin kept in touch with the shipping and travel agents who served his customers and contacted other *hoteleros* to learn of the availability of jobs. Further, the eight Aguirre children were raised at Casa Vizcaína, and all of them contributed to keeping the complicated enterprise going. Lucy, Antonia, Tomas, John, Valentina, Anita, Peter, and Mary primarily helped with domestic chores, cooking, serving, and escorting Basque travelers to and from the local docks and train stations.

As business at the Aguirre expanded, the family made several moves within the neighborhood. Their final *ostatu* was located at 82 Bank Street, on the corner of Bank and Bleecker Streets in Greenwich Village. In 1917 they converted the structure into three enterprises: the Santa Lucia Hotel, the Jai Alai Restaurant, and Valentin Aguirre's Travel Agency. Surely when Valentin passed away in 1953 an era had ended for Basques. Without doubt, Aguirre's played a more significant role in the settlement of Basques in North America than did any other *ostatu*, and it certainly was the most famous transit hotel.

On a smaller scale than Aguirre's, the Hogar Hotel in Salt Lake City also served an important function as a transit hotel. As with many other *ostatuak*, the Hogar's Second Street location was near the town's only train depot—on a major rail line that carried Basques to and from Los Angeles and Boise. The Hogar's owners, John and Claudia Landa, greeted Basques from the Intermountain area for more than fifty years. One description of *hotelero* John Landa is reminiscent of our impressions of New York's famous Valentin Aguirre: John Landa was "a tiny man with a powerful voice. He had all the connections. He was like the Basque ambassador."[17]

## The Spin-off Hotels

Because the transit hotels, by definition, moved people in and out of their doors rapidly, they may have contributed to the development of spin-off hotels in surrounding areas. For example, the hotels that developed as offshoots from Los Angeles's Basque town, in towns such as Chino, Bakersfield, and La Puente, could be called spin-off hotels because they grew up to serve Basque customers generated by the Basque town hotels. Similarly, the *ostatuak* that came into existence in outlying areas of southern Idaho and eastern Oregon as a result of Boise's Basque town could also be considered spin-off hotels, as could those in Paradise Valley, Nevada, as spin-offs of Winnemucca hotels.

## The Regional Hotels

Another type of Basque *ostatu* is the regional hotel. San Francisco's Basque hotels could be considered to be regional in that they served as vacation spots and honeymoon centers for many California and Nevada

Basques. Basque hotels in Ogden, Utah, also fall into this category because many incoming Bizkaians who changed railways in Ogden on their way to southern Idaho, and later Montana and Wyoming Basques, traveled through Ogden to reach southern California. Like San Francisco, Ogden became a regional focal point for Basque sheepmen in the Great Basin and Intermountain areas. The Basque hotels in Ely, Nevada; Marysville and Fresno, California; and Shoshone, Idaho, and other places that had a less potent drawing power but still attracted Basques from neighboring counties might be designated as semi-regional hotels.

By the early twentieth century, Basques seem to have favored three areas as vacation or honeymoon destinations. Those from the eastern seaboard region tended toward Valentin Aguirre's in New York City. Great Basin Basques usually picked hotels in Ogden or Reno. And during winter months, semiretired or elder Basque sheepmen from the Great Basin would congregate in southern California *ostatuak* to enjoy the comparatively warm weather. Nevada rancher Beltran Paris said that he developed the custom of leaving northern Nevada and "wintering" in the boardinghouses of Bakersfield,. California. Central California Basques from Stockton and Fresno, on the other hand, leaned toward the cooler clime of San Francisco in the summers.[18] Because of favorable climate or location, then, *ostatuak* in San Francisco, Bakersfield, Chino, New York, and Ogden became vacation hotels and regional hubs for the entire hotel network.[19] On a smaller scale, the hotels of Boise, Reno, and Los Angeles likewise served eastern Oregonians, northern Nevadans, and Basques of the Southwest. Basques congregating at these large and medium-size regional centers tended to support the longevity and vitality of the entire Basque hotel network in the United States.

## The Local Hotels

A fourth type of hotel might be called the local hotel. Serving the needs of local herders and their families, such a hotel was a small-scale local center serving counties or towns. Burns and Ontario, Oregon; Alturas and Oroville, California; Winslow and Flagstaff, Arizona; and Emmett and Mountain Home, Idaho, have been home to local hotels. An irony of the local hotel is that while it has depended upon those in rural agricultural occupations for its survival, it has been most successfully located in small urban centers. In the twentieth century, instances of Basque *ostatuak* in rural settings have been virtually nonexistent. The small-town or rural *ostatuak* of Firebaugh, Mendota, or McKittrick, California, for example, once had thriving businesses, but they disappeared decades ago.

## The Basque Town *Ostatuak*

In some localities, larger Basque populations have supported a number of hotels within one neighborhood district, in what we have called a Basque town. Such concentrations of hotels grew up in a number of cities. Throughout this book the term *Basque town* has been reserved for the largest or most intense concentrations of Basque *ostatuak*, such as those found in Los Angeles, San Francisco, Reno, Elko, Boise, and Stockton. But on a smaller scale many towns, such as Fresno, Bakersfield, Winnemucca, Shoshone, and Ely, have hosted important clusters of hotels as well. Even the comparatively small town of Yakima, Washington, at one time had its own Basque neighborhood.

A characteristic sometimes found among Basque town hotels is that they tended to take on the Old World Basque identity of their hotelkeepers. In the 1920s, for example, Stockton's Basque town had three French and two Spanish Basque hotelkeepers, and their customers were divided accordingly. Similarly, a decade earlier in Los Angeles's Basque town, customers distinguished between French Basque and Navarrese establishments. In Boise's predominantly Bizkaian Basque district, however, very little distinction was made between Bizkaian and Gipuzkoan hotels.

## Tourist Hotels and Basque Restaurants

The final type of Basque hotel would be the one that has developed most recently. The decline of the *ostatuak* in the last two or three decades has been accompanied by the emergence of the tourist hotel. The term is based on the fact that such hotels have to attract non-Basque clientele in order to survive. As opposed to the traditional *ostatuak*, these hotels offer room and board to Basques and non-Basques, or they rent rooms without offering board. They tend to employ non-Basques who dress in Basque costume, decorate their interiors more than traditional hotels tend to, offer a menu including non-Basque dishes, accept all major credit cards, and advertise in the local media. Such establishments are a step or two removed from the traditional *ostatuak*.

In California the devolution from hotel to restaurant has been apparent over recent decades. Basque hotels in Los Angeles, Stockton, Merced,

Tehachapi, McKittrick, Alturas, La Puente, and Santa Barbara have disappeared; and in Los Banos, Chino, San Francisco, Bakersfield, and Fresno hotels have either closed their doors to boarders or severely limited the number of new residents they take in. In Nevada the story is much the same: Basque hotels in Austin, Battle Mountain, Carson City, Ely, Eureka, Fallon, McDermitt, Paradise Valley, and Unionville have disappeared; only Reno, Elko, Winnemucca, and Gardnerville have boardinghouses today. But in many instances, upon closing their doors to boarders *hoteleros* have decided to focus on the restaurant part of their business. Of the ten remaining *ostatuak*, most have become Basque restaurants housed in an old *ostatu*. The Santa Fe Hotel in Fresno, for example, houses only a handful of boarders, but it relies on its restaurant and bar revenues for its livelihood.

## SOCIAL LIFE AT THE BASQUE BOARDINGHOUSES

In addition to being the herder's, miner's, seaman's, and lumberjack's home away from home, the *ostatuak* have served other important functions for Basque Americans and their families. In the earlier days wives living on remote ranches would come to stay at the nearest town or city hotel during the last stages of their pregnancies and frequently gave birth there. Not uncommonly, Basque ranchers in rural areas would send their children to the hotels to board during the school year.

Moreover, Basque hotels often hosted special occasions such as marriages, family celebrations, dances, and wakes. One Stockton Basque reported that when members of her family had a birthday, they expected all local Basques to gather at their favorite *ostatu* to help them celebrate.[20] In small towns where there was no Roman Catholic church, weddings, confirmations, and baptisms were often performed in the front room or lobby of the Basque hotel. And in a few instances elderly Basques have reported attending wakes and reciting the rosary in the hotel lobbies of remote boardinghouses.

Often Sunday was the day to visit the local hotel. Basques from outlying areas would pack up their families and make their way to a favored *ostatu*. There they might share a meal, cheer at a handball match, play a few rounds of *mus*, or attend a dance. For many hotelkeepers, Sunday was both dreaded and anticipated, because it was the most profitable day of the week yet it was also the day when they worked the hardest. As one *hotelera* stated, "Sunday was our toughest day."[21]

*A celebration in a Basque boardinghouse, probably in Alturas, California, ca. 1920. Courtesy of the High Desert Museum, Bend, Oregon.*

Hotels also helped create Basque-American families. Hotel owners often sent to Europe for Basque serving girls to work in their hotels. So frequently did these women meet their future husbands at the hotels that the Basque hotels have been referred to as "marriage mills."[22] In fact, many of the married people mentioned in this book married someone they met at a Basque hotel. In Ontario, Oregon, for example, *hotelera* Maria Echanis explained, "First, I would bring the young girls to work. First thing, they'd meet one of the young herders . . . then marriage!"[23]

Most of the social opportunities offered by the *ostatuak* are remembered fondly by Basque Americans. When interviewed, Basques are likely to speak of the friendships they formed there. Occasionally, a Basque couple will discuss their lifelong friendship with other newlyweds they met while honeymooning at an *ostatu*. Nevada Basques even developed a special term for this type of relationship, calling these friends their *urtekoak*, and they report celebrating anniversaries and special events with their special friends throughout their lifetime.[24]

The *ostatuak* directly or indirectly provided Basques with *urtekoak*, employment, storage space, a convalescent or retirement center, and even a place for Basque women to give birth to their children. Or a place to play handball, or jai alai, go dancing, or gamble. During Prohibition and earlier, ladies would gather in separate "women's parlors" where they might drink a coffee or chocolate and exchange news. If they preferred, wine or alcohol was available for them in the kitchen.[25] At Elko's Overland during Prohibition, women usually requested lemonade, grenadine, and soda. The more daring favored a mixture of beer and soda known as *panache* or a sherry served in the hotel's dining room. And around back, a more discreet alley entrance allowed Basques and non-Basques entrance to the Sabalas' speakeasy.[26]

The years between 1919 and 1933 were full of consternation for Basque hotelkeepers. Without exception, *hoteleros* during Prohibition were under pressure from two sides—on the one hand, their customers were urging them to serve alcohol illegally, and, on the other, the "prohibes" were constantly threatening to inspect them and shut them down at any hour. In some locations, such as in Bakersfield, *hoteleros* developed an elaborate system for distributing alcoholic beverages, and, more often than not, they successfully evaded the law. As the daughter of *hoteleros* Simon and Josefa Galdos at Charcha's in Emmett, Idaho, quipped: "Can you imagine the Basque people thinking it was wrong to serve wine and whiskey?"[27] In Los Angeles, a son of a *hotelero* reported that local police officers shamelessly took bribes in exchange for offering protection. All but two of the *hoteleros* interviewed in this study served alcohol illegally, because they were certain that not selling it would destroy them financially.

Many *hoteleros* in the northwestern states were able to get bootleg supplies from Canada without incident. Yet in Yakima, Washington, the Arraldes forbade the use of alcohol in their house and still managed a successful *ostatu*, because if their boarders wanted to drink, they sent them to other rooming houses in the neighborhood.[28]

Around Jordan Valley, Oregon, and McDermitt, Nevada, Basque bootleggers reported contacts who could supply alcohol across three state boundaries. Local Basques tell of one boardinghouse owner who usually sent boarders to the cellar to use his bottle, but on one occasion he suddenly realized he had left the bottle on the kitchen table unattended. As luck would have it, at that moment he overheard his wife talking with strangers in the front of the house, jumped to his feet, sneaked into the kitchen, and quickly stashed the evidence in a chamber pot.[29]

Whether it was the chamber pot, the water closet, the kitchen cabinet, or the cellar shelves, most *hoteleros* had a special spot where they stashed their supply of alcohol. Often they let regular customers know where to find the booze. Jonathan Sweet, current owner of the Landas' old Hogar Hotel in Salt Lake City, described his surprise a few years ago when he discovered a stash of "Prohibition whiskey" in the hotel's walls. Each of the unopened, full bottles was marked 1924. It seems that the Landas had not needed their reserves, had forgotten where they had stashed them, or found the first batches unacceptable.[30]

When describing "getting pinched" by federal or local agents, *hoteleros* often report feelings of betrayal and injustice. In Oregon, according to the account of an Oregon-born author, three agents who had just enjoyed a large meal accompanied by red wine at one place of business detained the *hotelera* and then searched the cellar for a wine press or still. They found neither, but they destroyed the foods stored in the cellar anyway, including the house's supply of canned fruits and vegetables. Although the charges against the woman were eventually dismissed and she was released, the authorities never offered to make up for the damage.[31]

The Oregon-born author of this account noted that the women of the boardinghouses were arrested instead of their husbands.[32] This may be an accurate description of what happened in Burns, Oregon, but the *etxe aitak* were less fortunate in other parts of the West. For example, Jose Uberuaga spent a few months in the Boise jail for selling alcohol to a federal agent, and his daughter remembers that as a young girl she waved to her father mornings and afternoons as she passed the jail.[33] In Bakersfield the local constabulary stormed the Amestoys' hotel on three separate occasions. In the course of the first two invasions, Francisco was arrested, and the third time his wife had a turn in the jailhouse. Thus in some communities the *hotelero* seems to have been just as vulnerable as the *hotelera*. Further, whether it was the *hotelero* or the *hotelera* who was arrested may have varied depending on a number of factors, such as local custom or who was on the premises at the time of the raid.

## THE PHYSICAL DESIGN OF THE BOARDINGHOUSES

Basques traveling from one hotel to another during peak years would have noticed that the physical layout of the *ostatuak* was fairly consistent. The lodgings were usually two- or three-story buildings with the kitchen, bar, dining hall, and card or parlor rooms occupying the first floor. Private quarters for the hotelkeeper and his family were often located on the first floor near the kitchen, toward the back of the building. Occasionally, the operators took a few rooms on the second floor with the boarders. The second and third stories contained dormitory-style rooms for boarders and hotel employees. Bathing facilities were most often found at the front and back of the long hallways that divided the upper floors. Breezes, the direction of sunlight, and street and kitchen noises were often factors boarders considered in selecting a room. Long-term boarders usually took the favored rooms, leaving the others for less frequent visitors. Some of the newer hotels provided wash basins in the individual rooms.

The lower floor and cellar of the boardinghouse were sometimes used to store foodstuffs or as a wine cellar. Outbuildings might be used as a toolshed or as a place to cure pork sausage and other meats. Attached to one side of the building there might be a handball court and, in earlier days, a stable and livery.

When the *ostatu* was not of the two- or three-story variety, the next most frequent type was a sizeable one- or two-story brick or wooden-frame home whose rooms had been converted to accommodate boarders. Examples include Uberuaga's in Boise, Arraldes' in Yakima, Landa's in Salt Lake City, Madariaga's in Jordan Valley, and Arrieta's in Battle Mountain. In fact, such converted homes seem to have been more common in less urban areas and in the Basque communities of the High Desert and Intermountain region than in Reno, Nevada, or in most of California.

## THE *Hotelero* AND *Hotelera*

Clearly, the hotel-keeping couple was crucial to the success of each *ostatu*. The hotelkeeper was oftentimes called upon to represent both New and Old Worlds. For the newly arrived Basque, he served as interpreter of American culture. For the New World Basque and his children, he provided a sense of Old World heritage. In essence, the hotelkeeper had to win the trust of the Old World Basques while also accommodating the demands of the younger generations of Basque Americans.

Very rarely was a hotelkeeper alone able to manage an *ostatu*. More often, a husband and wife team operated the hotels with the occasional assistance of other family members and/or hired staff. Traditionally, the *hotelero* ran the bar from morning until closing, while his wife supervised the preparation of noon and evening meals, the serving girls who waited tables, and the cleaning girls who maintained the rooms. If business was

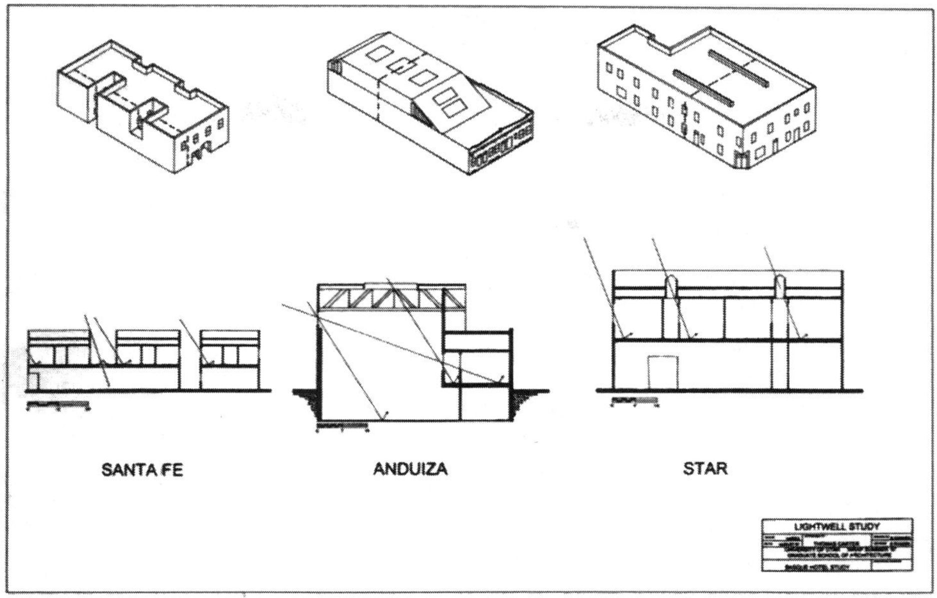


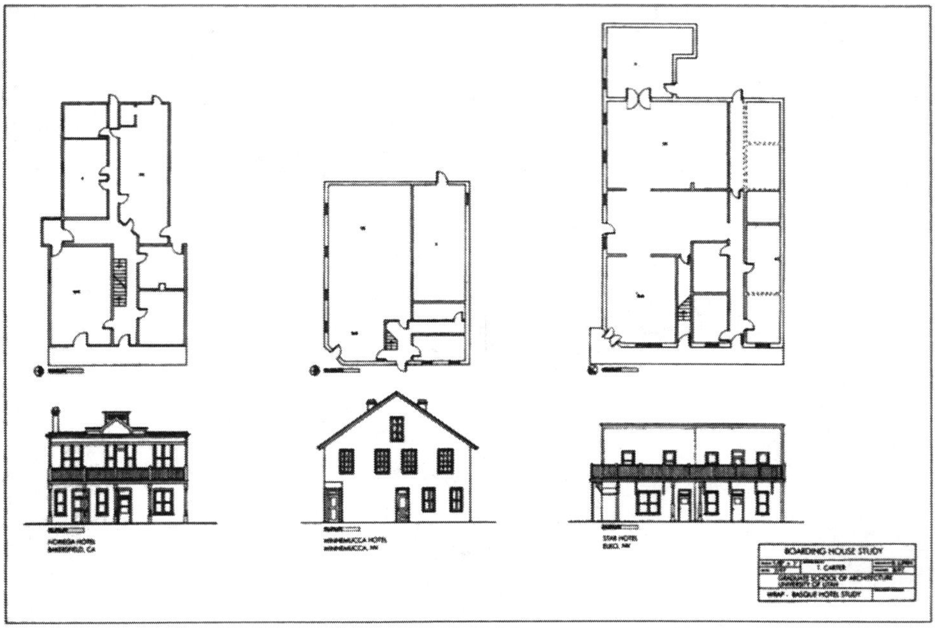


*Examples of hotel exteriors and their external light sources. Pictured here are the Santa Fe Hotel in Fresno, California; the Anduiza in Boise, Idaho; and the Star Hotel, in Elko, Nevada. Courtesy of the University of Utah Basque Boarding House Project. Examples of hotel fronts and their floor plans showing a variety of exteriors and interiors. Pictured are Noriega's in Bakersfield, California; the Winnemucca Hotel in Winnemucca, Nevada; and the Star Hotel in Elko, Nevada. Courtesy of the University of Utah Basque Boarding House Project.*

good and there was ample demand, hotelkeepers could hire additional bartenders, serving girls, maids, and cooks. If they could not afford to hire outside help, the husband and wife did all the work. Hotelkeepers rarely advertised to fill job openings since they preferred verbal recommendations.

Generally speaking, a Basque male born in the Old World and a Basque-American woman born in the United States have constituted the "perfect" hotel-keeping couple.[34] Among the eleven San Francisco hotelkeepers Jean Decroos interviewed for his study, for example, nine were Old World Basque men, and a majority had married New World Basque women who would escort boarders to "in-town" appointments.[35] With this combination, the first-generation customer could share common Old World concerns with the hotelkeeper in his native Euskara but turn to the *hotelera* when he needed assistance with New World dilemmas. The female hotelkeeper was generally more familiar with "American ways" and could serve as translator, escort, and adviser. Although this may have been the usual order of affairs in most locations, Boise residents have told me that in their experience it was more often the *hotelero*'s job to escort boarders to the local doctor, banker, or lawyer in town.

Based on the experiences of most of the hotelkeepers I interviewed, in most instances, *hoteleros*—male or female—found it particularly difficult to manage a boardinghouse alone; Santa Bilbao's boardinghouse in Twin Falls, Idaho, or Carmen Arruti's in Mountain Home, Idaho, were rare exceptions to this rule. In most cases a recently widowed *hotelera* or *hotelero* had to either quickly employ trustworthy help to fill the void of his or her former partner, consider selling, or eventually remarry, because doing the work of both people on a daily basis was impossible.

For many couples the rigorous daily schedules required of hotel operators undoubtedly contributed to their relatively short tenure in the hotel business. In fact, *hoteleros* rarely remained in operation beyond fifteen or twenty years, if that long.[36] Yet as we will see, the Jaureguis of Elko, Nevada; the Uberuagas, Ysursas, and Letemendis of Boise; and the Galdoses and Bicandis of Emmett, Idaho, were exceptions to this rule.

Hotel keeping could also be difficult on the families running the hotels. In one interview a *hotelera* said that in the hotels "there was no room for weakness," and that the daily demands of cleaning, cooking, and serving interfered with the family's desire to be together. Another interviewee stated that during the years she and her husband owned a hotel, they could "never get away together." In addition, a child of a hotelkeeper reported, "We kids never wanted to run a hotel. . . . [Y]our front room was always a bar."[37]

Children living in the hotels were expected to work. One woman remembered that as a child she visited friends whose parents were Basque hotelkeepers in Burns, Oregon. She stated that the *hotelera* there was "very tough" on her daughters, in that they "had lots more work than the rest of us."[38] One son of a hotelkeeper remembers vividly his more unpleasant daily chores in an early Los Angeles *ostatu*, which included cleaning sheepdog pens and horse stalls in the livery.

*Hoteleros'* families have recounted the less attractive aspects of living in Basque hotels as well as the more pleasant ones. In some locations and in certain eras hotel keeping was not highly regarded among Basque Americans. From around 1890 to 1920 in Stockton, for example, hotelkeepers were considered to be of inferior social status compared with local ranchers and stockmen.[39] The marked preference for making one's living directly from the land among recently arrived Basques probably related to the Old World distinction between *baserritarak* and *kaletarrak*. In the Basque Country, as in parts of the American West, it was considered far better to have an "honest" job working the soil or raising livestock on one's *baserri* than to depend directly on another for one's livelihood, as the town dwellers or *kaletarrak* often did. But this phenomenon is not peculiar to Basques; it has appeared among other immigrant groups in rural America.

Although *ostatuak* rarely passed successfully to the next generation, there were two exceptions in Boise: the Letemendi and Uberuaga boardinghouses, where the children of the *hoteleros* inherited and managed thriving business enterprises. Alustiza's California Hotel in Stockton was operated by father and son together until Fermin retired and Alfonso stepped in as sole proprietor. But for the most part second-generation hotelkeepers proved too far removed from the Old World village, the sheep camp, and the Basque language to earn the herders' trust.

## HOTEL NAMES

The name and ownership of the *ostatuak* are also noteworthy. Frequently Basques refer to an *ostatu* by the operator's last name. For example, Los Angeles's Basque town had hotels called Chotro's, Mayo's, Ballade's, and Hirigoyen's. Such names suggest that the building and business were the property of the operator, yet the operator was often a lessee rather than an owner. Establishing ownership of the *ostatuak* is especially problematic because very few operators appear in county records or courthouse archives.

That many of the *ostatuak* "owners" were lessees may also partially explain their relatively short tenure; indeed, Basque "owners" rarely operated a hotel for more than ten years. In Los Angeles, the practice of leasing rather than owning a hotel may also explain why the relocation of *ostatuak* was not unusual. The Hotels de France and the Hotel des Pyrenees, for example, both relocated three and four times, respectively, during their thirty years of existence.[40]

The names of *ostatuak* in Nevada, such as the Overland, differ from those we have seen in California. For the most part if California's boardinghouses were not named after the owner or operator, they boasted names such as the Pyrenees, the Chalet Basque, Woolgrowers'. But Nevada's Basques have more frequently referred to their *ostatuak* by the town's name, of which the Winnemucca, the Golconda, the Lovelock, the Ely, the Eureka, and the McDermitt are examples. Also names such as the Martin, the Star, and the Overland, which were common in Nevada, were rare in neighboring states.

### NETWORKS, ADVERTISING, AND COMPETITION AMONG THE HOTELS

Throughout their history, Basque *ostatuak* have been part of a larger network of hotels. Throughout the West, hotelkeepers came to know of other *hoteleros* from customers and through a referral system. But this was a gradual process. For example, in the 1890s Basques in southern California knew very little about their cousins in the Pacific Northwest. Editions of the Los Angeles–based newspapers *California'ko Eskual (California Basque Land) Herria* and *Escualdun Gazeta* include scant mention of Basques in Idaho or even in northern Nevada. A major factor contributing to the isolation of groups of Basques in the American West was that upon arriving in this country, Basques primarily sought out other Basques who were from their home villages or families. Thus through chain migration Idaho became a colony of Bizkaians, California became primarily a place for French Basques and Navarrese, and in the Great Basin there was a mixture of French and Spanish Basques.

Despite obstacles, a referral system and network for the hotels gradually emerged. As Basques became involved in the sheep industry in the American West, sheepmen needing herders began inquiring at local hotels. As Basques traveled from one area to another, they invariably stayed in *osta-*

*tuak*. One customer might praise the fine people at that "Bizkaian hotel in Ogden," and, eventually, another customer would hear about the place and stop there. Further, a Montana Basque vacationing in a Reno hotel would return home with opinions about the hotel, its service, and its hotelkeeper. Because the *hotelero*'s livelihood depended upon referrals from customers and from other *hoteleros*, he had made a point of talking with guests about services available elsewhere and tried to keep himself informed about the wider network of hotels.

In recent decades the annual circuit of festivals and picnics throughout Basque-American communities in the West has also supported the hotel referral system. Many California Basques, for example, travel to picnics in Chino, San Francisco, Los Banos, Reno, Fresno, Boise, and Bakersfield each spring and early summer. In addition, as the North American Basque Organization has grown, its annual meetings have given Amerikanuak the opportunity to meet and learn about Basque restaurants, clubs, and hotels in other parts of the nation.[41]

Complex familial connections among Basques throughout the hotel network have also supported the referral system among *ostatuak*. For example, *hotelera* Anselma Ballaz Amestoy of Bakersfield and *hotelero* Tomás Ballaz of Fresno were sister and brother; Jean Elizalde of Bakersfield and Jean Burubeltz of Bakersfield and Los Angeles were nephew and uncle; and Jean Pierre Martinto of Tehachapi was uncle to Lyda Esain of Fresno. There were also family ties among the hotelkeepers in Los Angeles's Basque town: the Errecas, Ballades, and Burubeltzes were all related by marriage. In Bakersfield, the ownership of the Basque Café, the Amestoy Hotel, and the Woolgrowers' Restaurant was temporarily complicated by marriages between Frank Maitia and Louise Amestoy and J. B. and Mayie Maitia. In Boise Lucy Garatea's aunt Gabina Aguirre ran the Star Rooming House while her niece Lucy operated the Plaza Hotel in Burns, Oregon.

As we have seen earlier, second-generation hotelkeepers rarely succeeded in carrying on with their parents' hotel businesses, but that did not stop Basque families from seeking out hotel keeping as a profession.

The second major means for *hoteleros* to expand their business, beyond word of mouth, was through advertising. *Hoteleros* frequently paid to have business-card-size advertisements appear in the issues of *California'ko Eskual Herria* and *Escualdun Gazeta* in the 1880s and 1890s. In addition, we know that all local hotelkeepers in East Bakersfield competed for business through advertising, because many of them took out advertisements in the City Directory between 1899 and 1915. Yet we do not find such advertising in the directories for Boise, Nampa, Cascade, Emmett, Twin Falls, Gooding, Pocatello, Mountain Home, and Hailey, Idaho, in the same time period. The general rule seems to be that *hoteleros* limited their use of "outside" advertising but purchased advertisement space in specialized newspapers, such as the *Voice of the Basques*, an English-language newspaper serving Basques in the 1970s, or in the annual picnic bulletins published by local Basque clubs.

There has been widespread, keen competition for hotel business among Basque *hoteleros*, even if the use of some form of advertising has been rare. Whether they were located in an urban center or small outpost, in communities with several Basque hotels or just one, *hoteleros* have kept a watchful eye on their competition. Rivalries among *hoteleros* have been generally regarded as the rule, as in the following observation from two Oregon residents:

> In any small community with a number of Basques, there will be several Basque hotels or boardinghouses. The rivalry between these hotels is most intense and often bitter. Each constantly attempts to do something a bit better than his competitor. Even the people who reside at the different hotels form factions in support of their respective landlords.[42]

For the boarders, the selection of a "favorite" hotel was based on an array of variables. For the recently immigrated, the prevalent Basque dialect used by the *hoteleros* was the foremost concern. As the French Basque Beltran Paris reported to author William Douglass, "The owners of the Star and Overland were Vizcainos and all the Vizcaino guys stayed there. Martin Inda owned the Telescope and he was a Navarro from Valcarlos. So that was my place. I always stayed there when I was in Elko."[43]

In many locations throughout the West, sons and daughters of Basque immigrants have reported taking their own children to a hotel or restaurant that reminded them of their parents or grandparents.[44] Subtle factors such as which hotel seemed the friendliest, or which seemed most festive might prove most persuasive. And if a town had more than one Basque hotel, the evidence suggests that most clients were pressured to select a favorite.

Since local boardinghouses almost always charged the same rates for room and board, and since the physical layout of the *ostatuak* was strikingly similar, one might wonder on what basis the businesses could compete. In one instance, a post–World War II *hotelera* in Fresno, California, reported that she and her husband realized that their income had decreased and that their three competitors were winning the lion's share of the local bar and dinner crowd. Instead of adding new food items or more dances, the couple decided to build a large *cancha* and host *pilota* tournaments every Sunday. As the *hotelera* summed it up, "From then on, boy, our business really took off. Of our thirty-five years in business, those were our best days, the fifties." Within five years of opening up the *cancha*, the hotelkeepers saw one neighborhood hotel and two smaller rooming houses close.

For some, the entertainment offered at the hotels or the meals served there were critical. During one period in the history of San Francisco's Basque colony, it was common for customers to hear *hoteleras* evaluating the kitchens, cuisine, and cooks at the competing *ostatuak*.[45] In most cases, however, once a change in the menu was initiated by one hotelkeeper, the others would copy the change.

Over the years the Basque hotels have provided a physical meeting place where Basques from Old and New Worlds could mix, where Basques from one of the seven European provinces could meet those from another, and where Basques from one state could visit with those from another. In fact, providing a physical environment where such mixing could occur has been a crucial function of the *ostatuak* in the United States. For example, Old World Basques who had trouble understanding unfamiliar Basque dialects assert that they learned to speak with one another in the hotels and sheep camps of the West. Some even claim that they learned English at the hotels because there they had gradual exposure to the language via non-Basque visitors and from barroom television sets in more recent years.

As the central and crucial gathering place for groups of European and American Basques over the past century, the *ostatu* has clearly served as a critical social and ethnic institution. In the first decades of Basque migration to the United States, when young herders arrived unmarried to seek their fortunes and return to Euskal Herria, the hotels served as the immigrants' job agency, extended family, and assistance league. Without question, the *ostatu* was the group's major social institution in those early years.

# 4

# The Earliest Hotels

Not surprisingly, the lure of California gold in 1849 brought a complement of Basques to the Golden State. As was the case for other ethnic Californians, Basques soon found work in alternative settings. Having failed in the gold mines, they turned to sheep- and cattle-raising enterprises. And a few turned to hotel keeping to accommodate the workers in these burgeoning industries.

## THE PLAZA HOTEL

Evidence of the earliest Basque hotelkeepers in North America is found in the mission town of San Juan Bautista, California. There a Basque named Julian Ursua operated a hotel that fronted on the old town plaza called the Plaza Hotel.[1] In 1844 Ursua was granted an enormous five-square-league tract of land known as the Rancho Panocha de San Juan y los Carrizalitos.[2] Unfortunately, relatively little else is known about Ursua beyond that at one time he owned the "Rancho Panoche" and later a hotel in San Juan Bautista.

Not far from Ursua's hotel, on the corner of Washington and Third Streets, an Italian named Angelo Zanetta ran another hotel known as the

Sebastopol.[3] After a few years, Zanetta married Maria Laborda, a French Basque from Bayonne whom he had met in San Francisco. Together the Zanettas purchased the Plaza Hotel from Ursua and reopened it on June 24, 1856.[4] According to one eyewitness, the opening was a "gala affair" featuring a band playing on the second-story veranda, the sporadic firing of the town's old cannon, and horsemen racing through the plaza at full speed plucking chickens' heads from their half-buried bodies.[5]

Under the Zanettas' ownership, the Plaza became a major gathering place for travelers, local ranchers, and businessmen. Favorably situated at an intersection of roads leading north, south, east, and west, the town of San Juan Bautista was a transfer point for seven stage lines including the famed Wells Fargo coach line.[6] As one early rancher stated, "San Juan was one of the best trading centers in the state. Cattlemen from as far away as Los Angeles and Santa Barbara used to bring their cattle here where the butchers from San Francisco would come buy them. There were no banks in those days and the Plaza Bar was their clearing house."[7]

Descriptions of life in San Juan Bautista from nineteenth-century visitors place the Plaza Hotel at the center of many town activities. According to one of the Zanettas' sons, the Plaza bar was regularly packed with out-of-town gamblers. They enjoyed Maria Zanetta's home-cooked meals, among which were steaks covered with mushrooms, served punctually at 9:00 A.M. and 4:00 P.M. in the dining hall next to the bar. A few years after opening the Plaza, the Zanettas leased the popular bar to an Englishman named John Comfort and continued to operate the hotel and kitchen.[8]

Not long after Comfort began tending bar at the Plaza, Angelo Zanetta decided that San Juan Bautista needed a livery barn and a city hall. He had the livery stable constructed near the town plaza and hired hands to oversee the stables. Then he bought an old adobe on the corner of the town plaza and hired men to construct a second story on the building. The upper level became San Juan Bautista's first city hall, and the lower part was used for hosting large banquets. Based on descriptions of the Plaza and on Zanetta's plan to expand his building, both the hotel and the bar were evidently popular stops and financially successful ventures for the Zanettas.[9]

Most likely, a number of the Basque ranchers living on the west side of the San Joaquin Valley visited the Plaza in the 1860s and 1870s. For example, the "three Johns" (Indart, Etcheverry, and Iribarri) operated the Sentinella Ranch on the San Luis Gonzaga Grant. One of the three part-

Table 4.1 Guests of Plaza Hotel, San Juan Bautista, California, 1863–1866

| Guest Name | From Ranch/Town | Date(s) of Stay |
|---|---|---|
| Jose Aurrecochea | Burns Creek | January 6, 1865 |
| Ramon Chevarria | San Juan | June 22, 1866 |
| Benito Echeveria | Santa Ana | August 12, 1866 |
| C. Echeveria | Los Banos | December 31, 1864 |
| Claro Echeveria | San Juan | June 26, 1865 |
| Franco Echeveria | Santa Ana | August 12, 1866 |
| Juan Echeverri | San Luis Gonzaga | September 1, 1864 |
| Juan Indart | San Luis Gonzaga | April 7, 1864 |
| Esteben Luyua | Rancho Quien Sabe | December 3, 1865 |
| Mendizabal | San Luis Gonzaga | September 18–20, 1865 |
| Julian Ursua | San Juan | October 5, 1863 |
| Julian Ursua | San Juan | November 6, 1866 |

*Source:* From "History of San Juan Bautista, Panoche, Los Banos," Talbott Papers.
*Note:* Entries are presented exactly as Zanetta recorded them, despite the fact that a few surnames were probably misspelled. Duplicate entries were deleted, and the guest names were alphabetized for the reader's convenience.

ners regularly traveled by horseback over the Pacheco Pass, arriving at San Juan Bautista by nightfall in order to buy, sell, and barter or stock up on needed provisions.[10] Other Basques, such as Juan Miguel Arburua, who owned the 22,000-acre Rancho Panocha de San Juan y los Carrizalitos, or Jean Baptiste Arambide of the Arambide Quicksilver Mines outside Mendota probably frequented the Plaza as well.[11] In addition, a veritable Basque colony had formed in western Merced County by 1860, as the Basque sheepmen Arrivallaga, Irigoyen, Anoitzbehere, Ayoigar, Gastimbide, Etcheaundi, and Oyarbide were all tending their flocks in the area at the time.[12]

Not surprisingly, a few of these Basque surnames can be found in Angelo Zanetta's hotel registers. Although the complete registers are not available, the small portion of the Plaza's guest lists that has been retained by the California Parks system is dated 1863–1866 and includes twenty-eight entries, with four of the registrants appearing more than once. Of the twenty individuals listed, fourteen appear to be Basques. The names of Basque guests, their hometowns or ranch names, and the date or dates of their visits are listed in table 4.1.

Why Zanetta's records contain only twenty entries is cause for speculation. First of all, it would stand to reason that the Plaza accommodated more than a couple dozen guests between 1863 and 1866. Possibly the complete records for these three years as well as those before and after were lost, misplaced, or accidentally destroyed. Since Zanetta recorded some of his guest names, it is likely that he listed guests' names during the other years that he and his wife were in business. By comparison, very few twentieth-century *hoteleros* have kept and/or shared their written ledgers, and therefore Zanetta's incomplete accounting is even more valuable. Is it possible that Zanetta listed some guests and not others? Could this ledger have been a record of special or important customers? Without further evidence these questions will remain unanswered. Whatever the case, the Plaza likely accommodated many more guests during, before, and after this three-year period.

Studying the available registers for the Plaza also raises some fundamental questions regarding the nature of Basque hotels and whether the Plaza ought to be considered the first Basque boardinghouse in the American West. For instance, the available guest lists indicate that the hotel's clientele was not exclusively Basque. Six of the twenty guests were clearly not Basques. But as a general rule, between 1890 and 1940 the majority of the Basque hotels catered more exclusively to Basques. Even if the Zanettas could have afforded to be exclusive, they probably would not have been so selective about their guests. Since the three business partners were of Italian, Basque, and English heritage, the ethnic combination probably appealed to a variety of local and visiting clientele.

Information gleaned from the census of 1870 leads one to question whether the Plaza should be considered a Basque hotel or an ethnic boardinghouse.[13] According to the census taker, for example, nine staff members were working and living at the Plaza in the summer of 1870, yet none appear to have been Basque. The name, gender, age, occupation, and birthplace of each staff member working at the Plaza that summer are listed in table 4.2. The census also reveals that Maria Laborda and her six children were the only Basques living at the Plaza at this time. Unfortunately, the Zanetta family and staff are not listed in the 1860 census for San Juan Bautista.[14] Had they been included, it might have been of interest to discover whether earlier employees of the hotel were of Basque descent and to analyze changes in the staff in the ensuing ten years.

Given that the evidence indicates that the Plaza catered to a wide sector of the population and not to Basques exclusively, we cannot consider the Plaza a Basque hotel in the truest sense. It was probably a hotel with a Basque owner that some local Basques frequented. The Plaza's Basque clientele must have enjoyed Maria's familiar style of cooking and exchanged news with her in their native Euskara.

Table 4.2 Staff of Plaza Hotel, San Juan Bautista, California, 1870

| Name | Age/Sex | Occupation | Birthplace |
|---|---|---|---|
| Yuck Ah | 30/M | Cook | China |
| James Engbrot | 30/M | Stablekeeper | England |
| John Karat | 30/M | Waiter | Prussia |
| John Oh | 30/M | Cook | China |
| Lu Oh | 23/M | Washman | China |
| Pietro Pironi | 27/M | Barkeeper | Italy |
| John Pompase | 89/M | Hotelkeeper | England |
| Mack Regan | 28/M | Stablekeeper | New York |
| Sim Tim | 45/M | Cook | China |

*Source:* From "History of San Juan Bautista, Panoche, Los Banos," Talbott Papers.
*Note:* Entries are presented exactly as Zanetta recorded them, despite the fact that a few surnames were probably misspelled. Staff names were alphabetized for the reader's convenience.

Since no witnesses remain from the mid-nineteenth century to describe the operation of the Plaza Hotel, because it did not cater exclusively to Basques and was not operated by two Basque *hoteleros*, it probably should not be considered a Basque hotel. Instead of thinking of the Plaza as the first *ostatu* in the American West, it is best considered a precursor.

### THE INDARTS' AT SENTINELLA RANCH

Another establishment that could be considered the first *ostatu* in the United States is a store and boardinghouse John and Mary Indart built in the 1860s on the Sentinella Ranch in the San Joaquin Valley between what is today Fresno and Stockton. Indart of San Benito County married Mary Erreca in Stockton, California, in July of 1863, and the newlyweds moved to the Sentinella Ranch, commonly known as the "Ranch of the Three Johns." There they formed a three-way partnership with John Etcheverry and John Iribarri to run the boardinghouse.[15] According to one of the Indarts' descendants, John and Mary owned a one-story adobe hotel on the ranch, and they later leased the business to a Basque named Valdemoro Media in 1864.[16]

From 1863 to 1865, when the Indarts worked the Sentinella Ranch, they lived in what was described in one account as a "small adobe house about twelve feet square" standing a few hundred feet from the old Salt

Slough Warehouse. The reference to the adobe as "a hotel" in the account of the Indarts' descendant is of interest and suggests that the Indarts accommodated travelers in the region. A pioneer claimed that "a sheepman and his wife [the Indarts] lived there during the gold rush and made lots of money selling butter and supplies to the gold hunters traveling by on their road to and from the mountains."[17] Possibly both of these accounts are speaking of the early Indart adobe, which was a familiar but small stopping place; another account described the Indart place as being among the stops that early miners made when traveling west from San Juan Bautista toward the Sonora Pass in search of gold.[18] After the Indarts left Sentinella in 1865, the adobe was expanded into a two-story wooden building, which remained standing until the 1930s.[19]

Although no proof exists that the Indarts' house served as a Basque hotel or boardinghouse, the Indarts may have catered to local Basques. There were numerous Basque-owned and operated quicksilver mines in the area, so there must have been an adequate Basque clientele in the area. The Richmond Gold, Quicksilver and Copper Mine in the Panoche, the Arambide Mines outside Mendota, and the New Idria Mines northwest of Fresno all attracted Basque employees.[20] Basque miners "passing through" were likely to visit the Indarts, purchase supplies, and stay the evening if it was convenient.

In some ways it makes sense to count the Indart adobe among the West's earliest Basque boardinghouses, as opposed to the Plaza Hotel in San Juan Bautista. Since both Indarts were Basque, it seems plausible that other Basques would prefer restocking supplies and exchanging news at their adobe. The presence of Basque miners and sheep ranchers in the local area meant that the Indart store and boardinghouse had a ready supply of Basque customers. In addition, given the small size and comparatively remote location of the Indart operation, it is likely that it served as a gathering place for early Basques. Basques would be less likely to frequent the large-scale Zanetta establishment.

In fact, identifying the first Basque hotel in the American West may be beyond our ability. Small boardinghouses and hotels may have existed throughout California and the West, but if they did, we have no existing records of them. For example, among the numerous hotels, butcher shops, and saloons in the Sonora area serving early forty-niners, some may have been run by Basques.[21] There was a sufficiently large Basque argonaut population in the area to support a boardinghouse or hotel in the early 1850s, but we have no evidence to substantiate its existence.

We have a lot more information about Juan Miguel Aguirre's hotel in San Francisco, however, so we can be more certain about numbering it among the first true Basque boardinghouses. After serving as a soldier on the losing side of the First Carlist War, Juan Miguel Aguirre left Spain for Montevideo, where he began a hide and tallow business. When he heard news of gold discoveries in California, he booked passage for himself and his wife, Maria Martina Aguirre.[22] After six months aboard the sailing vessel *Le Bon Pere,* they arrived in San Francisco on May 15, 1849. Unlike many other forty-niners, Aguirre remained in San Francisco. There he bought a donkey, which he outfitted with two large wooden barrels strapped onto a harness for transporting water. With his donkey, Aguirre began carrying water from the Presidio to the old downtown area around Dupont, Kearny, and Clay Streets, where he sold the water for a dollar a bucket.[23] As his business grew, Aguirre employed other Basques to help him cart and sell water throughout the city. Another Basque who had also arrived via South America, José Aurrecoechea, worked with Aguirre at this time. Years later, in 1872, Aurrecoechea bought the Idiart Ranch in Merced County from Jean Echeto.[24] Because Juan Miguel started a successful water transportation business, he is occasionally credited with designing San Francisco's first water system.

Encouraged by the success of his business, Aguirre decided to invest in real estate. Juan Miguel and Martina's first purchase was a lot at the intersection of what is now Grant Avenue and Ashburton Place.[25] Here, at 2 Dupont Place, Juan Miguel built the first handball court in San Francisco. Some authorities claim he used lumber imported from his Spanish Basque homeland.[26] In 1866 Juan Miguel began construction of the city's first Basque hotel at 1312 Powell Street.[27] In the spring of that year Aguirre sent for his nephew, Juan Miguel Arburua, to join him in San Francisco and help him construct the hotel. The twenty-two-year-old Arburua left his native village of Echalar, Navarre, arrived in San Francisco on June 27, 1866, and began working for his uncle at a wage of $20 per month. Within three months, Aguirre's hotel was completed and in operation. Interestingly, the name of Aguirre's new business is not documented in any source, but most other Basque hotels in the nineteenth and early twentieth centuries did not have their names recorded either. Even when hotelkeepers did name their establishments, local Basques often preferred to refer to the hotels by the owner's or employer's first name or surname, such as Aguirre's, Letemendi's, or Elizalde's.[28]

Aguirre's establishment probably operated much as today's Basque hotels do. By 1870, for example, Aguirre's was known as an employment agency serving newly arrived Basques. Consider the story of Italian rancher Alberto Trescony from the Salinas Valley.[29] While out walking one day in the early 1860s, Alberto happened across a Basque sheepherder named Echeverria. Discovering that they both spoke a broken but intelligible Spanish, the two struck up a conversation. Trescony was impressed with Echeverria and decided to begin importing Basque herders to tend his flocks. Because of this brief encounter, a steady stream of Basques flowed into the Salinas Valley—traveling by ship to New Orleans, by train to San Luis Obispo, and finally by stage to Trescony's. A few years later, when the transcontinental railway was completed, Trescony began turning to the Aguirres of San Francisco to help him locate good herders. A contemporary description of Aguirre's suggests that it was the perfect employment agency: "There was a Basque hotel in the center of town, where California rancheros in need of help were sure to find quiet gentle men from the Pyrenees."[30]

Aguirre's was also a gathering place for Basques. In 1870 Martina Aguirre sent for her niece Josefa Labayon from Areso, Navarre, presumably to help Martina with kitchen work, serving, and cleaning chores around the hotel.[31] Ten years later, Juan Miguel Arburua, Aguirre's nephew, married Josefa at the "French Church" in San Francisco. Also Albert Trescony's son Julius wed one of the Aguirres' daughters. As the story went, Trescony sent his son to Aguirre's hotel to procure a herder, but the young man returned with dreams of marriage to young Kate Aguirre instead.[32] Like the Arburuas and the Tresconys, many young Basques met their future spouses at Basque hotels, so much so that Douglass and Bilbao suggested that among its many functions, the Basque hotel served as a "marriage mill."[33]

Roughly twenty years later, in 1898, Francisca Arriola arrived in San Francisco with her mother and brother. The family stayed at the Aguirre hotel, then a two-story wooden building with a second-story veranda facing Powell Street.[34] As in the case of earlier couples, Francisca met her husband-to-be, Saturnino Celayeta, at the Aguirre. Years later the couple married at St. Mary's Catholic Church in Stockton, honeymooned at the Aguirre, and then made Stockton their permanent home.

The year before the Arriolas' arrival, on August 30, 1897, Juan Miguel had died at the age of eighty-four, but his widow and the couple's three sons and a daughter continued to oversee operations at the *ostatu*.[35]

By the turn of the century, Juan Miguel and Martina's hotel had become a central meeting place for the growing number of Basques living in San Francisco, Alameda, Sonoma, and San Jose Counties. Like the *ostatuak* of the twentieth century, the Aguirre saw a steady flow of Basque customers, both newcomers and locals. As we have seen, it served as an employment agency and a "marriage mill." In later years it became a vacation spot for Basques visiting from other parts of California and the West. The Aguirre hotel housed and fed Basques for almost forty years before it burned down in the San Francisco fires of 1906. In many ways, then, Aguirre's hotel may be considered the first authentic *ostatu* in the American West.

## THE TRES PINOS AND CHESTER HOTELS

In addition to Aguirre's San Francisco hotel, other California Basque hotels and boardinghouses were opening their doors for business in the 1870s and 1880s. For example, in 1874 Juan Etcheverry built a small hotel with a large livery stable in Tres Pinos just across from the railroad depot.[36] Three decades later, in 1903, Bernardo Yturriarte married Catalina Larrey, and the newlyweds received their guests at the same hotel, although by that time the Tres Pinos hotel was owned and operated by another Basque named Leon Yparraguirre.[37] Seemingly, the *ostatu* Etcheverry built in 1874 continued as a Basque boardinghouse throughout the early twentieth century.

In 1884 John Iribarne opened the Chester Hotel in Plumas County, a popular area for Basque herders and their flocks in the 1880s and 1890s. Iribarne's hotel could also be considered an early Basque hotel. In February of 1884 the Merced *Express* announced the opening of Iribarne's hotel as follows: "John Iribarne took possession of the hotel at Chester yesterday and hereafter will be found ready to greet old friends and minister to their physical comfort at that place."[38] Other Basque hotels and outposts in addition to the Tres Pinos and the Chester probably existed. Some sources suggest, for example, that the communities of Lemoore, Whitesbridge, Mendota, Firebaugh, Coalinga, Volta, and Sonora also had Basque boardinghouses serving "the sheep people" in California's central valleys in the decades spanning from 1850 to 1880.[39]

While Aguirre, Etcheverry, and Iribarne were operating their hotels in northern and central California, another Basque hotel was about to open in the sleepy southern California town of San Juan Capistrano. There, across the street from the old fenced-in mission, Domingo Oyharzabal and his partner Juan Salaberri, lifelong friends, purchased two of the town's original adobe buildings, the Yorba and Casa Mañuel Garcia Adobes, from Mrs. Maria Rios, the widow of Domingo Yorba,[40] and the purchase was made final on February 10, 1880.[41] Immediately thereafter the partners converted the Mañuel Garcia Adobe into the French Hotel and made the Yorba Adobe their home.[42]

That same year Oyharzabal began remodeling the second story of the French Hotel. How customers had gained access to the Garcia Adobe's second story prior to 1880 is unclear, but we know that Oyharzabal and Salaberri added a balcony running the length of the building with an external wooden staircase. With the expansion of the upper story to match the overall dimensions of the lower, Oyharzabal and Salaberri also doubled their capacity to accommodate visitors to the French Hotel.

Although there is not a comprehensive set of accounting records for the French Hotel, the one transaction for which we do have a record, a transaction between Domingo Oyharzabal and the State of California that took place in 1891, suggests that Oyharzabal might have kept careful note of income and expense accounts.[43]

Because the French Hotel was San Juan Capistrano's first hostelry, it is unlikely that its clientele was exclusively Basque. In fact, a non-Basque guest named Clifton Johnson provided an eyewitness description of the hotel, the earliest one we have. According to Johnson, he visited San Juan Capistrano's French Hotel, an old stage route tavern, on several occasions.[44] Johnson probably visited the hotel before 1887, since in his account he made no mention of the new railway that was completed in that year and passed within a block of the hotel's back lot.[45] Johnson described two large downstairs rooms; one serving as a grocery and provisions store, the other as a tavern. When he walked in, he most likely found Juan Salaberri minding the store while Domingo Oyharzabal tended bar next door.[46] To get to his room, Johnson walked out the back door, climbed a set of wooden stairs, and passed along the outside balcony. He reported that his room was a "rather bare and shabby apartment, with a bed that had two boxes under it to prop up the slats." From the top of the stairs in back of the hotel, Johnson was able to see "all sorts of whitewashed barns and sheds and shacks, including a kitchen and dining room which were under a roof by themselves." Not far away, hanging from a pepper tree, was a framed wooden box covered by fly netting that served as the hotel's refrigerator.

The partnership between Oyharzabal and Salaberri seems to have lasted until April 14, 1901, when Domingo Oyharzabal and his brother Etienne bought Salaberri's share of the property. Oyharzabal and Salaberri had first met onboard ship sailing for California, and, according to one Oyharzabal descendant, the families remained lifelong friends and continued to share the upstairs apartments of the Garcia Adobe for many years after Salaberri sold out his share in 1901.[47]

The life history of Domingo Oyharzabal is well documented. One of nine children born to Baptiste and Sabina Oyharzabal in the French Basque *département* of Basses-Pyrenees, Domingo left his birthplace for South America in the early 1860s, spent a few years there, and then set sail for California from Chile in 1868. On the boat from Chile the young Basque first met Juan Salaberri. The point of entry into the United States for the two friends was Alameda, California.[48] Between 1868 and 1878, when the two appeared in San Juan Capistrano, their activities and whereabouts are a mystery. Given the experience of many other Basque immigrants, the two likely found work in the Bay Area or the San Joaquin Valley with other Euskaldunak and joined up once they had saved enough money to invest in a business together.

About two years after settling in southern California, Domingo Oyharzabal was joined by two of his younger brothers, Etienne and William, who accompanied Domingo when he moved to San Juan Capistrano in 1878.[49] Not long after their arrival, William died, but Etienne, then a teenager, went on to work with his older brother for the rest of Domingo's life.

A number of Basques were already making San Juan Capistrano their home when the three Oyharzabal brothers arrived. For example, Bernardo Erreca's sheep ranch employed his two younger brothers, Juan and Miguel, and G. Etchevarran, D. Gastimbide, Juan Urulty, and Juan Mariliuss.[50] All of Erreca's ranch hands were most likely Basque, because records list surnames that could be Basque with French or Spanish birthplaces.[51] Other Basque residents of San Juan Capistrano at the time were Louis Dartiques; Juan, Maria, and Domingo Eramuspe; Bernard Ybarl; Juan and B. Arrambel; and Pedro, Juanita, and Maria Larra.[52]

Like other early pioneers in Orange County, Domingo Oyharzabal had an intense interest in real estate. As of 1893, when the county began recording deeds of sale, the elder Oyharzabal's name crops up frequently. Between 1893 and 1899, Domingo made nineteen land and building purchases in the Orange County area alone. In the following decade Oyharzabal's land investment activity continued at a similar pace.[53] On May 14, 1895, Domingo made his partnership with his younger brother official. The two shared town lots in San Juan Capistrano, the French Hotel, and livestock and ranching investments.[54] By 1910 Domingo had purchased more than 4,000 acres of land, planted 150 acres in walnuts, and owned vast herds of livestock in Orange and Inyo Counties.[55]

When they formed their partnership, both Oyharzabals were bachelors, but one year later, in 1896, Etienne married Lucille Darius of Bayonne. Lucy became the manager and overseer of the French Hotel until it closed in 1903.[56] Domingo, on the other hand, remained a confirmed bachelor until his death at the age of fifty-nine. Etienne and Lucy continued to manage the Oyharzabal properties and resided in the Yorba Adobe next door to the French Hotel until their deaths in 1934 and 1961, respectively.[57] Since neither Etienne nor Domingo had children, two of their nephews, Pedro and Esteban, inherited the property, and today the thick-walled adobes are still home to Domingo's heirs. The general store downstairs remained and is still open for business.

From the opening of the Plaza Hotel in 1856 to the 1880s when Oyharzabal and Salaberri ran the French Hotel in San Juan Capistrano, the *ostatu*, a new ethnic and social institution in the United States, was claiming its place in the American West. Not surprisingly, the California of "boom and bust" was the Basque *ostatu*'s first home. *Ostatuak* emerged as a result of increased Basque immigration, and the ebb and flow of the Basque hotels was often directly linked to fluctuations in the sheep industry. In fact, *ostatuak* in the nineteenth and twentieth centuries would appear soon after a critical number of Basques established their presence in any region of the American West. Whether the *ostatu* was located in a small-town setting or in an urban center, the link between the herder and the Basque hotel was ever present.

The historical record indicates that two major cities on the West Coast were home to Basque towns by 1890: San Francisco and Los Angeles. In San Francisco, Juan Miguel Aguirre's hotel played an important role in the lives of Bay Area Basques from 1866 through 1906, and in Los Angeles a small cluster of Basque hotels served a burgeoning Basque population by 1880. These two centers were critical to the development of other Basque communities and hotels throughout the state and eventually the other states of the American West. These two important early Basque towns are the subject of the next chapter.

# 5

# Los Angeles and San Francisco

## Two Early Basque Towns

By 1890, concentrations of Basque immigrants had appeared in small neighborhoods within San Francisco and Los Angeles. These communities, which we will refer to as *Basque towns*, featured clusters of *ostatuak* situated within compact geographical areas. At times as many as five Basque hotels were located in a two- or three-block neighborhood. Whereas the *ostatuak* that developed in California between 1850 and 1890 tended to be isolated resting spots frequented by travelers, the clusters of hotels that did business in the two Basque towns toward the end of the nineteenth century emerged as social centers for the greater Basque-American community in the state, and they also spurred the development of *ostatuak* in outlying areas. Decades later, Basque towns would also emerge in Bakersfield, Stockton, Boise, and Reno.

Despite numerous parallels, the patterns of growth and development of California's first two Basque towns differed slightly, specifically as regards their origins, their concentration of Basques, and their survival. San Francisco's first hotel, owned by Juan Miguel Aguirre and established in 1866, was critical to newly arriving Basques and to their northern California employers. For nearly three decades Aguirre's was the only San Francisco Basque hotel of record, until the 1890s when other hotels appeared in the Powell Street neighborhood. In 1906 the legendary earth-

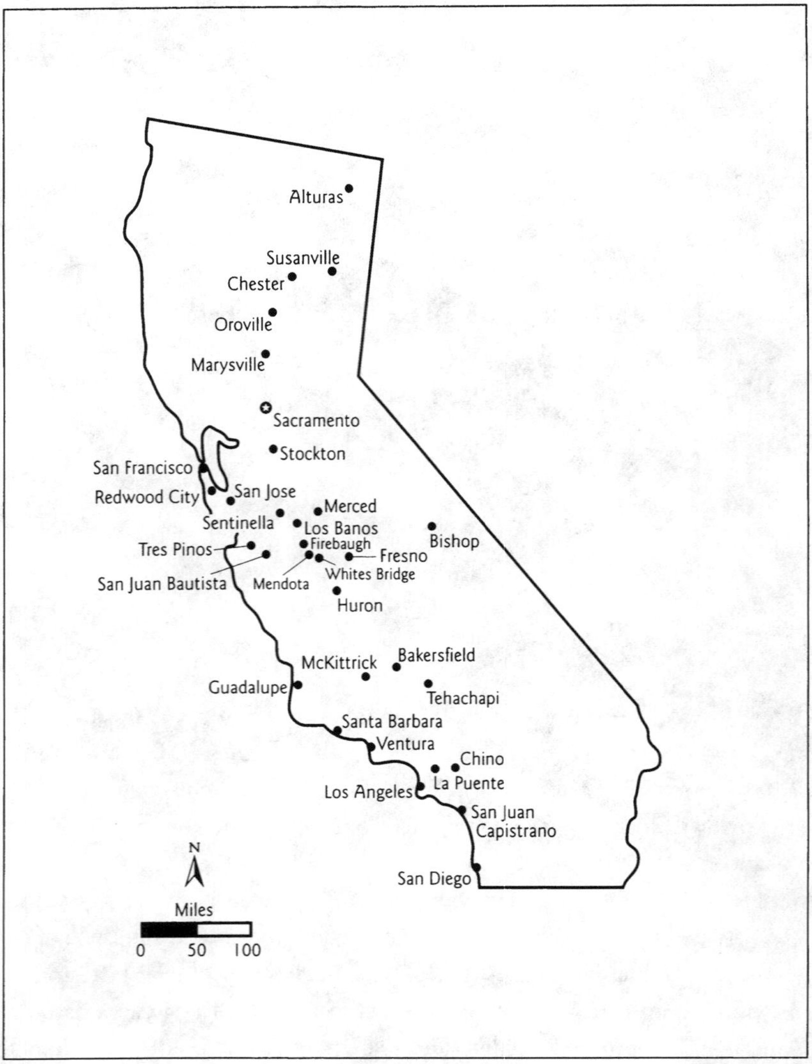


*Fig. 6. Communities with* ostatuak *in California.*

quake and subsequent fire brought down San Francisco's Basque town. In contrast, the Basque town of Los Angeles was based on a cluster of Basque hotels that were doing business in the neighborhood of Alameda and Aliso Streets as early as 1880, and possibly earlier. By 1940 southern California Basques had all but dispersed, and the Basque town of Los Angeles was defunct; whereas the Basque town of San Francisco still has one boardinghouse and a few Basque restaurants in operation today. Although

Los Angeles's Basque town was the more concentrated of the two during its peak years, 1890 through 1910, its northern counterpart has endured to the present day.

## THE BASQUE TOWN AND *Ostatuak* OF LOS ANGELES
### Peak Years

As Marie Pierre Arrizabalaga demonstrated in her statistical survey of Basque immigration, there were large increases in the number of Basques in southern California and Los Angeles County between 1860 and 1880.[1] As of 1881 Euskaldunak in Los Angeles County formed the largest Basque community in the American West. The city's first directory, dated 1872, includes nine Basque family names and merchants.[2] Six years later, the next directory available contains more Basques and lists one boardinghouse under the name of G. B. Levque.[3] The address of the Levque boardinghouse was 148–152 Alameda, in the heart of what would become Los Angeles's Basque town in the 1880s. Given the downtown Los Angeles location and the surname of the hotel owner, one could argue that as of 1878 Levque's boardinghouse was Los Angeles's first *ostatu* of record.

By 1881 the population of the city of Los Angeles was 11,200, and more first-, second-, and third-generation Basques lived in Los Angeles than in any other city or town in the United States.[4] Also as of that year five downtown lodging houses were either owned and operated by people with Basque surnames or were regularly serving Basque patrons. A few doors down from Levque's old establishment, Mrs. M. Ballade ran her first boardinghouse on the corner of Alameda and Aliso Streets with her husband Pascal who also worked at the grocery down the street at 35 Aliso.[5] Although Ballade is a French surname, the series of boardinghouses the family operated for over two decades should be considered Basque hotels because they were situated in Basque town and catered to Basque boarders.[6]

Martín Hirigoyen opened his hotel a few blocks away from the Ballades' on the corner of Labory and Alameda Streets.[7] And one street over Pascal Harotcavena took in boarders at 46 Commercial Street.[8] Although little is known about the operation of these early boardinghouses, the very fact that they were present in the area suggests that Los Angeles had an established Basque town by the 1880s, if not before.

The Hotel de France, located directly across from the Ballades' place on the northeast corner of Aliso and Alameda Streets, was another of the

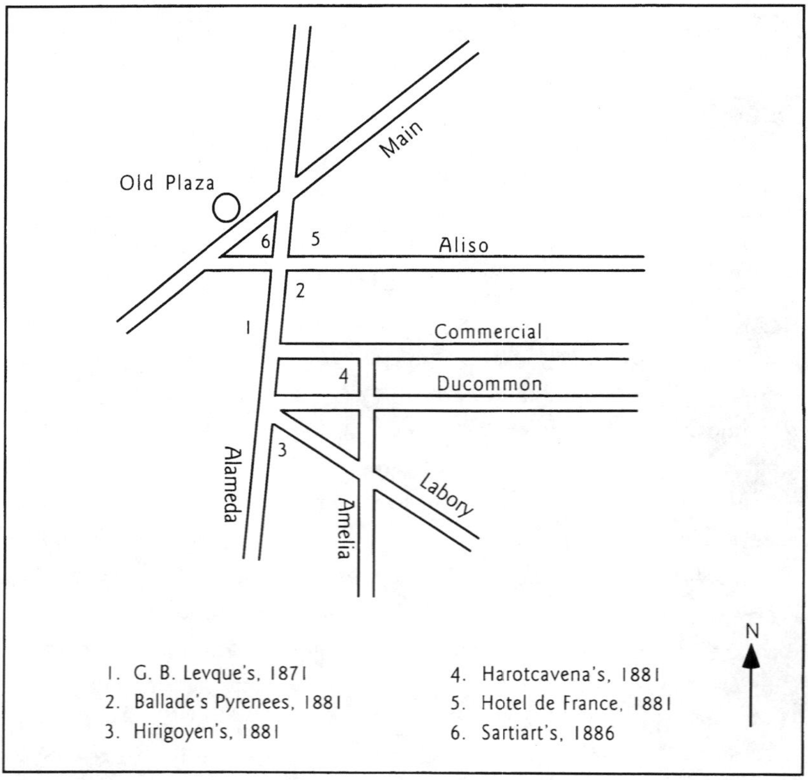


*Fig. 7. Los Angeles's Basque town ca. 1891. This map is based on a map that appeared in the* Los Angeles City Directory, *1891 (Los Angeles: W. H. L. Corran, 1891), fly leaf.*

early hotels in Los Angeles's Basque town.[9] Its owners, Louis Etchepare and Domingo Apestegui, operated the hotel from 1881 until 1890, when J. B. Archimaut purchased the business.[10] In 1886 Marie and Pascal Ballade renamed their boardinghouse the Hotel des Pyrenees.[11] To the west of these two Basque establishments were the Hotel de Gap, the Hotel d' Europe, and the Hotel de Grenobles, which catered to Los Angeles's growing French population.[12] G. P. Sartiart opened another small *ostatu* at 26 Aliso Street.[13]

Advertising in city directories suggests that competition among Basque town hotelkeepers was keen during the 1880s. In one city directory covering the last few years of the 1880s, each of the four existing establishments—the Hotel de France, the Ballades' Pyrenees, Sartiart's, and Hirigoyen's—added descriptive phrases extolling their virtues, but interestingly each promoted distinct attributes. The Hotel France, for example, claimed to be a "highly respectable house" where "strangers coming to the city will find good accommodations." The hotel also advertised that it offered good furniture, clean beds, and good meals at low rates.[14] Pascal Ballade at the Pyrenees guaranteed "good board at the lowest rates," and G. P. Sartiart, the newest member of the foursome, promoted his "clean and wholesome lunch house," which featured coffee "Fit for a King."[15] Hirigoyen singled out his dining room for its "accommodating waiters" and convenient location.[16] These advertisements indicate that the proprietors of the Basque hotels were keenly aware of their competition.

Los Angeles's Basque boardinghouses were likely to be of modest design, furnishings, and accommodations. Photographs taken in 1918 reveal that the Hotel de France was a modest two-story brick structure of Greek Revival architecture, for instance. In the late 1880s the Sanborn and Dakin Map Companies published the floor plans of the Hotel de France and the Hotel des Pyrenees (see figure 8).[17] The plans for the Hotel de France identify a dining room, saloon, sleeping rooms, a macaroni factory, and a bakery. According to the plans for both the Hotel de France and the Hotel des Pyrenees, alongside and behind the main building of each there were a number of sheds for cooking and a livery. Unfortu-

Table 5.1 Los Angeles's *Ostatuak*, 1872–1890

| Date | Operator | Location | Name |
|---|---|---|---|
| 1878 | G. B. Levque | 148–152 Alameda | Boardinghouse |
| 1881 | Mrs. M. Ballade | 141 Alameda | Lodging house |
| 1881 | M. Hirigoyen | Labory and Alameda | Boardinghouse |
| 1881 | L. Etchepare and D. Apestegui | Alameda and Aliso | Hotel de France |
| 1881 | Pascual Harotcavena | 46 Commercial | Boardinghouse |
| 1884 | P. Ballade | Alameda and Aliso | Hotel and grocery |
| 1886 | G. P. Sartiart | 26 Aliso | Boardinghouse |
| 1886 | Martin Hirigoyen | Labory and Alameda | Boardinghouse |
| 1886 | Pascal Ballade | Alameda and Aliso | Hotel des Pyrenees |
| 1888 | Dominique Apesteguy | Alameda and Aliso | Hotel de France |
| 1888 | Frank Esperance | 144 Alameda | Hotel de Basses-Pyrenees |

*Source:* This table is a compilation of information listed in city and county directories for this period (see Bibliography) and corresponds to the Basque town map in Figures 7 and 8. Spellings, addresses, and descriptions of the establishments are quoted precisely as found in directory sources.
*Note:* Entries such as those for 1881, Mrs. M. Ballade; 1884, P. Ballade; and 1886, Pascal Ballade represent the same establishment. The directory publishers list the hotels and owners differently from year to year.

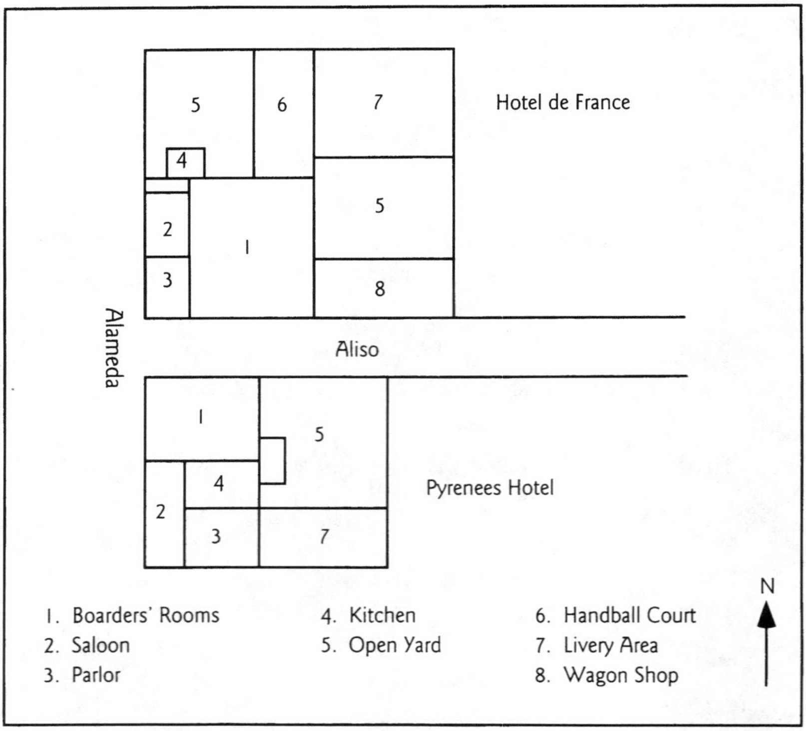


*Fig. 8. The physical layout of the Hotel de France and the Hotel Pyrenees, Los Angeles.*

nately, map work and photographs for the other boardinghouses in the neighborhood are not available.

Strangely, on the Sanborn and Dakin maps the Hotel des France is labeled a hotel and the Hotel des Pyrenees is labeled a boardinghouse. Yet in terms of floor plan, size, and layout, the two buildings were nearly identical. In local directories the Ballades listed their business as a boardinghouse until the mid-1880s, when they began advertising the same business as the Hotel Pyrenees, the Hotel des Pyrenees, or the Pyrenees Hotel. Why the change from "boardinghouse" to "hotel"? The upstairs rooms and the physical layout of the buildings remained exactly the same; only the terminology changed, probably because by 1890 a majority of the Basque town establishments were calling themselves hotels. Basques began referring to their *ostatuak* as "hotels" in this period, and the use of the term among Basques lingers still.

Establishing who owned the *ostatuak* is especially problematic because very few operators appear in county records or courthouse archives. That many of the *ostatuak* "owners" were lessees may also partially explain their relatively short tenure; indeed, Basque "owners" rarely operated a hotel for more than ten years. In Los Angeles, the practice of leasing rather than owning a hotel may also explain why the relocation of *ostatuak* was not unusual. The Hotel de France and the Hotel des Pyrenees, for example, both relocated three and four times, respectively, during their thirty years of existence.[18]

The construction of the Hotel de France in the early 1880s coincided with the arrival of the Atchison, Topeka, and Santa Fe rail lines, and followed a decade that witnessed the establishment of the city's wool industry;[19] the first woolen mill in Los Angeles had been opened by the Barnard Brothers in 1873.[20] Together these developments stimulated Basque migration to the City of the Angels, and the gradual and steady increase in their numbers must have been impressive to local Basques. Martín Biscailuz, an American-born attorney living in Los Angeles and the editor of the Basque-language newspaper *Escualdun Gazeta* (*Basque Gazette*), estimated that 2,000 Basques were living in Los Angeles in 1886.[21] Given that the entire city's population was only 18,000 in 1884, Biscailuz's claim seems unlikely.[22] Subsequent census records refute the suggestion that one out of every nine Angelenos was Basque; nonetheless the editor's claims are revealing. Perhaps for Biscailuz, Los Angeles seemed to be the mecca for American Basques. Biscailuz's overestimation is understandable given that many southern California Basques frequented the Los Angeles hotels on Sundays, holidays, and vacations. Many a Basque would travel to the city via horse and buggy to stock up on supplies and would then remain for an evening or two before beginning his journey home, temporarily adding to the city's Basque population.[23]

Los Angeles's Basque community supported the only two Basque-language newspapers printed in the American West. Martín Biscailuz believed that the emerging Navarrese and French Basque colony in southern California in the 1880s was sufficient to support a newspaper, so he started the *Escualdun Gazeta* around 1884, the first Basque-language newspaper in the United States.[24] Unfortunately this effort proved premature, and the newspaper folded three months later. It was not until José Goytino founded *California'ko Eskual Herria* in 1893 that Basques in the United States had a successful newspaper. A journalist by trade, Goytino established distributorships in San Francisco, San Diego, and Mexico City, thus maintaining ties between Basques in the American West and Latin America. In addition, each bimonthly issue featured columns with local news and advertising from other Basque colonies such as Tehachapi, San Francisco, and Bishop Creek, California.[25]

Since *California'ko Eskual Herria* was published for five years in the mid-1890s, we can theorize that the southern California Basque colony reached maturity during those years. We know that this publication contained many advertisements of the boardinghouses of the day. In the December 30, 1893, issue of *Eskual Herria,* for example, five Basque hotels in Los Angeles sponsored advertisements. They were the Hotel des Pyrenees, the Hotel d' Europe, the Buena Vista House, the Eskualdun Ostatua, and the Hotel de Bayonne.[26] One person who was interviewed for a study by Sonia Eagle described the Pyrenees' adjoining handball court and maintained that the Pyrenees Hotel was the largest of the Basque town hotels. He also stated that there were two private handball courts in operation in the neighborhood.[27] The *ostatuak* that could be found in Los Angeles's Basque town in the 1890s are listed in table 5.2 (those hotel names with an accompanying asterisk are hotels that advertised in *Eskual Herria*).

Given the keen competition that was evident among hotels in Los Angeles's Basque town, it is noteworthy that the old Hotel de France chose not to advertise in the only Basque newspaper available in the West. In a report on the Aliso Street area, Karen Weitz suggested that the Hotel de France was considered one of the "lesser" Basque establishments in Los Angeles's Basque town by 1895, because the city's Chinatown section of Los Angeles was beginning to press into the neighborhood.[28]

According to Weitz, for a brief period, when the Hotel de France was located at Aliso and Alameda Streets, alongside the hotel stood crude cribs housing Oriental, Black, and French prostitutes. Weitz insinuates that because of the intrusion of "outsiders" and prostitutes, the local Basque community may have shunned the hotel. Perhaps this could have happened, but we cannot substantiate this theory. Other reasons such as Old World resistance to modern advertising or a lack of resources may also explain the hotel's choice not to advertise in *Eskual Herria*.

The peak years in the life of Los Angeles's Basque town began with the founding of *Eskual Herria* in 1893 and lasted through 1910. Census information demonstrates that the Los Angeles County Basque population quadrupled between 1900 and 1910. In 1900 there were 269 Euskaldunak in the county, and ten years later the number had increased to 1,036.[29] There was also a well-established network of hotels within the city's Basque neighborhood during this ten-year period.

Table 5.2 Los Angeles's *Ostatuak* in the 1890s

| Date | Operator | Location | Hotel Name |
|---|---|---|---|
| 1890 | D. Hiriart | 144 North Alameda | Hotel des Basses-Pyrenees |
| 1891 | J. Ordoqui | 300 and 302 Aliso | Hotel des Pyrenees* |
| 1891 | J. B. Archimaut | 301 Aliso | Hotel de France* |
| 1891 | Clavere and Gouillardow | Southeast corner Commercial and Los Angeles | Hotel de Europe |
| 1891 | Burubeltz | 604 Alameda | Ballade House |
| 1893 | Clavere and Gouillardou | Southeast corner Commercial and Los Angeles | Hotel de Europe* |
| 1893 | Domingo and J. Larronde | 515 New High | Buena Vista House* |
| 1895 | Clavere and Gouillardou | 226 Aliso | Hotel de Europe* |
| 1895 | Jean and Mrs. L. Chotro | 302 Aliso | Hotel de France |
| 1896 | D. Hiriart | 312 Aliso | Pension Francaise* |
| 1896 | Felix Clavere and Gouaillardou | 226 Aliso | European House* |
| 1898 | Mrs. J. Larronde | 300 Aliso | Hotel des Pyrenees* |
| 1898 | M. Larinaneta | 515 New High | Buena Vista House |

*Source:* This table is based on Los Angeles directories covering the 1890s (see Bibliography).
*Note:* Occasionally, advertising in *California'ko Eskual Herria* offered conflicting pieces of information. For example, Hiriart's Eskualdun Ostatua appeared in the newspaper on December 31, 1893, but the establishment was called the Pension Francaise in local directories. In addition, the Hotels Maritonia and Bayonne purchased advertising from December 1895 through 1897 but were not listed in directories in those years.

Also one might notice the different spellings of *Clavere* and *Gouillardou*. Information in this table is presented as it appeared in the source material.

*All asterisked hotels advertised in *California'ko Eskual Herria*.

And, finally, establishments changed hands regularly. Note the Ordoquis and the Larrondes at the Hotel des Pyrenees, as well as the Larrondes and Larinanetas at the Buena Vista, for example.

The Basques have been in California for many generations. Los Angeles continued to be the largest of California's Basque communities until the census of 1910, when San Francisco's Basque population surpassed that of Los Angeles.

According to Arrizabalaga's study, when compared with similar statistics from San Francisco, Alameda, Kern, and Fresno Counties, the census data for Los Angeles for the years 1900 and 1910 presented in table 5.3 demonstrates the relative maturity of the Basque community in Los Angeles County. (In other words this community had a larger number of Basques from earlier generations.) Also the comparatively high male–female ratio in the population and the large number of Basque adults are

Table 5.3 Los Angeles's Basque Population, 1900 and 1910
(BY GENDER AND AGE GROUP)

| Sex | Number in 1900 | Percentage in 1900 | Number in 1910 | Percentage in 1910 |
|---|---|---|---|---|
| | | ALL BASQUES | | |
| Male | 145 | 53.9 | 564 | 54.4 |
| Female | 124 | 46.1 | 472 | 45.6 |
| Total | 269 | 100.0 | 1,036 | 100.0 |
| | | ADULTS | | |
| Adult Male | 81 | 54.4 | 363 | 56.5 |
| Adult Female | 68 | 45.6 | 280 | 43.5 |
| Total | 149 | 100.0 | 643 | 100.0 |

*Source:* Arrizabalaga, "Statistical Survey," 61–63.
*Note:* For the purpose of Arrizabalaga's study, an adult was defined as someone eighteen years or older.

primary indicators of the maturity of the community. Half the Basques in Arrizabalaga's study were either second- or third-generation citizens, which suggests that previous generations had probably settled in southern California and established themselves decades earlier. In both 1900 and 1910, the number of American-born Basques in Los Angeles was greater than the number of French and Spanish Basque immigrants who had recently arrived in the area; Basque-American citizens in the area constituted 54.7 percent of the Basque population of the county in 1900 and 51.1 percent in 1910.[30]

Occupations among Los Angeles County Basques according to the national censuses for 1900 and 1910 also tell us some interesting things about Basques living around Los Angeles in the early 1900s. Basques in this county were not exclusively involved in sheep and cattle raising, although agricultural occupations dominate the tally. But in other California counties, such as Kern and Fresno, an even larger percentage of the Basque population was engaged in agricultural occupations. By and large, the "newer" the Basque community, the more likely it was to be characterized by a high percentage of Basques working in agricultural occupations. According to the censuses, occupations of adult Basques in Los Angeles County for 1900 and 1935 indicate that after agricultural work, hotel work was the second most frequently mentioned occupation.[31] Unfortunately, there are no distinctions in the census data about the type of work Basques performed in hotels; thus Basques listed as working at hotels might have functioned as hotelkeepers, clerks, maids, or in a variety of other roles. (See table 3.1 for more on the employment statistics on Los Angeles Basques.)

## Decline

By 1905 Los Angeles's Basque town had begun a gradual decline. For the first time in two decades, Los Angeles Basques were closing their hotels rather than moving across the street or selling out to other Basques as they had in earlier years. Between 1900 and 1910, for example, several of the earliest Basque town hotels listed in table 5.2 closed, leaving only the five listed in table 5.4.

Yet hundreds of Basques still called the Aliso and Alameda neighborhood home in the 1910s, and thousands of Euskaldunak from other parts of the West visited the area. One such Basque was Pierre Sorcabal, who left his native village in Navarre, Spain, in 1877 at the age of seventeen and headed for the United States.[32] Before arriving in Los Angeles he worked for sheep outfits in Albuquerque, New Mexico, southern Utah, and Big Bear Valley, California. During a visit to the Basque town of Los Angeles, Pierre met a younger Basque woman, Marie Salthu, from Zuberoa, France, at a dance at the Hiriarts' Sempere Hotel on the corner of Turner and Alameda. In 1909 the couple married at the Old Plaza Catholic Church. With a loan from Casper Cohn, a Los Angeles financier who helped many Los Angeles Basques in those years, Pierre and Marie opened a hotel down the street from the Hiriarts' on Turner and Amelia.[33]

Table 5.4 Los Angeles's *Ostatuak*, 1900–1910

| Date | Operator | Location | Hotel Name |
|---|---|---|---|
| 1900 | Manual Ordoqui | 620 North Alameda | Pyrenees Hotel |
| 1900 | Domingo Hiriart | 312 Aliso | Hiriart House |
| 1904 | — | 503 Aliso | Hotel de France |
| 1904 | — | Aliso and Alameda | Hotel Español |
| 1909 | Ignacio Mayo | 610 North Alameda | Mayo's |

*Source:* This information is based on Los Angeles city directories (see Bibliography), except in the case of the Hotel Español, which was cited in the Etcheverria correspondence, Paquette Papers, Sonora, California, and mentioned by Frank Amestoy in an interview with the author on April 2, 1987, in Bakersfield, California.
*Note:* As in the other tables throughout this work, the dates listed for the hotels are based on the year when they first appeared in the city directories. Dashes indicate that no information was available for this entry.

The Hiriarts and Sorcabals became close family friends, and when the Sorcabals' first child was born in 1911, the Hiriarts became the child's godparents. Generally, despite keen competition for business, *hotelero* families maintained close family friendships.

Among the popular hotels operating during these years was Ignacio Mayo's hotel at 610 Alameda.[34] Mayo's, as it was known by its predominantly Navarrese Basque clientele, was a second home to the new arrivals from the Spanish Basque provinces and a meeting place for Basques living in southern California. Two Navarrese, Francisco Landa and Dominica Layana, from villages no more than ten miles apart in the Old Country, met for the first time at Mayo's. Not long after they were married on April 19, 1913, at the Plaza Church by the Basque priest Dominic Zaldivar. The couple then moved to Orange County, where they made their home on a small sheep ranch in Brea, California.[35] Thereafter, when they visited Los Angeles, the Landas made Mayo's their first stop.

Residents of Los Angeles's Basque town considered the half dozen *ostatuak* their homes. As one early resident remembered, "We butchered hogs right in the middle of what is now downtown Los Angeles."[36] Dominic Sorcabal remembers that one of his chores was feeding the sheepdogs that accompanied the herders to his parents' hotel. The Oyamburu, as the Sorcabals' place was called, had a small pen behind the hotel to accommodate the sheepherders' dogs.

Another of Dominic's pastimes was a daily visit to the handball courts on Alameda Street. His favorite was the one adjacent to the Olasso hotel, located around the block from his parents' hotel on Alameda and Aliso Streets. When Dominic was a boy, there were at least three courts available for use within a two-block area. Like other young boys, he loved to watch the *pilotariak* compete, and, when he had the opportunity, he would play against his neighborhood friends.

Dominic's memories of his childhood in Los Angeles are strikingly similar to descriptions of young Basques in Euskal Herria watching the *pilotariak* compete near the old plaza churches. Among the first and second generations of American Basques, the passion for sport—particularly handball—lived on. As we have mentioned before, the *pilota* court was built against the church walls in the Old Country and along *ostatu* walls in the New World.

Prohibition seemed to have little or no effect on Los Angeles's Basque town. As they had for decades, *hoteleros* made their own wine and whiskey in their cellars. Those hotelkeepers who procured wine and liquor

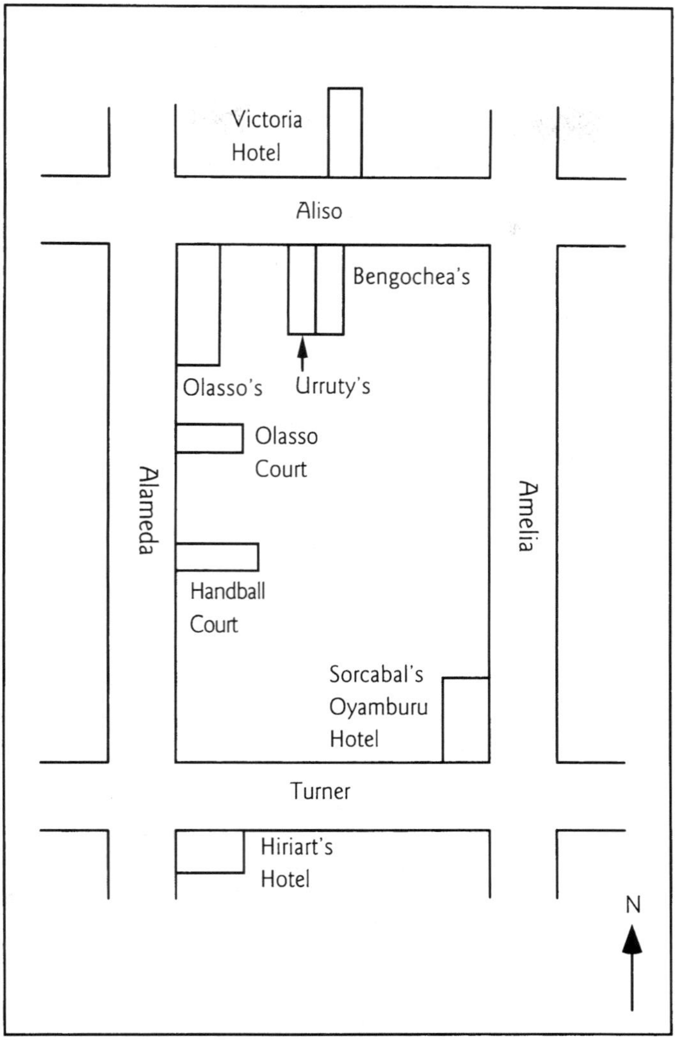


*Fig. 9. Los Angeles's Basque town ca. 1920. This map is based on Sorcabal's hand-drawn map of the hotels he remembered as existing in Los Angeles's Basque town between 1900 and 1920.*

from other sources continued with those arrangements during Prohibition. As one Basque I spoke with observed, some might consider Basques to be "big bootleggers" because they continued their lifestyle during Prohibition much as before;[37] of course, this was also true of other ethnic groups who consumed alcohol. The people I spoke with remember that they were able to buy a shot of whiskey at the Los Angeles Basque hotels for fifteen cents per shot, and that police raids of the Basque town *ostatuak* were quite rare. Sorcabal recalled that the police "had stopped by" the Oyamburu Hotel to ask the crowd to quiet down without checking for alcoholic beverages.[38] The good relationship that existed between the Los Angeles police and Basque town during Prohibition was not necessarily common to all Basque communities, however; for instance, the relationship was strained in the Basque enclave of Bakersfield, California. Perhaps "an arrangement" existed between Basque town hotelkeepers and the Los Angeles police, as has been suggested by a number of Basques I interviewed.

As has been noted before, only a handful of the Los Angeles *hoteleros* operated their *ostatuak* for more than ten years. The Ballade family, for example, managed the Pyrenees Hotel for three decades. The Eskualdun Ostatua (Basque House or Hotel), opened by Domingo Hiriart in 1893, was operated by Domingo and Catherine Hiriart and their descendants until around 1938. Within that forty-year time span, the Eskualdun Ostatua changed names a number of times; the Hiriart House, Pension Francaise, and Sempere's Hotel were three of the names for the same establishment.[39] In Los Angeles, as well as throughout the state, operating a hotel for longer than a decade was unusual. Perhaps, then, the staying power of the hotels run by the Hiriarts and the Ballades further demonstrates the relatively mature or stable nature of Los Angeles's Basque community in the early 1900s.

A slow exodus of Basques from the city to the outlying areas of Tehachapi, Bakersfield, Santa Barbara, and Orange County beginning in the 1910s and continuing into the 1920s eroded the community's Basque population. No doubt, the decline in the southern California wool industry, droughts, and large-scale urbanization were major factors contributing to the decrease in the Basque population in Los Angeles.

The 1920s and 1930s mark the final chapter for Los Angeles's Basque town. New and more involved transportation systems crisscrossed the area. The construction of an electric train line on Aliso Street in 1912, the new Pacific Electric, running through the heart of Los Angeles's Basque town, was the beginning of major changes for the neighborhood. A large highway severed Alameda and First Streets and eventually became an interstate. Older buildings were torn down so that roads could be widened, and a new mixture of ethnic groups, Chinese and Japanese in particular, began working and living in the old insular neighborhood, with "Japan Town" pressing in from the south. Eventually, when the construction of Union Rail station in 1930 entailed further demolition in the neighborhood, the death knell was sounded. By 1940 the downtown *ostatuak* had disappeared, and Basques had moved to outlying areas such as La Puente and Chino in significant enough numbers to support new *ostatuak* there.

## THE BASQUE TOWN AND *Ostatuak* OF SAN FRANCISCO
### The Early Days

California's other early Basque town, in San Francisco, continued to flourish through the war years. In fact, the Basque community to the north has lasted longer than Los Angeles's Basque town. As we have said earlier, the Basque community in San Francisco dates from the construction of Juan Miguel Aguirre's hotel on Powell Street in 1866, a hotel that could be considered the first complete Basque hotel in the American West. Unfortunately, we know very little about life in San Francisco's Basque neighborhood in the years between 1860 and 1900 as compared to what we know of its counterpart in Los Angeles. The earthquake and subsequent fires of 1906 are largely to blame for the gap in the historical record. In addition to breaking up many of the city's early ethnic neighborhoods, the disaster of 1906 destroyed large portions of civic archives and county records.

Nonetheless the city and county directories that remain provide sufficient information to indicate that San Francisco had a well established Basque town by the 1890s. By 1900, for example, the Hotel de France, the Hotel des Alpes, the Hotel de Basse-Pyrenees, and the Hotel Europa, located in the Broadway to Pacific Street area, constituted the city's Basque town.[40] Just as in Los Angeles, hotels had Basque proprietors and were clustered within a few blocks of one another.

Of the San Francisco *ostatuak* listed in table 5.5 for the period 1866–1906, most were not found in Sanborn Company maps from the prequake era. The New Pyrenees and Europa Hotels were included in the maps, and directories reveal four additional Basque hotels doing business in the area between 1888 and 1893 as shown in table 5.5.[41] A compilation of information discovered in directories, literature, and map work can be found in figure 10, which represents an approximation of San Francisco's Basque town in the closing years of the nineteenth century.

One of the hotels that was doing business in the 1890s was Yparraguirre's. In the early 1880s, young Juan Francisco Yparraguirre of Echalar

*One of the most important and earliest hotels in the American West, Aguirre's in San Francisco opened in 1866. Courtesy of the Basque Studies Collection, Getchell Library, University of Nevada, Reno.*

arrived in San Francisco. When visiting the San Joaquin Valley, Juan Francisco met Marie Etchebarren of Urepel, France, at her aunt's home in Tres Pinos, California, and a short time later the two were married at the Our Lady of Notre Dame Catholic Church in San Francisco.[42] In 1893 the Yparraguirres leased a hotel building on the corner of Powell Street and Broadway, which they named the Hotel Vasco. When it was originally constructed, the two-story wooden-frame building with a downstairs saloon stood between two private residences.[43] A year after opening their business, Juan Francisco sent for three of his brothers in Echalar to work for him at the hotel. Not long after, the four brothers built a handball court on 823 Broadway near the corner of Powell.[44]

Yparraguirre's was a popular location among Bay Area Basques in the 1890s. Juan Francisco loved music and often invited musicians to play in the restaurant and barroom. Juan Francisco's friend Vincent Arrillaga of the Arrillaga Musical College often frequented the Basque Hotel.[45] In addition, the owner was known for his singing, and he encouraged his clients to join him in Basque folk songs. The atmosphere and conviviality of the Basque Hotel, together with the handball court, attracted customers. In addition, Juan Francisco regularly advertised in *California'ko Eskual Herria*, luring Basques to visit from other parts of the West.[46]

When the fire of 1906 engulfed the peninsula from Van Ness Street to the bay, Juan Francisco whisked his family down to the docks where they boarded a barge and crossed to the safety of Oakland's harbor. Yparraguirre remained and attempted to protect the hotel from destruction until he was ordered to evacuate. By that time, evacuees were being directed to Golden Gate Park to wait until the crisis subsided. While Juan Francisco waited and watched, his hotel and the old Aguirre burned to the ground. Neither family attempted to rebuild their former businesses after the disaster.

The destruction of the city's first two *ostatuak* and the neighboring hotels marks the end of San Francisco's first Basque town. Although new Basque establishments emerged in the twentieth century, the two earliest hotels represented particular periods in Basque hotel keeping and Basque migration to the United States: one was reminiscent of gold-hungry adventure seekers, and the other of California's "boom and bust" period.

Comparisons of the censuses for 1900 and 1910 for San Francisco and Los Angeles Counties help us clarify the development of the two Basque centers. In 1900 San Francisco's Basque community was the second most populous in California after Los Angeles's.[47] Ten years later, however, San

Table 5.5 San Francisco's *Ostatuak*, 1866–1906

| Date | Operator | Location | Hotel Name |
|---|---|---|---|
| 1866 | Juan Miguel Aguirre | 1312 Powell | — |
| 1888 | Yparraguirre and Matias Jauregui | 1347 Powell | Hotel Vasco |
| 1890 | Armand Dehay | 618 California | Hotel de France |
| 1890 | Cuyala and Labarere | 614 North Broadway | Hotel des Basse-Pyrenees |
| 1893 | Juan Francisco Yparraguirre | 1347 Powell | Hotel Vasco |
| 1896 | Louis Savart | 616–18 California | — |
| 1899 | — | Stockton Avenue | New Pyrenees |
| 1899 | — | Broadway | Europa Hotel |
| 1904 | J. E. Eustache | 621 Pacific | Hotel des Alpes |

*Source:* City directories for San Francisco (see bibliography).
*Note:* As in the other tables throughout this work, the dates listed for the hotels are based on the year when they first appeared in the city directories. Dashes indicate that no information was available for this entry.

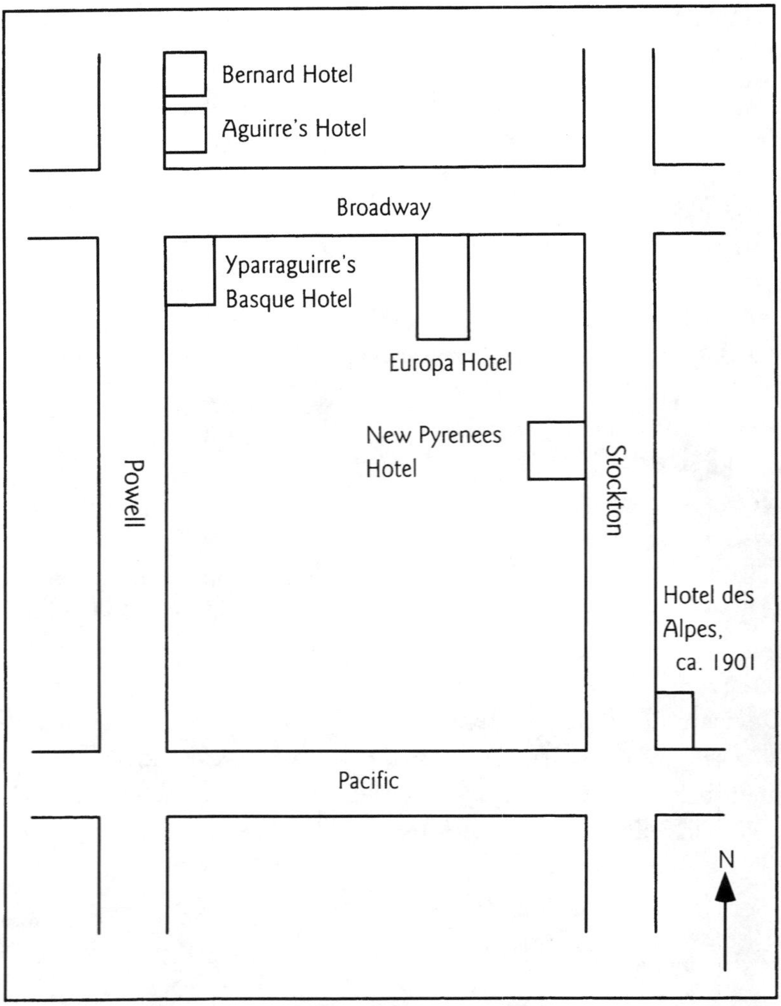


*Fig. 10. San Francisco's Basque town ca. 1899.*

Francisco's had surpassed Los Angeles's Basque town as the largest Basque community in the state. The Basque community in San Francisco expanded despite the disaster of 1906 and despite the fact that as compared to Basques in other enclaves in the Western states, residents of that community were the least involved in sheep raising.[48] For Basques in California and other parts of the West, San Francisco was becoming a major point of entry, a regional cultural center, and an ideal vacation spot for Basque families living in the San Joaquin Valley and a resting place for tired herders.

Another characteristic of San Francisco's Basque community revealed in the 1900 and 1910 censuses was the relative youth of its population. San Francisco's Basques were on average three years younger than the Basques living in other parts of the state. The implication of this statistic is that the population was dynamic, and the community was experiencing an influx of newcomers. The statistics bear this out as the numbers and percentage of foreign-born Basques in San Francisco increased between 1900 and 1910 (see table 5.6).

## After the Quake

As we have seen, San Francisco's first *ostatuak* played an important role in the history of Basque immigration to and settlement in the United States. But tragically the buildings housing these early businesses were destroyed in the earthquake and fires of 1906. These disasters are among the most spectacular in California history, and they had a dramatic impact on the Basque colony living in the city. The quake struck shortly after five in the

*Bernardo Altube (with the beard) and others standing in front of the Hotel Vasco on Powell Street in San Francisco, ca. 1870. Courtesy of the Basque Studies Collection, Getchell Library, University of Nevada, Reno.*

morning on April 18, 1906; the initial shock lasted for about one minute, with subsequent waves continuing for much of the day. Although it is impossible for us to know how the event rated seismically, it has been estimated that the San Francisco quake would have measured 8.3 on the Richter scale. About five thousand buildings were destroyed, railways and roads were mangled, and public services came to a halt. Sporadic fires broke out immediately after the first quake, and within two hours the east end of Market Street, Chinatown, city hall, and the North Beach area were ablaze. An area measuring four square miles was destroyed, and the fire burned for seventy-four hours after the initial quake before it was finally put out.[49]

The hotels of Jose Aguirre and Juan Francisco Yparraguirre were two of the thousands of buildings that were destroyed in the inferno of 1906. The 1906 disaster provides a convenient close to the nineteenth-century chapter of San Francisco's Basque neighborhood. Immediately after the conflagration, a second Basque district emerged in the Broadway and North Beach neighborhood. The available evidence suggests that Ambrosio Yrionda's *ostatu* at 734 Broadway was the first post-quake hotel. According to 1907 directories, "lodgings and furnished rooms" were available at Yrionda's; none of the pre-quake *ostatuak* were included in these directories.[50] By the following year, the Hotel España was listed at 785 Broadway, and Justino and Manual Yriarte had opened the Hotel Yberico at 1034 Pacific.[51] In 1907 the adult Basque population living in San Francisco was only 949, a markedly small portion of the 342,782 residents of the City by the Bay.[52]

By 1916 the neighborhood of Broadway and North Beach was home to a number of hotels that may have been Basque owned or operated. Among some of the most likely candidates, based on the names of the hotels, were the Hotel des Alpes, the Hotel de France, the Hotel de España,

Table 5.6 Origins of San Francisco's Basque Population, 1900 and 1910

| Origin | Number in 1900 | Percentage in 1900 | Number in 1910 | Percentage in 1910 |
|---|---|---|---|---|
| France | 47 | 42 | 374 | 28 |
| Spain | 15 | 13 | 511 | 38 |
| United States | 50 | 45 | 456 | 34 |
| Total Basque Population | 112 | 100 | 1,341 | 100 |

Source: Arrizabalaga, "Statistical Study," 67.

Table 5.7 Post-Quake Hotels

| Date(s) | Operator(s) | Location | Hotel Name |
|---|---|---|---|
| 1907–ca. 1920 | Ambrosio Yrionda | 734 Broadway | Yrionda's |
| 1908–1970s | Miguel and Ramon Lugea<br>Henry Urigoyen<br>Jose Echamende and M. Daniel<br>Fermin Huarte and Louis Elu<br>Louis and Marie Elu | 785 Broadway | Hotel España |
| 1908–1930s | Justino and Manuel Yriarte<br>Gernika Basabe | 1034 Pacific | Hotel Yberico<br>Hotel Iriarte and Jai Alai Bar |
| 1910s | Jose and Dionisia L. Yriberri | — | — |
| 1920s–1970s | Dominca Olarque<br>J. P. Arretche and Lucy Etchemendi | 787 Broadway | Hotel du Midi |
| 1930s–present | Jean and Marie Cazahous<br>Ganish and Ana Iriartborde<br>Ciriaco and Elaine Iturri | 732 Broadway | Hotel des Alpes* |
| 1040s–1970s | Jean and Amelie Sorhondo | 517 Broadway | Sorhondo's Pyrenees |
| 1943–1992 | Juan and Nieves Yriarte<br>Pierre and Catherine Goyenetche<br>Arnaud and Marie Mendisco<br>Bambi McDonald | 1208 Stockton | Obrero Hotel |
| 1960s–1998 | Martha Biguet and family<br>Joe Gestes<br>Sauveur and Anna Anchartechahar<br>Antoinette and Daniel Francisco Oroz<br>Rebecca and Jean Idiart | 15 Romlulo Place | Basque Hotel |
| 1960s | John Etchevers and Claude Berhouet | 780 Broadway | Hotel de France† |

*Directories indicate that this hotel was opened in 1916 but did not include information about its operators.
†Four Hotels de France have graced San Francisco's Basque town: in 1890 at 618 California; in 1912 at 1312 Powell; in 1916 at 776 Broadway; and from the 1960s to the present at 780 Broadway.
Dashes indicate that no information was available for this entry.

the Hotel des Pyrenees, and the Hotel du Midi.[53] We are certain that the Hotel España was Basque because it was under the management of two Basque brothers, Jose and Miguel Lugea.[54]

In 1907 Jose Lugea invited his brothers Miguel and Ramon to join him in San Francisco. Jose Lugea had arranged a long-term lease of a lot at 785 Broadway, and he wanted his brothers to help him build a hotel there. He hoped that his oldest brother, Miguel, who was a carpenter, would supervise construction of the building.[55] Miguel was living in Elko at the time, but reluctantly he consented to move to San Francisco to take on the

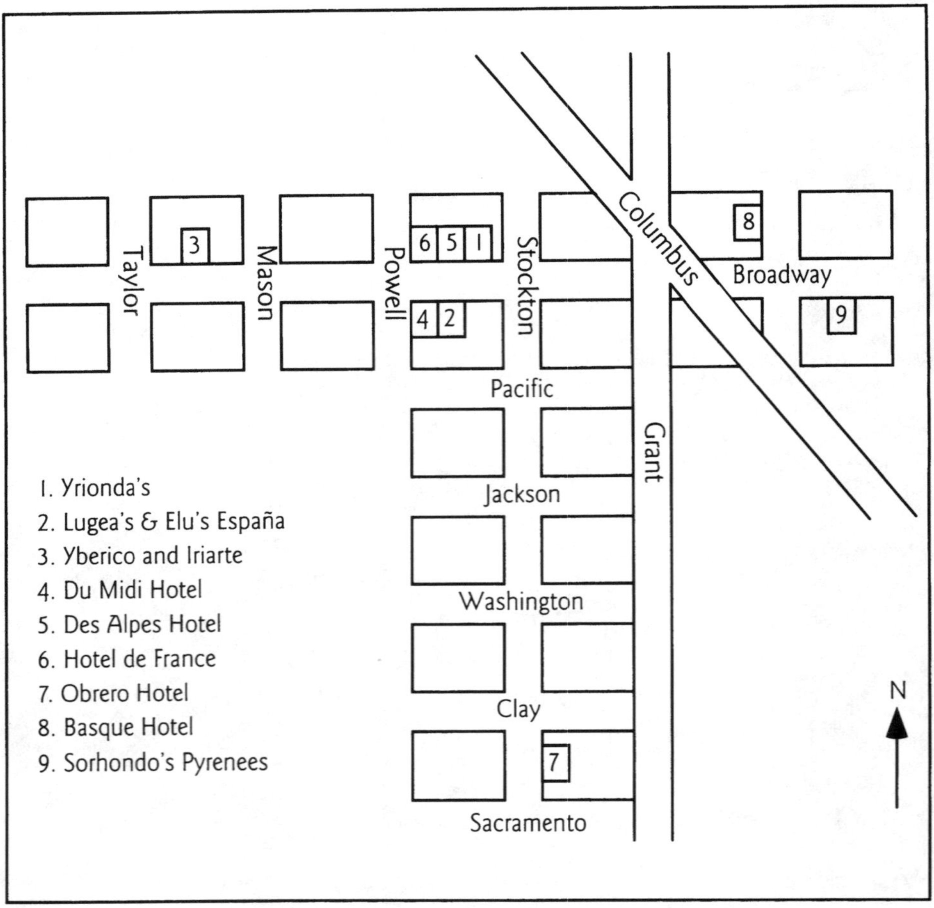


*Fig. 11. San Francisco's post-quake hotels. The hotels on this map correspond to those listed in table 5.7 and date from 1907 to the present.*

project. Once the hotel was built, Miguel and Jose operated it until 1924, when Miguel passed away. After Miguel's death, Jose sold his interest in the Hotel España and joined Ramon in Fresno, where he dedicated his efforts to sheep ranching.[56]

Despite competition, the Lugeas' hotel seems to have been one of San Francisco's most popular *ostatuak* in the decade between 1910 and 1920.[57] The hotel of Jose and Dionisia Lusaretto Yriberri is often cited as the other major neighborhood competition.[58] Old-timers recall the Lugeas' popular Sunday night dances. There young John Bidegaray, whose father owned Fresno's Bascongado Hotel, often played his accordion until the early morning hours.[59] San Francisco's Basque residents and visitors also remember games at Jeronimo and Selernia Meabe's handball court, which could be reached by going out the rear exit of Lugeas' and proceeding "down the alley."[60] It was another favorite gathering place on Sunday afternoons.

By 1920, and perhaps earlier, San Francisco's Basque town had become a regional center for Basques from the northern portions of the San Joaquin Valley. In 1929 Tomas and Maria Ballaz, who later settled in Fresno and operated the Victoria Hotel, honeymooned at the Hotel Español, which was then operated by Martin Ayoleta Abaurrea.[61] Occasionally out-of-town Basques took up temporary residence in San Francisco *ostatuak*. For example, Elena Etcheverry of Los Banos lived at Henry Yrigoyen's Hotel España for ten months while completing a business school course, and Dominica Arambel enjoyed a long visit to Dominica Olargue's Hotel du Midi in 1928.[62]

Many Basque families from the Stockton area would spend a few summer months in San Francisco to avoid the oppressive valley heat and enjoy what San Francisco's Basque town had to offer.[63] In addition to those hotels already mentioned, an early favorite was the three-story brick Hotel Iriarte on the southeast corner of Powell and Pacific. "Gernika" Basabe owned the hotel in the 1920s and reopened it in 1932.[64] The bar in the lower floor was called the Jai Alai, and adjacent to the building stood one of the city's larger handball courts.[65]

San Francisco's Broadway area continued to be home to about half a dozen Basque boardinghouses and hotels up to and during World War II. During the war years San Francisco restaurateurs and hotelkeepers were obliged to report to the War Price and Rationing Board, under the Office of Price Administration, on menus and pricing every week, so we have records of what Basque establishments served and the prices they charged. Jean and Marie Cazahous, owners of the Des Alpes Restaurant and Hotel, attempted to cooperate, as did other *ostatu* owners.

In conformity with the Office of Price Administration, the Des Alpes reported its six-course evening meals on a weekly basis. For the week of April 4, 1943, for example, the evening meals included soup, hors d'oeuvres, an entrée, a roast of some sort, salad, coffee, French bread, and dessert. On Friday and Sunday nights, the price of dinner was $1, and on the other evenings customers were charged eighty-five cents.[66] It is clear from the menus that diners were not offered a choice of entrée, and that meals were served family-style. Among the offerings were dishes such as steak with spinach, fried sole, lamb stew, broiled chicken with sweet peas, tripe à la mode, or calf's head, and roast beef with lentils. One can only imagine the reaction of a non-Basque city dweller attending the Wednesday evening meal and being presented with a calf's head for dinner! The Des Alpes Restaurant enjoyed a fine reputation among its customers and is still noted for its cuisine among San Franciscans.[67]

From 1956 through 1975 Ganish and Ana Iriartborde managed the Des Alpes. During those years the establishment was both a restaurant and a boardinghouse. Fifteen rooms on the second and third floors accommodated boarders comfortably, and because there were so many Basques visiting San Francisco in those days, the Iriartbordes claim that they never rented rooms to non-Basques.[68] Ciriaco and Elaine Iturri began operating the Des Alpes in 1975.[69] Today the boardinghouse function is nearly defunct, yet food from the Des Alpes kitchen is still regarded as a treat by locals and out-of-towners, Basques and non-Basques.[70]

By the late 1950s and early 1960s a full assortment of hotels had emerged in the Broadway district, including the more well known Hotel España, Hotel de France, Hotel du Midi, Cosmopolitan, Obrero, Pyrenees, Hotel des Alpes, and the Basque Hotel. Around 1960 Fermin Huarte and Louis Elu began managing the España, formerly owned by Jose and Miguel Lugea; John Etchevers and Claude Berhouet constructed the Hotel de France restaurant and boardinghouse on 780 Broadway; Jean Pierre Arretche and Lucy Etchemendi were at the Hotel du Midi; Juan and Nieves Yriarte managed the Hotel Obrero on Stockton Street; John Bordalampe took over for the Iriartbordes for a two-year period at the Hotel des Alpes; and Amelie and Jean Sorhondo opened a lodging house at 517 Broadway called the Pyrenees.[71]

Eventually Fermin Huarte sold his interest in the España to Louis and Marie Elu, and the Elus opened a new family restaurant and bar on the lower floor.[72] For over two decades, Elu's Basque Restaurant was a favorite of visiting Basques and local San Franciscans. Advertisements for Elu's appeared regularly in the Boise-based *Voice of the Basques* newspaper, an English-language publication that folded in the 1970s. One advertisement claimed that Elu's was the "Headquarters for Wool Sheep Cattlemen."[73] The claim was undoubtedly correct insofar as Elu's was a central meeting place for Basques throughout the 1960s and 1970s; yet the restaurant tended to cater exclusively to Basque sheepmen, not cattlemen.

Down the street and around the corner from Elu's was the Obrero Hotel. Juan and Nieves Yriarte managed the Obrero for nine years, until

1952, when they discontinued their lease on the three-story building. Then Pierre and Catherine Goyenetche began their fourteen-year term as managers of the hotel. They rented out ten rooms to boarders and used three rooms for their private quarters.[74] When they began at the Obrero, the Goyenetches' eleven-year-old daughter served tables, and their thirteen-year-old son helped with cleaning up and washing dishes. Catherine cooked all the meals, and Pierre tended bar. At the evening meals, which were priced at $2.50 a person, up to sixty diners might appear. If more people showed up, the Goyenetches had to turn customers away.

Many San Francisco Basques ate in the Obrero's compact dining room and claimed that it was their favorite place to dine. They describe plentiful and tasty meals and a warm atmosphere, enhanced by Catherine Goyenetche's jovial spirit. One old-timer recalled that Catherine would get people who had been strangers before dinner to sing together after their meals. Passers-by might have heard anything from "Frere Jacques" and "Oh Susanna" to "Gernika'ko Arbola" as they walked down Stockton Street past the restaurant in the evenings.

In 1975 the Goyenetches retired from business. Catherine's niece Marie and Marie's husband Arnaud Mendisco leased the Obrero for two and a half years. They continued to manage the hotel in much the same style as their aunt and uncle had, but they encouraged the restaurant more than the boardinghouse business, as one can see in one of their advertisements, which reads, "The Obrero—Where Old Friends Meet . . . Distinctive French Basque Cooking."[75] During their years at the Obrero, the Mendiscos took over more rooms for their own personal use and rented only five rooms to boarders.[76]

From 1978 to 1992 an Irish-American woman named Bambi MacDonald owned and managed the Obrero. At that time the hotel's situation struck many a Basque as ironic: the owner was Irish, the cuisine was Basque, and the surrounding neighborhood was Chinatown. When Bambi came to the Obrero, she intended to maintain the hotel and offer the same cuisine, but doing so was tougher than she anticipated. As Bambi correctly claimed, "One does not have to be a Basque to cook Basque," but the local Basques could not be expected to act according to such logic.

Painted, scrubbed, and redecorated, the Obrero appealed more to those interested in a unique dining experience or a weekend getaway than to local Basques looking for a place to socialize. Increasingly, the Obrero attracted American clientele interested in a dose of ethnicity, but at the same time the old Basque clientele dropped off. A few people I interviewed stated that they occasionally went back to the Obrero to reminisce but that "it wasn't the same anymore." Quite possibly this feeling had more to do with nostalgia for the "good old days" and was less related to Bambi's cooking or the Obrero's face-lift.[77]

When Catherine and Pierre Goyenetche were still running the Obrero, around 1964, a Basque family named Biguet leased and reopened a twenty-five-room hotel at 15 Romulo Place, on an alley off Broadway.[78] The Basque Hotel, as it was called, underwent several managerial turnovers in roughly five-year intervals. After the Biguets, Joe Gestes operated the hotel until 1975, when Sauveur and Anna Anchartechahar took over.[79] Then Antoinette and Daniel-Francisco Oroz leased the place from 1979 to 1985.[80] When the Orozes bought the Chalet Basque Restaurant in San Rafael in 1985, Rebecca and Jean Emile Idiart moved in to the Basque Hotel and Restaurant, and their business flourished until 1998, when they sold out to non-Basques.[81]

Across the street from the intersection of Romulo and Broadway was perhaps the most authentic of San Francisco's Basque boardinghouses in recent existence—the Pyrenees. Owned by Amelie and Jean Sorhondo, the boardinghouse was located on the second and third floors of an old Broadway hotel building. The Sorhondos leased the space from 1957 to 1993 and rented out twenty-six rooms to single Basque men who worked in the city. Because the front door was unmarked, few people other than Basques would have known about this small *ostatu*.

After ringing the bell and gaining entry, one ascended a narrow and creaky stairway to the second floor. If it happened to be midday, the aroma from the kitchen might give one the hope of an invitation for lunch. But as an "outsider" one would be lucky to be invited for a meal at the Sorhondos' because it was a "true" boardinghouse in that meals were served almost exclusively to boarders. The dining room and kitchen were practically the only common rooms in the Pyrenees, with the exception of a television room that was seldom used.

Within San Francisco's Basque neighborhood, Jean and Amelie Sorhondo were fondly regarded. As one local Basque observed, "Amelie still helps the old-timers and boarders and is a great cook."[82] Many local Basques would stop in at the Pyrenees on Sunday afternoons to play *mus* in the dining room. When asked why the couple had continued for so long at the Pyrenees before retiring, the octogenarian Amelie responded that she and Jean were "too old to go to work now."[83] Probably closer to the truth is that for their Basque customers and the Sorhondos themselves, the Pyrenees was synonymous with the Sorhondos. No one could imagine one without the other.

Although the Pyrenees might be considered a "classic" *ostatu* model, there were other forms of lodging offered by Basques in San Francisco. For instance, a hotelkeeper might not offer cooking or kitchen services to his or her customers. Such an establishment was more like a Basque-run apartment building, and it might not cater exclusively to Basques. Around 1980 Grace Iribarren began operating the Liguria Hotel on Columbus Street, where she supervised the leasing and upkeep of thirty apartments.[84] Not far away, Martin Minaberry at the Hotels Trevore and Cable Car and Terese Huasqui at the Castro ran similar businesses. These establishments do not resemble the *ostatuak* that are the focus of this work, but their presence suggests that there was some flexibility in the forms of lodging offered by Basques in San Francisco—that there were variations on the more traditional Basque hotel.

On February 15, 1982, the San Francisco Basque Cultural Center opened, and in some ways it offered Basques an alternative to congregating at the *ostatuak* in North Beach. Built with funds generated by local Basques, the new South San Francisco complex features a large enclosed handball court with grandstands for spectators, a spacious restaurant with individual tables, a variety of meeting rooms, a dance hall and bar, and a recreation room or day care area for children. The center also has a small library of Basque books and offers classes in Basque dancing and singing and Euskara.

Downtown hotelkeepers have claimed that the center has hurt weekend business at the *ostatuak*. The reported loss of Saturday and Sunday business among hotelkeepers may also be the result of customers choosing more modern hotels over the older boardinghouses. Also, as many hotelkeepers will admit, their customers are increasingly non-Basques, so it is not surprising that local Basques are choosing to frequent the cultural center. At the risk of oversimplifying, San Francisco's cultural center can be seen as the next step in the evolution of Basque institutions that promote social and cultural interaction.

Although the San Francisco Basque Cultural Center may have rivaled the downtown hotels for clients over the past decade and a half, it has not completely taken over the role that the Broadway district's hotels have fulfilled for a long time. Author Jean DeCroos identified four neighborhoods where Basques were concentrated in San Francisco, pointing out that only one hosted *ostatuak*. He further suggested that the Broadway neighborhood's function was distinct from the others and probably cannot be replaced.[85] Nonetheless, the fact that the former owners of the Hotel des Alpes were also the first managers at the cultural center suggests that there is a strong link between the cultural center and the Basques on Broadway.[86] At the Basque Cultural Center, Ana and Ganesh Iriartborde and their clients have enjoyed a new, spacious environment, but they have never attempted to replace the boardinghouse atmosphere. In a sense, they have been aware that they are providing something new, perhaps a cousin twice removed from their Hotel Des Alpes.

San Francisco's early Basque town shared some characteristics with that of Los Angeles. In both cities clusters of *ostatuak* sprang up in a particular neighborhood and formed a nucleus for Basques living in the immediate area and outlying towns. Both Basque towns became regional centers for the wider Basque population, and both contributed to the growth of offshoot communities on their periphery. The Basque neighborhood in Los Angeles had dwindled and collapsed by World War II, yet San Francisco's Basque town has expanded, even though in San Francisco hotels continued to flourish up through the 1960s. Perhaps the nature of urban development in the Los Angeles metropolitan area was the most important factor pushing Los Angeles Basques to relocate to surrounding areas. In contrast, Basques in San Francisco were able to adjust to urban growth by taking "town jobs" as gardeners, janitors, bakers, and laundry workers.[87] In Los Angeles, Basques were often directly tied to sheep raising and wool production or other agricultural endeavors.

Although both early Basque towns share the distinction of being the first two in North America, this status should not be overemphasized. Instead, important consideration should be given to the role these two early neighborhoods played in contributing to the development of many new Basque communities in outlying areas and spurring the establishment of hotels in less urban settings around the turn of the century.[88] In the next chapter, we focus on southern California, where Basque towns and *ostatuak* cropped up based on the earlier models of those found in Los Angeles, and in a later chapter we explore offshoots of San Francisco's Basque town.

# 6

# Southern California's Spin-Off Hotels

## The Legacy of Los Angeles's Early Basque Town

Although the Basque populations in Los Angeles and San Francisco declined rapidly with the urbanization of these regions, colonies of Euskaldunak developed elsewhere in southern and northern California as a result of the relocation of Basques. Los Angeles's Basque hotels served as the early training ground for those who later became hotelkeepers in Bakersfield, Tehachapi, Santa Barbara, Chino, and La Puente; and San Francisco's *ostatuak* provided on-the-job training for *hoteleros* who would eventually relocate in San Jose, Sacramento, Stockton, and Reno, Nevada.[1] A review of the hotels throughout the San Joaquin Valley reveals that the area once attracted numerous Basque ranchers between 1907 and 1970. In the twentieth century the towns of Bakersfield and Fresno, as well as Stockton (see chapter 9), grew to be better known for their Basque populations than the coastal cities of Los Angeles and San Francisco. And just as hotels spun off from California's two early Basque town populations into outlying areas, this pattern would repeat itself in other Basque-American communities of the West in the early decades of the twentieth century.

The substantial presence of Basques in Kern County is reflected in census material for 1900 and 1910. In 1910 the county had the fifth largest Basque population in California, after San Francisco, Los Angeles, Alameda, and Fresno Counties.[2] Compared to the other California counties with large Basque populations, Kern County had a large number of single adults (59.4 percent), most of whom were males. Among the adult Basques in Kern there were 213 males and 54 females; thus 79.8 percent of the adult Basque population of the county was male. Put another way, there were nearly four times as many Basque men as there were Basque women. Because the ratio of men to women approaches one to one in more mature Basque colonies, the numbers for Kern County suggest that it was in an earlier stage of demographic development as compared with Los Angeles, San Francisco, Fresno, and Alameda Counties.[3] In Kern County in 1900 and 1910, Basques were younger, were more frequently first-generation Americans, and were more often aliens than in the other counties.[4]

## Bakersfield

By 1870 Basques were beginning to move into southern portions of the San Joaquin Valley of California, specifically to Bakersfield and the small neighboring town of Tehachapi. The Miller and Lux Ranch and the Kern County Land Company, two of Kern County's largest ranches, drew a number of the earliest Basques to the county and employed many Basque sheepherders between 1870 and 1900, thus functioning as a "Basque pipeline" to the Bakersfield area. Ironically, the first of Bakersfield's numerous Basque hotels was built in Kern City (later renamed East Bakersfield, and incorporated into the city of Bakersfield) by a non-Basque named Faustino Mier.

Mier was born in Santander, Spain, on February 15, 1856.[5] At the age of fifteen he traveled to America to join his uncle Vincent Noriega in Tulare, California, and took his uncle's surname as his own. Faustino Mier Noriega began working as a herder for the large Miller and Lux outfit in 1882 and became a foreman of one of the outfit's Kern County ranches a few years later. He worked there until February 1893, when he married a French Basque woman, Louise Inda.

A few months before the Noriega-Inda wedding, Faustino formed a partnership with Fernando Etcheverry, a French Basque from Aldudes.

Having secured a loan of $3,500 to finance their business investment the year before, Noriega and Etcheverry opened their Iberia Hotel in Kern City in 1893.[6] The new hotel immediately became a center and a meeting place for Basques from Bakersfield, Tehachapi, Wasco, Tulare, and other surrounding towns.[7] Before the Iberia, several Dauphinois French–owned hotels had served the French and Basque communities in Bakersfield.[8] Not accidentally, the Iberia was located directly across the street from Bakersfield's train station. For decades Basques arriving in Bakersfield by rail have spotted the hotel upon stepping from the train. In fact, one 1899 advertisement ran, "Iberia Hotel, F. M. Noriega, proprietor, first class accommodations, everything neat and clean, for reliable information as to pasturage and fat stock of all kinds . . . opposite freight depot."[9]

After the turn of the century, Noriega and Etcheverry renegotiated their partnership, divided the profits from the hotel, and began investing elsewhere in Kern County. Not more than a block away, the two built a second Basque hotel, which they named the Pyrenees. Construction costs for the new brick building were $9,000.[10] To recoup their initial investment, the two leased the Pyrenees to a series of other Basque hotelkeepers until they finally sold the building years later. During their first eight years of managing the Iberia and the Pyrenees, Faustino and Louise Inda Noriega, with their young children and Fernando and Mathilde Etcheverry, all lived at the Iberia. In 1901 the Noriegas left the Iberia, and the partners began leasing it to other operators. Five years later, while still in partnership with Etcheverry, Faustino changed the name of the Iberia to Noriega's. Today Noriega's is the oldest *ostatu* still operating in the West; that is, it is the oldest Basque hotel still taking in Basque boarders and serving family-style meals at one sitting.

For its first fifty years, Noriega's was a long two-story building. There was an enclosed wooden handball court against the back wall of the hotel. Old-timers tell colorful stories about the bats that lived in the rafters of *la cancha*. Chicken pens, a few livestock, a livery, and a vegetable garden could be found in the empty lots alongside and behind the hotel.[11] In 1928 a fire damaged the livery area and ball court, and a new *cancha* was constructed.[12] The present bar, card room, and dining area were added in 1940, nearly doubling the area of the lower floor.[13] Today Noriega's reminds one of the self-sufficient complex it once was; one can still see vestiges of its former supply areas, courts, kitchens, parlors, and barrooms.

Taking a walking tour through the century-old Noriega Hotel, one can appreciate the lifestyle and demands of earlier days. When facing the

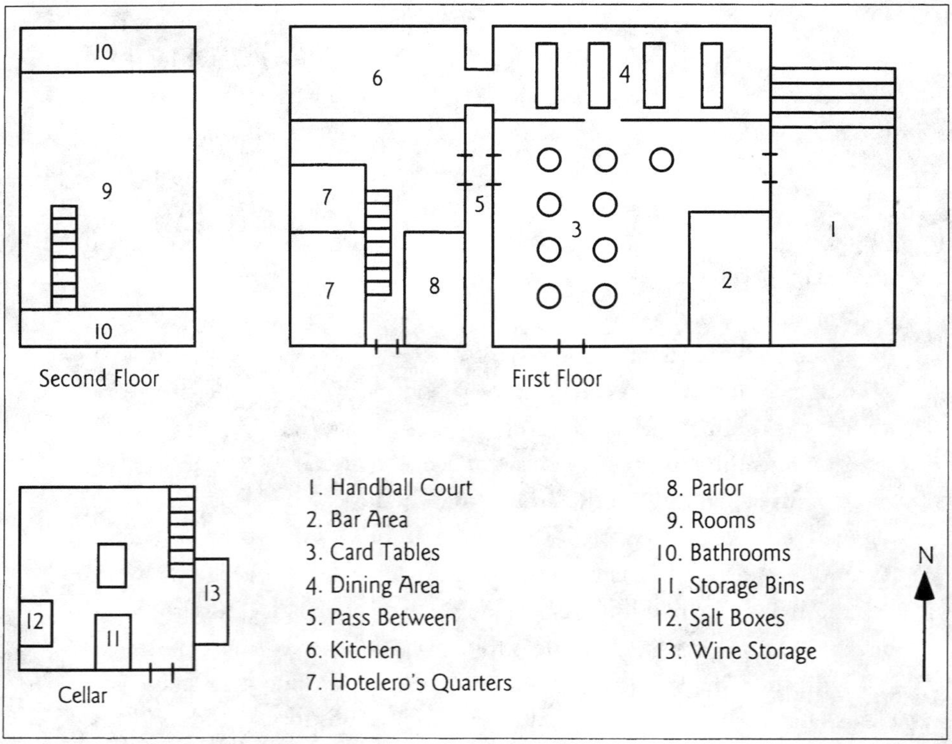


*Fig. 12. The physical layout of the Noriega Hotel today, Bakersfield, California.*

façade of the building, one can barely distinguish the 1893 construction on the left from the 1940 extension on the right. Upon entering the building, however, the difference becomes more discernible. Today the visitor entering the front door walks into a large barroom with tables for playing cards or private visiting. Most of the socializing occurs in this area, which also serves as a sort of lobby to all other portions of the hotel. Crossing from the newer to the older section of the downstairs, one can easily get a sense of stepping into the Prohibition Era or earlier. The parlor, for example, was separated from the main area and used by the ladies before the 1920s for visiting, while their men socialized in the barroom or played handball in *la cancha*. In the cellar directly beneath the parlor, the ramp that hotelkeepers once used for rolling enormous wine barrels down to the cellar for storage still leans against the wall. Also in the cellar are large wooden salt boxes once used for curing meats, as well as pipes suspended overhead where *txorizo* (sausages) were hung and dried, and a screened-in cupboard where dry goods were stored.

To accommodate its boarders and visitors, Noriega's has thirteen upstairs rooms, with washrooms at either end of a long corridor. Guest rooms appear as they must have earlier in the century. Each is small, sparsely furnished, and clean. Interestingly, visitors know which rooms are preferred. For instance, the rooms at the back of the building tend to be the last ones chosen because of the noises that tend to rise from the kitchen early in the morning, and rooms in the front of the hotel are considered less pleasant because they get baked by the hot Bakersfield sunshine in summer months. The hotel's thirteen rooms are numbered one through fourteen—there never has been a room "13" at the Noriega, reflecting a tendency among Basque boarders to share widespread superstitions.[14]

In the years since 1901, when the Etcheverrys left the Iberia, a number of hotelkeepers have made the hotel their home. From 1901 through 1906, Jean and Jeanne Burubeltz operated the hotel. Before moving to Bakersfield, Jean Burubeltz had managed the Ballade House in Los Angeles's Basque town. A native of Lasse, France, Burubeltz had arrived in southern California in 1873, where he began herding sheep and struck up a friendship with Pascal Ballade. The Hotel des Pyrenees in Los Angeles became his "second home" and was also where he met Jeanne Erreca, the niece of Marie Ballade, who would later become his wife. After the two were married in 1890, Burubeltz sold his sheep interests and went to work for Ballade. In the early 1890s J. Ordoqui and Sons leased the Hotel des Pyrenees, and the Ballades relocated to 604 Alameda Street, which became the Ballade House.[15] Directories for 1891 listed Pascal Ballade as manager and restaurateur, with Jean Burubeltz as proprietor.[16] The Burubeltzes continued to work at the Ballade House until 1901, when they learned that Faustino Noriega of East Bakersfield was looking for someone to manage the Iberia Hotel.

The Burubeltzes then moved to Bakersfield to manage the Iberia until 1906, and they made the town their permanent home. In one account, Jean and Jeanne Burubeltz are credited with opening the Hotel d' Europe in 1901, but more than likely this date is incorrect.[17] The records indicate that the couple managed the Iberia until 1906, when they moved to the Hotel d' Europe, owned by "Frenchman" Pierre Roux.[18] Jean Burubeltz died in 1911, and Jeanne continued to operate the Hotel d' Europe until 1915, when she purchased the hotel from La Roux.[19] She then operated the Hotel d' Europe until 1921, when the it faded from East Bakersfield history.

Information on Noriega's during the period from 1906 until 1920 is sketchy. One account mentions that a Jean B. Estribou managed the Metropole Hotel during this period, even though biographical sketches and supplementary materials do not include the hotel.[20] From 1915 through 1920 a Spaniard named Fernandes-Aja managed the hotel. Other than his unusual nickname, Rothschild, very little has been reported on his five years at the Noriega.

On the other hand, information regarding the Noriega Hotel since 1920 is more accessible. A fire at the hotel caused some structural damage in 1920. Afterward Faustino Noriega offered a month's free rent to Francisco Amestoy if he would manage the hotel and make the needed repairs to the building.[21]

Francisco Amestoy was born in Navarre and went to the Philippines to work the sugar plantations with his two older brothers after the death of his parents. In 1904 he left the Philippines and traveled to southern California. Arriving with $15 in his pocket, he first stopped in Los Angeles at the Hotel Español on Aliso and Alameda Streets, where he enjoyed visiting with other Euskaldunak and playing handball at the Español's court.[22] Not long after his arrival, he began herding sheep for Pierre and Jacob Loustalot and, later, for the Anchordoquy brothers.[23] Eventually Amestoy made his way to Bakersfield, where Faustino Noriega hired him to work at the hotel.

Amestoy met his future wife, Anselma Ballaz, at the hotel in 1912, the year she began working at Noriega's as a maid.[24] After they were wed the two Amestoys ran the Noriega from 1920 to 1931. In 1927 they purchased the Cesmat Hotel, located a few blocks away on East Twenty-first Street. Descendants of the Amestoys claim that Anselma never considered making Faustino Noriega an offer on his property because she was worried about the building burning down; she had already seen two fires in the hotel (one in 1920 and the other in 1928), and she detested the bats that lived in the hotel attic and the old handball court. As the story goes, Anselma purchased the two-story brick Cesmat Hotel without consulting Francisco and signed a loan agreement with Ardizzi and Olcese, a firm that helped many early Bakersfield Basques with loans and financing.[25]

In comparison to the experience of Basques in Los Angeles, Bakersfield Basques had a difficult time with Prohibition. Indeed, there are a number of bootlegging stories from the decade when the Amestoys were in business at Noriega's. In Bakersfield, hotelkeepers kept wine and other alcoholic beverages on hand for Basque clients but did not serve non-Basque customers. As one observer noted, "[A]ll Bascos drank and made their own wine, . . . and if you didn't have wine [at your hotel], the Bascos wouldn't stay."[26] Anselma, whose Basque friends called her "Txaparita," reportedly developed a number of clever ways of hiding alcohol from "the public": she kept a private bottle in the upstairs bathroom, a teapot on the kitchen stove, and a flask tucked into her brassiere.[27] Any local Basque knew he could go into the kitchen, pour himself a shot of whiskey from the teapot, put fifty cents in the cigar box above the stove, and return to his card game, dinner seat, or courtside perch without attracting attention.[28]

Despite such ingenious tricks, the Bakersfield police "pinched" the Amestoys three times.[29] One time the police entered Noriega's, marched downstairs to the cellar, and axed every wooden cask of wine in the supply, causing a minor flood and an eventual mud-bath in the dirt-floored cellar.[30]

On other occasions, however, the local hotel operators were more successful at serving alcoholic beverages without arousing the suspicions of the local constabulary. One of the favorite stories told among locals involved using "chicken orders" as a decoy for ordering bottles or kegs of wine. Since orders were placed by telephone on party lines, hotelkeepers and their customers had to be careful about what they said to one another. It was privately understood, for example, that an order for "three chickens for Sunday dinner" really meant three barrels of wine by Sunday dinner.[31]

After eight years of managing the Noriega without a vacation, the Amestoy family spent four months in the Basque region in the spring of 1928. Upon returning, they renewed their lease at Noriega's and extended the lease agreement with the operators of the Cesmat. On January 31, 1931, after making their home at Noriega's for eleven years, the Amestoys moved to the Cesmat. For a brief time, Marcelina Noriega Recatune and her husband took over at Noriega's, and then the operation of the place was passed on to the Elizaldes. On East Twenty-first Street at the Cesmat the Amestoys posted their family nameplate, which the building still bears today. The Amestoys' comparatively modern brick structure underwent a thorough cleaning, light remodeling, and downstairs reinforcement before they opened for business.[32] The Amestoy was open in the ensuing decades. In 1953 Josephine Amestoy purchased the business from her mother (Anselma) and managed it until 1964, when she sold it to Raymond Maitia.

By the mid-1930s, three *ostatuak* were prospering in Bakersfield's Basque neighborhood. Late in 1931, Jean and Grace Elizalde had taken over at

Noriega's, Francisco and Anselma Amestoy were at Amestoy's, and Jenny Iribarne Dunns and Inocencio "Jack" Juarena were partners at the old Pyrenees, which Noriega and Etcheverry had built three decades earlier. Lunch at the Pyrenees cost fifty cents and dinner seventy-five. Some patrons claimed that the Pyrenees served the very best Basque meals in town, and for a time it was the most popular stop in Basque town.[33] When Jenny Iribarne Dunns died in 1943, sole ownership of the Pyrenees Café went to Inocencio (rooms were no longer let at the Pyrenees), but Jenny's third-generation descendants are still running the business today.

Another Basque establishment operating in Bakersfield from the mid-1920s through the 1930s was the Metropole Hotel, a second-story hotel located at the corner of Sumner and Baker Streets, across the street from Bakersfield's train depot.[34] Although dates and information regarding the Metropole when it was run by Jean Estribou are sketchy, we know that its later operators, Jacques and Grace Iriart, moved to Bakersfield from Tehachapi in 1926, when they became managers of the hotel.[35] Directories indicate that the Iriarts were at the Metropole for at least fifteen years. Curiously, however, people I interviewed who would likely have remembered the hotel rarely mentioned it. Perhaps meals and drinks were limited exclusively to the hotel's boarders or the family's close associates, which has occasionally been a practice at some *ostatuak*. If the Metropole wasn't the type of place where a lot of people gathered to socialize, it might have gone unnoticed by some Basques.

Possibly the most well-known and loved managers of any Basque hotel in Bakersfield were the Elizaldes. In the Bakersfield community, Graciana (Grace) Elizalde's legacy is enormous. At the age of twenty, in 1914, she came to Tehachapi to work as a maid at a hotel owned by family friends from her hometown of Anhauze.[36] There, at the old Franco-American Hotel, she met Jean Elizalde, who had come to California in 1905 under the sponsorship of his uncle Jean Burubeltz (who operated the Iberia and later the Hotel d' Europe). Grace and Jean married, and when they later lost their sheep in the crash of 1929, Grace went to work at the Old Commercial Hotel in Tehachapi. After two years there, the Elizaldes relieved Marcelina Noriega Recatune at the Noriega in late 1931.

Bakersfield Basques rarely fail to remember at least one of Graciana's kind acts. In part, the legacy of "Mama Elizalde" is a result of Graciana's unusually long stay at Noriega's from 1931 to 1974. But it was the *hotelera*'s kindness and generosity that made her loved in the community. Whether it was buying a large burial plot in the local cemetery for a bachelor herder, tending to the needs of an infirm boarder, or making a quiet loan to a local rancher, Graciana touched most Bakersfield Basques.[37] As one woman stated, "Grace was very, very Basque. She was like the oak tree in the forest; she had a place for every bird who came to the tree."[38] If an elderly boarder needed special care or bathing, for example, Grace would climb the stairs and harass the old-timer until she succeeded in persuading him. Oftentimes she would give or loan herders suits of clothing to wear to funerals, weddings, and baptisms. Although she never learned to drive, Grace insisted on helping others when they needed a ride. Her kitchen help and children knew they had to be ready to drop whatever they were doing and escort her or a friend at a moment's notice.

One of the most charming Elizalde stories is told by Mayie Maitia, who came to Bakersfield in March of 1947. Mayie worked as a serving girl at the Amestoy until she met Jean Baptiste Maitia, who worked at the neighboring Pyrenees. The two married, and Mayie went to work for Grace at Noriega's a few years later. When Mayie and J. B. were expecting their first child, Grace, who loved to gamble, decided to wager on the gender of the expected child. By the time the baby girl was born, Grace had wagered more than $200. As luck would have it, she bet on the correct gender. With her winnings Grace opened a savings account in the child's name.[39]

Grace Elizalde managed Noriega's continuously from 1931 until she became too sick with cancer. On April 14, 1974, she died. Even on a casual visit to Bakersfield today, however, one gets the sense that Graciana lives on in the memory of many local Basques. Her two sons, Albert and Louie Elizalde, took over management of Noriega's after their mother's death, and today her descendants still manage the hotel.

The Noriega Hotel, the Pyrenees, and the Metropole were located directly across the street from Bakersfield's train station. Frank Maitia remembers spotting the three hotels as he got off the train in 1930. Following in the footsteps of his two older brothers, J. B. and Raymond, Frank left Donibane-Garazi (St. Jean Pied de Port) to come to America. He herded sheep around Bakersfield for twelve years until he eventually saved enough money to buy the French House on East Twenty-first Street. Marius Plantier had put up the French House in 1898, and the old hotel had long served as headquarters for stockmen from all over the southern San Joaquin Valley.[40] Maitia renamed the business the Basque Café, and the establishment became a landmark for Basques in the 1930s and 1940s.[41] After renovating the building, Frank and his family lived upstairs at the Basque Café, but they did not take in boarders. During these years, Frank Maitia acted as an employment agent for ranchers in Madera, Fresno, and Bakersfield. He would wire associates in the Basque Country, stating that a certain number of men were needed for ranch jobs. Upon the arrival of the prospective group of herders and ranch hands, Maitia would arrange rooms for them at Noriega's or Amestoy's. Then he would gather the men together, write their names on slips of paper, drop the names in a hat, and then he would draw names to decide which man would work for which rancher.[42]

Another service that Frank Maitia particularly enjoyed providing was scheduling handball matches and tournaments between local players and out-of-town visitors. Frank would collect teams of players from Orange County, Chino, and La Puente, for example, and schedule Sunday matches against local competitors. Such tourneys brought out the local Basque community and attracted Basques from other southern California towns as well. Maitia was probably well aware that arranging for regular handball games also boosted weekend business for the Basque Café and the neighboring hotels.

On July 21, 1942, the quake that devastated Tehachapi's downtown and ruined all its remaining *ostatuak* buildings also caused damage in Bakersfield. It destroyed only the Metropole, which had long since ceased to function as a Basque establishment. Photographs of the destruction of the Metropole Hotel appeared on the front pages of larger newspapers, such as the Los Angeles *Times* and the Denver *Post*.[43] The old brick Amestoy and Pyrenees, and even the older wooden Noriega, withstood the quake without a major interruption in business.

By 1950 Bakersfield's Basque town began to undergo changes as the businesses were passed on to a new generation. In 1954 J. B. and Mayie Maitia opened the Woolgrowers' Restaurant down the street from the Pyrenees and Noriega's. Twenty years later, they moved to a new location on Twenty-first Street, which Mayie and her daughter Jenny still operate today. Also in the 1950s, one of the Amestoy daughters, Josephine, purchased her parents' business from Anselma and operated it for eleven years until she sold out to Frank's brother Raymond Maitia in 1964. By the early 1960s, the Frank Maitias had sold their Basque Café to Raymond Echeveste.

By the 1960s and 1970s perhaps the only strand of continuity in the rapidly changing Basque hotel business in Bakersfield was Grace Elizalde at Noriega's. As many have lamented, when Grace passed away, an entire era of Bakersfield's *ostatuak* was sealed.[44] Most of the restaurants have discontinued the practice of serving food at one sitting, one meal at noon and another at six in the evening, a practice Grace had insisted upon; they have switched to serving individual tables family-style. Today a majority of the area's Basque restaurants offer their customers a variety of choices; whereas at Grace's the customer was expected to eat whatever was being served that day without complaint.

Recent years have also seen the closing of Bakersfield's Basque boardinghouses. Only Noriega's offers room and board today, and it continues to offer rooms only to Basques. Yet Bakersfield still has numerous successful restaurants in the old Basque town area. The Woolgrowers', Noriega's, and the Pyrenees are three excellent examples. There are also several Basque restaurants in other parts of town. In the early 1970s Frank Maitia and his son moved up Union Avenue and built Maitia's Basque Restaurant, an enterprise that received early acclaim but has since closed.[45] In addition, J. B. and Marie Curuchague's Chalet Basque, the Echevestes' Chateau Basque on Union Avenue, Dominique's Basque Restaurant on New Stine Road, and Benjie Arduain's restaurant, Benjie's, continue to offer Basque cuisine.[46] In the three decades since Grace Elizalde stopped serving food, many restaurants have opened and closed. Only Noriega's hangs onto a dwindling Bakersfield tradition, as the town's other *ostatuak* have disappeared.

## Tehachapi

Bakersfield was not the only Kern County town welcoming Basques in the late 1880s, however. Approximately forty miles southeast of Bakersfield, nestled in the foothills about four thousand feet above sea level, is the small town of Tehachapi. Founded in the summer of 1876, when the Southern Pacific Railway finally conquered the difficulties of the grade and reached the little valley, Tehachapi still lies along a major highway and rail route connecting the San Joaquin Valley to the southern deserts and the Mojave.[47] In the 1870s the town sported four or five saloons, one hotel, and a population of about three hundred residents.[48] In the next twenty years, the small town began to expand with the influx of miners and stockmen. A combination of events in 1894 spurred the migration of Basques from different parts of California to Tehachapi. In the summer of that year the Wilson-Gorman Tariff went into effect, allowing foreign wool to compete more easily with domestic wool. In addition, a severe drought that year forced sheepmen to "retreat to the mountains," and Tehachapi proved a true refuge for stockmen.

A year earlier, in 1893, the Los Angeles–based Basque-language newspaper *California'ko Eskual Herria* published an article claiming that Tehachapi was the largest Basque colony in the United States.[49] Although this statement was inaccurate, the publication of this boast suggests that an increasing number of Basques were settling in the vicinity. The article also announced a day of festivities, including a regional handball tourney between local Basques and French Bearnais. For a few years around the mid-1890s, the Piute Hotel in Tehachapi operated by Austin and Marianne Goyehen Young served local Basques and may have accommodated these early handball matches. An 1893 advertisement appeared in *California'ko Eskual Herria* listing the Piute as an "Ostatua Eskualduna," or Basque hotel.[50] Unfortunately, a fire destroyed the Piute in 1895.[51]

One Basque who migrated to Tehachapi in the 1890s was Jean Pierre Martinto. A native of Osses, France, Martinto had come to Los Angeles in 1887.[52] After herding sheep in southern California for a year, he began herding for one of his older brothers, J. F., in Kern and Fresno Counties. After suffering an economically disastrous year in 1894, Martinto decided to invest what remained of his savings in Tehachapi. He had come to know the town during a visit with one of his older sisters, Marie Martinto Laffargue, who had settled in Tehachapi with her family.[53] With the help of his brother Dominique, Martinto purchased six unimproved lots on Main Street, Tehachapi, built the largest hotel in town, the Basses-Pyrenees Hotel in 1895, and put up an adjoining livery barn.[54] He also constructed a handball court of stone and cement on the premises. One account described the court as "substantial and complete as good workmen and good material could make it and said it to be the best in the country."[55] The handball court received much attention from local players as well as Basques throughout the state. In fact, in an 1897 issue of *California'ko Eskual Herria* featured the court in an article with the headline JEAN MARTINTO BUILDS BALL COURT AT HIS HOTEL.[56]

Jean Pierre married Veronica Borda in 1896, and for the next twelve years the couple expanded the Basses-Pyrenees. In 1908 they decided to retire from the business and leased the hotel to Vicente Iriarte.[57] From Tehachapi, the Martintos moved with their three children to a home on California Avenue in Bakersfield, and a few years later Martinto opened a saloon on Nineteenth Street in the heart of Bakersfield's Basque town.[58]

In the same year that Jean Pierre married Veronica, George Esponda built the Basko Hotel in Tehachapi. Esponda's wife, Marie Alzuet Borda, had been married to Jean Borda and had borne three children. When Borda died, she placed the children in an orphanage and moved to Tehachapi to find work, and there she met and married Esponda. Unfortunately, the Espondas suffered financial setbacks in their hotel business—including the loss of their home on West E Street—and they ended up selling the Basko to Jacques and Grace Iriart. By 1914 the Iriarts had taken on a French Bearnais partner, L. Escoulie, and the old Basko Hotel was renamed the Franco-American Hotel.[59]

In addition to Martinto's Basses-Pyrenees, the Espondas' Basko Hotel, and the Goyehen-Young's Piute Hotel, a fourth Basque hotel, the Hotel Cesmat, emerged in Tehachapi in the decade between 1893 and 1903. Its owner, John Iribarne, had arrived in Tehachapi in 1886, and, together with two non-Basque partners, he built the town's first warehouse at the railway station in 1889.[60] He owned the Cesmat for only three years, from 1900 to 1903, and not much else is known of Iribarne's hotel venture, except what can be gleaned from an advertisement in the *Tehachapi Tomahawk* a few years later:

> HOTEL CESMAT, JOHN IRIBARNE, PROP. FIRST CLASS HOUSE, NEW AND MODERN. MEALS 25 CENTS; REGULAR FRENCH DINNER FROM 5:30 TO 8:00, 50 CENTS; NO CHINESE COOKING. STABLE IN CONNECTION. TELEPHONE MAIN 74. 1 MO.[61]

In addition to telling us a bit about Iribarne's hotel, the advertisement suggests a community hostility to the Chinese who had settled in town after the railway was built.

Unfortunately, Tehachapi's city plans for 1901 feature only two of the hotels we have discussed, the Basses-Pyrenees and the Cesmat. Strangely, the Martinto and Iribarne properties, located within one block of the Southern Pacific Railway, appear, yet Esponda's Basko Hotel does not.[62] The omission of the old Piute Hotel is understandable, however, since it had been destroyed by fire in 1895.

By 1920 Basques were steadily moving from Tehachapi to Bakersfield. Still in 1922 Jacques Iriart of the Franco-American Hotel and his brother Samson constructed the Iriart Building across the street from their hotel in Tehachapi. The building contained a pool hall, two bars, a drugstore, a barbershop, a beauty salon, and two restaurants. Upstairs in the brick structure was the Juanita Hotel. Whether this establishment was an *ostatu* is doubtful, yet it is likely that Jacques Iriart sent overflow customers from the Franco-American Hotel across the street to the Juanita. As mentioned earlier, the Iriarts left Tehachapi in 1926 and moved to Bakersfield to manage the Metropole Hotel on Baker Street. In 1931 they returned to Tehachapi as the proprietors of the Tehachapi Hotel on Second Street. After only two months they leased the hotel to Pete Errecart and returned to Bakersfield. Errecart and his wife ran the hotel until 1936, when Francisco and Hortense (Anchordoquy) Ciaurritz, formerly of Santa Barbara, began their tenure at the Tehachapi, which lasted until 1942 when Francisco died.[63]

Front-page headlines in the Bakersfield *Californian* announced the devastation of Tehachapi's downtown by earthquake on July 21, 1952.[64] Although the temblor ruined all the buildings that once housed Tehachapi's *ostatuak*, such as the Iriarts' Franco-American, many of the Basques and their families had already moved to Bakersfield. One of Bakersfield's *ostatu* was also flattened by the quake, however. The effect of the 1952 quake on Tehachapi's remaining Basque community was significant. After the disaster, little remained of the Basque colony; many of the old-timers left for Bakersfield or other farming communities in the San Joaquin Valley. And, none of the old *ostatuak* remained intact.

## McKittrick

In addition to Bakersfield and Tehachapi, other Kern County towns were home to Basques in the early part of this century. About thirty-five miles due west of Bakersfield, near the highway that leads west over the coastal mountains toward Santa Maria and San Luis Obispo, lies the small town of McKittrick. After leaving Tehachapi's Cesmat Hotel in 1903, John Iribarne appeared in McKittrick, where he married Bernarda Arrache.[65] In one account of early ranching days in the San Joaquin Valley, Sodie Arbios mentioned that John Iribarne's saloon, named the McKittrick after the town where it was located, was a popular stop for Basques and local oil-field workers.[66] The leasing agreement signed by Iribarne and the building's owner in 1924 indicates that there was a boardinghouse on the premises: "Headquarters, Pool Hall, Rooming House, Grainery, and Stable from 1 November, 1924, through 1 November, 1925."[67] Thus the McKittrick might have been among Kern County's Basque hotels.

Not all Basques leaving Los Angeles or San Francisco moved to the southern San Joaquin Valley and Kern County. During the latter half of the 1870s the central and northern San Joaquin Valley began emerging as the principal sheep-raising district in California. As the number of sheep recorded in the censuses for in Los Angeles and Monterey Counties declined, flocks of sheep and their herders became increasingly common sights in the central San Joaquin Valley.[68] By 1880 Fresno County had the state's largest sheep population with 383,243 head of sheep.[69]

One practice that distinguished sheep raising in the San Joaquin and Sacramento Valleys from techniques found in the formative years of the southern California sheep industry was that of summering herds in the High Sierras.[70] Sheepmen of the southern San Joaquin Valley would trail their sheep from the Bakersfield area southeast through Tehachapi to the Mojave. To the north, outfits from Fresno, Los Banos, and Stockton grazed their sheep on the valley floor in the winter and trailed them into the Sierras for the hot months of July through September. With the seasonal east-to-west flow of herders and their flocks and the north-south transportation lines that developed in the basin, *ostatuak* sprang up throughout the San Joaquin Valley.

Basque sheepmen began to appear in Fresno County in the 1870s and 1880s, many of them taking their first jobs with the Miller and Lux Ranches in Merced, Madera, and Fresno Counties.[71] Some Basques joined family members who had arrived earlier to work Fresno County's fertile soil.[72] In 1872 the Southern Pacific Railroad replaced the Overland Stage, which had served Fresno since 1852.[73] Access to Fresno via north-south rail routes was augmented in 1896 when the Santa Fe rail system opened.[74] In addition to calling attention to the small town of Fresno, both rail services eventually became conduits carrying Basques north from Los Angeles and Bakersfield, south from Stockton, and southeast from San Francisco.

## Firebaugh, Mendota, and Huron

In the 1890s Basque *ostatuak* appeared in Fresno and in the three nearby towns of Firebaugh, Mendota, and Huron.[75] The Firebaugh Hotel was owned and operated by "Idiart and Son" in the 1890s, and it was one of only three hotels, four saloons, and one restaurant in town during the decade.[76] At that time, Miller and Lux continued to dominate the area's sheep business on the west side of the valley. Tiny Firebaugh swelled into a commercial center at the same time every year—when shearers gathered from throughout the state to crop the enormous herd.[77] During the high point of shearing season, local newspapers reported shooting scapes, street fights, brawls, and other violent activity.[78]

Because of Firebaugh's "unruly" reputation, the management of the Southern Pacific Railroad decided not to construct a switching station there in 1890. Instead, the company chose to create its own town ten miles southeast of Firebaugh in 1891. The new town, named Mendota, grew to two hundred residents by the mid-1890s. There French Basque Alfred Joseph Arnaudon built the Arnaudon Hotel and General Merchandise Store in 1893 on Main Street and hired Pierre Arripe as his clerk. By 1900 the building housing the hotel and store had become a major town center, containing the water company, telephone exchange, and post office.[79]

Before establishing himself in Mendota, Arnaudon had opened a hotel at White's Bridge, Fresno County, in 1886.[80] He also ran a small store, served as assistant postmaster of White's Bridge, and owned approximately four thousand sheep, which pastured in the White's Bridge area. Some thirty years after moving to Mendota, Arnaudon left the hotel business in 1917 and went into ranching full-time.[81]

Because of Southern Pacific Railroad, it was Mendota, and not Firebaugh, that would become the sheep-shearing center for the ranches on the valley's west side. In 1896 one Fresno newspaper reported that Arnaudon had "erected a new sheep corral and will probably shear the great majority of sheep in this district. Already have arrived many 'Knights of Golden Fleece.'"[82] It is not surprising that Arnaudon arranged for the shearing to be done near his hotel property given that he was a hotelkeeper and grocer. One would assume that many local sheepmen were Basque and that the hotelkeeper profited from this arrangement.

In another newspaper clipping from the pioneer days in Mendota a writer mentioned the Arnaudon Hotel and described a walking tour through the alleys of the town, complaining that "something must be done" to clean up the town.[83] Behind Arnaudon's, according to the article, were large unkempt pens containing horses, cows, chickens, ducks, dogs, cats, and pigeons. It is unusual to discover a description focusing on hotel livestock, and one can only imagine based on this particular narrative that locals must have been repulsed by the stench and squalor behind Arnaudon's.

Directly southeast of Firebaugh and Mendota, Huron was a very small outpost in the late nineteenth century, and it remains so today. In fact, one early correspondent quipped that the town had "four buildings, a visible population of five men, and one dog."[84] Joseph and Angela Mouren purchased the Central Hotel in Huron in 1890. Joseph had worked as a sheep buyer throughout the San Joaquin Valley since the 1870s. He met and married Angela in San Francisco in 1889.[85] In addition to the Central Hotel, Joseph and his wife bought a livery stable in town, operated a grocery store, and raised sheep.

The Central's last two operators, Pierre Oxoby and Alfred Quintana, closed down the business in 1919.[86] By that time the total population of Huron had dropped to below fifty, and the town could no longer support a hotel. The building, located at the corner of what are now Tenth and M Streets, later became headquarters for the Mouren Farming Company.

So three small towns east of Fresno had Basque-owned or operated hotels in the 1890s. Each had strong ties to the sheep business through their hotelkeepers. All of them had disappeared by 1930, as had the area's sheep outfits. As Douglass and Bilbao have suggested, hotel operations were often dependent upon the sheep industry, so the most effective hotel proprietors were often those with personal experience with sheepherding, as was the case with Idiart, Arnaudon, and Mouren.[87]

## Fresno

In comparison with Huron, Firebaugh, and Mendota, the town of Fresno was a thriving metropolis in 1890, with 10,890 residents. By the turn of the century the population had grown to 12,470.[88] Among California's five largest Basque communities, Fresno numbered fourth in 1900 and 1910.[89] As in Bakersfield, Basque males outnumbered Basque females in Fresno County by a ratio of nearly four to one, so demographically speaking Fresno was a relatively young Basque community as of the turn of the century. In addition, 86.2 percent of the Basque population in Fresno County was involved in sheep or cattle raising as of 1910.[90]

As the Fresno city directories suggest, the Hotel Bascongado at 1223 G Street was probably Fresno's first Basque *ostatu* and probably opened in 1897 or 1898.[91] Martin Iribarren built the hotel in the late 1890s, and when his friend John Bidegaray approached him proposing a partnership at the hotel, Iribarren was skeptical. According to one of Iribarren's daughters, "Papa didn't believe in partners. 'Either you buy or the other way,' he told Bidegaray."[92] Evidently, Iribarren convinced Bidegaray to purchase the Bascongado, and by 1902 Iribarren had built another hotel on the other side of town, across the street from where the new Santa Fe Depot had been built.[93] Iribarren's second hotel was officially named the Fresno Hotel, but old-timers in Fresno remember it as the "Sheepcamp" Hotel.

John Bidegaray, who had arrived in the United States in 1892 at the age of eighteen, first worked in Huron and Coalinga as a ranch hand and stockman. From these ventures he saved $800, which he used to buy Iribarren's small hotel and store located west of Fresno's Southern Pacific Railroad Depot.[94]

John Bidegaray managed the Bascongado for more than twenty years, subleasing it to others off and on. He took in other partners for his business, such as Martin Echeverria in 1902 and Gratian Indart in 1904, but each of these arrangements was short-lived.[95] In 1910, for example, he signed a two-year lease arrangement with John Echeverry and Angelo Iruleguy.[96] Between 1912 and 1918, Madame Chabriolet made her mark on the Bascongado's history, distinguishing herself with the tasty impromptu omelettes she prepared in the kitchen after regular hours.[97] Sodie Arbios, then a young non-Basque herder who was new to the area, claimed he could never forget Madame Chabriolet's kindness and compassion during his difficult bout with malaria.[98]

Photographs of the Bascongado and a Sanborn Fire Insurance Map of the neighborhood help us imagine what the hotel must have been like in its heyday.[99] In one photograph, the building is a two-story wooden-frame structure with a deep second-story balcony. The porch under the balcony must have provided an inviting shaded area below, where visitors could gather on hot summer afternoons. High above the balcony, J. BIDEGARAY & CO. HOTEL BASCONGADO was emblazoned in letters two to three feet tall. To the right, another sign reading GENERAL MERCHANDISE indicates that there was also a neighborhood grocery located within. The bar, general quarters, and kitchen seem to have been downstairs to the left, and entrance to the second story was gained via a wooden stairway on the exterior of the building.

Finally, in 1918, Bidegaray sold the Bascongado to George Bazterra from Abaurrea Alta, Navarre, who had come to Fresno in 1891 at the age of five with his father.[100] Although the Bazterra family returned to Navarre when George was nine, he came back to work for Miller and Lux driving wagon teams in Firebaugh. Eventually, he returned to Fresno, bought the Bascongado, sold it after four years, in 1922, and took a job with a neighborhood grocer on G Street.[101]

A third Basque hotel, the Hotel des Pyrenees, appeared at the corner of Kern and O Streets in Fresno in 1901.[102] Listed as the original proprietors for the hotel were Dominic Bordagaray and Frank Frechou.[103] Bordagaray reportedly worked at the Pyrenees for two years, and, upon saving $350, he sold his portion of the business to Frechou. He then moved to the Coalinga area, raised sheep, and homesteaded 140 acres.[104] Frechou is listed as the proprietor at the Hotel des Pyrenees, 2504 Kern, for each year thereafter until 1909, when his wife Eulalia is listed as the owner and operator of the business for the first time.[105]

Between 1910 and 1920 the boardinghouse was renamed "the Frechou House." It had fourteen rooms. Two downstairs rooms were occupied by the Frechous; there was a bathtub on the lower floor with a toilet outside. The Frechou property also included a small livery.[106] Sometime between 1915 and 1933, the old hotel was torn down, and the Frechous' sons, John and Michael, opened a gas station on the same lot.[107] Mrs. Frechou then moved to a private home on the northeast corner of the lot, and the two brothers ran the gas station.

Jose M. and Raymond Lugea, two American-born Basque brothers who had been Nevada sheep ranchers before coming to Fresno, opened the Hotel de Spanio in 1907.[108] The Lugeas managed the hotel and their local sheep interests for ten years, until 1917, when they sold the Spanio and returned to full-time sheep raising.

By 1924 the Spanio, the Frechou House, and the Bascongado had become part of Fresno's past. The following year, Baptiste Laxague opened the tiny Laxague House on F Street, which folded by 1926.[109] The closing of these four *ostatuak* in the mid-1920s marks a turning point in the history of Fresno's Basque hotels, because with the demise of the old hotels, the "newer" hotels—the Victoria, the Basque, and the Santa Fe Hotels—became increasingly popular among area Basques.

Tomas and Maria Ballaz married in Bakersfield in 1929, and that same year they bought a ten-room boardinghouse, at 1018 N Street in Fresno, which became their first home and their first place of business. Locals refer to the boardinghouse as the "old Vitoria," but the small *ostatu* never had an official name.[110] Business expanded, and within three years, the Ballazes were looking for a larger hotel.

With their move to their new thirty-room hotel at 2520 Tulare Street in 1932, Tomas and Maria tripled the capacity of their old house. At the "new" Victoria, all rooms were located on the second floor. The Ballaz family reserved three rooms for their private use and rented out the remainder. For the first time they hired a full-time bartender and cook. In the early days they charged fifty cents for lunch, and twenty-five cents each for dinner and breakfast. Eventually the Ballazes hired one woman to clean the upstairs rooms and another to wash dishes and work in the kitchen. As was the custom, hired help lived on the premises and received room and board in lieu of part of their wages. As their business expanded in the 1940s, the Ballazes hired additional help to relieve their small staff. Within fifteen years of purchasing the larger hotel building, Tomas and Maria had paid off the building in full.

Their days at the Victoria began with cooking breakfast for the children downstairs in the hotel's kitchen and getting them ready for school. Boarders willing to fix their own breakfasts could be found cooking at the large stoves between seven and ten in the morning. After ten, kitchen privileges were terminated, and serious preparation for the large noon meal began.

In the early 1950s, Tomas and Maria moved to a private home on Peach Street. Roughly ten years later, Tom Ballaz suffered a stroke and was confined to home. After Tomas's stroke, the Ballazes leased the Victoria to Javier and Rosana Sanchez and retired. The Victoria was later sold in 1964. After thirty-two years of good food, warm family events, and fine hospitality, the Victoria Hotel closed. The building was torn down a few years later.

Back in 1929, when the Ballazes opened their first *ostatu*, John Villanueva managed a boardinghouse across town at 1102 and 1106 F Street.[111] Villanueva's name dropped from public records shortly thereafter, and George Bazterra's widow Marie's name appeared as the manager of the *ostatu* for a few years. Then in 1935 Felix and Lyda Esain bought the building and renamed the establishment the Basque Hotel.[112] Before that time Felix Esain had worked with Javier Eleano and Ascension Curutchet at the Santa Fe Hotel.[113]

Felix and Lyda were married in 1932, and for the first three years of their marriage they worked at the Santa Fe and ranched outside of town. In 1935 they sold their ranch, purchased the boardinghouse they called the Basque Hotel, and moved back to town. In their sixteen-year tenure at the hotel, Felix and Lyda played an important role in the local Basque community, and they are fondly remembered throughout Fresno.

In many ways, Felix and Lyda were the ideal hotel-keeping couple. Felix had been born in Euskal Herria, and his command of Basque and Spanish exceeded his abilities in English by far. Lyda, on the other hand, had been born and raised in the San Joaquin Valley. Her father, Dominique Martinto, had come to California from the Basque Country to join his older brother Jean Pierre at the Basses-Pyrenees Hotel in Tehachapi.[114] Dominique worked in the Tehachapi lime kilns for a few years, married Marie Amestoy, started a family, and eventually moved to Fresno County. Thus the Old World Basque Felix and the New World Basque Lyda together had a broad array of experiences and were able to offer their clients and friends an ideal combination of skills and services.

If a boarder needed assistance with some aspect of surviving in the greater Fresno community, for instance, he would ask Lyda to advise him. Oftentimes, Lyda accompanied her boarders and served as their translator at the doctor's or lawyer's office and in local banks, where she helped herders open accounts. Felix tended to represent and maintain the Old World social and cultural aspects of the Basque community, which were also vital to Basque boarders. For example, he organized all the *mus* and handball competitions at the hotel. He also made a point of dropping in to visit other hotelkeepers in Fresno; he would buy drinks for their customers and encourage neighborliness on a regular basis. While in his own hotel, Felix discussed local ranching and the concerns of his customers, and he shared relevant information with his boarders and clients.

Felix, Lyda, and their son Victor lived in the small downstairs apartment at the Basque Hotel. The lower floor also included a kitchen, dining hall, bar, and small office.[115] Upstairs, the hotel had twenty-eight rooms for boarders, who, in the 1930s, paid $1 a day for room and board, including three meals and wine. At some point the downstairs was remodeled, the kitchen and dining hall were expanded, and a dance area was added. The Esains also constructed a partially covered handball court along the north side of the hotel, and it is still in use today. When the court was constructed, the Santa Fe was the only other hotel in town to have a *cancha*, and according to the Esains, their new handball court greatly improved business at their hotel. In 1951, after the Esains sold out to Jean and Marie Nouqueret, they opened the Villa Basque Restaurant on Blackstone Avenue in Fresno.[116]

In 1929, the same year that Maria and Tomas Ballaz opened the Victoria and Juan Villanueva managed the boardinghouse that would later become the Basque Hotel, the Santa Fe Hotel appeared for the first time in Fresno directories, although it had opened in 1926. In an account from Maria and Bicenta Ibarrola of Bakersfield, the sisters claim that they worked at the Santa Fe as maids in 1902.[117] Yet local Basques and the Santa Fe's present owners insist that the boardinghouse did not open until

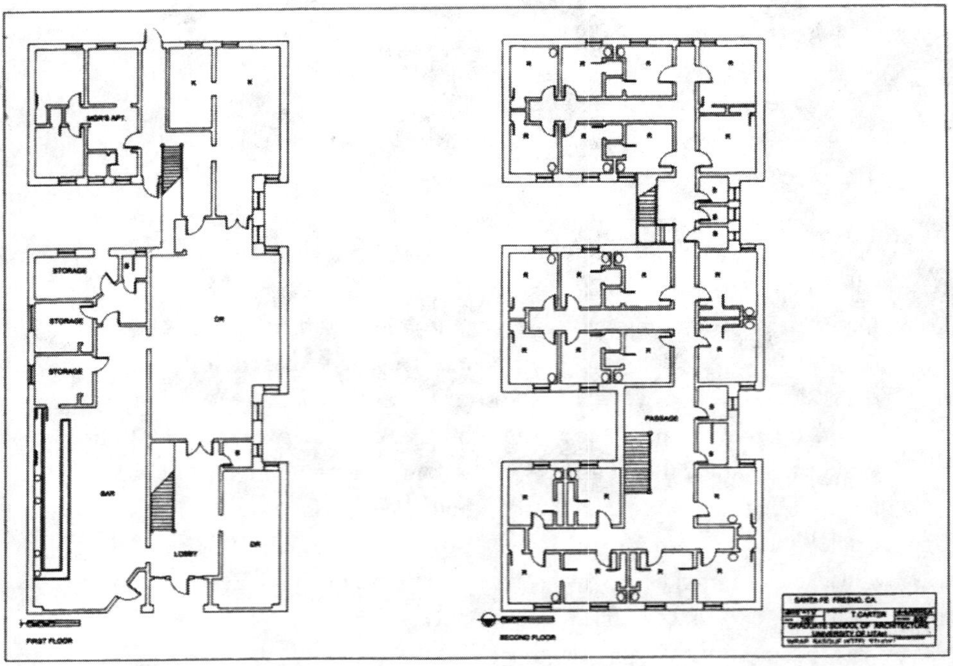

*First- and second-floor plans for the Santa Fe Hotel, Fresno, California. Courtesy of the University of Utah Basque Boarding House Project.*

1926. Perhaps the Ibarrolas got the Santa Fe confused with Iribarren's place: it stood across the street from the Santa Fe terminal; it occupied a lot next to what is now the modern Santa Fe Hotel; and the informal names of the establishment—the "Sheepcamp" and Iribarren's—were greatly preferred over the hotel's legal name, which was the Fresno Hotel.[118]

In any case, when the Santa Fe appeared in the 1929 directory, Javier Eleano was listed as the hotelkeeper. In 1932 John Baptiste and Asuncion Curutchet leased the business, but during their first year at the Santa Fe, J. B. died. Unable to afford either cooking or cleaning help, Asuncion continued to work as the hotel's only cook for the next four years, and she would clean the boarders' rooms between meals, early in the mornings, and whenever she had the chance. As Asuncion describes this period in her life, "I had four years of work with thirty minutes off per day."[119]

In 1936, when the Dolagarays assumed the lease at the Santa Fe and began managing the hotel, Asuncion went to work for J. P. Bidegaray at the Europa Cafe on G Street.[120] Martin and Marcelina Dolagaray operated the Santa Fe Hotel through the war years and were followed by the Toqueros and, eventually, by Segundo and Benita Garcia.[121] Today J. P. and Manuela Etchechurry successfully and enthusiastically own and operate the Santa Fe.

The Yturri Hotel once stood about a block east of the Santa Fe. Paul and Marcelina Yturri built the hotel in the early 1940s.[122] The Yturris had married in 1932 and farmed in neighboring Reedley for a time before they decided to take up hotel keeping in Fresno. After Paul's death in 1957, Marcelina leased the hotel to a series of managers, including Bernard and Marie Uhart, Pete Idiart, and Frank and Rosana Sanchez. The City of Fresno purchased the property and tore down the building in the early 1990s when Fresno underwent renovation downtown. Ironically, the Yturri had been both the youngest of the community's *ostatuak* and the youngest in North America.

Today Fermin and Margaret Urroz's Basque Hotel and the Santa Fe Hotel, the only remaining *ostatuak*, are crucial to the Fresno Basque community, as they have been for the past seventy years. Before the Fresno Basque Club purchased its own building, the group's meetings were regularly held at these two hotels, with the meeting sites alternating from one meeting to the next. Today the Basque and Santa Fe Hotels continue to take in boarders, although the hotels' rooms are no longer filled to capacity.

## Los Banos and Merced

About sixty miles north of Fresno, in the two small Merced County communities of Los Banos and Merced, three Basque hotels came into being between 1915 and 1930. The first opened in Los Banos, located at the eastern terminus of the Pacheco Pass, a route once traveled by ranchers heading to and from the Plaza Hotel in San Juan Bautista in the 1850s and 1860s. Anton and Josefa Lassart arrived in Merced County after the turn of the century and purchased property in what is now downtown Los Banos.[123] They opened the Lassart Hotel in 1914, but unfortunately after the hotel had been in business for only four years the two-story wooden structure was completely destroyed by a fire.[124]

The second Basque hotel in Los Banos, the Woolgrowers', has a more fortunate history. Joe Goñi finished building the Woolgrowers' on H Street near the train station by 1925, and the hotel has been in operation continuously since.[125] Local residents speak fondly of Sunday festivities at

Goñi's in the late 1920s and 1930s. The Barcelona family, for example, would leave their ranch in the Panoche just after sunrise in order to reach Los Banos in time for nine o'clock Mass. After church they would go to Goñi's to visit with friends and family, play cards, and eat Sunday dinner. In the late afternoon, a group might attend a movie or another social gathering before heading back to the Panoche. In any case, Sunday outings to the Woolgrowers' were part of a full day's excursion.

Since the 1930s, there have been a number of hotelkeepers at the Woolgrowers', including Valentin Pozueta, Andrea Larrainzar, and the Arretches.[126] Today the Woolgrowers' occupies the same building as Goñi's old hotel, but the business is limited to a restaurant and bar; the rooms once reserved for boarders are now under separate management. The current owner, Michel Iturbide, left Euskal Herria in 1962 and came to work for Joe Gestes at the Basque Hotel in San Francisco.[127] From there Iturbide moved to Stockton, where he cooked at John and Pete Ospital's Villa Basque before buying the Woolgrowers' in Los Banos. Like many Bakersfield Basque *hoteleros* who trained in the early Basque hotels of Los Angeles, Iturbide trained in San Francisco and Stockton before moving to Los Banos.[128]

On the east side of the county on Highway 99 in Merced, at the corner of I and Sixteenth Streets, a small Basque hotel, the Hotel des Pyrenees, appeared in 1929.[129] John Elgart built the hotel and operated the business for ten years until he sold it to Bartolo Goñi and his family in 1939.[130] The Goñis managed the small two-story hotel together with their daughter and son-in-law, Angie and Fortunato Anaut.[131] The family occupied the three small downstairs rooms at the back of the hotel, leaving thirteen private rooms upstairs for boarders and customers.

In the 1940s and 1950s, before the Highway 99 overpass was built and traffic was diverted away from downtown, the Hotel des Pyrenees was located on the main highway passing through Merced. According to the Anauts, their clientele was always a mixture of Basques and non-Basques. Because of its size and location, this small *ostatu* probably welcomed more "outsiders" than the larger and more selective Basque hotels of Fresno and Bakersfield did. Non-Basque truck drivers were welcome to stay at the Pyrenees, and during the five-month period in the 1940s when crews were expanding Castle Air Force Base in nearby Atwater, the Pyrenees was jammed with construction workers who came for dinner every evening. By 1955 the Anauts had built a home on Merced's Alexander Street, expanded the Pyrenees Bar, and closed the kitchen portion of the hotel. When the family sold their business in 1968, that was the end of Basque hotel keeping in Merced.

As we have seen, traveling north from Los Angeles along California's State Highway 99 during the earliest decades of the twentieth century, one might have encountered numerous Basque communities and their *ostatuak* in the San Joaquin Valley, ranging from Bakersfield at the southern extreme to Stockton in the north. Between these locales lie a number of towns with smaller Basque colonies, such as Tehachapi, McKittrick, Mendota, Firebaugh, White Bridge, Los Banos, and Merced, as well as Fresno with its more substantial collection of Basques.

## COASTAL TOWNS IN CENTRAL CALIFORNIA: SANTA BARBARA, VENTURA, AND GUADALUPE

Not all Basques leaving Los Angeles chose the inland towns of Kern, Tehachapi, Fresno, or McKittrick, however. A few selected the coastal communities of Ventura and Santa Barbara about eighty to ninety miles north of Los Angeles. For instance, Jose Borderre, a French Basque from Urepel, arrived in Los Angeles with an older brother in about 1880. Jose began herding in the Cucamonga area, and within a few years he had acquired more than eleven hundred head of sheep, which he pastured near Ventura, Santa Barbara, Santa Paula, and Simi Valley.[132] One account notes that Borderre occasionally drove his herd through downtown Santa Barbara, using the dusty road that eventually became State Street.[133]

In his travels through southern California, Jose often stopped in Los Angeles's Basque town. There he met Jennie Alfaro, also a native of Urepel, who was working as a maid at a Basque hotel on Aliso Street. In 1898 the two married and moved to Santa Barbara. The following year they purchased a hotel from the estate of Leander Sawyer[134] on the city's busy Plaza de la Guerra, a prime piece of property that extended to Anacapa Street.[135] At the north end of the plaza stood the old red-tiled De la Guerra Adobe, built in 1826. Borderre's French Hotel was three buildings away, on the east side of the Plaza. Ironically, by the turn of the century the old Spanish plaza featured three French-owned businesses, one of which was Borderre's French Basque hotel, the French Hotel.[136]

One photograph of Borderre's French Hotel from the period shows a crowd of Basques standing in front of a two-story wooden building, with a

*Joe Borderre's French Hotel in Santa Barbara with a horseless carriage parked in front, ca. 1915. Courtesy of the Santa Barbara Historical Society.*

broad sign atop reading BORDERRE FRENCH HOTEL.[137] The original French Hotel faced the Plaza, and within ten years the Borderres constructed a two-story home nearby that faced Anacapa Street. There was also a free-standing handball court between the hotel and the Borderre residence, and that a shed, workspace, and livery were also part of the complex.[138]

By 1910 the Borderres were taking in boarders in both two-story buildings—the hotel and their home. In fact, directories show that Jose Borderre lived at 721 Anacapa and rented furnished rooms there, and, under the Borderre Hotel listing Antonio Bastanchuri was renting rooms from the Borderres' hotel at the Plaza de la Guerra address.[139] It appears that the Borderres took Bastanchuri on as a partner when they expanded their business, and that he may have taken up residence at the Borderre earlier, as directories have Bastanchuri listed as a boarder at the Borderre as early as 1901.[140]

Jose and Jenny Borderre and their French Hotel were central to Basque social life in Santa Barbara and Ventura for the first two decades of this century. The Amorena family, for example, would leave Ventura early in the morning and travel a good distance to the Borderres' in order to make it in time for the Sunday midday meal.[141] Another Basque American noted that Borderre's was very popular with the non-Basque middle and working classes of Santa Barbara, especially during Prohibition, when Jenny Borderre "always held a bottle of wine in her ample white apron."[142]

In 1925 the Borderres sold their property to Tom Storke, founder of the Santa Barbara *News Press*, the offices of which still stand on the south end of De La Guerra Plaza.[143] But the Borderres continued to operate the French Hotel for the next six years until Jose passed away in 1931. Jenny retired, and the Storke family in turn rented the building to Pierre and Hortense Anchordoquy Heguy.

Before coming to the French Hotel, Hortense had run a small boardinghouse near the beach west of the Santa Barbara train station, and, as one observer noted, Basques could get "*traguitos bajo la ley*" at Anchorodoquy's.[144] Not long after the Heguys began operating the French Hotel, Pierre died, leaving Hortense to manage the hotel alone. During this period, she contracted with the City of Santa Barbara to feed the inmates and jailers at the city jail across the plaza. In 1932 Hortense married Francisco Ciaurritz, and the newlyweds moved to Los Angeles. Later, in 1936, they moved once again to Tehachapi, where they managed the Tehachapi Hotel. The Ciaurritzes' departure from Santa Barbara marked the final chapter for the Borderre French Hotel.

Although Borderre's was the major Basque hotel in Santa Barbara, early residents remember other, smaller Basque boardinghouses. Besides the Anchordoquys', there was a boardinghouse in the two-story home of Jose and Martina Layana Campos near Chapala and De la Guerra. The Campos rented out six rooms to Basque field workers and ranch hands between 1933 and 1937. During the summer months and during Santa Barbara's annual Fiesta week, the small house swelled with family and friends from around southern California.[145]

Two other boardinghouses were in operation during the years when the Borderre was open. Jose Egu and his wife rented rooms to two or three boarders at a time. The Egus were open for business for only two years, in 1917 and 1918.[146] The second such boardinghouse was the Hotel España on Haley between State and Anacapa Streets. Eduardo Linzuaín and his family owned and operated the small hotel in the late 1920s. It had a large dining hall that attracted many locals. The España closed its doors in 1932.

Northwest of Santa Barbara some eighty miles, however, another Basque hotel may have existed at one time in the small town of Guadalupe. Today a restaurant called the Basque House occupies part of a century-old hotel building there.[147] Basques might have frequented this spot at an earlier time; this theory is made even more plausible if one considers that Guadalupe lies on the western end of the highway that leads across California's coastal mountain range to the small town of McKittrick mentioned earlier. Basque herders, ranchers, and travelers in the 1920s and 1930s may have traveled between Guadalupe and McKittrick, using either extreme as a stopover.

## GREATER SOUTHERN CALIFORNIA

In addition to heading northeast to Bakersfield and Tehachapi and north to Santa Barbara and Ventura, a number of Basques who left Los Angeles went outside the metropolitan basin, heading south toward Orange County, and east toward Chino and La Puente. There is one mention of a Basque hotel even further south in San Diego in 1893—an advertisement for the Hotel d'Europe operated by a P. Etcheverry appeared in an edition of *California'ko Eskual Herria* in December 1893.[148] San Diego city directories spanning from 1887 through 1905 do not list the hotel or its operator.[149] Given the size and location of San Diego, one would imagine that the city might have had an *ostatu* or two, but only this one reference has come to light thus far.[150]

To the north of San Diego, in San Juan Capistrano, Oyharzabal's French Hotel was in operation until 1903. Other Basques followed Oyharzabal and Salaberri south from Los Angeles, but not all of them relocated in San Juan Capistrano. From 1910 through 1930, for example, the Bastanchury Ranch near Fullerton, California, employed numerous Basques and became a meeting place for Euskaldunak south of Los Angeles, among them Lentxo Echanis and his family (see the Prologue). In 1913 the Bastanchurys built a handball court near their main farmhouse, and Sunday gatherings under their grape arbors became popular events for Orange County Basques. When interviewed independently decades later, the Echanises, Ondaros, Oxandaboures, Yriartes, Arroues, and Oxararts all described Sunday gatherings at the Bastanchury Ranch.[151]

Sunday functions at local southern California ranches provided Basques the opportunity to get together, socialize, and keep cultural values alive.

Around the Orange County area between 1910 and 1920, there were thirteen Basque-owned citrus ranches of ten acres or more.[152] One American-born Basque remembers that nearly every Sunday the county's ranchers would alternate hosting Sunday gatherings.[153] In the 1930s the Chilibolosts in Chino and the Changalas in El Toro offered their ranches to host large gatherings. Both had big barns that were used for dancing, listening to music, playing cards, and visiting.

As the number of Basques in the La Puente, La Habra Heights, and Chino area mushroomed, so too did the demand for a local *ostatu*. Finally in the 1930s two Basque hotels opened in La Puente. The Puente Hotel in the Bidart Building, on the corner of Main and Second Streets, remained open until 1948, when a gas explosion demolished the entire structure.[154] Across the street, on another corner of the same intersection, stood the Old Roland Hotel, which was purchased by Jean Nogues in 1930. He renamed it the Valley Hotel, and a few years later he put up a thousand dollars to begin funding the construction of a handball court adjoining his property. Local Basques who contributed $25 or more to the construction of the court could become charter members of the La Puente Handball Club.[155] The neighborhood was also home to the French American Bakery, which employed many Basques. Ironically, the Valley Hotel was torn down in 1964, but the court still stands and is part of the parking lot for employees of the French American Bakery.[156]

About a thirty-minute drive southeast of La Puente is the town of Chino, California. There, nearly sixty years ago in 1940, Jean Baptiste and Grace Robidart built the Centro Vasco Hotel on Central Avenue.[157] The two added a handball court and went on to manage the business until 1947, when they sold to Valentin and Victoria Juarena. After ten months, the Juarenas sold to the current owners, Ben and Melanie Sallaberry.[158] The Sallaberrys operated the hotel themselves for a few years and then began leasing out the business to others. The hotel is still open today.

In the period between 1957 and 1963, when Henry Idiart leased the Centro Vasco, one advertisement described it as "the Centro Basque Hotel and Trailer Court," indicating that Basques could bring their trailers and stay on property adjoining the hotel. The Centro Vasco's accommodation of trailers underscores the more contemporary nature of this *ostatu*. Rather than facing the local train station, as did so many of the other hotels we have described, the Centro Vasco is located on a broad street with easy access to a southern California freeway. And in its years of operation the Centro Vasco has probably attracted more workers from the local meat packing house as well as gardeners and dairymen in the area than most other *ostatuak*, which have appealed primarily to herders, stockmen, and ranchers.[159]

The distinct nature of the Centro Vasco reflects in part its southern California setting and in part its comparatively recent construction. Still, despite its relatively modern characteristics, the Centro Vasco offers local Basques many of the same amenities that other *ostatuak* do. The old handball court, once the scene of many weekend tournaments, stands at the back of the property lot and is still used. The small garage that used to be located alongside the front wall of *la cancha* and served as a dance hall for decades is gone. Also gone are the grape arbors that once shaded picnic tables used for special functions and festivities. In their place is a building extension, added in 1970, that contains banquet rooms, an expanded kitchen, and a large room to accommodate indoor dances and banquets. Today Basques and non-Basques dine in a front dining room and order from a menu on a regular basis. A few interior rooms offer long tables with family-style dining reminiscent of earlier days.[160]

In 1970 Pierre and Monique Berterretche took over the management of the Centro Vasco, and they continue there today. The Berterretches own and operate the motel, hotel, restaurant, and bar.[161] In the early 1970s, Monique reported that their seven upstairs rooms held twenty-two boarders, but only a few Basques reside there currently.[162]

In addition to Chino's Centro Vasco, for a time there was another southern California outpost for Basques in San Juan Capistrano. In 1903, the Oyharzabal family retired the old French Hotel, but there were still a number of local Basque families residing in southern Orange County. Occasionally they would gather at the Changala Ranch in El Toro, but in the 1940s and 1950s they often preferred to meet at the cantina run by Nick (Nicomedes) and Carmen Arbonies in downtown San Juan Capistrano.[163] The cantina was in an old two-story building located within half a block of the Oyharzabals' French Hotel. The downstairs housed a bar, liquor store, and soda fountain, and in the upstairs there were a few rooms that were rented for a small fee to visiting friends and family. An outdoor handball court stood behind the premises. Whether this was the same court that the Oyharzabals had constructed decades earlier is unclear.

The *ostatuak* of Bakersfield, Santa Barbara, and southern California have the same roots—their origins can be traced to the Basque town of Los Angeles—just as the origins of San Jose, Stockton, Sacramento, and Marysville *ostatuak* (to be covered in chapter 9) can be traced to the earlier hotels of San Francisco. Those *ostatuak* of the smaller outlying towns were spin-offs of hotels of an earlier day, but beyond that they also differ in particular circumstances. To the north of Los Angeles, for example, Bakersfield's and Santa Barbara's Basque colonies had developed by the twentieth century and formed Basque towns of their own, one with a San Joaquin Valley agricultural base, the other with a coastal town flavor. To the east, La Puente's and Chino's hotels matured differently. First, large ranches took on part of the social role that the Los Angeles *ostatuak* would have filled. Then, forty and fifty years after their fellow hotels had developed in Santa Barbara and Bakersfield, La Puente and Chino produced three hotels that catered to an urban southern California lifestyle, in a time when comparatively few Basques were immigrating to the United States.

Farther north, however, in the central and northern San Joaquin Valley as well as the Sacramento Valley several colonies of Basques had been clustering. These valleys had provided ample territory for sheep raising, and, when the sheep industry declined, many Basques turned to ranching and farming in the area. Towns like Fresno, Merced, Marysville, Los Banos, and Stockton provided the setting for many *ostatuak* during this period (the northern California Basque communities of Marysville and Stockton are discussed in chapter 9). There were also emerging Basque settlements in other locations outside California, such as Winnemucca, Reno, and Carson City, Nevada; and Boise, Idaho. Those "golden years" in the Great Basin and beyond are the subject of chapter 7.

# 7

# The Golden Years in the Great Basin & Beyond

In the years between 1890 and 1930, Basque hotel keeping reached its zenith in the United States. Whereas in the mid- to late nineteenth century we saw the *ostatuak* get their first foothold in California, in the first decades of the twentieth century the distribution and numbers of new boardinghouses throughout the Western states expanded dramatically. In fact, every Basque colony in the American West and in New York City that was to have an *ostatu* already had at least one by 1930.[1]

A number of factors may have contributed to the exodus of Basques from the Golden State into the Great Basin around the turn of the century. As we have seen so far in our exploration of the Basque hotels of California, the growth pattern of *ostatuak* has been intimately linked to and dependent upon expansions and contractions in the sheep industry and was also accelerated by the completion of the transcontinental railway system.[2] Largely owing to the increase in California's population and the diminishing of its open range land, Basques began to spread east and trail their sheep into the Great Basin area. Another factor contributing to the Basque exodus from the Golden State in the 1860s and 1870s was the inland mining boom, drawing Basque men to northern Nevada and southern Idaho.[3] Basque sheepmen were also lured by the opportunities provided by the increased demand for food in mining camps, just as they had been during California's gold rush, and to take advantage of that demand, they eventually crisscrossed the Silver State as well. Between 1870 and 1890 over two million sheep were trailed from California through northern Nevada via three basic routes that had been established by early trail masters. The first route originated in the Red Bluff, California, area and proceeded east through Paradise Valley, Nevada, and along the Snake River toward Montana and Wyoming; the second began near Independence, California, followed the Owens River north through Esmeralda County, Nevada, then joined the first route along the Snake River and continued east; and the third started further south at Bakersfield, California, headed up the Owens Valley to Tonopah, Nevada, then through Ruby Valley, Nevada, en route to Wyoming, Montana, and Nebraska.[4]

## NEVADA

Although Nevada has occasionally been presented as the state through which Basque immigrants passed on their way to more alluring destinations, this perception is not completely accurate. In fact, an examination of Basque boardinghouses in Nevada's history demonstrates a broad and steady settlement pattern throughout the golden age of Basque hotel keeping, as well as the establishment of regional centers for Basques in Reno, Elko, and Winnemucca. In fact, according to historian Wilbur Shepperson, by 1910 Nevada had grown into the most significant Basque center along with southern Idaho and southeast Oregon.[5]

The three migratory routes and the herders who walked them left their mark on the Nevada landscape. The well-known Altube and Garat cattle-ranching families moved from California to establish their Spanish Ranch in Independence Valley, Elko County, in 1871 and remained in that area through 1907. French Basques Jean and Grace Garat, after nineteen years of ranching on California's San Joaquin Valley, moved their cattle to a new ranch outside Golconda, Nevada, in 1871. Among the others who put down roots in Nevada around the same time were Jose Bengoechea, who settled in the Elko area; and Jose Ugarriza, Mateo Badiola, Jose Erquiaga, and Juan Aldamiz, all of whom settled in the Winnemucca area.[6]

Thomas Dufurrena left Spain near the turn of the century, crossed the Atlantic as a stowaway, jumped ship upon arrival in Mexico, and, like many other Basques, made his way to Humboldt County, where he was hired on as a herder. Within a decade, Dufurrena's forty thousand sheep

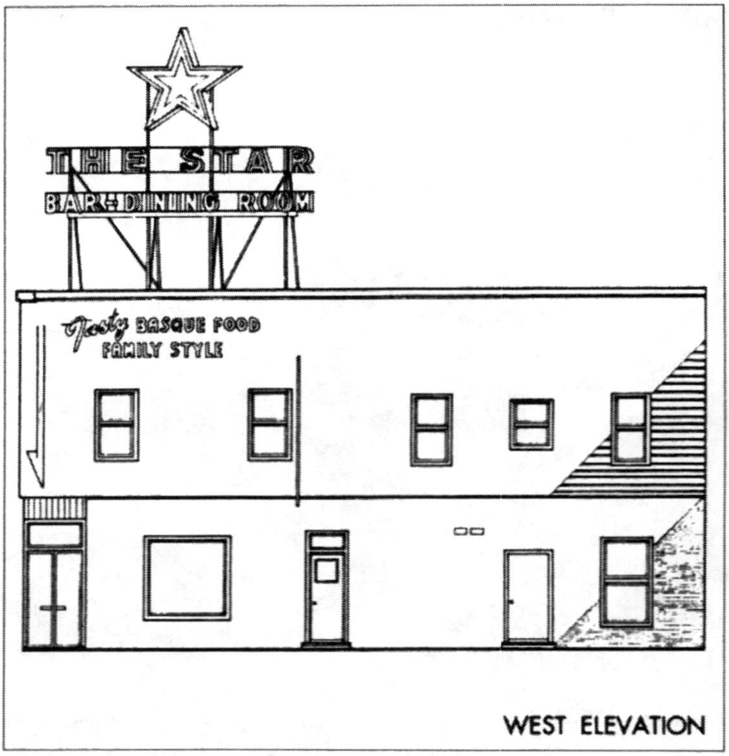


*The Star Hotel with sign, Elko, Nevada.*

roamed the open range under the guidance of other countrymen, friends, and relatives who had joined him.

Another similar tale involves Pete Itçaina, who arrived in northeastern Nevada in 1898. Although Pete began with literally no resources, by 1940 his sheep and livestock operations were valued at around a million dollars.[7] One oft-told story around Elko depicts Pete Itçaina as follows:

> So Pete Itçaina, who was a big Basque sheepman in those days, comes into this new saloon with his herders. They was all dusty and sweaty from shipping lambs. The bartender, who didn't like sheepherders, says he won't serve 'em, and he locks 'em out. So Pete Itçaina goes straight to his lawyer and says, "You know that new saloon down the street? I want to buy it." The lawyer does and tells Pete Itçaina the price is $30,000, which was a small fortune in those days, you know. Pete Itçaina says, "You tell him we be right over and make

> out a check, huh?" So they go over to the saloon and give the check to the owner, and the owner signs the deed over. Then Pete Itçaina goes out to the bar and says to the bartender, "A little while ago, you were the big boss man in this bar. You tell me to get out of here. Now it's me who is the big boss man, and I'm telling you to get out of my saloon." Well, now that's the most expensive drink that wasn't bought in Elko, but you got to remember Pete Itçaina didn't come to America to be treated like dirt.[8]

Not as expansive as the Dufurrena, Garat, or Itçaina operations, the Jack Creek Ranch in Independence Valley near Tuscarora also drew numerous Basques, such as Mateo Arregui, Francisco and Andres Ynchausti, Balbino Archabal, and Feliz Plaza, to name only a few.[9]

In addition to following the sheep trails into Nevada, newly arrived Basques also sought their fortunes in Nevada's mines. The Viscaíno Ledge Spanish Company in Unionville, for example, attracted an early *ostatu*. And Tomas Alcorta's discovery of red ore deposits in the hills above McDermitt led to the founding of Alcorta's Cordero Mine, the largest cinnabar mine in North America.[10] The Cordero attracted Basque miners, and it was largely responsible for the emergence of an *ostatu* in McDermitt. Once the Central Nevada and Eureka-Palisade railways began transporting Basques to mining operations in Austin and Eureka between 1862 and 1885, Basques eventually established *ostatuak* in those towns as well.

Because of the draw of sheepherding and mining, then, Basques gradually settled in the greater Winnemucca region, bordered on the west by Reno, Nevada; on the north by Jordan Valley, Oregon; and on the east by Elko, Nevada. As opposed to the Basques who had settled in California twenty or thirty years earlier, the majority of Basques arriving in Nevada between 1870 and 1910 were from Spanish Basque provinces. Their settlement in Nevada before 1900 had been quite gradual,[11] but between 1900 and 1910 the state's Basque population increased more than fivefold from 180 to 986. As in California, the flow of Basques into the state peaked in 1907, and by 1910 Nevada's Basque colony constituted slightly over 1 percent of the state's population.[12] Further, nearly 800 of the 986 Basques chose to set up house in Humboldt, Elko, Washoe, and Lander Counties.[13]

As one might expect, the emergence of Basque boardinghouses in Nevada followed closely on the heels of Basque migration and settlement. As of 1900, only 2 of the 136 Basques for whom Arrizabalaga could identify occupations were directly involved in hotel keeping. Just ten years later, 50 of the 986 Basques in her study were *hoteleros*.[14] Recollections recorded in the Holbert-Osa Oral History Collection and mentioned in Nancy Zubiri's *A Travel Guide to Basque America* reveal that *ostatuak* could be found in over a dozen sites in Nevada by 1910, including Reno, Winnemucca, Elko, Ely, Eureka, Gardnerville-Minden, Carson City, Paradise Valley, McDermitt, Golconda, Fallon, Austin, Battle Mountain, Jack Creek, and Unionville, but it is likely that a few others went unrecorded.[15]

Among these locations, Reno, Elko, Winnemucca, and Gardnerville-Minden were the four with the most concentrated Basque populations; Reno and Elko each developed a Basque town that sustained a concentration of hotels lasting over a decade or two. In fact, Reno maintained four *ostatuak* in the 1920s, and Elko maintained three. Although these two Nevada Basque towns were located in smaller and less urban settings as compared with the Basque communities of Los Angeles, San Francisco, Bakersfield, Boise, and Stockton, their significance for area Basques and their influence on the surrounding towns were the same.

As Marie Pierre Arrizabalaga has demonstrated in her study of Basque immigration, all Nevada Basque communities enjoyed consistent and steady growth after the turn of the century, but increases in the numbers of Basques were gradual rather than dramatic. In addition, Nevada towns that were home to *ostatuak* usually served as regional centers for non-Basque Nevadans as well. Of the sixteen Nevada towns where Basque boardinghouses appeared, for example, nine were county seats, such as Elko, Ely, Carson City, Austin, Minden, Winnemucca, Eureka, Fallon, and Reno. One would assume that these towns provided many other similar amenities for the growing non-Basque regional population as well. Nonetheless, by 1910 Basque herders had established a firm foothold in northern Nevada and began trailing their flocks northward into southern Idaho and east into Colorado. Throughout Nevada, in towns already mentioned and others like them, *ostatuak* flourished during the peak years of Basque hotel keeping and began disappearing in the late 1930s.

## Reno

Of all the Nevada cities and towns with boardinghouses mentioned thus far, Reno has had a particularly important function. Because Reno is located on one of the major transportation corridors that has been used by Basques moving east and west, Reno's Basque hotels have had an important role in facilitating travel to and from the Great Basin region.

In fact, Reno's origins are firmly established in its role as a transportation hub. In the mid-1860s early Nevadan Myron Lake convinced railroad man Charles Crocker that Lake's Crossing was the ideal location for the proposed junction of the Virginia-Truckee Railroad and the transcontinental line. Even before the town received its new name, Crocker had the land surveyed and divided into lots. Then in May 1868 the *Carson City Appeal* announced the auction of town lots. What Crocker and several others knew was that since Reno would serve as the main conduit for Virginia City's mineral wealth, Reno would get its start as a vital link to other destinations. What Crocker and Lake did not realize, however, was that Reno would outlast the Comstock Lode.[16]

The first Reno *ostatu* for which we have a written reference is the Commercial Hotel, operated by George Etchart in 1904 and then by Jean Etchebarren and J. P. Aldaz around 1911.[17] Also in 1900, a J. F. Davin and Z. Martin owned the French Hotel at 210 Center Street. This establishment was likely to have been Basque owned as well.[18] Given that Basques had been settling in and traveling through the Reno area for some time before the turn of the century, it is likely that the French and Commercial Hotels were preceded by other Basque boardinghouses that reach back beyond modern memory and remain unrecorded.

Correspondence from a descendant of a Winnemucca *hotelero* indicates that her grandfather roomed and boarded with other Basques in Reno around 1912 in an oddly named *ostatu*, the Butcher House, which was operated by Augustin and Elisa Martin around that time.[19] We also know that by 1906 Francisca Elia and her first husband had finished building the Español Hotel on the corner of Plaza and Evans Avenues in Reno. For a few years, Francesca sublet the business to Felix Turillas and A. Iriarte. Later that building also housed Francisca and her second husband, Eusebio Barcos, as well as their successful boardinghouse business. The building still stands near Reno's downtown rail yard today. Some have claimed that the Español and the Indart Hotel at 222 Lake Street were the most popular because they both had *pilota* courts in the 1920s and 1930s.[20] According to Reno's early residents, there were about eight or nine Basque boardinghouses during the interwar years in the area of Lake, Commercial, and Center Streets. Some of them were small establishments, where the owners of a first-floor business rented out a few rooms on the second floor.[21] In fact, the Alturas, the French, and the Toscano Hotels once stood in the space that Harrah's Casino occupies today.

Perhaps the best known of Reno's more recent *hoteleros* were Martin

Table 7.1 Reno *Ostatuak*, 1900–Present

| Date(s) | Operator | Location | Name |
|---|---|---|---|
| 1900 | J. F. Davin and E. Martin | 210 Carter Street | French Hotel |
| 1904–ca. 1948 | G. B. Etchart | 213 Center Street | Commercial Hotel |
| (1911) | Jean D. Etchebarren | | |
| (1920) | Justo Garcia | | |
| (1924) | John Etchebarren and Felix Turillas | 207–209 Center | |
| (1930) | Dominic Lartirigoyen | | |
| (1935) | Felix Turillas | | |
| (1940) | Lucas Ituarte | | |
| (1944) | Paul Toquero | | |
| 1906–ca. 1944 | Jose and Francisca Elias | 239–241 East Plaza | Español Hotel |
| (1920) | F. Turillas and A. Iriarte | | |
| (1925–1944) | Eusebio Barcos | | |
| 1906–ca. 1934 | Peter Indart | 222 Lake Street | Hotel Indart |
| 1911–1918 | Y. W. Inchausti | 37 West Plaza | Colonial Hotel Español |
| 1914 | — | — | Yriberri's |
| 1927–1936 | Martin Orriaga | 213 Lake | Alturas Hotel |
| 1927–1950 | Martin Orriaga and Joe Elcano Sr. | 238 Lake | Old Toscano Hotel |
| 1929 | E. Aniotz | 220 North Center | French Hotel |
| (1935) | Ancleto Goñi | | |
| 1929–1999 | Martin Orriaga and Josephine Inda | 235 Lake | Santa Fe Hotel |
| (1936–1941) | J. P. and Louise Etcheverry | | |
| | Dominic and Grace Lartey | | |
| | Martin Esain | | |
| | Aurelie Esnoz and Anita and Joe Zubillaga | | |
| 1932–ca. 1948 | Louis and Segunda Lataysa | 359 North Virginia | Altona Hotel |
| 1941–1948 | Martin and Josephine Orriaga | 32 East Commercial Row | Martin Hotel |
| 1960s | Louis and Lorraine Erreguible | 301 East Fourth Street | Louis' Basque Corner |

Data based on Reno and Sparks city directories, 1900–52; dashes indicate no available information.

and Josephine Orriaga, who simultaneously owned and/or operated four hotels between 1927 and 1950.[22] Their Alturas Hotel at 213 Lake Street was open from 1927 until 1936, when the couple sold out to Harrah's. In 1927 the Orriagas also bought the Toscano at 238 Lake with Joe Elcano Sr., who lived on the premises and managed the business until 1950. Both the Alturas and the Toscano were razed; the former was replaced by a parking lot, and the latter was overtaken by Harrah's new casino.

A third operation co-owned by the Orriagas was the Santa Fe Hotel at 235 Lake Street. Josephine Inda and John Etcheberry entered into partnership with the Orriagas at the Santa Fe from 1929 to 1936, followed by John and Louise Etcheberry from 1936 through 1941. Dominic and Grace Lartey periodically assisted the Orriagas in the operation of several of their hotels. In 1948 the Santa Fe burned down, and in the following year it was rebuilt at the same location by its new owner, Martin Esain.

The fourth and final Orriaga hotel property was the Martin Hotel located at 32 East Commercial Row, which Martin and Josephine ran themselves from 1941 through 1948. Ironically, the Orriagas' fourth *ostatu* was known for being their most traditional in that it rented rooms exclusively to Basques.

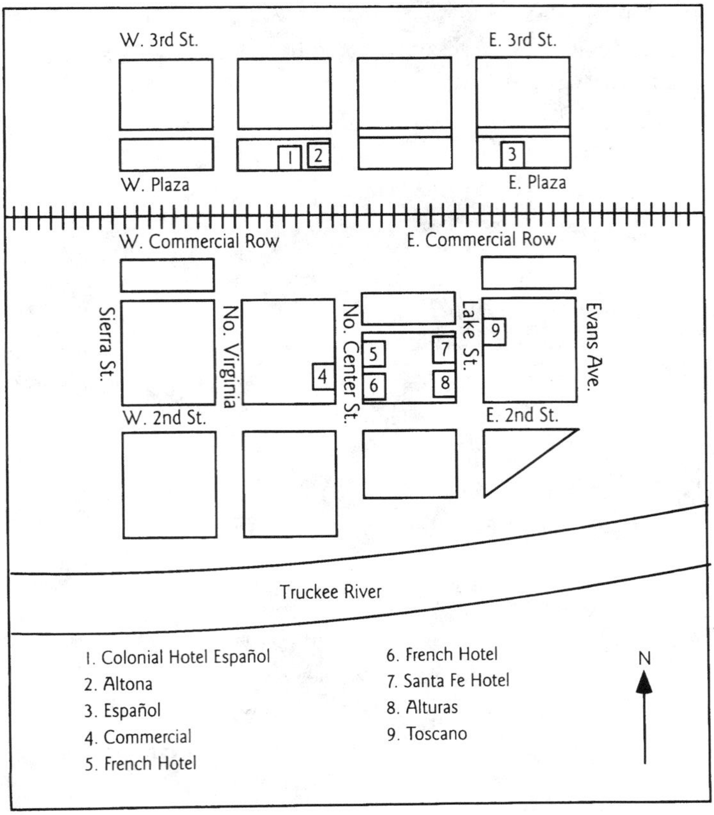


*Fig. 13. Reno's Basque town. Louis' Basque Corner is located north of this area on East Fourth Street.*

When Martin Esain passed away, he willed the Santa Fe to his niece and nephew. Aurelie Esnoz and Anita and Joe Zubillaga continued to run the Santa Fe, even refusing a generous offer from their wealthy neighbor, Harrah's Casino. The Zubillagas served Basque meals in their comparatively small brick hotel until they closed it in 1999.

For over thirty years now, Louis and Lorraine Erreguible have operated their hotel, restaurant, and bar at East Fourth Street, known simply as Louis' Basque Corner. Still a popular stop for local Basques as well as non-Basques, it is the only remaining Basque *ostatu* in Reno. Although the Erreguibles still operate the hotel upstairs, non-Basque guests have replaced their old patrons.

During the late nineteenth century and into the twentieth century, Reno's *hoteleros* benefited from the numerous Basques who have regarded Reno *ostatuak* as regional centers, vacation sites, honeymoon spots, and points of transfer. Although Reno's Basque town never reached the concentration of the Basque communities in Los Angeles, San Francisco, Boise, or Stockton, the *ostatuak* of the neighborhood of Lake and Commercial Streets in Reno flourished during the 1920s and 1930s. Further, the role Reno's Basque town has played in hosting Intermountain and Great Basin Basques has been significant.

## Winnemucca

It could be said that the greater Winnemucca region provided a staging platform for a second wave of Basque migration within the Western United States. As William Douglass and Jon Bilbao have noted in *Amerikanuak*, two Bizkaians named Antonio Ascuenaga and Jose Navarro left Winnemucca in 1889 and headed northward. After a difficult desert crossing, they reached Jordan Valley, Oregon, where they established sheep outfits, eventually extending their operations into southeastern Idaho. Two years later, Jose Uberuaga and two of his Basque shepherds left to relocate his sheep outfit to the Treasure Valley of Idaho.[23]

By 1900 many of the Bizkaian sheepmen in the Jordan Valley area had extended their sheep operations into the Boise Valley. Thus Basques from the greater Winnemucca region eventually moved north to settle the Boise area and even moved into more remote areas of eastern Oregon and Washington State. Further, by 1910 Boise had become a springboard for sheep outfitters operating throughout southern Idaho as far east as Pocatello.[24]

*Two of western Nevada's best-known hotelkeepers, Louis Erreguible of Louis' Basque Corner and J.T. Lekumberry of J and T's, ca. 1980. Courtesy of the High Desert Museum, Bend, Oregon.*

*The Martin Hotel as seen from the Winnemucca train station across the street. Courtesy of the University of Utah Basque Boarding House Project.*

Table 7.2 A Chronological Listing of Nevada's *Ostatuak*

| Location | Hotel Name |
|---|---|
| Reno | French Hotel |
| | Commercial Hotel |
| | Butcher House |
| | Español Hotel |
| | Hotel Indart |
| | Colonial Hotel Español |
| | Yriberri's |
| | Alturas Hotel |
| | Old Toscano Hotel |
| | French Hotel |
| | Santa Fe Hotel |
| | Altona Hotel |
| | Martin Hotel |
| | Louis' Basque Corner |
| Winnemucca | Larre's Boarding House |
| | Winnemucca Hotel |
| | Busch Hotel |
| | Martin Hotel |
| Paradise Valley | Bridge Street Hotel |
| | Gastenaga's |
| | Paradise Valley Hotel |
| Elko | Jauregui's Telescope Hotel |
| | Sabala's Overland Hotel |
| | Star Hotel |
| | Amistad Hotel |
| | Uriarte's Elko Boarding House |
| | Garretch's Railroad Depot Hotel |
| | Nevada Hotel |
| | Arrascada's Elk Hotel |
| | West Hotel |
| | Errecart's Clifton Hotel |
| Gardnerville-Minden | Overland Hotel |
| | East Fork Hotel |
| | French Hotel |

In Winnemucca, perhaps the best known *ostatuak* are the Winnemucca and the Martin. The Winnemucca, at 95 Bridge Street, stands alongside a major highway that runs through town.[25] The adobe portion of the hotel building dates back to 1863. In 1866 and 1867 owners Frank Baud and Louis Lay enlarged the hotel and added a large wooden bar. Five years later, a new owner added a two-story wooden structure to the bar and two brick floors to the hotel. Over the past 125 years, the edifice has survived fire, flood, and earthquakes and has undergone several structural revisions.[26]

In 1919, when Martin Arbonies and John Esparza first leased the Win-

Table 7.2 *Continued*

| Location | Hotel Name |
| --- | --- |
| | Pyrenees Hotel |
| | J & T Hotel |
| Carson City | French Hotel |
| Ely | Mariluch-Cordana's Spokane Hotel |
| | Irigaray's Ely Hotel |
| | Cordana's Ely and Plaza Hotels |
| | Orueta's Commercial Hotel |
| | Beltran Paris's Scott Rooms |
| | Joe Gamboa's Scott Rooms |
| Currie Ranch | Mariluch's Currie Ranch Hotel, outside of Ely |
| Eureka | Inda's Spanish Hotel |
| | Laborde's Eureka Hotel |
| | Landa's Hotel |
| | Sallaberry-Labarry's Colonnade Hotel |
| Austin | Aldape's Silver State Bar and Hotel |
| Gold Creek | Arrascada's |
| Battle Mountain | Arrieta's |
| | Commercial |
| | Mendive |
| | Silver State Hotel |
| Fallon | Morning Star Hotel |
| | Grand Hotel |
| Golconda | Arrascada's |
| | Star Hotel |
| Jack Creek | Jack Creek Hotel |
| Lovelock | Lovelock Hotel |
| McDermitt | Alcorta's McDermitt Hotel |
| Unionville | Unionville or Evans Exchange Hotel |
| Wellington | Goñi's Hotel |

*Source:* This table is a compilation of the Holbert-Osa Oral History Collection, Basque Studies Collection, Getchell Library, University of Nevada, Reno; additional interviewing; material published in Jai Aldi 1990 Commission, *Jai Aldi '90 International Basque Cultural Festival Program Booklet* (Boise: Idaho Centennial, 1990); and Nancy Zubiri's, *A Travel Guide to Basque America.*

nemucca, it became an *ostatu*. Esparza was able to buy the building five years later, and in 1929 he passed it on to his brothers Daniel and Epifano, who took in a third partner, Frank Escabel. From 1946 through 1965, the Winnemucca was owned and operated by Angel and Eugenia Mendiola, who then sold to Miguel and Margaret Olano and Claudio and Jesusa Yzaguirre. Finally, the Olanos bought out their partners in 1971, and today they run the business with their son Michael.

In the summer of 1913 a young French couple named Augustin and Elisa Martin bought a smaller hotel located across town by the railroad station; it was known as the Martin. Henri and Elisa had fled San Fran-

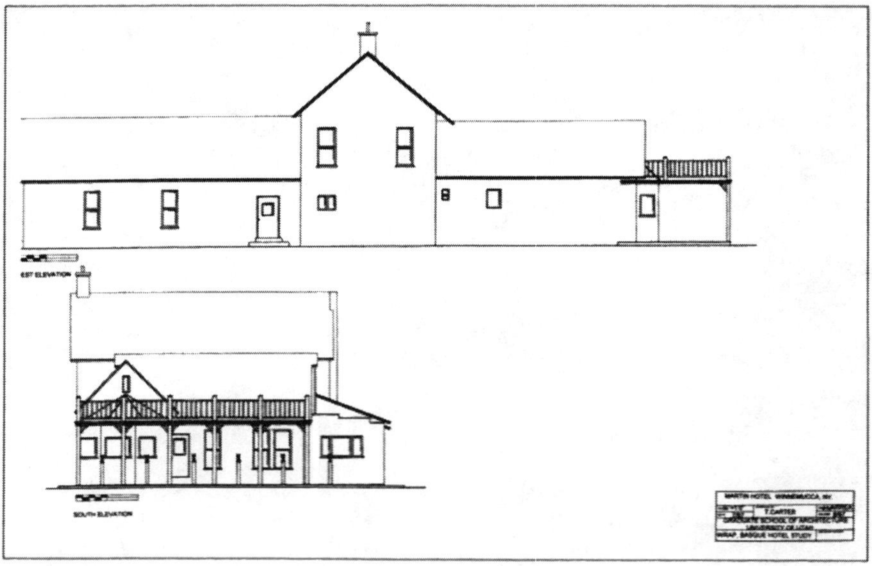


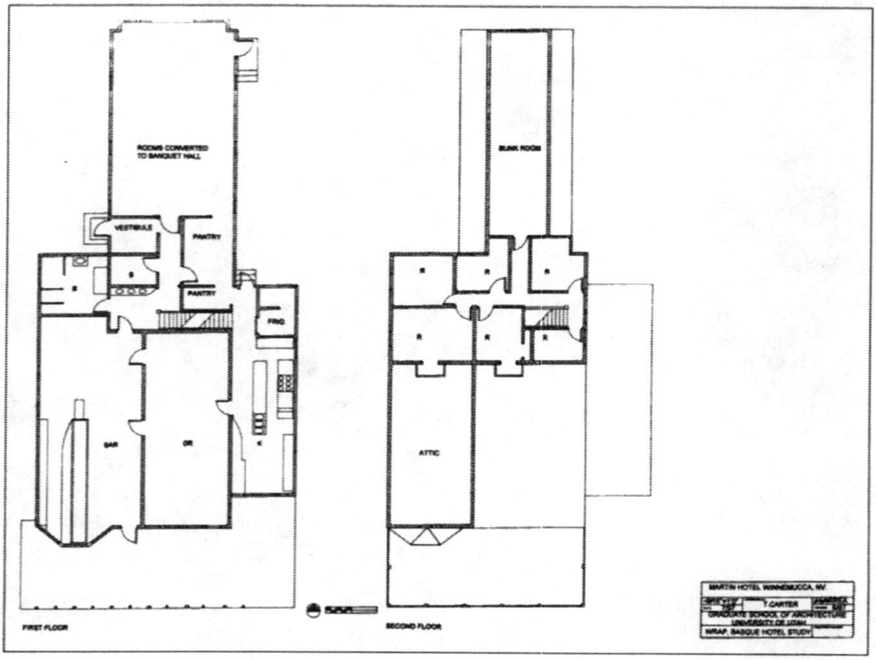


*The Martin Hotel. The exterior from the southern and eastern perspectives, and the first and second floors. Courtesy of the University of Utah Basque Boarding House Project.*

*Tomasa Alcorta standing in front of the Martin Hotel in Winnemucca in 1937. Courtesy of the High Desert Museum, Bend, Oregon.*

cisco after losing their possessions in the 1906 quake and fire. Before relocating to Winnemucca, the two had operated a small boardinghouse in Reno known as the Butcher House. Although the Martins were not Basques, they certainly attracted a large Basque clientele. Their business in Winnemucca prospered, but around 1920 Augustin contracted a debilitating case of Bright's disease, and the couple decided to return to San Francisco. Nonetheless, the Martins' successors decided to keep the name of the hotel's former owners, and from 1925 until the 1970s it was owned and operated by Basques.[27]

## Paradise Valley

Between 1875 and 1920, Basques responded to the promise of rich mineral deposits in Humboldt County, Nevada. Landowner and developer

*Bridge House, Paradise Valley, Nevada, as it appears today. Courtesy of the University of Utah Basque Boarding House Project.*

Alphonso Pasquale leased his building, Kemler Hall, in Paradise Valley, to a series of Basque hotel-keeping families who settled in the area beginning in the mid-1890s. Hotelkeepers such as the Mendiolas and the Arriolas changed the name of the establishment to the Humboldt House and later to the Paradise Valley Hotel.[28] After leasing the Valley Hotel for a time, Jose Gastenaga purchased the home of fellow-Basque Antoni Letemendi.[29] The modest wooden-frame structure stood on the corner of Main and First North Streets, and, after the Gastenagas moved in, theirs became the longest running *ostatu* in Paradise Valley, in operation from 1910 until the early 1940s.

Alphonso Pasquale refurbished his former Bridge Street residence, adding a large room on the back of the structure, which eventually would be used as a bar and a cellar for storage. Pasquale later leased the building out to Basque hotelkeepers. The Bridge Street residence stands on the western bank of Cottonwood Creek in Paradise Valley. One can still see where a second and smaller building was dragged down the creek side and attached to the original building. By the 1920s, when Basques from the greater Winnemucca region visited Paradise Valley, they enjoyed catching up with the Uriguens, Echevarrias, Rubianes, Ugaldeas, Gastenagas, and several other Basque families who had settled there.

## Elko

A number of boardinghouses emerged due east of Reno and Winnemucca in the town of Elko.[30] As author Robert Laxalt claimed, "Everyone must have his favorite small town, and Elko in northeastern Nevada is mine. In the near distance loom the turrets and minarets of the Ruby Mountains, green in summer, snow-buried in winter, and splashed in autumn with entire hillsides of gold aspen."[31] Elko's existence, like that of so many Nevada towns, was cemented with the arrival of the Central Pacific Railroad in 1868. From that time forward, Elko has served as a freighting and supply center for the region.

Between 1868 and 1870 Elko changed from a rough, tent-lined frontier town to a thriving center of four thousand to five thousand, with twenty-two merchandise stores, two hotels, three hardware stores, four drug stores, four wagon shops, eight stables, sixteen physicians and attorneys, and ten blacksmith shops.[32] This dramatic growth was not sustained, however. In part owing to a devastating fire in October of 1871 and in part owing to the booming northern mining camps of Edgemont, Aura, Midas, Jarbridge, and Gold Creek, Elko's population dropped to eight hundred in 1900.

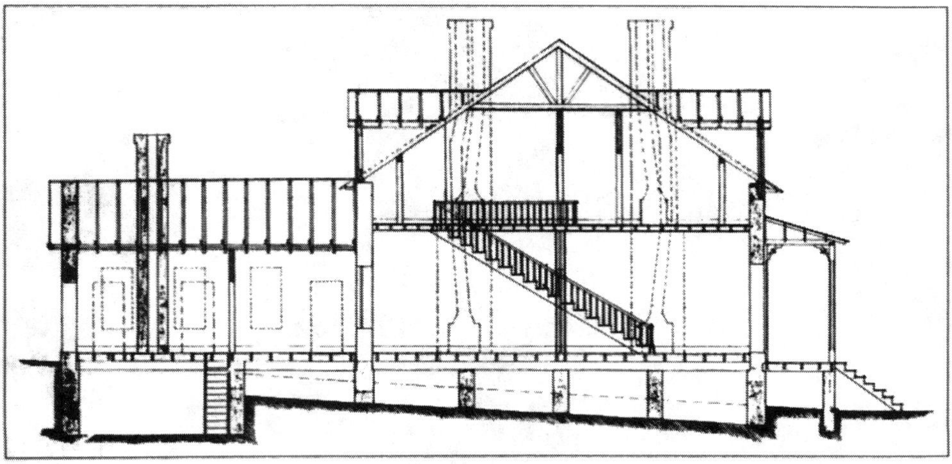

*Bridge House, Paradise Valley, Nevada. Exterior, section drawing. Courtesy of the University of Utah Basque Boarding House Project.*

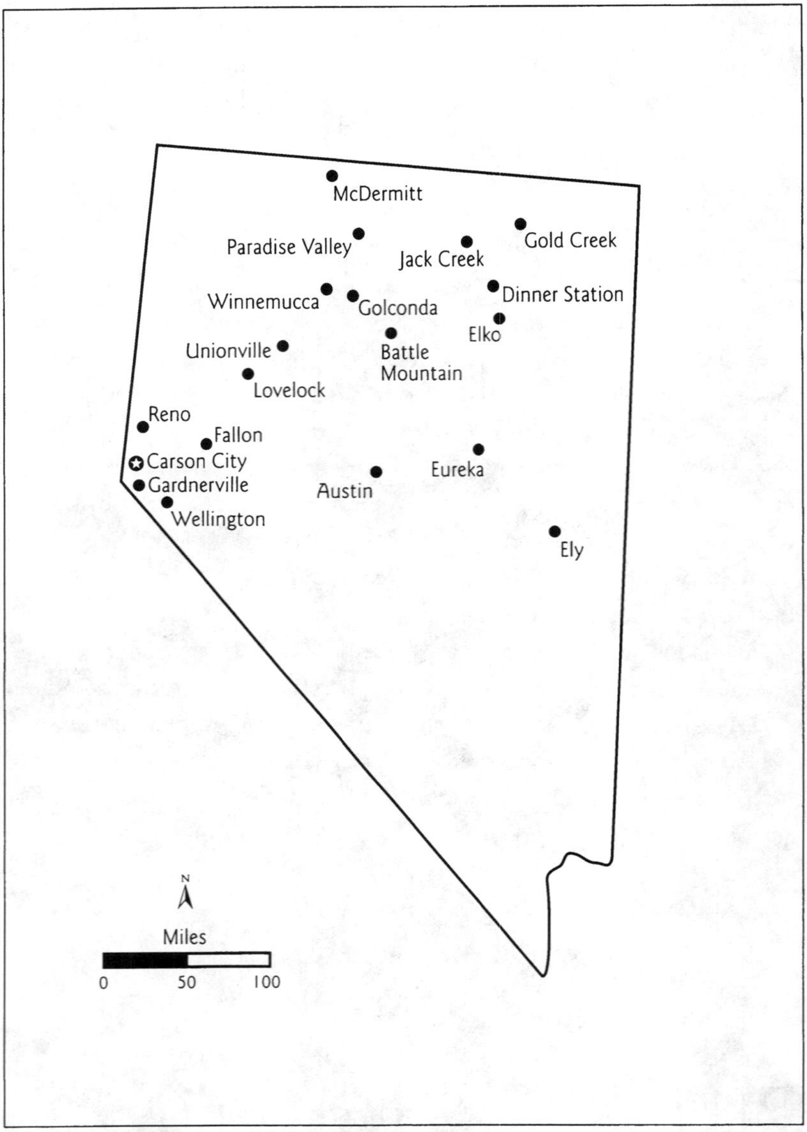


*Fig. 14. Communities with* ostatuak *in Nevada.*

Although very few Basques seem to have taken up residence in Elko between 1868 and 1900, we have evidence of several Basque families moving into the surrounding area, such as the Altubes and Garats mentioned earlier. One of Elko's earliest Basque *ostatuak* was built and managed by Gregorio and Domingo Sabala.

Domingo and Gregoria Sabala met in Elko in 1907, and soon thereafter they decided to marry.[33] After a short-lived cattle and sheep venture, the Sabalas returned to downtown Elko in 1908 to build the Overland Hotel on Fourth Street. The first floor of the three-story brick structure included a cigar counter, a bar, a lobby, a dining room, a kitchen, and, at one time, an indoor handball court. The second and third floors held twenty-four rooms to be rented out, the Sabalas' family quarters, and rooms for serving girls and hired help. The Sabalas operated the hotel successfully for twenty-five years, but then the Great Depression hit hard, and business at the Overland took a decided turn for the worse. The Sabalas struggled to keep their business afloat during the lean years, but ultimately they were forced to sell in 1938. Since that time, the Overland Hotel has been annexed by the Commercial Hotel and is now part of Elko's Anacabe Building. Sadly the sale of the Overland marked the end of the building's years as a Basque *ostatu*.

Another pair of legendary Elko *hoteleros* were Pete and Mathilde Jauregui, who defied the model for Basque hotelkeepers in that they spent nearly fifty years in the hotel business. Based on the existing evidence, the Telescope Hotel, which Pete Jauregui and Guy Saval opened in 1907 at 346 Silver Street, was the first Basque hotel in Elko.[34] The Telescope opened with an indoor handball court, which was converted to a large dance hall in 1911 when an outdoor court was built. After managing the place for three years, Jauregui and Saval sold their business to Francisco and Julianna Goicoechea, Martin Inda, and Pedro Orbe. Before that sale occurred, however, a young Basque woman named Matilde entered the picture. Bound for Elko from her hometown of Berriatua, Bizkaia, the newcomer missed her train in Salt Lake City and was delayed.[35] Overland Hotel partners Domingo Sabala and Eulalia Onandia had been expecting Mathilde to work for them, but when she failed to arrive when she was expected, they hired another Basque girl in her stead. According to one account, "the thoughtful bartender at the Telescope Hotel had heard a young woman was coming and sent two men to meet her. That bartender, Pete Jauregui, became her husband four months later."[36]

A few months after marrying Mathilde and after dissolving his partnership with Saval at the Telescope, Jauregui built the Star Hotel at 246 Silver Street with investment partner Emilio Dotta. The Jaureguis operated the Star from 1910 through 1929, when they sold it to Joe Corta, who in turn sold the business to G. F. Arrascada and Albert Garamendi. The Jaureguis then disappear from the public record for two years, 1929 and

*An early photograph of the Elko's Star Hotel and its proprietors, ca. 1920. Courtesy of the Basque Studies Program, Getchell Library, University of Nevada, Reno.*

1930, but they reappear when they began their one-year sheep partnership with Domingo Calzacorta in the Battle Mountain area. According to one account, Pete's "only pleasure out of the venture was the time he spent as camp cook during lambing season."[37]

In 1932 the Jaureguis returned to Elko to manage the Star for three years. In the following seven years they operated Stockman's, spent one year back at the Star, and then seven more years at Stockman's. After forty-three years of hotel keeping in five distinct Elko establishments, Pete and Mathilde "retired"; that is, if what they did next could be considered retiring: from 1954 through 1960 they managed the non-Basque Townhouse nightclub, the El Dorado Hotel, the Traveler's Motel, the El Neva Motel, and the Marquis Motel. They were the only Basque *hoteleros* who "turned to American hotel keeping" during their retirement years.

The Jaureguis were also unique in that they sold the same hotel twice, and twice they owned the Nevada *ostatu* with the longest history of continuous Basque proprietorship.[38] As the first owners of the Star Hotel, in operation since 1910, the Jaureguis seem to have set a record in terms of

*The Star Hotel, Elko, Nevada. The north elevation and the first and second floors. Courtesy of the University of Utah Basque Boarding House Project.*

operating several different hotels. When they sold the Star a second time it was to Fred and Bibaina Bengoa in 1944. Nine years later the Bengoas sold to Domingo Ozamis, who then sold the hotel to Jose Juaristi and Luis Alfonso Esnoz in 1959. Sometime between 1959 and 1964, Esnoz sold his share to Bernard Yanci, who with Juaristi sold to Joe Sarasua and Juan Aldazabal in 1964. Miguel and Teresa Leonis and Severiano Lazcano purchased the business in 1979 and continue to this day as the proprietors.

Although the Star is Elko's oldest Basque boardinghouse, the Telescope Hotel, which closed to boarders around 1970, is the town's oldest Basque-owned business. Henry Samper bought the Telescope in 1936. In 1950 he had the old handball court removed and replaced it with a small eight-lane bowling alley. Members of the Samper family continue to operate the Telescope today. And the Clifton Hotel, a small nine-room hotel at 516 Commercial Street that has been owned and operated by Jack and Barbara Errecart since 1960, is located in one of the town's oldest buildings. In fact, the owners claim that the Clifton once stood in the heart of Elko's Chinese district. The Errecarts have reported that during one rainy winter, their pickup truck sank right into the ground, and in the process of unearthing it they discovered a stash of opium bottles in underground tunnels![39] Across the street from the Clifton, Anastasio and Jeanne Viscarret built their Nevada Hotel in 1927. Twenty years later the Viscarrets sold to the Aguirre family, who moved the popular *ostatu* next door to the Telescope. In the late 1960s the Nevada closed its doors to boarders but retained the Aguirres' Nevada Dinner House on its first floor.

A visitor driving through downtown Elko today will observe some remnants of Elko's Basque town of the 1920s and 1930s. The façades of the Clifton, Telescope, and Star Hotels can still be appreciated. Elko's old-timers discuss small lesser-known boardinghouses, such as Uriarte's Garretech's, Arrascada's, and "the West" when they remember those peak decades today. The Star, Elko's solitary remaining *ostatu*, is still serving family-style meals to its handful of boarders, and in its dining room photographs of all of her *hoteleros* commemorate days gone by. Nearby the Clifton retains a few Basque residents, but the Errecarts no longer serve meals, and the Telescope has restricted its business to the bar and restaurant. In the 1970s the Sabalas' Overland was torn down and replaced by a parking lot. The Amistad, owned by Basque Joe Marisquerena in the 1920s and 1930s, was sold to non-Basques who converted it to a bar. The Aguirres' Nevada closed in 1987. In addition to these hotels and boardinghouses there were several Basque-owned bars and clubs in Elko's

Table 7.3 Elko's *Ostatuak*

| Date | Operator | Location | Hotel Name |
|---|---|---|---|
| 1907–ca. 1970 | Pete Jauregui and Guy Saval | 346 Silver | Jauregui's Telescope Hotel |
| | Francisco and Julianna Goicoechea | | |
| | Martin Inda and Pedro Orbe | | |
| | Henry Semper | | |
| 1908–1938 | Domingo and Gregoria Sabala | Fourth Street | Sabala's Overland Hotel |
| 1910– | Pete and Mathilde Jauregui | | Star Hotel |
| | Joe Corta | | |
| | G. F. Arrascalda and A. Garamendi | | |
| | Fred and Bibaina Bengoa | | |
| | Domingo Ozamis | | |
| | Jose Juaristí and Luis Alonso Esnoz | | |
| | Bernard Yanci | | |
| | Joe Sarasua and Juan Aldazabal | | |
| | Miguel and Teresa Leonis and Severiano Lazacano | | |
| 1920s/1930s | Joe Marisquirena | — | Amistad |
| 1927–ca. 1970 | Anastasia and Jeanne Viscarret | 516 Commercial | Nevada Hotel and Dinner House |
| | Johnnie Aguirre | 351 Silver | |
| 1960s– | Jack and Barbara Errecart | — | Errecart's Clifton Hotel |

*Source:* This table is a compilation of the Holbert-Osa Oral History Collection, Basque Studies Collection, Getchell Library, University of Nevada, Reno; additional interviewing; material published in Jai Aldi 1990 Commission, *Jai Aldi '90 International Basque Cultural Festival Program Booklet* (Boise: Idaho Centennial, 1990); and Nancy Zubiri's *A Travel Guide to Basque America*.
*Note:* El Dorado (1947–1950), El Neva (1960–1961), and the Travelers' Motels (1960s) discussed in the narrative are not Basque *ostatuak*. These motels were operated by former *hoteleros* Pete and Mathilde Jauregui and became popular stopping points for out-of-town Basques in the 1950s and 1960s. Dashes indicate that no information was available for this entry.

Basque district. The Lenizes' Blue Jay Bar on Third, the Biltoki at Fourth and Silver, Shorty's on Railroad Street, and the Silver Dollar Bar on Commercial Street were among them.

## Gardnerville–Minden

As with Reno, Winnemucca, and Elko, Gardnerville–Minden's location made it an attractive stopover for Nevada and California Basques. For many decades, Gardnerville–Minden, situated at the foot of the Sierra

*J. T. Lekumberry tending bar at the J and T Bar, Hotel, and Dining Room in Gardnerville, Nevada, in the early 1960s. Courtesy of the High Desert Museum, Bend, Oregon.*

Nevadas in the Carson Valley, has put up sheepmen moving their herds in and out of mountain ranges, as well as Basques traveling north and south along Highway 395.

Today the only remaining Gardnerville *ostatu* is the Overland Hotel, which was built by non-Basques in 1906. John Etchemendy bought into the hotel in 1921 and operated it until 1967, when Eusebio Cenoz bought the business. Cenoz managed the boardinghouse by himself until he married Elvira in 1980. Elvira has been running the Overland single-handedly since Eusebio's death in 1989.[40]

A touching description of the Overland's *hoteleros* was offered by Gretchen Holbert in a recent paper. In Holbert's words,

> At dusk Eusebio switches on the 50s-style, electric image of a giant martini glass on Main Street and Elvira, his Guipuzcoan wife, stirs the huge cauldron of soup expectantly. Sometimes he forgets the neon sign and she chides him, but it doesn't matter. The Overland does not advertise; the regulars know the way and one assumes that the hungry straggler will find the front door.[41]

Across Main Street and a block over from the Overland stands the J & T Bar and Restaurant. Although the building's origins are unknown, it is estimated to be 100 to 130 years old. In 1960 Jean Lekumberry bought the building and opened it as a Basque boardinghouse. After thirty-three years of business, in 1993, the elder Lekumberry died, leaving J & T's to his three children. Today the colorful establishment is decorated with cowboy hats, memorabilia, and photographs. The restaurant's menu continues to draw numerous customers, but the Lekumberrys no longer take in boarders.

Gardnerville was home to other *ostatuak* between 1930 and 1970 and likely enjoyed its heyday of Basque hotel keeping during the 1930s and 1940s. The East Fork Hotel was operated by Ramon and "Mama" Borda in the 1930s. Next door the Bordas' cousin, Baptiste Borda, ran the French Hotel until he leased it to Joe and Jeanne Micheo, who operated the hotel from 1937 to 1947. In 1947 the Micheos bought their own place across the street and called it the Pyrenees. They finally sold that business in 1972.

### Carson City

North of Gardnerville, in Carson City, Teresa and Dominique Laxalt operated the French Hotel during the first two decades or so of this century.[42] There Teresa raised her children and tended to her boarders while her husband, Dominique, helped out when he was not working in the sheep camps or tending his sheep outfits. Their son Robert Laxalt, an author, has provided a rich literary description of growing up in a boardinghouse in his recent book, *The Basque Hotel*.[43]

### Ely

In eastern Nevada the town of Ely was once one of the state's largest towns. The opening of the Kennecott Copper Mines in the region in 1902 initiated a large and steady population growth up until the early 1940s. During those forty-some-odd years Basque miners were drawn to the downtown Ely Hotel, which Sebastian Irigaray operated in the early 1920s. North of Ely, in southern Elko County, Gregoria and Pete Mariluch opened and operated the Currie Hotel near Currie Ranch. Years later, Gregoria and her family moved to town and started the Spokane Hotel, eventually buying the next-door Plaza Hotel to accommodate additional boarders. Years after her husband Pete passed away, Gregoria remarried and took over the Ely Hotel in the late 1920s (Cordana's Spokane Hotel, after Gregoria's maiden name). Eventually the Goyhenetche family purchased the business, and today Marianna Goyhenetche is most frequently associated with the now defunct hotel.

Beltran and Marie Paris bought a small rooming house in Ely known as the Scott Rooms. Marie operated the business during the depression years and then sold to Joe Gamboa at the end of that decade. Jean and Eva Orueta ran Ely's Commercial Hotel in the 1930s and 1940s. For a brief period in the 1940s and early 1950s, there were a few other Basque-owned hotels, but they were not *ostatuak*, for instance, Zubizarreta's Club Rio.

### Eureka

As compared to Ely, the silver mining town of Eureka, Nevada, was never very large. Yet the discovery of silver in the area in 1864 attracted miners and hastened the completion of the Eureka and Palisade Railroad in 1875.[44] References to Basque *ostatuak* in this mining town, however, seem to postdate the dramatic increase of Basque sheepherders in the area around 1907, when the Eureka Livestock Company and others began trailing their herds into the Diamond Mountain area. Advertisements found on the curtain of the Eureka Opera Theater list three Eureka *ostatuak* in 1924: Laborde's Eureka Hotel and Café, John Landa's boardinghouse, and Martin Inda's Spanish Hotel.[45] Perhaps a better known *ostatu* was the Colonnade Hotel on Clark and Monroe Streets. The popular Gracieuse and Jean Sallaberry purchased the sixty-seven-year-old hotel building in 1947 and operated their hotel business there until 1973 when their daughter Mary Jean Labarry returned to Eureka to help her mother run the boardinghouse. Labarry and her mother continue to run the Colonnade, although it is no longer frequented by Basque boarders and does not serve Basque cuisine.

Throughout the Silver State, the story of Basques moving into an area for opportunities in mining and sheep ranching have been told many times over. When their numbers were substantial, Basque boardinghouses sprang up. Just west of Eureka in Austin, for example, Frank Aldape opened and operated his Silver State Bar and Hotel for thirty-one years. Likewise, the Arrascadas opened an *ostatu* in Golconda before moving to Gold Creek and starting another.

Although the success of the earliest *ostatuak* closely paralleled the fluctuations in Basque migration and immigration to the Silver State, one can also observe that the few *ostatuak* remaining in Reno, Elko, Winnemucca, and Gardnerville today stand at major transportation crossroads along interstate highways. In a sense, then, the *ostatuak* continue to benefit from the Great Basin vacationers and visitors passing through.

It has been noted that, with the possible exception of herding in southern California in the 1850s, Basques did not initiate open-range herding in the Western United States. In many locations, such as Winnemucca, a marked Basque presence appeared within a decade after other groups had introduced herding into a region.

In addition to establishing themselves as sheepmen in California, Nevada, and Idaho, Basques eventually participated in the smaller but emerging sheep industries found in Arizona, New Mexico, Utah, Colorado, Montana, Wyoming, Oregon, and Washington. As one would imagine, as Basque residents accumulated in these states, Basque *ostatuak* subsequently opened and were operated in these states as well.

## ARIZONA

Although there are comparatively few contemporary indications that Basques once settled in Utah, Colorado, Arizona, and New Mexico, news of small Basque colonies in these states was mentioned in the Basque language newspaper *California'ko Eskual Herria* between 1893 and 1896. The Basque-language newspaper further informs us that a small Basque colony existed in and around Tuscon, Arizona, in 1894.[46] Another early account explains that Basques migrated into portions of Arizona and northern New Mexico to flee the disastrous California drought in 1870 and 1871. The eventual result was small populations of itinerant Basques living in Flagstaff, Phoenix, and Tucson, Arizona, as well as in Raton and Grants, New Mexico, between 1891 and 1906.

In the first decade of this century, young Fermin Echeverria left Navarre headed for Jesus's boardinghouse in Flagstaff, Arizona, where he joined his older brothers Matias and Miguel. Jesus' was relatively easy for Fermin to find, since it stood a block and a half from Flagstaff's railroad station on the corner of a large intersection. Ironically, both Fermin and Matias met their future wives at that *ostatu*, and both women were the proprietor's nieces.[47] Later, when Fermin's extended family gathered, they sometimes traveled to Carmen Serrabia Chacon's small boardinghouse in

Winslow, Arizona. And during the summers Fermin's children especially enjoyed staying with the Chacons, who had children their own age and whose doting boarders Arnaud Etchemendy, Esteban Uriz, and Nicomedes were favorites among the children.

## NEW MEXICO

In neighboring New Mexico, specific mentions of Basques and their *ostatuak* have been sparse. Yet three centuries before Fermin Echeverria reached Arizona, Basque visitors arrived in the area during a famous expedition from Nueva Vizcaya. Juan de Oñate made his first expedition in search of the lost city of Quivira in 1598. His was also the very first recorded sheep trailing venture into present-day Arizona and New Mexico, as well as the first recorded entry of a contingent of Basques in the area.[48] After serving as governor of New Mexico for a few years, and after undertaking a second and a third southwestern expedition searching for Quivira in 1601 and 1604, the frustrated Oñate resigned his post as governor of New Mexico.[49]

Although some descendants of the Oñate contingent undoubtedly remained in New Mexico and the greater southwestern United States, their offspring did not establish a distinctly Basque colony. Centuries later the California-based Basque newspaper *California'ko Eskual Herria* contained a solitary mention of an *ostatu* in Grants, New Mexico. A few old-timers report having heard of it. The boardinghouse was most likely connected with Basques trailing sheep in the area in the late nineteenth century.

## COLORADO AND UTAH

### Grand Junction and Montrose, Colorado

One article in *California'ko Eskual Herria* revealed that because of crowded conditions in the Golden State, four Bakersfield Basques left California with their sheep outfits to settle in western Colorado and eastern Utah in 1894.[50] For a time, the westernmost portions of Utah and Colorado were popular grazing regions for itinerant Basque herders and their sheep. As a result, the Basque colony in Grand Junction, Colorado, supported a local *ostatu* called the Star Hotel (which operated in the 1910s), and the Basques in Montrose, Colorado, had another one.

In 1919 in Grand Junction, Colorado, Tony Coscorrozza opened a big

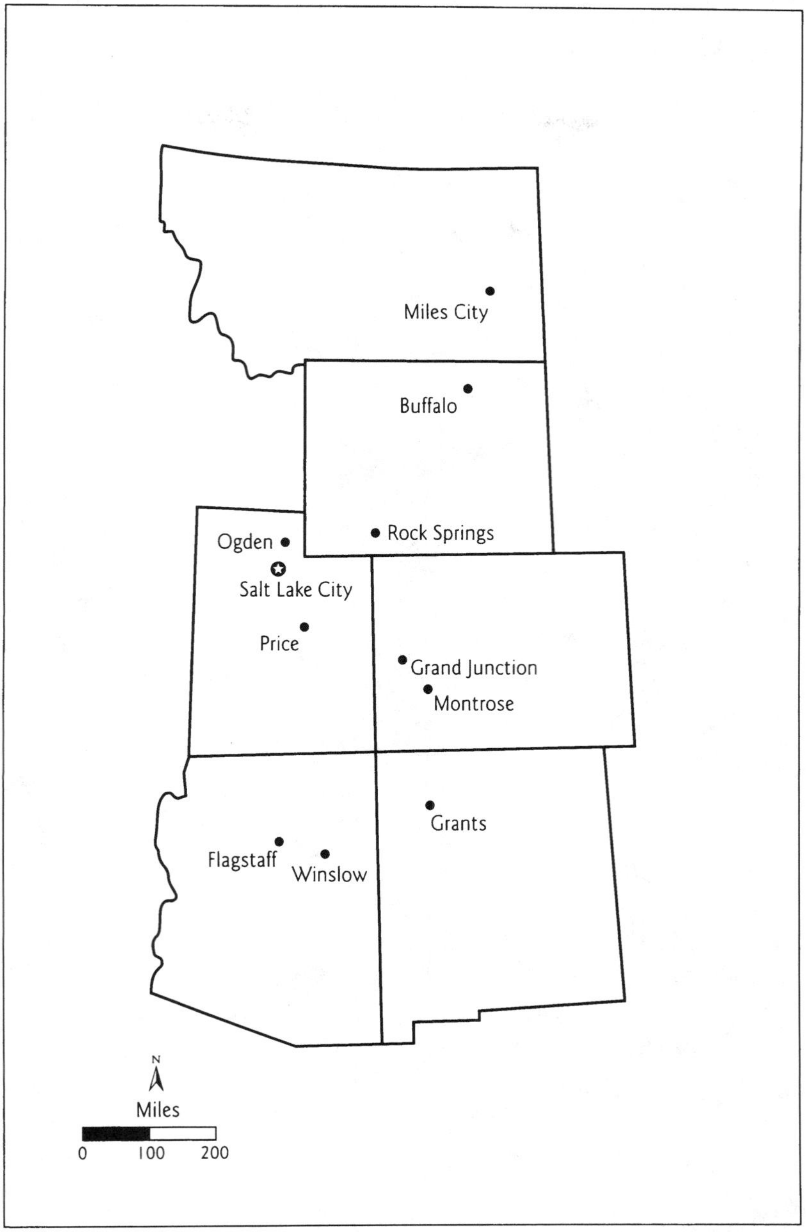


*Fig. 15. Communities with* ostatuak *in Utah, Colorado, Arizona, New Mexico, Wyoming, and Montana.*

boardinghouse at 224 Colorado Avenue called the Cantabarria. The following year, his nephew Antonio Retolaza and his wife Magarita took over and operated the combination grocery store, pool hall, and boardinghouse until 1946. Between 1936 and 1946 Louie and Isadora Eisaguirre—who had moved from Salt Lake City—ran an *ostatu* at 234 Ute Avenue. During the same period Basques visiting Grand Junction often stayed at Jean and Benny Urruty's LaSalle Hotel on the corner of Colorado and Second. Guests there walked two doors down to eat at Retolaza's, however. And in nearby Montrose, Colorado, there was the Basque-owned Mesa Hotel. Although the establishment was not a boardinghouse that served meals, Basques traveling through Montrose between 1904 and 1970 enjoyed the Arruabarrenas' hospitality.

### Ogden and Price, Utah

In Ogden, Salt Lake City, and Price, Utah, small but important hotels could also be found in the 1920s and 1930s.[51] Two Ogden, Utah, hotels are of particular interest because they were located in a key transportation center of the 1890s. Since Ogden served as the main rail switching terminal for travelers bound for southern Idaho and points west of Boise, many Basques disembarked in Ogden and waited for a connecting train in the small Basque district that contained one French Basque and one Bizkaian boardinghouse. No further information could be gleaned on these establishments. These Ogden *ostatuak* also became popular stopover spots for vacationing Great Basin Basques, places for local and regional Basque ranchers and sheepmen to conduct business, and the scene where young couples gathered with their families to conduct marriage ceremonies and the festivities afterward, as well as spend their honeymoon.[52] Ogden is unique in that it had a comparatively small Basque population, yet its two *ostatuak* were supported by a constant flow of out-of-town Basques.

Another small Utah town, Price, is also of interest. Although Basque herders were relatively rare in the state of Utah, owing to the dominance of the sheep industry by early Mormon settlers, some Basques were known to have wintered their sheep in southeastern Utah between Grand Junction, Colorado, and Price. There, between 1915 and 1933, the French and Allies Basque hotels flourished for a brief time.

### Salt Lake City, Utah

Less than an hour south of Ogden, in Salt Lake City, John and Claudia Landa converted a small two-story hotel, the Hogar, on Second Street to an *ostatu* in 1927.[53] Their successful business, based largely on Claudia's legendary cooking skills and John's ability to place Basque herders on the ranches of Intermountain Basques, kept the Hogar's doors open for fifty years.

The Hogar Hotel has been mentioned in several pieces of literature. In *Amerikanuak* William Douglass and Jon Bilbao reminded us that the Hogar served as a regional medical center for Utah Basques, who sent injured herders there for Claudia and John's care. In several articles in *The Voice of the Basques*, Bob Ithurralde reminisced about the eight years he boarded at the Hogar. And, in Nancy Zubiri's recent work, Mary Gaztimbide from Wells, Nevada, described living at the Hogar during her college years from 1954 to 1963.

In 1977, two years after John died, the then eighty-seven-year-old Claudia reluctantly closed the boardinghouse. Although Landa's may have been the most well known of Salt Lake City's Basque hotels, others also flourished in the 1920s and 1930s, especially because travel through Salt Lake City increased during that period. A street away from Landa's, Fred Otasue and his family operated the Fonda Español, a favorite among many Bizkaians and Gipuzkoans passing through Salt Lake City.[54]

## MONTANA AND WYOMING

In Montana and Wyoming a similar pattern of initial Basque settlement followed by *ostatuak* can be observed.

### Miles City, Montana

In Montana, a group of Basques got their start working for a sheep outfit owned by a French Bearnais near Deer Lodge.[55] By the 1890s additional itinerant Basque sheepmen were also grazing their flocks in the Plentywood and Glasgow areas of Montana, and immediately thereafter an *ostatu* was established in Miles City.

Although a few dozen itinerant Basques and their *ostatu* were present in Miles City in the late 1890s, according to the census of 1900 only two Basques had settled in Wyoming by the beginning of the new century.

## Buffalo and Rock Springs, Wyoming

About 160 miles south of Miles City, in Buffalo, Wyoming, the Healy and Patterson Sheep Company hired a French Basque named Jean Esponda in 1902. As one Wyoming author described that day:

> Buffalo, Wyoming, 1902, Jean Esponda straightened his shoulders, squinted his dark eyes approvingly at the Big Horn Mountains, and stepped off the train. Beside him was his new employer, Mr. Patsy Healy, and with this simple act of employment a web began to spin which eventually blanketed the land from the Big Horn Mountains to Powder River in Johnson County, Wyoming, with a unique race of people.[56]

Within a year of his initial employment, Esponda began attracting other Basques from St. Etienne de Baigorry and Arneguy to the Buffalo area to work with him at the Healy and Patterson Sheep Company.[57] By 1910, three years after Esponda had purchased his own ranch land, there were 43 Basques in Johnson County, and the population of Basques in the state had climbed to 126.[58]

In the next two decades, Buffalo would become the nucleus of the largest concentration of Basques to be found outside the states of Idaho, Nevada, California, and Oregon. The Basques in Johnson County frequented a number of downtown Buffalo *ostatuak*. Although they are no longer Basque-owned or operated, the sixty-room Occidental Hotel and Simon and Madeline Harriet's Idlewild are still standing along Buffalo's Main Street. Within a few blocks of these hotels, Madeline Ardans, Dominica Mendine Bejino, and Mrs. Irigaray once offered room and board to young Basque men and women in their small boardinghouses.[59]

In Rock Springs, in the southwestern part of the state, Casimiro and Aniseta Larrabaster opened the first Basque boardinghouse in Sweetwater County in 1909. In the subsequent decade, Cecilia Tayo opened another boardinghouse near the railroad station in Rock Springs, followed by a third, which was opened by Mary Loisate in 1921.[60]

### TEXAS AND OKLAHOMA

Although there is no evidence of Basque *ostatuak* in Texas and Oklahoma, a handful of Basques have settled in those two states. *California'ko*

*Eskual Herria* ran several advertisements in 1893 and 1894 in which Basques were invited to join their countrymen in the Lone Star State's Basque colony.[61]

The columns suggested that there was a blossoming colony of Basques, but there is nothing in the Texas State Archives that substantiates this claim. And despite a few subscribers in Van Horn and in Corpus Christi, the claim seems to have been a fabrication or an advertising ploy.

To the north, in the Oklahoma Territory, a few Basque priests founded a Sacred Heart mission in the late 1870s. The Benedictines corresponded with *California'ko Eskual Herria* regularly, announcing the arrival of visiting Basque prelates and authoring a column on the lives of the saints.[62]

Although evidence has been found of a handful of Basques living for a time in Texas, Oklahoma, and in other states, their numbers are relatively small as compared with the number of Basques who settled in California, Nevada, Idaho, Oregon, and Wyoming, and they do not seem to have established *ostatuak*.

The emergence of two large Basque towns between 1890 and 1930 remains to be discussed. As we will see in chapters 8 and 9, Boise and Stockton played an important role in maintaining the vitality of the Basque community in the upper High Desert area and in north central California. Further, the two communities developed downtown Basque districts that were similar to the Basque towns of Los Angeles, San Francisco, Bakersfield, and Reno. The stories of these two Basque communities, as well as the *ostatuak* of eastern Oregon and Washington and northern California, are the subject of the next two chapters.

# 8

# Boise's Basque Town and Its Spin-Offs

## THE BASQUE TOWN AND *Ostatuak* OF BOISE

The eight decades of Basque hotel keeping in Boise that ended in 1978 generated one of the most popular and visible Basque communities in the American West. As we will see in the discussion that follows, Basque *ostatuak* were key to establishing what is today a still-thriving Basque colony in southern Idaho.

Not unlike the neighboring states of California and Nevada, Idaho's earliest population boom was primarily the result of gold and silver discoveries. A native of Ireland, Elias Davidson Pierce is credited with initiating Idaho's first gold rush on the south branch of Clearwater River in 1861. News of his Oro Fino Mining District spread, and discoveries in Florence (1861), Owyhea and Boise Basin (1863), Wood River (1880), and Coeur d'Alene (1882) followed.[1]

By and large, Idaho's earliest Basques were not lured by the gold, silver, and lead mines found in the Idaho Territory. Evidence suggests that Basques began arriving in significant numbers decades after the gold rush began, and that they were attracted by fertile grazing land in the Owyhees and the Great Basin. Later in the twentieth century, however, some Basques worked the mining camps and sawmills near Mullan, Cascade, and other towns.

As has been stated earlier, the greater Winnemucca, Nevada, region provided a staging platform for Basque migration within the Western United States between 1890 and 1930. Several accounts of early Basque settlement north of Winnemucca tell of the lengthy and treacherous voyage of Antonio Azcuenaga and Jose Navarro who crossed the High Desert and arrived in Jordan Valley, Oregon, in 1889.[2] By 1900 several Bizkaian sheepmen had followed the two sheepmen to the Jordan Valley area and then extended their operations into the Boise, Ada, and Owyhee Counties of Idaho. Eventually, the Basques in the predominantly Bizkaian colonies of Boise and Jordan Valley would fan out into other portions of southern Idaho, eastern Oregon, and southeastern Washington. In 1891, for example, the Boise City Directory listed only 35 Basque surnames in a population of 4,400.[3] In the 1900 national census 61 Basques were identified in Idaho, and only 1 was of French Basque origin.[4] But the total number of Idaho's Basques increased dramatically in the earliest decades of the 1900s.

## Boise's Early *Ostatuak*

By 1920 Boise's Grove Street neighborhood had mushroomed into a Basque district with nearly a dozen *ostatuak*. As historian Patrick J. Bieter stated:

> Boise's Grove Street area was a Basque enclave in this period. Indeed, there were so many recently arrived immigrants in the area that it was possible to start school speaking only Basque, since all of the children in the neighborhood were foreign- or American-born Basque-speaking children. Basque was the language of home and of the streets.[5]

Although we have ample evidence of Boise's Basque town since 1920, the decades between 1890 and 1920 are more scantily documented.

The Boise City Directory in 1891 listed a Jose Gestel who lived and worked at the Spanish Restaurant at the corner of Eighth and Idaho Streets. A Mrs. E. Gestel, Manual Gestel, and Victor Guisasola were also living at the Spanish Restaurant; there is a possibility that the Spanish served as a small boardinghouse or rooming house.[6]

According to local author Julio Bilbao, Boise's first Basque may have been a Bizkaian woman who reportedly operated a florist shop on East Idaho Street. Bilbao mentions a Mrs. Narcissa Gustel, a Basque woman who reputedly married a Spaniard of that surname. One can wonder about whether directory editors may have misspelled the family name as Gestel.[7] In fact, one could speculate that the Spanish Restaurant may have been the town's first Basque hotel or rooming house based on the assumption that the City Directory misspelled Gustel as Gestel, that Mrs. Narcissa's florist shop was located close to the Spanish Restaurant, and that the Spanish Restaurant took in boarders as well as served food. Unfortunately, though, the Spanish Restaurant cannot be traced in subsequent years. The only subsequent record of the Gestels was ten years later when they were managing the Boise City Green Houses on Warm Springs Avenue.[8]

Another early Basque boardinghouse in Boise was the Oregon Hotel, located at the corner of Ninth and Front Streets. Jordan Valley *hotelero* Antonio Azcuenaga built the hotel in 1900, when he arrived in Boise.[9] His selection of location was logical, and probably ideal, because during that time the Oregon Short Line Railroad deposited its passengers at the depot directly across Front Street from the Oregon Hotel. Azcuenaga is said to have operated the hotel for only a few years before leasing it to longtime Boise *hotelero* Mateo Arregui.

The first Boise boardinghouse in living memory, however, was Jose and Felipa Uberuaga's Star Rooming House on Idaho Street. Ironically, the Star was also one of the last of Boise's *ostatuak* to close. The Star appeared in city directories in 1903, although it may have been in operation for a few years before that time. The Uberuagas managed the Star until 1915, selling to Francisco and Gabina Aguirre, who kept the business going for another fifty-seven years. The Uberuaga family then opened the Uberuaga on Grove Street and continued their long tradition of hotel keeping until 1971. As it would turn out, one of Boise's earliest *ostatuak*, the Star, and its last were owned and operated by Uberuagas.

Other Basque establishments in the 1912 neighborhood, in addition to Aguirre's Star and the Uberuaga included Juan and Juana Saracondi's on Sixth Street, Siriaco and Maria Cruz Bicandi's at 706 Grove, and the DeLamar Rooming House at 887 Grove. As in other communities we have explored, Boise's rooming houses (such as the DeLamar) offered simple rooms with or without very limited kitchen privileges; whereas at boardinghouses (such as Saracondi's, Bicandi's, and Aguirre's) tenants rented rooms and expected prepared meals daily. Discussion regarding types of boardinghouses has been considered in earlier chapters, but it is noteworthy that among those Basques I interviewed, Boise Basques most consistently made a distinction between rooming houses and boardinghouses.

*The Anduiza Hotel in Boise, Idaho, as it appears today. Courtesy of the University of Utah Basque Boarding House Project.*

In 1918 Juan and Juana Anduiza opened their new *ostatu* at 619 Grove Street. Its physical layout is perhaps the most unique among Basque boardinghouses in the American West because it was constructed around a handball and *pala* court. Its first floor contained eleven rooms for boarders with two bathrooms at the rear of that floor. Its basement contained a *hoteleros'* apartment, a dining room, kitchen, bathrooms, and storage rooms. Apparently Juan Anduiza knew the importance of *pilota* to Basques and wanted to provide a year-round indoor court for his countrymen. According to Jay Hormaechea, who worked at Anduiza's in the early years, "the court was the largest covered court of its kind in the northwest."[10] Visitors to Boise today can still see *pilota* being played on the Anduiza's court, although the *ostatu* has long since closed.

At the age of thirteen Jay Uberuaga Hormaechea left school and went to work for the Anduizas at the urging of her parents. The young Hormaechea was saddened to leave school and unhappy at Anduiza's. As she reported, it was an unseasonably cold winter, and "my room was upstairs, a terrible location because the boardinghouses had no heat." After working there for three months and three days, Jay decided to quit. "On my last day," she stated, "the pee pots were frozen sold. I decided then and there I had had enough!"[11]

From Anduiza's Jay got a job at Estaquio and Guillerma Ormaechea's boardinghouse, also known as Barberos. They hired her to work as a hostess. "I loved working there," Jay remembered. "I was outgoing and was hired to encourage boarders to play cards, billiards, and dance. I love people and enjoyed working there much more than Anduiza's." A few years later, in 1921, when new owners Benito, Asuncion, Thomas, and Antonia Ysursa purchased the *ostatu,* they retained Jay's services.

The boardinghouses and rooming houses in operation in Boise between 1891 and 1920 are listed in table 8.1. Because a few Basque rooming houses were central to Boise's Basque town they are also included in the tables for this chapter. Some of the more notable rooming houses doing business between 1891 and 1920 include the DeLamar, Martin's, and the Capitol.

## Boise's *Ostatuak* of the 1920s

Contemporaries comment that any Boise Basque who is "middle aged or older" remembers the boardinghouses that lined Grove Street in the 1920s.[12] Although Grove was still a shady residential street at that time, local Basques might recall Anduiza's fronton where they wagered on *pilota;* or Barbero's player piano at nearby Idaho Street, where they staged

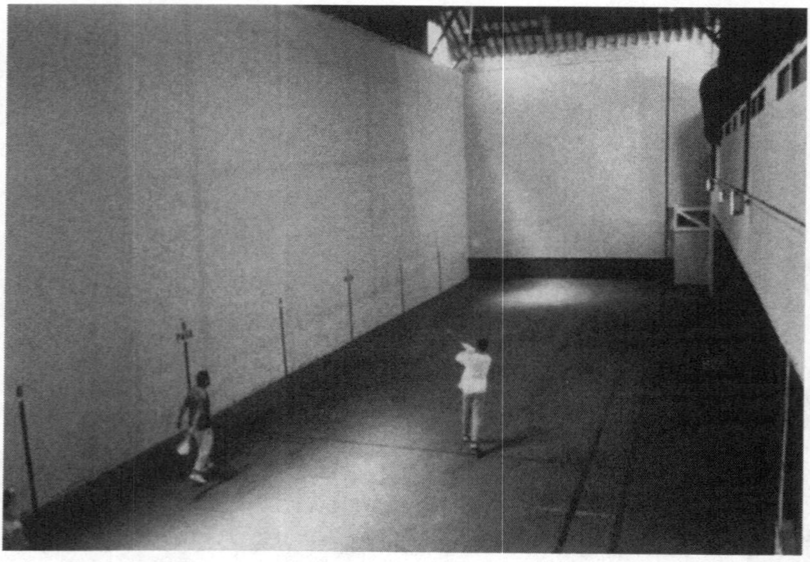

*Anduiza's interior ball court with* pala *players. Courtesy of the University of Utah Basque Boarding House Project.*

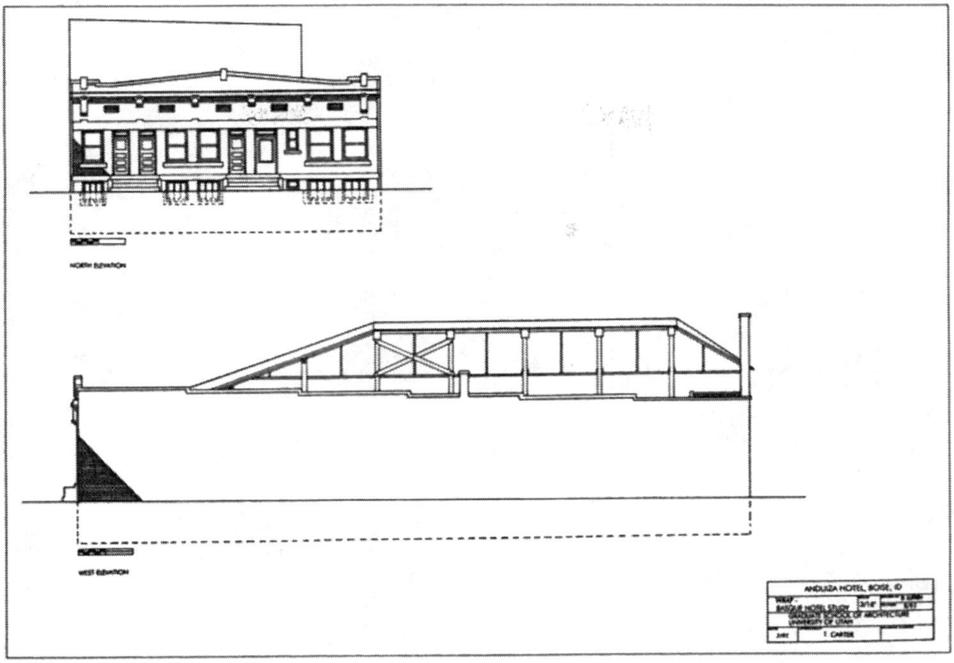


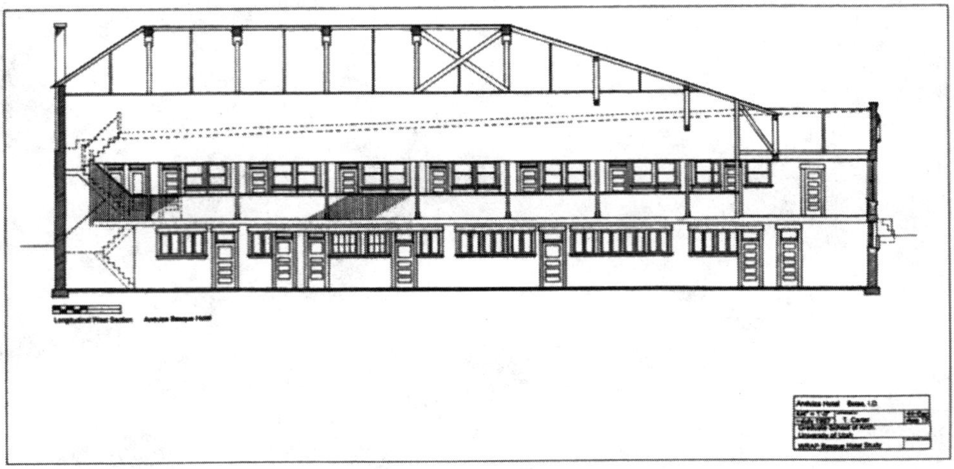


*The Anduiza Hotel, Boise, Idaho. The front of the hotel, the transverse view of the building, and a cutaway diagram showing the basement and first floors. Courtesy of the University of Utah Basque Boarding House Project.*

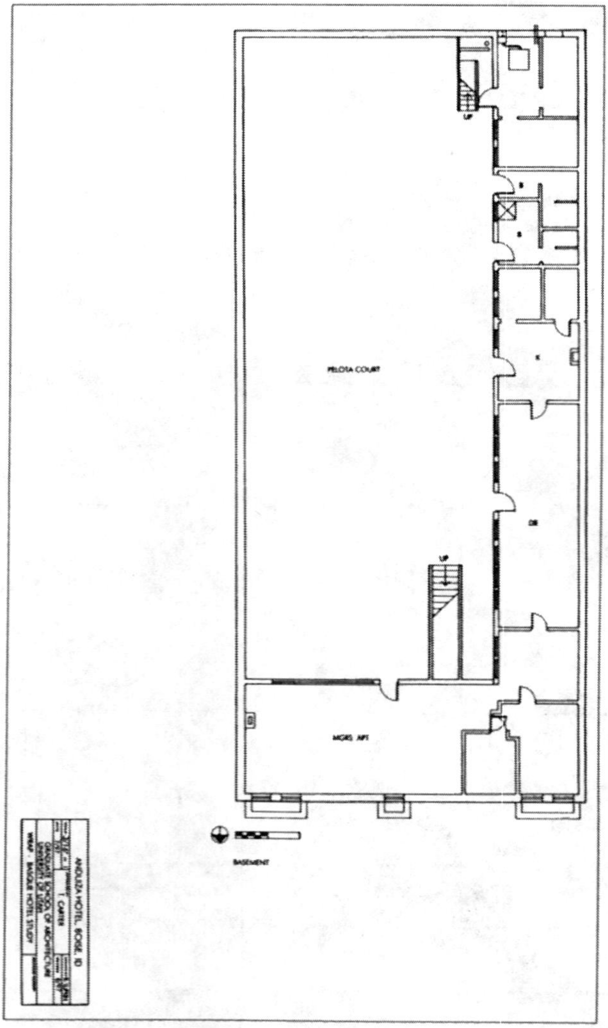


impromptu sing-alongs; or Sunday evenings spent at Letemendi's, where they danced late into the night and talked Leandra into cooking early-morning breakfasts.

Antonio Letemendi and Leandra Ondarza met and married near the turn of the century in Bizkaia. Not long after they arrived in the United States they went to Paradise Valley, Nevada, where Antonio worked as a cook for a sheep outfit. In 1907 they decided they had saved enough money to move to Boise. In 1912 the Letemendis began managing the DeLamar Rooming House. Nine years later they moved to 216 Ninth

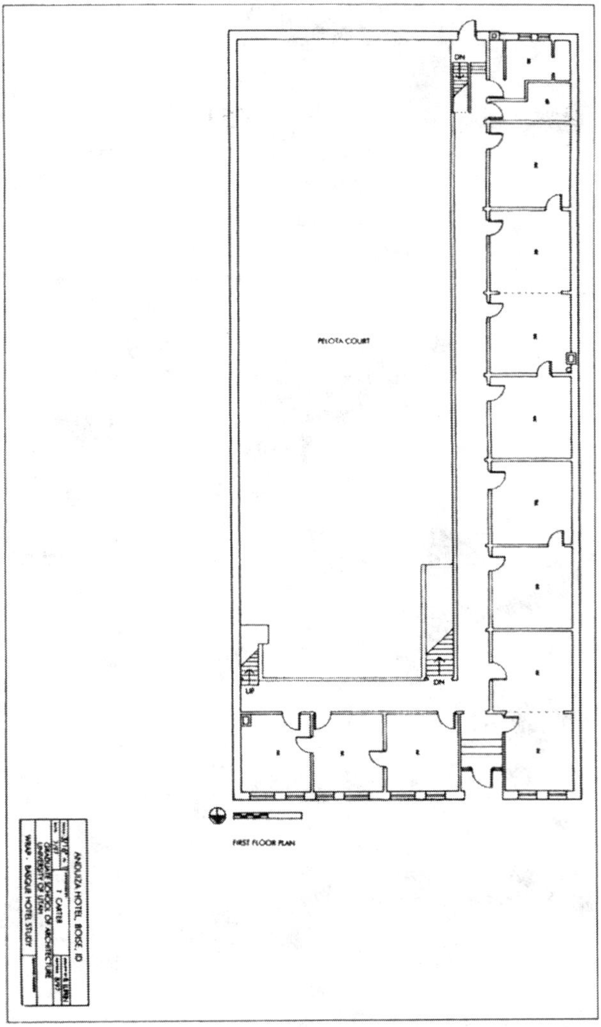


opposite and left: *Basement and first floor plans of the Anduisa Hotel, centered around the handball/*pala *court. Courtesy of the University of Utah Basque Boarding House Project.*

Street, where they opened an *ostatu*. And in 1926 they purchased a large three-story wooden-frame house at 521 Grove. As local historian Patrick Bieter has written, the house "was to become for hundreds of young Basque men and women their entree to America. The house was home for the seven Letemendi children, up to twenty boarders when filled, and later some of Leandra and Antonio's grandchildren."[13]

Like Jayo's at Ninth and Front Streets, Ysursas at 613 West Idaho, Arego's at 217½ South Ninth, Yribar's at 118 South Seventh, or Uberuaga's at 607 Grove, Letemendi's was much more than a building to its

Table 8.1 Boise's Early Boardinghouses and Rooming Houses, 1891–1920

| Date | Operator | Location | Hotel Name |
|---|---|---|---|
| 1900– | Narcissa Gustel | Eighth and Idaho | Spanish Hotel and Restaurant |
| 1900– | Antonio Azcuenaga | Ninth and Front | Oregon Hotel |
| 1903–1915 | Jose and Felipa Uberuaga | 512 Idaho | Star Rooming House |
| (1915–1972) | Francisco and Gabina Goitia Aguirre | | |
| 1910–1918 | Simon and Josefa Galdos (owners) Siriaco and Maria Cruz Bicandi (operators) | 607 Grove | Bicandi's Boarding House |
| 1910s | Ysidro Madarieta | Main Street | Madarieta's |
| 1911–1918 | Juan and Juana Arriola Uberuaga | 211 South Sixth | Saracondi's |
| 1912–1921 | Antonio and Leandra Letemendi | 887 Grove | DeLamar Rooming House |
| 1912–1914 | Jose and Hermengilda Uberuaga | 206½ West Idaho | Capitol Rooming House |
| (1914) | Jose Arregui | | |
| (1914–1916) | Jose and Crusa Arostegui | | |
| (1916–1965) | Jose and Crusa Arostegui and Pedro and Marie Epeldi | | |
| 1914–1918 | Arrego family | 217½ South Ninth | Arrego's |
| 1914–1918 | Juan and Juana Anduiza | 216 South Ninth | Anduiza's |
| (1918–1950) | Juan and Juana Anduiza | 619 Grove | |
| 1914–1925 | — | 611 Grove | Martin's Rooming House |
| 1915–1921 | Estaquio and Guillerma Ormaechea | 613 West Idaho | Ormachea's (Barbero's) |
| 1918–1978 | Jose and Hermengilda Uberuaga | 607 Grove | Uberuaga's |
| 1918– | Juan and Juana Arriola | 211 South Sixth | Arriola's |
| 1918– | Arrego and Arguinchona families | 217 South Ninth | Arrego/Arguinchona |
| 1918– | Agustin and "Pacha" Bilaustegui | 117 South Seventh Moved to Sixth Street "Chico Club" | Bilaustegui's |
| 1918–1932 | Juan and Teresa Yribar | 118 South Seventh | Ybar's/Yribar's |

Dashes indicate that no information was available for this entry.

Table 8.2 Boise's *Ostatuak* in the 1920s

| Date(s) | Operator | Location | Name |
|---|---|---|---|
| 1912–1921 | Antonio and Leandra Letemendi | 887 Grove | DeLamar Rooming House* |
| 1914–1920s | Arrego family | 217½ South Ninth | Arrego's* |
| 1915–1972 | Francisco and Gabina Goitia Aguirre | 512 Idaho | Star Rooming House* |
| 1915–1921 | Estaquio and Guillerma Ormaechea | 613 West Idaho | Barbero's* |
| 1916–1965 | Jose and Crusa Arostegui | 706½ West Idaho | Capitol Rooming House* |
| 1918–1950 | Juan and Juana Anduiza | 619 Grove | Anduiza's* |
| 1918–1978 | Jose and Hermengilda Uberuaga | 607 Grove | Uberuaga's* |
| 1918–1932 | Juan and Teresa Yribar | 118 South Seventh | Ybar's/Yribar's* |
| 1921–1940 | Benito and Asuncion Ysursa and Tomas and Antonia Ysursa | 613 West Idaho | Ysursa's/Modern Hotel |
| 1921–1960s | Mateo and Adriana Arregui | Idaho Street | Arregui's |
| 1921–1929 | Antonio and Leandra Letemendi | 216 South Ninth | Letemendi's |
| (1929–1968) | Antonio and Leandra Letemendi | 521 Grove | |
| 1923–1950 | Anastasio and Anunci Jayo | Five locations on Ninth, Main, and Grove Streets | Jayo's |
| 1925–1931 | Victor Gabica | 118½ South Ninth | Gabica's Metropole Hotel |

*Indicates a boardinghouse that existed pre-1920 that also can be found in table 8.1.

residents. Nicasio Beristain described the significance of Letemendi's in the following way: "Almost everything I became in America I owe to Letemendi's. I met my future wife in their kitchen. I learned to speak English talking to Vicki Letemendi's children. I got my first job in America through the boardinghouse. They helped me send money to my mother. I don't think I would have made it without them."[14]

Another oft-recounted Boise tale is the story of Benito, the now legendary penniless Bizkaian who arrived in town in the 1920s and bet $75 on himself in a *pilota* game. Fortunately for Benito, he prevailed, and the winnings became his grubstake in the New World.[15] Regardless of which colorful story one hears about Boise's Basque district of the 1920s, it is clear that the neighborhood was vibrant during that decade, and that the twenty blocks adjacent to the Oregon Short line hosted several important Basque establishments, as can be seen in figure 16.

Most of Boise's Basque town *ostatuak* were located, as one observer stated, "between the church off Idaho Street and the DeLamar Hotel on Eighth and Front," and many of them remained in business for a relatively long time as compared to *ostatuak* in other parts of the West.[16] For example, the Bicandi-Uberuaga, the Star, the DeLamar, and Capitol Rooms (all mentioned earlier) all opened their doors before 1920 and remained in business until 1978, 1972, 1973, and 1968, respectively. Anduiza's opened during the same period but remained in business for "only" thirty-six years. The Letemendis opened their *ostatu* slightly later, in 1921, but enjoyed forty-seven successful years in Boise's Basque town. Other popular and fondly remembered *ostatuak* were Jayo's, Ysursa's, and Martin's, each of which were in business for over twenty years. The staying power, sheer number, and concentration of these Basque hotels in Boise suggest that that community saw a convergence of Basques over a period of some fifty years.

The Ysursa family is a hotel-keeping family that made a significant impact on Boise Basques. As was mentioned earlier, Eustaquio and Guillerma Ysursa Ormaechea operated a boardinghouse at 613 West Idaho Street. Mrs. Ormaechea was an Ysursa and sister to Benito and Tomas Ysursa. In 1921 Benito and Asuncion, Tomas and Antonia took over the *ostatu* from their sister and brother-in-law who had decided to return to Spain. Benito's daughter Ruby recalled that the *ostatu* could hold forty or fifty herders at one time.[17] In 1941 the Ysursa brothers bought the building across the street and moved their business to 612 West Idaho. There they also opened a Basque restaurant they named the Valencia, which was open from 1941 through 1966. According to one native Idahoan, "The food at the Valencia was so satisfying and plentiful that it became known throughout Idaho and far beyond. . . . Whenever the Valencia was mentioned, someone would invariably say, 'That soup. Have you tasted that soup?'"[18] The Valencia closed in 1966, marking the last year of Ysursa's four decades of hotel keeping in Boise's Basque town. In 1976 the family sold the building to non-Basques.

The endurance of Boise's *ostatuak* and the fact that the boardinghouses were owned and operated primarily by Bizkaians or Gipuzkoans makes Boise's Basque town unique among others in the American West. As in California's Basque districts of Los Angeles and San Francisco, Basque customers often favored one or two boardinghouses over others. Their choice may have been influenced by a combination of factors, including

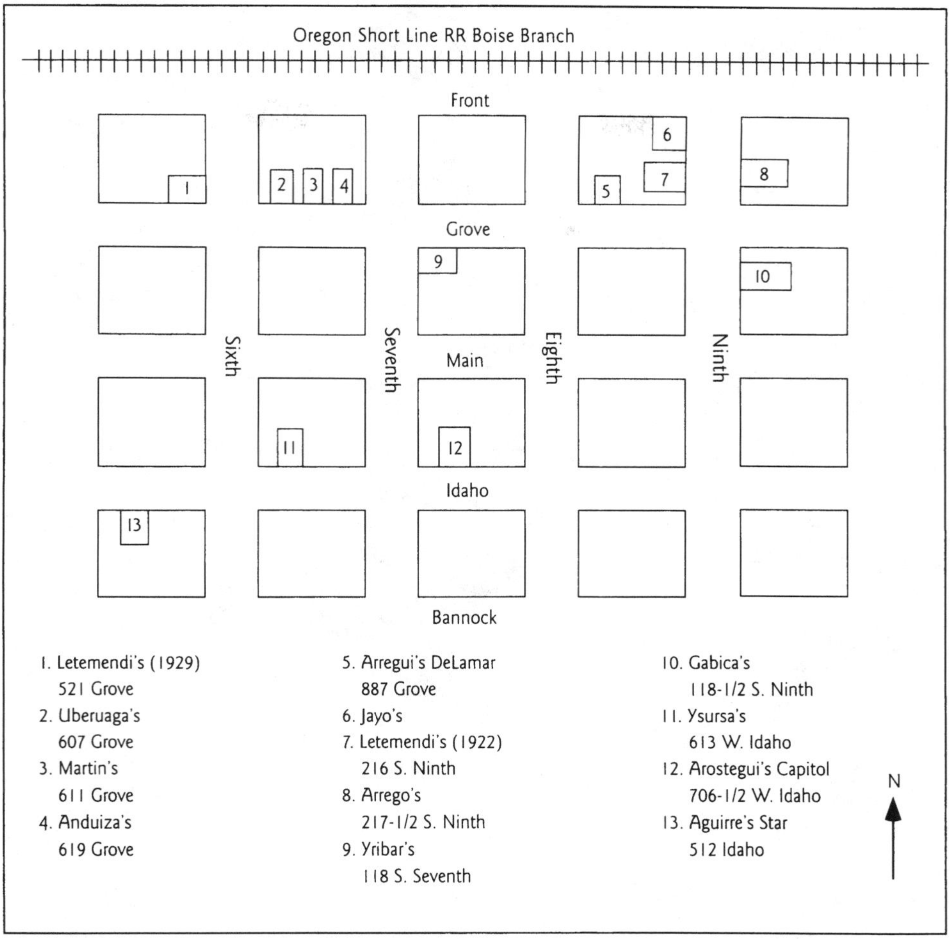


*Fig. 16. Boise's Basque town in the 1920s.*

whether they shared a hometown with the *hotelero* or *hotelera*, or whether the *ostatu* was the favorite of their family and friends. Barbero's in Boise, for example, attracted newcomers from the coastal villages of Gipuzkoa, primarily owing to the fact that Barbero and his wife were from that part of Euskal Herria.[19] Also some clients may have been swayed by minor dialectical differences in Euskara. Overall, the practice of selecting boardinghouses "most like home" extended throughout Basque communities in the American West.

Boise's *hoteleros* commonly relocated their businesses several times during their careers (see tables 8.1, 8.2, and 8.3). By casual study of the tables one can see that Boise's hotel-keeping families were quite mobile. For instance, Mateo and Adriana Arregui operated two different boardinghouses on Idaho Street before moving to the DeLamar on Grove, and finally to another on Seventh Street. Likewise the Jayos had businesses located at the corner of Ninth and Front, 1103 Idaho, 1107 Grove, 118 South Ninth, and 607½ Main Streets. And, in similar fashion, the Arregui, the Arostegui, and the Epeldi families lived in and conducted business in the same edifice, the Capitol Rooming House, at different times.[20] One could claim that Boise's hotel-keeping families were prone to relocate and managed to be successful when they did so, although the same could not be said about hotelkeepers in other Western states.

*Hotelero* Mateo Arregui's arrival and settlement in the Western United States is in many ways representative of a sheepherder turned *hotelero*, and of the longevity of some of Boise's Basque *hoteleros*. In 1907, at the age of twenty-two, Arregui left Bizkaia and headed directly for the Winnemucca region, where he had heard he would find work. Upon arrival he checked into Martin's Hotel Lafayette where he paid fifty cents per day for room and board. With just $20 left in his pocket, Arregui was eager to start working. When Jose Saval, a Basque employed by the John G. Taylor outfit, offered Arregui a herding job, he gladly accepted. Mateo's first job grazing sheep in the Rye Patch and Golconda areas earned him $15 per month. During his years in northern Nevada, Arregui also worked for F. O. Bacon, Pedro Altube, and Jose Bengoechea. In his final herding job at Bengoechea's, his pay had increased to $35 per month by around 1919. Having saved enough and having decided to put down roots in the High Desert area, Arregui returned to Bizkaia in search of a bride. When he came back to the States with Adriana, Arregui chose to settle down in Boise. There the couple leased their first boardinghouse on Idaho Street in 1921, purchased a band of sheep, and settled into four decades of hotel keeping.[21]

Jose and Hermengilda Uberuaga also enjoyed a relatively lengthy run as *hoteleros*. They lived in, owned, and operated a Basque boardinghouse at 607 Grove Street from 1918 through 1978. The two-story brick house they purchased in 1918, the oldest brick building in Boise, began as a private residence for Cyrus Jacobs and his family when it was built in 1864. In 1910 Jacobs's descendants sold the house to Simon and Josefa Galdos, who opened a boardinghouse there in 1910. A few years later, Siriaco and Maria Cruz Bicandi were hired to operate the business, and, in 1918, after short stints at the Star and the Capitol Rooms, the Uberuagas purchased the home from the Galdos family.

Table 8.3 Boise *Ostatuak* Since the 1920s

| Date | Operator | Location | Hotel Name |
|---|---|---|---|
| 1915–1972 | Francisco and Gabina Goitia Aguirre | 512 Idaho Street | Star Rooming House* |
| 1916–1965 | Jose and Crusa Arostegui and Pedro and Marie Epeldi | 706½ West Idaho | Capitol Rooming House* |
| 1918–1978 | Jose and Hermengilda Uberuaga | 607 Grove | Uberuaga's* |
| 1918–1932 | Juan and Teresa Yribar | 118 South Seventh | Ybar's/Yribar's* |
| 1932–1935 | Juan and Teresa Yribar | 118 Capitol | |
| 1918–1950 | Juan and Juana Anduiza | 619 Grove | Anduiza's* |
| 1921–1960s | Mateo and Adriauna Arregui | Idaho Street | Arregui's* |
| 1921–1929 | Antonio and Leandra Letemendi | 216 South Ninth | Letemendi's |
| 1923–1950 | Anastasio and Anunci Jayo | Five Locations on Ninth, Main, and Grove Streets | Jayo's* |
| 1927–1940 | Benito and Asuncion Ysursa | 613 West Idaho | Ysursa's Modern Hotel* |
| 1929–1968 | Antonio and Leandra Letemendi | 521 Grove | Letemendi's* |
| 1936–1938 | Justo and Angeles Murelaga | 811½ Idaho | Murelaga's Economy Hotel |
| 1936–1937 | Elias Echevarria | 912 Grove | Echevarria's Blue Bird |
| 1936–1938 | Hilario and Petra Urresti | 716½ Main | Urresti's Eagle |
| 1939–1940 | Carmen Bilbao | 612½ Main | Bilbao's |
| 1941–1966 | Tomas and Antonia Ysursa | 612 West Idaho | Ysursa's Valencia Hotel |
| 1945–1973 | Hilario and Laura Arguinchona | 887 Grove | DeLamar Rooming House |
| 1950–1969 | Hipalito and Maria Sabala | 716½ Main and 910 Grove | Sabala's Del Rio Hotel |
| 1970s | Juan Uscola | — | Uscola's Nuevo Viscaya |

*Indicates a boardinghouse that existed pre-1920 that also can be found in table 8.1.
Dashes indicate that no information was available for this entry.

The Uberuaga remains distinct among Boise's *ostatuak* in a number of ways. First, the boardinghouse business operated successfully under the same hotelkeepers for six decades, and this is a record for local *ostatuak*. Second, the old boardinghouse is one of the few still standing, and it looks much as it did near the turn of the century. Thanks to recent conservation efforts by local Basques, the *ostatu* at 607 Grove Street has been further distinguished from others around Boise.

In 1978, when the Uberuaga children decided to close the family *ostatu* after seventy-five years of operation, they were closing Boise's last boardinghouse. Six years later a Boise-born Basque American named Adelia Garro Simplot purchased the Uberuaga and formed a nonprofit corporation called the Basque Museum and Cultural Center. In the brief twenty-year period since then, the building has been placed on the National Register of Historic Buildings, the exterior and interior of the home have been restored, and an annex with display cases, exhibit rooms, and a museum store has opened next door. Locals still enjoy John Anduiza's *pilota* court next door to the annex. In short, the project has successfully preserved an *ostatu* and part of the old Basque neighborhood for future generations of Basques and Basque Americans to appreciate. The Basque Museum and Cultural Center is the only undertaking of its kind in the Western Hemisphere.

## BOISE'S SPIN-OFF HOTELS

Just as spin-off hotels sprang up in the areas surrounding San Francisco and Los Angeles, so too did offshoots of Boise hotels develop in parts of Idaho. In Mullan, Cascade, Emmett, Parma, Caldwell, Nampa, Mountain

*Originally built as a private home for the Cyrus Jacobs family in 1864, the Uberuagas' place became home for many Basques from 1918 through 1978. It has since become home to Boise's Basque Museum. Courtesy of the University of Utah Basque Boarding House Project.*

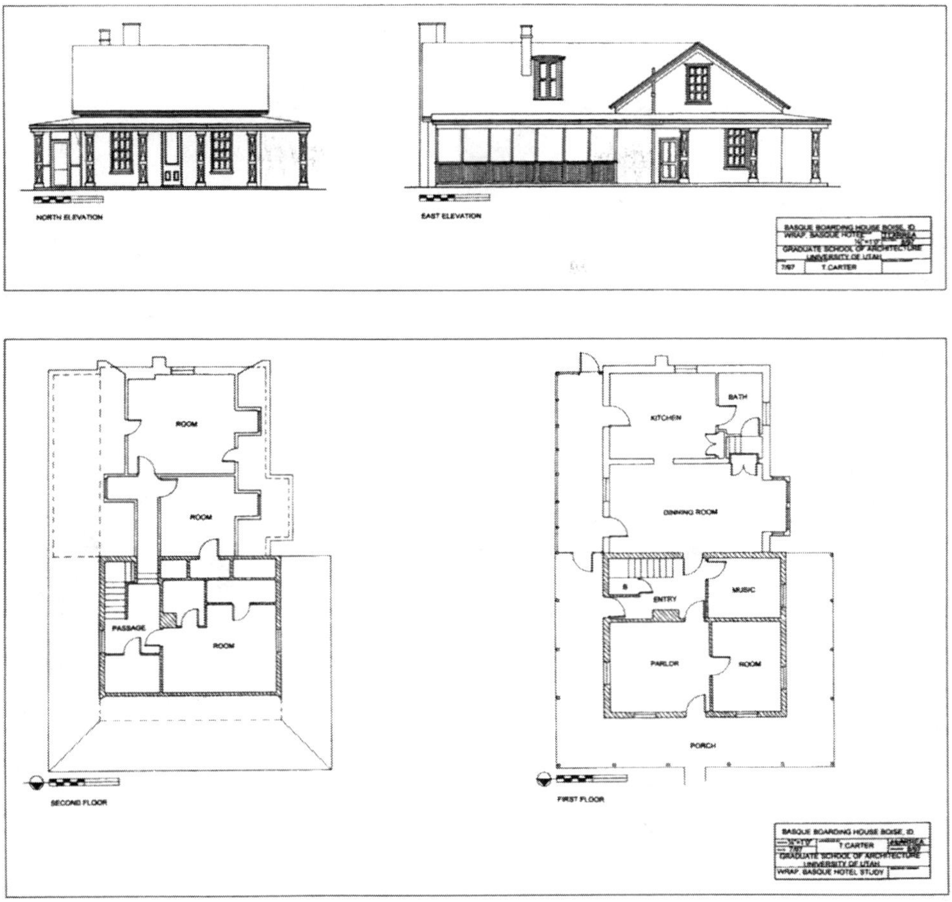


*The Uberuaga, Boise, Idaho. Exterior drawings from the north and east, and the layout of the first and second floors. Courtesy of the University of Utah Basque Boarding House Project.*

Home, Gooding, Hailey, Twin Falls, Rupert, Pocatello, and other towns in southern Idaho and eastern Oregon small local boardinghouses sprang up along the state's major highways and railways within a few decades of the establishment of Boise's earliest *ostatuak*. *Hoteleros* such as Siriaco and Maria Cruz Bicandi lived and worked in Boise's early Basque district and watched their cousins and offspring open *ostatuak* in Cascade and other Idaho locations. Lucy Garatea began working at Boise's Star Hotel for her aunt Gabina Aguirre at the age of fifteen, and years later Lucy became the *hotelera* at the Plaza Hotel in Burns, Oregon, in 1948.[22] There was a pattern to who opened their own boardinghouses in the surround-

Table 8.4 Other *Ostatuak* in Idaho

| Date(s) | Operator | Location | Hotel Name |
|---|---|---|---|
| 1925–1939 | Eugenio and Dominic Soloaga Mingo | Mullan | Mingo-Soloaga's |
| 1940s | — | Cascade | Echeverria's |
| 1940s | — | Cascade | Onaindia's |
| 1945–1972 | Frank and Frances Bicandi Bilbao | Cascade | Bilbao's Valley Club and Emery Hotel |
| 1910s | — | Hailey | Mendiola's |
| 1911 | — | Hailey | Arriaga-Unamuno's |
| 1920s | — | Hailey | Menchaca's |
| 1934 | Julio and Maria Astorquia | Hailey, South Main | Astorquia's Rialto Hotel |
| 1936–1958 | David and Epi Inchausti | Hailey, West Bullion | Inchausti's |
| 1930s | — | Mackay | Urresti's |
| 1907–1909 | Claudio "Makusa" Ascuena | Gooding, North of RR station | Ascuena's Casa Española |
| (1909– ) | Timoteo Serdiga | | |
| 1920s | Marcelino Goicoechea | Gooding | Goicoechea's |
| 1922–1935 | Florencio and Antonia Uriaguereca | Gooding, 121 Second Avenue | Uriaguereca's |
| 1940s–1978 | Florencio and Antonia Uriaguereca | Gooding, 121 Second Avenue | Uria's General Store |
| 1940s–1960s | Felix and Henrietta Gamboa | Gooding, Fourteenth Avenue West | Gamboa's |
| 1909–1920s | Eugenia Mingolarra and Domingo Soloaga | Shoshone | Solaga's Basque Hotel |
| 1910–1938 | Manuel and Fernanda Beitia | Shoshone, North Street | Beitia's |
| 1917–1925 | Pete Mendiola | Shoshone, Greenwood Street | Mendiola's |
| 1918– | J. Oneida | Shoshone, South Rail Street | Oneida's |
| 1920s | Pagoaga family | Shoshone, South Rail Street | Pagoaga's |
| 1923 | Atiyeh family | Shoshone, South Rail Street | Atiyeh's |
| 1925–1929 | Ramon Urrutia | Shoshone, Greenwood Street | Urrutia's |
| 1929–1989 | Carlos Berriochoa | Shoshone, Greenwood Street | Berriochoa's |
| 1930s | Jose and Gertrude Ansola | Shoshone, North Alta Street | Ansola's |
| 1907–1984 | Pedro Anchustegui | Mountain Home, Northwest Third | Anchustegui's Basque Hotel |
| 1910 | Jose Bengoechea | Mountain Home | Bengoechea's Mountain Home Hotel |

| | | | |
|---|---|---|---|
| 1945–1956 | Agapito Bideganeta, owner<br>Carmen Arruti, operator | Mountain Home, South, Second East | Bideganeta's Royal Hotel |
| 1957–1986 | Carmen Arruti | Mountain Home, 325 East Second | Carmen Arruit's |
| 1917–1967 | Simon and Josefa Galdos and<br>Anastasio and Teresa Jayo | Emmett, 109 South Commercial | Charcha's |
| 1925–1957 | Eugenio and Dolores Bicandi | Emmett, 327 Main | Bicandi's Boarding House |
| 1910–1930s | Luis Bermensolo | Nampa | Bermensolo's |
| 1920–1944 | Tomas and Tomasa Jausoro | Nampa, 119 Twelfth Avenue | Jausoro's Spanish Hotel |
| (1920s) | G. Uriquiaga | | |
| 1936–1947 | Juan and Regina Bastide | Nampa, 16 1/2 Eleventh Avenue | Bastide's Modern Hotel |
| (1947) | Sam and Rosa Arana | | |
| 1930s | Bilbao and Bengoechea families | Jerome | Bilbao-Benogechea's |
| 1939–1955 | Gogenola family | Jerome | Gogenola's |
| 1920s | — | Parma | Parma Hotel |
| 1910s | — | Pocatello | Pocatello Hotel |
| 1930s | Etcheverry family | Pocatello | Etcheverry's |
| 1930s | Jean and Louis Etcheverry | Rupert, Eighth and J Streets | "La Chata's" |
| 1920–1952 | Francisco and Florentino Sabala | Twin Falls, 214 Second Street | Sabala's |
| 1925–1946 | Lorenzo and Benita Selaya | Twin Falls, 564 Main Street | Selaya's |
| 1930s–1937 | John and Santa Bilbao | Twin Falls, Main Avenue South | Bilbao's |
| 1937–1949 | Santa Bilbao | Twin Falls, 302 Second Avenue | Bilbao's |
| 1940s | Adelia Olaverria | Twin Falls, 461 Second Avenue | Olaverria's |
| 1950–1976 | Aniceto and Alma Bengoechea | Twin Falls, 302 Second Avenue | Bengoechea's (formerly Bilbao's) |

Dashes indicate that no information was available for this entry.

ing region: serving girls and semiretired herders who had had a taste of boardinghouse life in Boise's Basque town went on to open their own *ostatu* either in the Basque town or in an outlying area.

Boise's spin-off hotels have a few traits in common. Whether it was Jausoro's Spanish Hotel on Twelfth Street in Nampa, or Santa Bilbao's in Gooding, or Carmen Arruti's in Mountain Home, rarely did the smaller Idaho towns have more than one or two *ostatuak* at any one time. Also many of the earliest boardinghouses outside Boise flourished between the 1920s and early 1940s and then faded rapidly.

### Mountain and Forest Towns

Far north of Boise in Mullan, near the Coeur d'Alene Mountains and the Montana border, where gold, silver, and lead had drawn pioneers as early as the 1870s, Eugenio and Dominica Soloaga Mingo operated a Basque boardinghouse from 1925 to 1939. For most of their fourteen years there, Eugenio worked in the local mines, and Dominica ran the *ostatu* for Basque miners.[23]

Due south, in Cascade along the Payette River between the Payette and Boise National Forests, the Echeverrias and Onaindias ran boardinghouses in the late 1930s and early 1940s. In 1945 Frances and Frank Bilbao opened their Valley Club and Hotel in Mullan, which for nearly thirty years housed and served Basques who grazed their sheep in the Boise Forest, worked at nearby dam construction sites, or worked in the Boise Cascade mills in Cascade and McCall.[24]

Similarly, Basques were drawn to the Sawtooth National Forest area around Hailey and MacKay, where they mined the region's rich iron ore deposits. Eusebio Arriaga and Pia Unamuno, Pete Mendiola, Julio and Maria Astorquia, David and Epi Inchausti, the Menchacas, and the Urrestis all operated thriving *ostatuak* in the area between 1910 and 1935. Further south in Gooding, Florencio and Antonia Uriaguereca, Claudio Ascuena, and Marcelino Goicoechea operated *ostatuak* during the 1920s.[25] Lucia Uriaguereca Osa, daughter of *hoteleros* Florencio and Antonia Osa, described living in their Gooding *ostatu* in the years between 1922 and 1936:

> I remember helping my mother make chorizos and murcillas. I also remember one night my mother left *arroz con leche* (rice pudding) on the window ledge so it could cool off. Two of the *mutillak* ("boys," or

boarders in this case) came home in the wee hours and ate the whole thing!

My dad was an accordion player and mother played the tambourine. The rest of us would dance. The "boys" called mother "Ama." There were two other *ostatuas* [*sic*] in Gooding at the time. One was Claudio Ascuena and one Marcelino Goicoechea. Both are gone now. What wonderful times and memories.[26]

## Shoshone

Located between twenty and thirty miles northeast of Gooding, the town of Shoshone has played an important role in the development of Idaho's Basque settlement. Near the turn of the century, Shoshone served as a major rail center, with four lines running down Rail Street. Basques coming from and going to the transcontinental rail artery in Ogden, Utah, enjoyed stopping in Shoshone, where they could find *ostatuak* named Beitia's, Soloaga's, Mendiola's, Ansola's, Urrutia's, Pagoaga's, Atiyeh's, or Berriochoa's, depending upon the years when they were traveling (table 8.4 contains specific dates and locations). Of particular interest are the boardinghouses owned and operated by the Mendiolas. When winter set in along the Sawtooth National Forest, they closed their boardinghouse there and moved south to Shoshone, where they enjoyed a thriving trade at their other *ostatu* during the winter and early spring months.[27]

## Mountain Home

Another Basque community existed about sixty miles east of Shoshone and fifty miles south of Boise. In the town of Mountain Home, in Elmore County, a comparatively well known Basque-owned tavern, *pilota* court, hotel, and restaurant was built by Jose Bengoechea in 1910.[28] The elegant three-story building was commonly called Bengoechea's for nearly three decades, but later it was identified with its official name, the Mountain Home Hotel.[29] Bengoechea entered the country in 1897 and got his start working in Elko County, Nevada, at Pedro Altube's Spanish Ranch.[30] Within two decades of arriving in the United States, Bengoechea became one of the largest sheep and cattle owners in northeast Nevada and southern Idaho. In that timespan he also became vice president of the Mountain Home Bank and constructed the town's best hotel. The building must have drawn commentary from locals because it loomed over not only the small Basque Hotel next door, but every other edifice in town. Jose claimed that he built his hotel so that out-of-town Basques would be welcome in Mountain Home, but the Mountain Home Hotel also attracted many non-Basques during its day and should not be considered a traditional *ostatu*.

### The Greater Boise Area

North and south of Boise in Canyon and Ada Counties a number of *ostatuak* appeared in the towns surrounding Idaho's capital city. In 1917, after selling their property at 607 Grove Street to the Uberuagas, Simon and Josefa Galdos moved north to Emmett, where they opened Charcha's boardinghouse on Commercial Street. About eight years later, in 1925, Eugenio and Delores Aguirre Bicandi opened Bicandi's Boarding House on Main Street in Emmett; it survived until 1957.[31]

In Nampa, Tomas and Tomasa Jausoro bought the Spanish Hotel on Twelfth Avenue from G. Uriquiaga in 1920, and Juan and Regina Bastida opened the Modern Hotel on Eleventh Avenue in 1936. The Jausoros and the Bastidas were in business for twenty-four and eleven years, respectively.[32]

## OREGON

### Jordan Valley

Just as the *ostatuak* of southern Idaho followed the development of Boise's Basque town, Treasure Valley Basque establishments encouraged the distribution of boardinghouses in southeastern Oregon and Washington.

As we mentioned earlier, Basques began settling in Jordan Valley, Oregon, as early as 1890, but their boardinghouses seem to have cropped up decades later. In February of 1914, Eulogio and Trinidad Arriola Madariaga left Boise's Star Hotel and moved to Jordan Valley, Oregon. After a few years, they added on to their home and converted it into a boardinghouse, which they operated until 1958. Although Madariaga's rooms are no longer for rent, the Old Basque Inn still greets travelers passing through Jordan Valley today.

Across the highway and about a city block from Madariaga's stood another Jordan Valley *ostatu* owned by Sotero and Eustaquia Marquina commonly called "the yellow house" or Marquina's, which remained open until 1945. Next to the "yellow house" stood a fronton, which was constructed by five early Jordan Valley Basques. Nearby there was also Am-

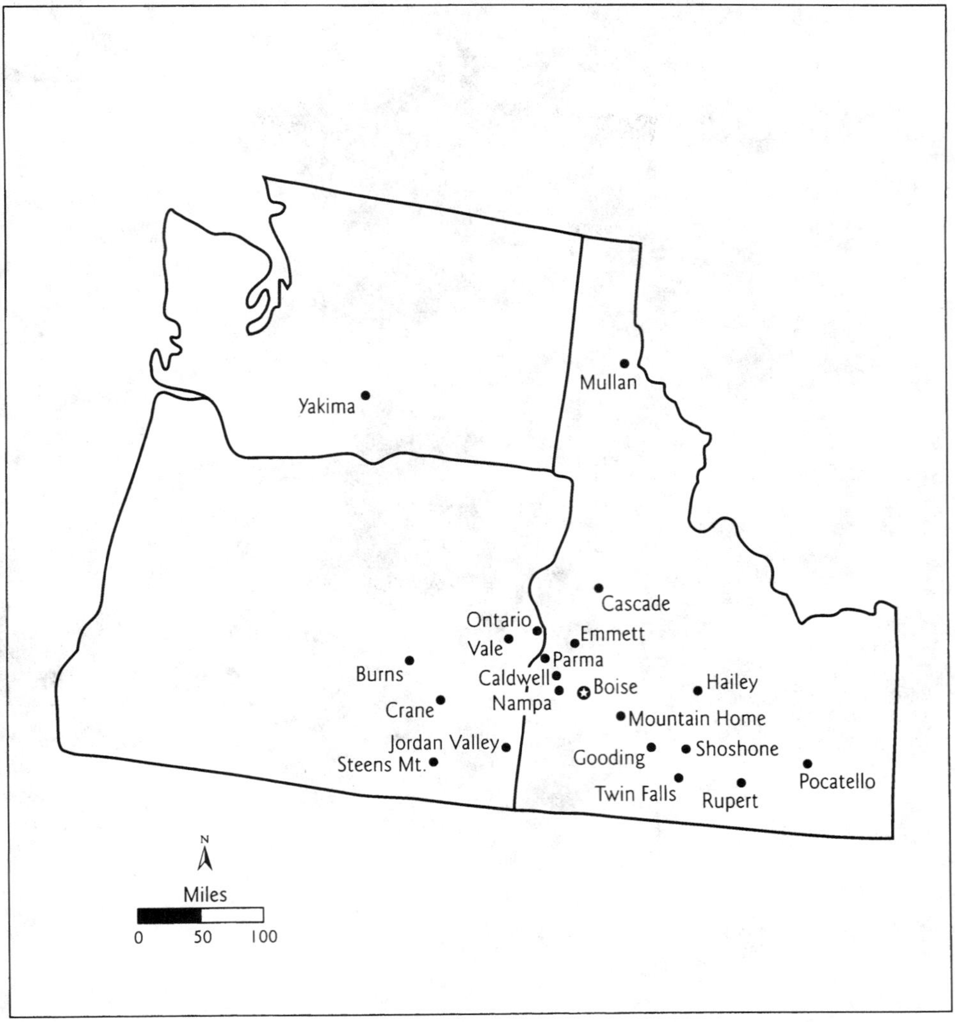


*Fig. 17. Communities with* ostatuak *in Idaho, Oregon, and Washington.*

brose's *ostatu* run by Ambrose and Maria Elorriaga.[33] Unfortunately, passing through town today, one can see only part of the nearly ruined fronton and the Old Basque Inn.

## Ontario

North of Jordan Valley near the Oregon-Idaho border, Lentxo's older brother Jack and his wife Maria opened Ontario's first boardinghouse in 1922. Before coming into town, Maria Echanis had cooked on the open

*A sign post in front of Madariaga's boardinghouse in Jordan Valley, Oregon, advertising meals and rooms, ca. 1930.* Left to right: *Jim Barlow, owners and operators Trinidad Madariaga and Eulugio Madariaga, and an unidentified boarder. Courtesy of the High Desert Museum, Bend, Oregon.*

range for the Echanis brothers, John Egurrola, and for the Andres Urquidi sheep outfit.[34] The original Echanis home on North Oregon Street burned down in 1929 and was replaced in 1930 by a large two-story wooden-frame house that could easily accommodate forty boarders. Although no other *ostatuak* seem to have appeared in Ontario besides the Echanises', in interviews Maria mentioned three small out-of-town boardinghouses south of Ontario. The first was located in Crane, Oregon, the second was near Steens Mountain and owned by the Arreguis, and the third was in Vale. According to Maria, the Crane boardinghouse appeared shortly after Malheur and Harney sheepmen began trailing their herds to the new railhead in Crane.

## Burns

In the town of Burns in northern Harney County, southwest of Ontario, the first Basque hotel, the Star Hotel, appeared in 1926.[35] It featured five bedrooms upstairs and three downstairs, and a bathroom on each floor. The owners, Felix and Cecilia Urizar, had previously owned a rooming house in the Andrews area of Harney County, but after losing it to a fire they decided to open a boardinghouse in Burns.[36] After operating the business for twenty years, the Urizars sold to Tomas Zabala, who in turn sold the Star to his brother Pedro and wife Elbira in 1958.

In 1929 Marcelino and Margarita Osa bought the Plaza Hotel in Burns, which they managed until 1945,[37] selling it to Joe and Paulina Lizundia, who in turn sold it to Lucy Garatea in 1949. Garatea managed the Plaza until 1965, when she sold it to Bernardo and Maite Andueza, who then sold it to Domingo Lete in 1968. By the early 1980s, both the Star and the Plaza had closed, as had the two Basque-owned rooming houses in Burns, the Ebar's and Larraneta's Commercial.[38]

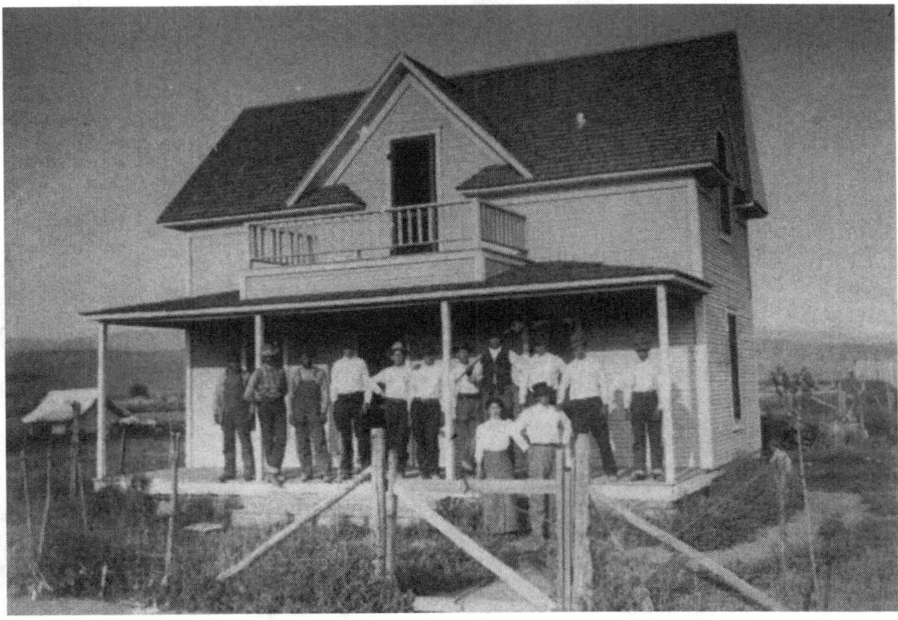

*The Madariaga boardinghouse in Jordan Valley, Oregon, ca. 1918. Pascual stands on the porch with a hoe on his shoulder. Courtesy of the High Desert Museum, Bend, Oregon.*

## WASHINGTON
### Yakima

One also finds *ostatuak* further north in Yakima, Washington. In 1912 Jose and Expectacion Elizalde and their children traveled north to Yakima from San Francisco by train.[39] Their daughter Elena remembers her father repeating, "No sheep or ranches for me" regularly while the family was en route to their new home. After they arrived, he proved that he meant what he said when he bought a two-story wooden-frame home on South Fourth Street and immediately opened it as a boardinghouse for local shepherds and ranch hands. Jose supplemented the family's income by operating the Independent Bakery from 1912 until 1916, when he died unexpectedly from an infection that began with a toothache. Expectacion and her children retained the boardinghouse for the next twenty-one years, and when Expectacion died in 1937, young Elena and her husband stepped in to operate the twenty-five-room house.

In the 1920s and 1930s, six large sheep and cattle outfits surrounded the town of Yakima. Sheepherders and cattlemen from the ranches came into town when they were off the range or during the winter season. During the peak decades there was a handful of additional *ostatuak* and rooming houses in Yakima, including Esain's, Maria and Francisco Alvarez's, Itçaina's, and Ramon Garay's. As in other locations, the small rooming houses and boardinghouses of Yakima competed with one another for business. Although the Arraldes lost some boarders because they would not allow hard liquor in their place during Prohibition, their regulars were satisfied with the Arraldes' homemade wine. Other Yakima residents reported that the lure of hard liquor enticed the Arraldes' boarders to other establishments during after-dinner hours.

At the heart of Idaho's Basque colony was the cluster of *ostatuak* that attracted Basques to downtown Boise in earlier years. In addition, much like the earlier Basque towns of Los Angeles and San Francisco, Boise emerged as a social and ethnic center for the greater American Basque community. Similarly, it generated "spin off" hotels—Boise *hoteleros* relocated in Shoshone, Cascade, or Hailey. This Basque town and Stockton's (discussed in the next chapter) had peaked by World War II, and their Basque populations began declining in number dramatically soon thereafter.

# 9

# Stockton's Basque Town & Northern California *Ostatuak*

## THE BASQUE TOWN AND *Ostatuak* OF STOCKTON

Of all the towns in the American West that contained *ostatuak*, only one other twentieth-century town seems to compare with Boise in terms of the level and degree of Basque activity. Stockton's location and particularly close relationship to the San Francisco and Reno Basque communities explain why the Basque colony there grew so rapidly and was home to so many *ostatuak* in the earlier part of this century.

By 1881 the city of Stockton had become an ideal terminus for regional transportation and shipping. Situated at the head of the Stockton Diverting Canal, just two miles from the Sacramento River, Stockton was connected with San Francisco via a ninety-one-mile route on the Central Pacific Railroad.[1] In 1871 the Stockton Woolen Mills had been erected on the south bank of Mormon Channel. There about 200,000 pounds of wool went into producing blankets and wool flannels on an annual basis.[2] Area wool production undoubtedly encouraged Basque migration to Stockton in the late nineteenth century, since Basques would have reason to trail their sheep in the surrounding areas.

Between 1880 and 1905, the population of the small agricultural town nearly tripled from 12,000 to 30,000.[3] Judging from the city's census records, much of this influx consisted of immigrants, and the largest increase in Basques immigrating to Stockton occurred during this period. County and city directories for the 1880s list only a small number of Basque surnames, but by the first decade of 1900 there is evidence of the presence of a sizeable contingent of Basques. Nonetheless, it was not until 1905 that the first Basque hotel appeared in Stockton.

Evidence indicates that the Basque Hotel at 203 East Hazelton was Stockton's first *ostatu*. Raymond Narbaitz and his brother-in-law Jean Ospital, the original owners, opened the hotel in 1907.[4] In the following year Ospital sold his share to Joe Oyarbide and opened Ospital's Basque Hotel at 548 South Hunter. Oyarbide and Narbaitz remained partners at the original Basque until 1916, when they sold to Peter Mantaberry, who in turn sold to Victor Badaya the following year. Throughout these years Narbaitz also ran between three thousand and seven thousand head of sheep in Fresno, Merced, and San Joaquin Counties and was considered one of the valley's finest sheepmen.[5] As we have seen elsewhere, the tie between hotel keeping and sheepherding was very close, and several Stockton Basques worked in both businesses simultaneously.

A third early hotel was opened on Hunter Street by the popular Basque Pierre Recault between late 1907 and early 1908. Although Recault named his *ostatu* the Hotel de France, locals sometimes referred to it as "the Camino" because Pierre's brother-in-law (named Camino) was a well-liked jokester who entertained the guests with his witticisms, practical jokes, and pranks. Elena Celayeta Talbott recalled that one evening Camino performed a one-man vaudeville act that brought the house down.[6]

Between 1912 and 1970 at least fifteen Basque hotels opened after these three early Stockton *ostatuak*. In several instances hotels and boardinghouses changed owners and names but remained in the same buildings. For example, 325 South Hunter appears to have been a popular location for *ostatuak*, as it was occupied by Recault's Hotel de France, Olano and Legarra's Hotel La Bilbaina, Aldamos and Edoyaga's Hotel Basco, and, finally, Domenech's Hotel España. As we can see by comparing table 9.1 to the tables in chapter 8, turnover in *ostatuak* occurred more frequently in Stockton than in Boise.

Because Stockton's Basque neighborhood sprang up after *California'ko Eskual Herria* (in Los Angeles) had ceased publication, local hotel owners did not have a statewide Basque newspaper in which they could advertise. But they found other publications in which to advertise. Local competition among hotelkeepers was keen, and between 1908 and 1910 there were three or four hotels competing for the same clientele. In fact, an English-language publication dated 1908 contained two business-card-size advertisements for Basque *ostatuak*. One promoting Narbaitz's Hotel Royal stated the hotel name, address, and telephone number, and below "*Eskualdun Bilkura. Establia Eta Pilota Plaza*" ("Where Basques Gather. Stable and Handball Court").[7] In another advertisement, although the establishment was named the Hotel de France, the message appealed to both Spanish and French Basques, described the hotel's location, and then boasted, using three languages, "*Hescualdun Etchea, Pension Francaise I Espanola, Pilota Plaza Eta Cabellerisa*" ("Basque House, French and Spanish hotel. Handball Court and Horse Stable").[8]

Like Los Angeles, San Francisco, Bakersfield, and Fresno, Stockton had a Basque town of its own by 1915. The neighborhood was located on San Joaquin and Hunter Streets between Main and Hazelton. On the southern edge of Stockton's Basque town was the Mormon Slough, and across the trench, the Santa Fe Depot. The northern border of the neighborhood was formed by Main Street and Stockton's early Japanese and Chinese neighborhoods.

According to Stockton Euskaldunak, the local Basque community was aware of each hotel and the clientele who frequented it. For instance, a Spanish or "Bizkaino" hotel might be less preferable to a French Basque whose friends regularly frequented another hotel. In a study of the Basques of Stockton, Carol Pagliarulo interviewed a Basque woman who reported visiting her favorite Basque hotel: "I can remember, when I was young, going every Tuesday and Sunday night to the Basque Hotel. The entire family would go, dance, eat, and have a good time."[9] When asked why they went to that hotel, she responded, "That's where we always went. It's where 'our crowd' went and there was always something happening there."[10] Her comments, backed up by other Basques who were interviewed for the same study, underscore that Stockton's Basques were aware of who frequented which hotel.

By 1917 there were four well-established *ostatuak* in Stockton. An article in the Stockton *Record* in that year featured the local Basque colony, its hotels, and handball courts. Among *hoteleros* and their customers it was considered advantageous for a hotel to have a handball court. If the court was sufficiently large, players could strap on their wicker jai alai *xistera* and play full-court jai alai. The *Record* article featured Jean Ospital's Basque Hotel, Pierrre Mentaberry's Hotel Royal, Pierre Recault's Hotel Basco, and Fermín Alustiza's Hotel Central. A handball court adjoined each hotel, and, according to one resident, the Basque Hotel was the only establishment with a court long enough to accommodate jai alai.[11] That all four *ostatuak* had adjacent courts seems unusual, since in other Basque

Table 9.1 Stockton's Basque Hotels, 1907–1970

| Date(s) | Operator | Location | Name |
|---|---|---|---|
| 1907 | John Ospital and Raymond Narbaitz | 203 East Hazelton | Basque Hotel |
| (1908–1911) | John Ospital | | |
| 1912 | Fermín Aluztiza | | |
| (1913–1924) | John Ospital | 548 South Hunter | Basque Hotel |
| (1925) | Elroy Perez | | |
| 1908–1916 | Raymond Narbaitz and Joe Oyarbide | 341 South Hunter | Hotel Royal |
| (1917) | Peter Mentaberry | | |
| (1918–1919) | Victor Badaya | | |
| 1907–1909 | Pierre Recault | 325 South Hunter | Hotel de France |
| 1909–1910 | Miguel Olano and Severiano Legarra | 325 South Hunter | Hotel La Bilbaina |
| (1911) | Miguel Olano | | |
| 1912 | Nicolás Aldamos and Marcos Edoyaga | 325 South Hunter | Hotel Basco |
| (1913–1915) | Marcos Edoyaga | | |
| (1915–1916) | Pierre Recault | | |
| 1916–1924 | Severiano Legarra | 303 South Hunter | Hotel Español |
| (1924–1925) | Mrs. Eulalia Legarra | | |
| 1916–1917 | Victor Badaya | 122 West Main | Hotel Central |
| (1917–1919) | Fermín Alustiza | | |
| (1920) | Victor Badaya and Nicolas Ylarraz | | |
| (1924) | Bernardo Yoldi | | |
| (1925) | Victor Badaya | | |
| (1931) | Frank and Richard Artozqui | | |
| (1933–1937) | Frank Artozqui | | |
| (1938–1941) | Manual Artozqui | | |
| (1942–1943) | Mrs. Irene Artozqui | | |
| (1945–1946) | Julia Beamish | | |
| (1947–1948) | Mrs. I. F. Artozqui | | |
| (1949–1958) | M. A. Artozqui | | |
| (1960) | Mrs. Irene Artozqui | | |
| 1917 | Saturnino Domench | 325 South Hunter | Hotel España |

communities only one half or two thirds of the *ostatuak* might have their own handball courts. The higher percentage of frontons at Stockton *ostatuak* might reflect the degree of competition among hotelkeepers there, or it might be an indication of the size of Stockton's Basque community.

Another Basque who lived in Stockton in the late 1920s noted that "two of the Basque hotels in town dispensed with [their] boardinghouse services and served the general public with Basque and Italian dinners. They also opened the bars."[12]

Table 9.1 *Continued*

| Date(s) | Operator | Location | Name |
|---|---|---|---|
| 1921–1924 | Joseph Solaequi | 401 South Hunter | Estrella Hotel |
| (1925–1926) | Tomás and Florentino Uriarte | | |
| (1931) | Tomás and Florentino Uriarte | | |
| 1924–1952 | Fermín Alustiza | 403 South San Joaquin | California Hotel |
| (1953) | Alfonso and Fermín Alustiza | | |
| (1955–1956) | Fermín Alustiza | | |
| (1958–1969) | Alfonso Alustiza | | |
| 1924 | Peter Baigorri | 310 South Hunter | Royal Hotel |
| (1925) | John Errecart | | |
| (1952–1956) | Clifford T. Ito | | |
| (1958) | Mrs. Francisca Contrera | | |
| (1960) | Herbert Yuerra | | |
| 1935 | John Idiart | 343 South San Joaquin | Hotel Basque |
| (1936–1937) | W. P. Aluiso | | |
| (1938) | Teresa Idiart | | |
| (1939–1941) | John Idiart | | |
| (1942–1943) | Paul Etcheberry | | |
| (1945–1946) | G. A. Russell | | |
| 1935 | Mrs. Dominica Predagne | 335 South San Joaquin | Pyrenees Hotel |
| (1940) | Mrs. Louise Olson | | |
| 1935 | Dominic Olcomendy | 243 South Hunter | French Hotel |
| (1940) | Ellen Lamar and Jean Marlow | | |
| 1936 | Michael Coron | 39–43 South Hunter | La Coste |
| (1937–1946) | Etienne La Coste | | |
| (1949–1950) | Peter Iturria and Joaquin Erro | | |
| (1955) | Mrs. Damasa Erro | | |
| 1949–1958 | Benjamin and Teresa Mariones | 325 South Hunter | Woolgrowers' Hotel |
| (1959–1971) | John and Pete Ospital | | |
| 1949–1952 | Mrs. Jesse Gainza | 343 South San Joaquin | Basconia Hotel |
| (1953–1955) | John Gainza | | |

In a history of Stockton prepared under the auspices of the Works Progress Administration (WPA) in 1938, only two Basque town hotels were mentioned. At that time, however, there were a total of forty-six hotels throughout Stockton, and Basque town had five *ostatuak*. The two mentioned by the WPA seem to have been selected because of their size. Fermín Alustiza's California Hotel had forty-two rooms, charged fifty cents per day and up for room and board, and offered garage rates.[13] Across San Joaquin Street and one block away, the Idiarts' Hotel Basque

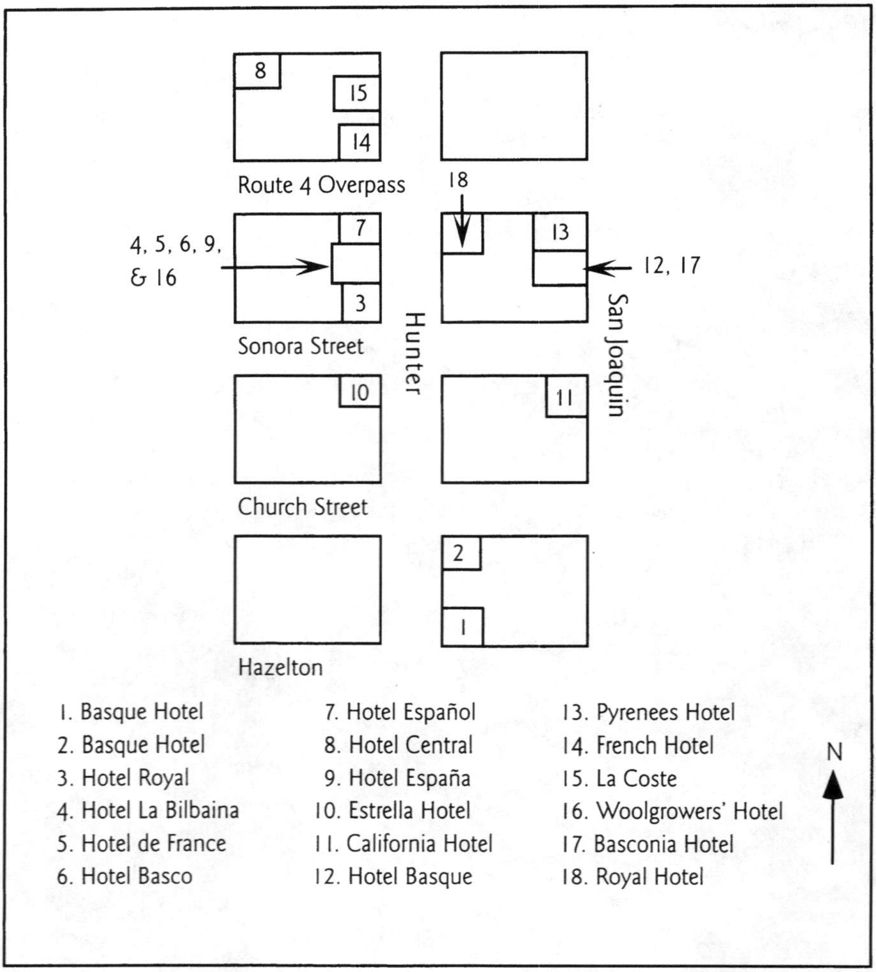


*Fig. 18. Stockton's Basque town. The dates of operation for these eighteen* ostatuak *are listed on page 197.*

had sixty-six rooms. It charged the same daily rate as the California Hotel but also offered weekly rates of $2.50.[14] These two three-story hotels were exceptionally large compared with Basque hotels in other locations. The three *ostatuak* not mentioned in the 1938 publication were the La Coste, the French Hotel, and the Pyrenees Hotel; they were probably dismissed as boardinghouses.[15]

As we can see in the chronological listing below of the life span of Stockton Basque hotels, only three Stockton *ostatuak* were in business for more than twenty years, and just one lasted between fifteen and twenty years. The Artozquis at the Hotel Central and the Alustizas at the California Hotel were at their hotels for thirty and forty-five years, respectively. Much more frequent in Stockton, however, were shorter terms in hotel keeping. In fact, by dividing the number of distinct family proprietors by the number of years all Stockton *ostatuak* were in operation we get an average tenure of four years.

During the first ten years that *ostatuak* were present in Stockton—1907–1917—eight Basque hotels opened. In the subsequent decade, four new boardinghouses were launched, and eight of the combined total closed. Between 1927 and 1937 four new Stockton *ostatuak* opened, including John Idiart's Hotel Basque, Dominica Predagne's Pyrenees Hotel, Dominic Olamendy's French Hotel, and Michael Coron's La Coste. The total number of *ostatuak* in 1937 was five. From 1937 through 1947, the third decade in Stockton's Basque hotel-keeping history, no new *ostatuak* were introduced. But between 1949 and 1952, the last three hotels to come into existence in Stockton's Basque town were opened. Clearly, then, the peak years of Stockton *ostatuak* occurred between 1915 and 1935 as follows:

| *Hotel* | *Years in Operation*[16] |
|---|---|
| Basque Hotel | 1907–1911 |
| Basque Hotel | 1912–1925 |
| Hotel Royal | 1908–1919 |
| Hotel La Bilbaina | 1909–1911 |
| Hotel de France | 1907–1909 |
| Hotel Basco | 1912–1916 |
| Hotel Español | 1916–1925 |
| Hotel Central | 1916–1960 |
| Hotel España | 1917–1918 |
| Estrella Hotel | 1921–1931 |
| California Hotel | 1924–1969 |
| Hotel Basque | 1935–1946 |
| Pyrenees Hotel | 1935–1940 |
| French Hotel | 1935–1940 |
| La Coste | 1936–1955 |
| Woolgrowers' Hotel | 1949–1971 |
| Basconia Hotel | 1949–1955 |
| Royal Hotel | 1924–1960 |

By the 1940s and 1950s, Basque hotel owners in Basque town were focusing on their restaurants, catering to a non-Basque dinner trade, and deemphasizing their hotel business. Since the late 1940s, four of the seven Basque restaurants in Stockton have been located in former Basque hotels. Among them was Alustiza's, which opened the year after Fermín Alustiza closed the California Hotel on San Joaquin. Over thirty years earlier, in 1924, Fermín had purchased a building at 403 South San Joaquin and named it the California Hotel. In 1953 Fermín took on his son Alfonso as his partner. For a few years father and son ran the hotel and Alustiza's Restaurant. Not long after Fermín's death in 1958 Alfonso sold the business. There was also the Artozquis' place in the Hotel Central building. For the last five years that the Hotel Central was in business, the Artozquis operated only a tavern and restaurant on the premises. Likewise, the proprietors at La Coste and the Woolgrowers attempted to increase their business by opening their boardinghouse restaurants to the general public in their last few years of operation.

| *Restaurant* | *Year(s) in Operation* |
|---|---|
| La Coste Inn<br>(41 South Hunter) | 1949–1955 |
| Jessie's Place<br>(347 South San Joaquin) | 1952–1955 |
| Sofi's Place<br>(27 South Hunter) | 1955–1965 |
| Hotel Central<br>(124 West Main) | 1955–1960 |
| Woolgrowers' Inn<br>(325 South Hunter) | 1955–1971 |
| Alustiza's<br>(403 South San Joaquin) | 1970–1982 |
| Ospital's Villa Basque<br>(448 South Hunter) | 1972–present |

In 1948 Carol Pagliarulo conducted a study of 219 Euskaldunak, including eighty-seven family groups, all of whom lived within Stockton city limits.[17] The purpose of the study was to ascertain the degree to which Stockton Basques had assimilated by 1948. Pagliarulo reported that 58 percent of Stockton's Basque population at that time had been born in America, and most of the second-generation Basques were living in urban areas, as opposed to the earlier generations, who tended to live in rural settings. Pagliarulo also reported a change in the nature and function of the city's Basque hotels. As she stated, "They are no longer exclusively Basque boarding houses; they now cater to other guests; serve the general public food, and have added public bars."[18]

Another Stockton Basque stated it another way: "Oh yes, we always went to these gatherings [at the hotels]. But as our children grew older, they would stay a few moments, and then go off with their American friends."[19]

The last and most recent Basque establishment in Stockton's Basque town to close was Ospital's Villa Basque restaurant. Located at the corner of Hunter and Church Streets, it stood in what was once the heart of one of the busiest Basque communities in California's history, that is, until 1993. On the northern edge of the neighborhood, the new Highway 4 overpass bisects Hunter and San Joaquin Streets. Nearby, the old La Coste and Central Hotels and Saint Mary's Catholic Church, where so many early Basques were baptized, married, and worshipped, are now part of Stockton's Chinatown. South of the highway, closer to where Ospital's Villa Basque restaurant was located, a few of the old hotel buildings have been destroyed and replaced with a market and a parking lot, and the street has been widened. Since Ospital's closed, the only way to bring Stockton's *ostatuak* back to life is by talking with the elderly Basques of Stockton, or by taking a walk with them through the "old neighborhood."

## NORTHERN CALIFORNIA *Ostatuak*

Additional Basque boardinghouses emerged in California between 1890 and 1930.[20] Just as Basque colonies developed in southern California around Los Angeles, several enclaves developed in northeastern and north central California during this period. Marie Pierre Arrizabalaga pointed out in her study that the county of Alameda, just east of San Francisco, was home to the third largest California Basque colony in 1910.[21] By comparison with Basques in other counties, Basques in Alameda did not primarily raise sheep, cattle, or farm. Atypically, about one out of every three Basques in the county was involved in the laundry industry.[22] Although evidence of Basque hotels and boardinghouses in Alameda is lacking, a few probably existed. Further south, in San Jose, there is a record of a Basque hotel in the late nineteenth century: Madame D.

*Urbano, Albert, Mary, and Elvida Pedroarena in front of their recently opened Buena Vista Hotel in Alturas, California. Courtesy of the High Desert Museum, Bend, Oregon.*

A. Bayle's New Lake House ran an advertisement in *California'ko Eskual Herria* claiming that the house was an "*Ostatu Eskualduna.*"[23]

## Susanville, Alturas, and Cedarville

Far to the north and east, the small lumber towns of Susanville and Alturas also developed Basque populations. Most Basques in that area found work in the sawmills and lumber camps. Bartolo Goni and his family, for example, ran a fourteen-room boardinghouse, which they called the Pyrenees, near the Pickering Lumber Company.[24] The sawmill in Alturas employed numerous Basques, hired the Gonis to operate the *ostatu*, and encouraged the mill's Basque employees to live at the Pyrenees.[25] In 1923 Urbano Pedroarena and his bride Marie Barnetche met and married at the Overland Basque Hotel in Gardnerville and then moved to Alturas. There the skilled blacksmith and his wife opened the Arena Blacksmith Shop and Boardinghouse. The *ostatu* did not survive beyond the 1950s, but the couple's son Albert also became a blacksmith and still runs his father's shop today.[26]

Directly south, in Susanville, another lumber town, John and Marie Beterbide ran a boardinghouse at the old Lassen Mill from 1930 to 1942.[27] Because most of the Beterbides' boarders were mill workers, dinners at the boardinghouse were served after the plant's second shift closed down around nine in the evening. Marie tended to cooking, cleaning, and raising the children; while John Beterbide worked a twelve-hour shift at the mill and then returned home to help with chores at the boardinghouse.

Not far away, in downtown Susanville, Jane Goñi purchased the thirty-six-room St. Francis Hotel. Before coming to Susanville in 1947, Goñi had managed hotels in Reno and Wellington, Nevada.[28] The St. Francis Hotel was constructed by non-Basques and was not designed to cater exclusively to Basques. But the hotel and downstairs restaurant served as a gathering place for local Basques in the 1950s and still draws several Amerikanuak today.

Across the Warner Mountains to the east, the small town of Cedarville, California, also had an *ostatu* for Basque men working in the local mills and in the area's forests. Owned and operated by Valentin and Victoria Juarena, Valentin's at one time boasted a large *pilota* court and was part of a circuit of courts that hosted tournaments for players from Susanville, Alturas, Maxwell, Fort Bidwell, Oroville, and Marysville.[29]

## Oroville

Another California community that witnessed the influx of Basque herders during the first decades of the twentieth century was Oroville, California, just west of the Sierra Nevada. During the 1920s Martina Estea's Hotel was a popular stop for sheepmen returning from summer grazing in the Sierra Nevadas. Estea's catered mainly to nomadic herders and a few local lumbermen.

## Marysville

Nearly equidistant between Oroville and Sacramento, Marysville is also located at the foot of the Sierra Nevadas. For decades, sheepmen wintered their bands in Marysville because of the mild weather and the good land in the Sacramento Basin. Between 1910 and 1915 there were six Basque *ostatuak* in Marysville's Basque neighborhood near the intersection of A and Fourth Streets. Two were owned by French Basques Ferdinand Tehesta (Tehesta's) and John Belza (Belza's); one was owned by a Navarrese, Fabio Ugarte (the Bark Hotel); and three were owned by Bizkaians, Luthio Agulia, Sabino Uriz, and the Mendiola family.[30] There were also three or four rooming houses in the vicinity wherein Basque families provided rooms for rent without meals. One of the favorite activities in the neighborhood was competing in and gambling on the regular *pilota* tourneys at Tehesta's. In 1922, when Tehesta's Hotel and handball court burned to the ground, the *pilota* action moved to the old Belza Hotel whose management had just been taken over by the Uriz family; the Urizes had just finished building a larger court of their own.

In 1932 the Marysville Basque colony's population peaked at about three hundred, and the Basques who had primarily resided in a four-square-block area in the center of town began moving to other locations. One of the more recent hotels in Marysville, the Estrella, was owned and operated by Helen Mendiola for years.[31] But today there are no more than seventy Basques living in the area, and the old Uriz, standing directly across from the former train depot without its once popular fronton, serves as a reminder of the town's short-lived early Basque colony.

## Sacramento

In comparison to the cities and towns of the San Joaquin Valley, the states capital was home to only two Basque hotels in the 1920s and 1930s. Mostly likely rapid urbanization drove Basques to outlying areas.[32]

In Sacramento, an hour's drive southwest of Marysville, an *ostatu* named the Español opened at 114 J Street in 1923. The Español was especially dear to Basque ranch hands working with large outfits in and around the state capital. Although its peak years were 1923 through 1932, the Español continued as a boardinghouse until 1952, when it moved into the Commercial Hotel on Third and I Streets; it was later purchased by the Luigi family.[33] Longtime residents report that when the Español's rooms overflowed in the old days, nearby Basque-operated rooming houses took in boarders as well. Occasionally elderly Basques have mentioned a Basque hotel named the España, but it is unclear whether they were referring to the Español or a second boardinghouse in the downtown area.

Basque restaurants, ranches, and surnames appeared in the Walnut Creek area, in Dixon, and in Oakland, and a small Basque restaurant in Maxwell, thirty minutes north of Sacramento, has flourished. So whereas there is a Basque presence in the foothills between San Francisco and Sacramento, no evidence of Basque hotels has been found in these towns. Similarly, Sacramento Valley sheepmen trailed sheep throughout the Monterey Peninsula, but they seem to have been temporary visitors.[34] Most likely area Basques preferred traveling to the already established hotels in San Francisco and Stockton.

Stockton, with its clusters of *ostatuak,* was a social and ethnic center for the greather American Basque community. Hotelkeepers moved out from Stockton to create hotels in Modesto, Merced, and Sacramento. But the *ostatuak* of Stockton had peaked by World War II.

The *ostatuak* of Stockton and those of the other Basque districts we have explored are part of a broad panorama of boardinghouses spread throughout the eleven Western states. Many of these boardinghouses have differed in size, shape, prosperity, and staying power. An important aspect that they have shared, however, has yet to be discussed. The critical role of the *ostatuak* within the greater Basque community, their importance to the Basques who called them home and how they functioned is the subject of chapter 10.

# 10

## Inside the *Ostatu Euskalduna*

### A HOME AWAY FROM HOME

As has been suggested earlier, the *ostatuak* of the American West reached their zenith in influence and breadth in the forty years between 1890 and 1930. During these years and since, the ebb and flow of Basque hotel businesses have been linked with the expansions and contractions of the sheep industry in the American West. For the single Basque sheepman who came to earn his fortune and then return to the Basque homeland, the *ostatu* became a "home away from home." In the absence of an extended family in the New World, the *ostatu* became the major social institution of this immigrant group.

As a second home, the hotel was likely to offer a number of amenities for the newcomer to the United States. Many of the Basques who entered the United States via New York, for example, went directly to Valentin Aguirre's hotel, where the hotelkeeper and his family assisted them with their travel plans, briefed them on the "ways of the New World," and sent them on their way properly labeled with nametags, instructions written in English for train conductors, and names of people to look up along the way and to contact at their future destinations.[1]

When the traveler arrived at his final train depot—say Boise, Shoshone,

Winnemucca, Los Angeles, Ontario, or Yakima—he was often greeted by a local Basque sent to meet him at the station. If not, as may have happened in Bakersfield, Reno, Elko, Ogden, and Fresno, in most instances he had only to look across the street to find the Basque hotel that had been recommended to him. In fact, the percentage of Basque boardinghouses located within one or two blocks of a train depot in the American West is impressive. Of the over three hundred hotel sites that I have studied, only five were beyond the train conductor's whistle.

Once inside the *ostatu*, the newcomer would find that his native language was spoken, and that familiar food and drink were served. The Basque boardinghouse felt familiar to the boarders because there they could live with customs not too different from what they had grown up with in the *baserri* and the town. The practice of gathering at the American *ostatuak* before lunch was no doubt similar to the Old World custom of frequenting the local tavern in the town's plaza before lunch. In both European and American settings, locals congregated to exchange the most recent news and gossip or to discuss a wide variety of topics. Although this pre-luncheon ritual is not exclusive to Basques, its presence in both the New and Old Worlds suggests a modest parallel between the gathering places of the two settings. In the Old World village, the local tavern, or *taberna*, was the place for Basques to gather. In the *ostatu* of the New World the Basque American encountered a larger facility in which he could get room and board if he needed to, and he could eat, play handball, dance, or play cards. Thus it could be suggested that the hotels became the American extension of the Basque *taberna*.

The hotelkeeper was likely willing to help the newcomer make his transition from Old World to New as smooth as possible. Many hotelkeepers provided a number of services. In some instances, *hoteleros* arranged employment for herders and then sent for them in the Old Country. If a Basque did not have a job upon arrival, a *hotelero* was likely to set out in search of work for him in the community, on a neighboring ranch, or with a sheep outfit in the area. In the meantime, many a hotelkeeper would extend liberal credit and room and board in exchange for the newcomer's future business and eventual repayment. In his later years an elderly or retired Basque herder might also be given light jobs around the *ostatu* to earn his keep.

Throughout we have seen the Basque boardinghouse referred to as a "home away from home" for Basque bachelors. We might readily accept this notion, but do we really understand how much it meant to immigrants to find a second home in a strange land, when in most cases they could not speak English and thus could not make a request of English-speaking people without going through an embarrassing series of pantomimed antics? Because the young Basque immigrants had no extended and immediate family to rely upon, it is understandable that so many of the Basques called their favored *hoteleros* either *etxeko ama* or *etxeko aita*.[2] When asked why they considered the boardinghouses their second homes, boarders most likely gave the following reasons:

Basque language
Basque cooking
Basque games
Basque music and dance
Help finding work
Short-term loans and/or credit
Advisers/*etxeko amak, etxeko aitak*
Place to find a mate
Place to find other Basques
Help with translations
Help with travel to other towns
Storage place
Place to receive mail
Place in town to deliver children
Place to recuperate from injury or illness
Place in town to board children
Place to celebrate family's special occasions

The sheepherders' stay at the *ostatuak* often was seasonal because of the seasonal nature of the sheep industry. In the summer, when the herders were on the high mountain ranges of the Sierra Nevada, for example, they might individually tend up to one thousand ewes and lambs, so they would not have much need for lodgings, but in the fall, when the lambs were sold and the remaining ewes were grouped into winter bands, about half the herders would be released until the next lambing season. Many would come into town, rent a room in a Basque hotel, and begin looking for additional work to tide them over until spring. If a herder was injured or fell ill on the job and needed medical care, his boss was likely to send him to the nearest Basque hotel to recuperate. Upon retirement, many elderly herders without families made the hotels their home.

*Interior hallway and a room at the Star Hotel, Elko Nevada. Courtesy of the University of Utah Basque Boarding House Project.*

Whether they were on the range or in the hotels, herders used the *ostatu* as their permanent mailing address and as a storage facility for their Sunday suit and extra gear. Many a hotel set a room aside for storing bedrolls, suits, camp gear, dated mail, and personal papers. In Noriega's upstairs corner room and in Uberuaga's upstairs hall closet, for example, rows of moth-eaten Sunday suits awaited their owners' return for up to four decades. While renovating Elko's Overland Hotel in the late 1930s, for example, one hotel operator brought in two bank officials to oversee a "safe cracking." Upon opening the vault, the group discovered a series of locked compartments containing decades-old personal papers, long-forgotten documents, cash, and jewelry.[3] In good faith, the previous owners had guarded their vaults carefully.

An account of Basque hotel keeping collected in Nevada by Gretchen Holbert-Osa suggests that Basque men and women viewed life in the *ostatuak* differently. As Holbert-Osa has pointed out, some sheepherders clung to the independence afforded them by life on the open range:

> The hotels, however, were a mixed blessing to the independent herder. This woman-tended haven was both solace and confinement to him, fellowship blended with the loss of absolute freedom. Like

*Basque herders and sheepmen dancing the* jota *to music from the jukebox. Courtesy of the High Desert Museum, Bend, Oregon.*

*Christmas eve dinner for Basque herders at the Buena Vista Hotel, Alturas, California, 1947.*

the sailor come home to a landlocked village, the herder entered the hotel conditionally, determined to leave. The hotels would be there, red-bricked sentinels of a new order, awaiting his return.[4]

## HOUSE RULES

Throughout the American West, hotelkeepers and their boarders generally policed their own hotels. As we will see later in the chapter in the story of what happened when a boarder brought a prostitute into his room, hotel residents were aware of whether others were violating house rules. Even so, challenges to house dictates were likely to create a confrontation among customers and boarders. At some point, for example, a loud or obnoxious drunk stretching the local sense of propriety was likely to be physically ejected from the bar by the hotel residents.

Internal policing was sometimes less effective when it came to hotelkeepers collecting payment from customers, however. *Hoteleros* reported that getting itinerant herders to pay what they owed was occasionally a problem. When a Basque herder requested room and board, he was assigned a room number and asked how long he intended to stay. During "signing in" it was rare for the boarder to put down money. Usually *hoteleros* kept some form of a tally, but only seldom did they maintain a formal register. The understanding was that the customer would pay upon departure, or if his stay was to exceed seven days, he would pay at the end of the week or at some other prearranged time.

Hotelkeepers knew that during "hard times" they might absorb some losses until herders or sheepmen earned enough to pay their debts. But it was probable that they would collect back payment if the customer was known, according to the *hoteleros*, although itinerant herders occasionally used hotel facilities, ran up a tab, and left town before paying. One recourse for the hotelkeeper was to embarrass the delinquent herder by telling others that "this one did not pay his bills." If it was a hardship case, *hoteleros* might absorb the loss quietly in hope of future payment, or they might ask the boarder to work on the premises to earn his keep.

If a herder who stayed at the hotel left without paying, apologizing, or making some arrangement to pay in the future, he was likely to face the threat of ostracism from the community in the future. All the *hoteleros* I interviewed reported a few "bad deals" and failures to collect. Generally speaking, this problem was viewed as a part of doing business. Notably, although retired hotelkeepers remembered who had failed to pay their bills, they were hesitant to reveal the names of those people. Basques pride themselves on being honest, straightforward people, so it is difficult for *hoteleros* to admit that there are a few exceptions to this generalization.

## INSIDERS AND OUTSIDERS

For the unsuspecting non-Basque in the past, a visit to a Basque hotel might have brought the reward of good food, conviviality, and ethnicity. To the Basque who made the hotel his home, however, the non-Basque visitor—the outsider—might have been a target for speculation and discussion. Indeed, as one "outsider" who studied such behavior at Basque establishments has suggested, Basques working and residing in the *ostatuak* displayed "front" and "back" behavior.[5] Douglas Hale, the author of that study, observed the differences when non-Basque visitors and Basque immigrants entered a boardinghouse, and he recorded what happened. When non-Basque visitors arrived a few minutes before noon to eat lunch at the hotel, they waited in the barroom until lunchtime seating was announced. When they entered, Basques at the bar stopped speaking and turned to see who had just arrived. After a moment, they returned to their conversation in Euskara, Spanish, French, or English and often asked, "Who is that?" or jokingly, "What is that?"

Were a non-Basque able to engage a Basque in conversation at the bar or during lunch, he might have been treated to stories of the Old Country, herding, or the "mysterious" Basque character. Such an exchange would have been an example of "front" behavior, where an "outsider" was allowed to penetrate a bit of the façade of Amerikanuak culture as encountered in the hotels.

If, at the other extreme, a newcomer had just arrived from Gernika and was in pursuit of promised employment on a local ranch and could speak Basque fluently, he would be welcomed into what has been called "back" or "insider's" behavior. Hale reported several instances of ready acceptance, a welcoming acceptance, and sharing of information, all traits, he concluded, that constitute "back" behavior.

The few non-Basque hotelkeepers I interviewed in the course of preparing this work had had plenty of experiences with "front" and "back" behavior among Basques and other *hoteleros*. In two instances, not being fully accepted by their Basque customers made them uncomfortable and jeopardized business. In one case, an embittered Irish-American hotelkeeper felt forced to pursue non-Basque customers owing to the local Basques' cool reception. She managed to do so with moderate success until recent years when she was forced to close her boardinghouse.

Yet Basques living in and operating the *ostatuak* have had close alliances with neighboring ethnic groups that visited the hotels occasionally. In Tehachapi, for example, the positive and close relationship between the local Bearnais French and the area Basques has been documented.[6] For instance, early hotel operator Jean Martinto organized handball competitions between the two groups at his Basses-Pyrenees Hotel, and afterward he hosted large picnics for all attendees.[7] Three decades later, in nearby Bakersfield, French, Italians, and Basques regularly attended Saturday night dances at the Basque Café and the Amestoy Hotel.[8] Numerous marriages between Basques and Italians in Bakersfield and San Francisco also testify to the close relationship between these two groups.[9]

Fresno's *hoteleros* likewise reported having a good relationship with the Mexican-American farm laborers who have frequented their bars and restaurants. Many Basque herders learned Spanish for the first time listening to Mexican radio broadcasts on their transistor radios at night in their sheep camps.

The people I interviewed rarely complained about other ethnic groups, but the *hoteleros* in California did take measures to avoid problems before they might occur; by renting rooms exclusively to Basques they diminished potential problems in dealing with "outsiders." A non-Basque asking to rent a room heard a politely stated, "I'm sorry, there are no rooms." In order to separate out non-Basques, the *hotelero* took into consideration the newcomer's language, birthplace, looks, and state of cleanliness. On the other hand, hotelkeepers in Jordan Valley and Burns, Oregon; Boise; and Winnemucca and Elko, Nevada, have indicated that non-Basques were welcomed and occasionally rented rooms in their *ostatuak*.

## PROSTITUTION AND GAMBLING

Whereas Basque couples and families visited regional centers to honeymoon and vacation; the bachelor herder might journey to a local or regional Basque center with a slightly different intention. For some Basque men, a vacation in town without a visit with "the ladies of the night" would have been incomplete. Given that herders were single men isolated from social contacts for months on end, it is no wonder that some of them sought out prostitutes. Non-Nevada *hoteleros* interviewed for this project insisted that such a transaction had to be negotiated and completed outside hotel premises (prostitution is legal in Nevada). There is a story about a herder in California who attempted to bend house rules, and other boarders reported to the hotelkeeper that "old Dave in room twelve" had just taken a lady upstairs. In that instance and a few others, the *hotelera* on duty stormed the door, key in hand, and insisted that the visitor leave, threatening to enter immediately and escort her to the door. As one can imagine, the direct confrontation of prostitution at a hotel would embarrass a few customers, but it curtailed a potentially troublesome situation for *hoteleros*. Such a scene had to occur only once for residents to understand house rules.

But what went on outside the boardinghouses was another matter. One Basque living in Boise recorded his commentary on local prostitution in an improvisational verse or rhyme that is reminiscent of Old World *bertsolariak* (Basque troubadours). In his verse he recalls the prostitutes who worked in Boise's red-light district at house "Number 52." Based on the poet's account, one senses that many Basques and non-Basques frequented "Number 52" on a regular basis.[10]

Number 52

1

| | |
|---|---|
| We are plenty in here | We are plenty in here |
| Euzkadi-tik eginak. | Hechos desde el País Vasco. |
| And we want to advertise | And we want to advertise |
| pasatzendan egiak. | las verdades que pasan. |
| Tran la ran la ra la rai | Tran la ran la ra la rai |
| pasatzendan egiak. | las verdades que pasan. |

2

| | |
|---|---|
| To-day neskatillak | Las chicas de today |
| Jasten dira pretty, | Se visten pretty, |
| Powder ipini eta | se ponen powder y |
| ensegida all ready. | enseguida all ready. |
| Tran— | Tran— |
| ensegida all ready. | Enseguida all ready. |

3

| | |
|---|---|
| Sidewalk—ien pasatzendan | Al pasar por el sidewalk |
| People gustiari | a todo el people |
| Begia ginatu eta | guiñan el ojo y [dicen] |
| come on right in honey. | come right on in honey. |
| Tran— | Tran— |
| come on right in honey. | come right on in honey. |

4

| | |
|---|---|
| Sartun barrura eta | Pasan adentro y |
| ensegida all ready | enseguida all ready |
| lenik erraten dabe | Lo primero que dicen es |
| gimme me first my money. | gimme me first my money. |
| Tran— | Tran— |
| gimme me first my money. | gimme first my money. |

5

| | |
|---|---|
| How much money—suk | How much money—tú |
| cobratu horregaz | cobras con eso [?] |

Besides the war taxes
Bakarrik two dollars.
Tran—
Bakarrik two dollars.

Besides the war taxes
Solamente two dollars.
Tran—
Solamente two dollars

6

Two dollars gaitikian
skirts—ak altzatu.
All right erran eta
chewing gomies maskatu
Tran—
chewing gomies maskatu.

Por two dollars
levantan las skirts.
Dicen all right y
mascan el chewing gum.
Tran—
mascan el chewing gum.

7

Two dollars joaten diras
Kaltza barrenera.
Oh sweety etora [*sic*] berris
sure mamma ikustera.
Tran—
sure mamma ikustera.

Los two dollars van
Al interior del calzón.
Oh sweety, ven de nuevo
a ver a tu mamma.
Tran—
a ver a tu mamma.

8

Pretty soon juaten dira
begira looking glass—eri
Euran munak gorriturik
begi beltzakin pretty
Tran—
begi beltzakin pretty.

Pretty soon van
a mirar a los looking glass.
pintados sus labio de rojo [y]
con los ojos negros pretty.
Tran—
con los ojos negros pretty.

9

Laster juaten dira
window ondora.
Kaleko people—ari
begia ginatzera.
Tran—
begia ginatzera.

Pronto van
al lado de la window.
A la people de la calle
a guiñarles el ojo.
Tran—
a guiñarles el ojo.

10

| | |
|---|---|
| Palo Suria juaten da<br>kalien erraten.<br>Come on everybody<br>good time pasatzen.<br>Tran—<br>good time pasatzen. | El Palo Blanco va<br>diciendo por la calle.<br>Come on everybody<br>a pasar un good time.<br>Tran—<br>a pasar un good time. |

11

| | |
|---|---|
| Baltza sein txinua<br>we don't matter who it is.<br>Dirue dakarrelata<br>come right on in honeys.<br>Tran—<br>Come right on in honeys. | Negro or chino<br>we don't matter who it is.<br>Ya que traen dinero<br>come right on in honeys.<br>Tran—<br>Come right on in honeys. |

12

| | |
|---|---|
| Urten campora eta<br>aztera begiratu.<br>We can find tomorrow<br>it is number fifty-two<br>Tran—<br>It is number fifty-two. | Salen a la calle y<br>miran hacia atrás.<br>We can find tomorrow<br>it is number fifty-two<br>Tran—<br>It is number fifty-two. |

13

| | |
|---|---|
| Juan Marvin's—en caferata<br>gimme piece of apple pie.<br>Orain au jan eta<br>we will be feeling fine.<br>Tran—<br>we will be feeling fine. | [Van] al café de Juan Marvin's<br>y [dicen] gimme piece of apple pie.<br>Ahora comemos esto y<br>we will be feeling fine.<br>Tran—<br>we will be feeling fine. |

14

| | |
|---|---|
| I had amalau bertso<br>in this paper jarriak<br>Idaho-ko estaduko | I had catorce estrofas<br>in this paper puestas<br>del estado de Idaho |

| | |
|---|---|
| Euzkaldunen berriak. | las nuevas [estrofas] del vasco. |
| Tran— | Tran— |
| Euzkaldunen berriak. | las nuevas [estrofas] del vasco. |

Despite the legalization of prostitution in Nevada, Basque *hoteleros* in that state also discouraged in-house prostitution. In Reno the downtown hotels were adjacent to the bordellos, such that one child of *hoteleros* reported that when she was a young woman she was embarrassed when her dates picked her up and brought her home to the hotel in the evenings. Occasionally she would meet her date elsewhere. Similarly, the houses of prostitution in Elko were located within a city block of that town's Nevada and Star Hotels. As in other areas, over the years the houses of prostitution have also profited from the cyclical nature of the herders' work. Further north, in Hailey, Idaho, one child of *hoteleros* remembers the numerous brothels that lined one end of Bullion Street: "Mother would absolutely not let us go down Bullion Street through the Red Light district."[11] One might understand that although the brothels and the boardinghouses shared the same neighborhoods and each profited from the proximity of the other, *hoteleras* were justified in being unhappy with the arrangement.

Basque herders themselves, in their own way, may have helped to keep prostitution out of the Basque hotels. In the Steens Mountain area in Oregon, for example, there was a field near an aspen grove that was informally named Whorehouse Meadows. One can still find tree carvings in this grove depicting clothed and unclothed women, including names and dates from the 1920s through the 1940s. During these decades, prostitutes regularly came up to meet Basque herders at the aspen grove, plied their trade, and scheduled their next visits.[12] In similar fashion, prostitutes from Casper, Wyoming, serviced a sheep camp circuit including Hazelton, Uncle Billie's Flats, Pass Creek, Bear Trap, and Scotch Corrals.[13] It is probable that the availability of "on-site" and "in the neighborhood" prostitutes for Basque herders helped spare the *hoteleros* the trouble of confronting prostitutes within their hotels.

Although in-house prostitution was strongly discouraged among hotelkeepers, many forms of small-stakes gambling seem to have been considered part of a visit to the hotels. Frequently card players gambled for rounds of drinks, handball players competed for a percentage of the afternoon's wagers, and others placed bets on anything from the outcome of a televised sporting event to which sheepdog could corral six sheep the fastest. Instances of enormous wagers, say of over $100, were comparatively rare, but the frequency of smaller bets was striking.

### SOME NOT SO POSITIVE ASPECTS OF BOARDINGHOUSE LIFE

Although most Basques reacted positively when asked to recall the *ostatuak*, a few shared negative aspects. One person I interviewed observed that the hotels could also be "prisons"—that they limited job possibilities for Basques and delayed mastery of English.[14] For example, this particular man remembered a few elderly Basques who had come to America seeking their fortunes, had worked as herders most of their lives, but had been unable to amass savings. Upon retirement, these herders had neither the finances nor the will to return to the Basque Country as they had hoped. Although the boardinghouses were not to blame for the herders' failures, they were part of a system that may have kept the herder dependent.

Because many Basques had depended upon the hotels for their social and employment contacts for years and spoke only Euskara, their choice of residence upon retirement or unemployment was usually limited to the most familiar hotel. There they might live out their days in relative solitude. In so many words, the hotel eased the herder's transition to the New World while at the same time limiting his ability to become part of it.

As mentioned in chapter 3, hotel keeping was difficult for some of the Basque families running the hotels. The lack of privacy, the difficulty of arranging for vacations, the inability of family members to leave the premises together, and the tough daily workload were among the many challenges faced by those who owned and managed the *ostatu Euskaldunak*.

# 11

# *Etxeko Amak*, Second Mothers

## The Women of the Basque Boardinghouses

Although Basques have often referred to a specific boardinghouse by the name or surname of the *etxeko aita* (father of the house), the personality, hospitality, and graciousness afforded by the *etxeko ama* (mother of the house) often influenced the quality of the boarders' stay much more. Thus a boardinghouse might have been referred to as Arrieta's, Barbero's, or Fermin's, but its popularity may have been more dependent upon the *hotelera*. In fact, as we shall see, some of the *hoteleras* were much more critical to the success of their enterprise than is often imagined.

### SECOND MOTHERS

Perhaps the most basic characteristic shared by *hoteleras* was that they were in the hotels at all times, with very rare exception. Their husbands or business partners may have also worked seasonally in sheep camps or on ranches, or locally as blacksmiths, lumberjacks, miners, or construction workers, but the women dedicated their entire effort to the concerns of the *ostatu*, raising their own children in and around the steady demands of hotel keeping. Thus a Basque seeking any sort of assistance from the *hoteleros* knew he or she would be able to locate the *etxe ama* on the premises at all times. Further, there are abundant examples of *hoteleras* dropping their work to respond to a customer's emergency.

The powerful association between maternal figures and one's home is another factor that explains the significance of the *etxeko amak*. Perhaps the young men and women of Euskal Herria, once having established an *ostatu* as their second home, found it comparatively easy to associate the familiar language, foods, and nurturance provided by *hoteleras* with their own mother. Eventually there seems to have been a symbolic acceptance of the *hoteleras* as surrogate maternal figures. Whether Basques consciously considered the strong association between their "new homeplace" and accepting a "second mother" as adviser and parental figure is doubtful; nonetheless, the fact that it happened frequently is unquestioned.

## EXEMPLARS

From what we know of Maria Echanis, for example, she was the heart of the boardinghouse she operated with her husband, Jack, in Ontario, Oregon. After herding sheep in eastern Oregon for five years, Jack Echanis returned to Mutriku, Gipuzkoa, to seek the hand of Maria, his childhood sweetheart, in marriage. Maria accepted, and when the two returned to Oregon, they joined Jack's partners in a sheep outfit in Stinking Water. There Maria cooked for two of her brothers-in-law, the two Urquidi brothers, and a few hired hands. She also worked a bit at the Urquidi boardinghouse in nearby Crane.[1] Based on her popularity as camp cook and her experience at Urquidi's, the men finally talked Maria into opening her own *ostatu*. When she and Jack moved into Ontario, they opened their home on Oregon Street as a boardinghouse. That wooden-frame structure burned down in 1929, and it was replaced by a new twelve-bedroom structure in 1930.

In addition to raising her own five children in that *ostatu*, Maria treated her young customers as if they were her own offspring. Many of them called her *etxeko ama* or simply *ama*. In Maria's words, "These boys and girls were so far away from home. They not only needed good food and a room they could call their own; they needed companionship."[2] Thus "Mom Echanis's place" became a second home for many of Oregon's young Basques, and Maria Echanis became known as a maternal figure who would provide comfort, advice, and encouragement.

Throughout the four decades she served the Ontario Basque commu-

*Elvira Cenoz of Gardnerville's Overland Hotel with William Douglass, director of the Basque Studies Program at the University of Nevada, Reno. Courtesy of the Basque Studies Collection, Getchell Library, University of Nevada, Reno.*

nity, Maria Echanis was known for her generosity. As her daughter once stated,

> In looking back, I don't see how Mother managed it all. Sometimes, during fair time, she would be cooking breakfast, dinner, and supper for as many as forty people. Then, in the middle of the morning would come a younger brother who was hungry and would ask her to fix him some *txorizo* or something. She always did everything for them, and so cheerfully.[3]

There are accounts of other well-loved *hoteleras*. One Boise Basque remembering mother and daughter Letemendi stated that, "Almost everything I became in America I owe to Letemendi's. . . . I don't think I could have made it here without them." Boise author Patrick Bieter suggested that the term "tough love" best described Leandra Letemendi.[4] Anyone who showed up late for one of Leandra's meals was subjected to a serious tongue-lashing. Yet one young Basque who learned the importance of punctuality in Leandra's house also benefited from her compassion. When she discovered him alone crying on the first birthday he had spent away from home, Leandra put her chores aside, sat down, and talked the young man through his homesickness.

In Elko's Overland Hotel, Gregoria Sabala was known for taking young herders and serving girls under her wing, acting as their mother, counselor, and nurse. Expectant mothers in their final months of pregnancy would leave their Nevada ranches and travel to Elko's Overland so that in case of problems they would be closer to a midwife or physician. By necessity, most of the babies were delivered by Gregoria instead. As Gregoria was known to quip, by bringing so many lives into the world, she specialized in "rural free delivery."[5] And when the dreaded influenza epidemic of 1918 struck Elko, the Overland's rooms and hallways were strewn with fifty to sixty afflicted patients. Once again, Gregoria called upon her nursing skills and, as she later boasted, she did not lose a one.

As was mentioned in chapter 6, Bakersfield's "Mama Elizalde" was one of the San Joaquin Valley's most well known and well loved *hoteleras*. Like many of her boarders at Noriega's, Graciana Elizalde loved to gamble and wagered on an array of events ranging from *pilota* matches in the adjacent *cancha* to the vagaries of human nature. As one might suspect, betting has not been unusual among Basques of either gender. Graciana's generosity upon winning, however, was. As readers might recall from earlier in the book, Graciana bet on the sex of a serving girl's baby, and upon winning she bestowed the takings on the newborn infant, opening a savings account in the baby girl's name. "Mama Elizalde" is a legend in part because of her forty-two-year tenure at Noriega's, but also because she shared her resources and time whenever she thought someone needed her help.

In 1955 Catherine and Pierre Goyenetche came to the United States for the second time. They selected San Francisco as their new home. Catherine went to work at Loustou's French Laundry, and Pierre found work as a gardener. After six years of intense saving, the couple leased the Obrero Hotel, reserving three of the Obrero's rooms for themselves and renting the remaining seven to boarders. Only on special occasions did Catherine hire help, for she usually served as cook, Pierre as bartender and host, their son as busboy and dishwasher, and their daughter as waitress and hostess. At the Obrero the family successfully produced legendary meals for sixty to seventy people at one evening seating, charging as little as $2.50 per meal.[6]

Catherine and Pierre leased the Obrero from 1961 through 1975. To their consternation, they were never able to buy the building because the owners refused to sell. During the 1960s the Obrero and the Goyenetches were a central part of San Francisco's busy Basque neighborhood. Catherine regularly passed Basques on Broadway and Powell Streets as she ran errands or shopped in the afternoons. As in other locations, the young men called out to her using the familiar "*ama*" in their greeting. Older San Francisco Basques fondly remember Catherine's delicious meals and the raucous after-dinner singing that she often directed.

In Carson City, Nevada, Teresa and Dominique Laxalt opened their small French Hotel a few streets from the state capitol. In *Sweet Promised Land*, *The Basque Hotel*, and *Child of the Holy Ghost*, their son Robert described how Teresa stepped in to attend to family business matters, discipline children, manage and cook for the small hotel, and generally keep things going while Papa was away in the sheep camps.[7] In *The Deep Blue Memory*, Robert's daughter Monique recounts early memories of her "strong, sturdy, and imposing" grandma, who

> took a lease on a boarding house on Main Street, just across from the capitol grounds. She hired a girl to tend to the two baby boys, and for eighteen hours a day she cooked and cleaned and washed. The father [grandpa] would appear at intervals, tending bar until he became sick with cabin fever, then disappearing back into the hills.[8]

Monique's depiction of her grandmother and Laxalt's of his mother remind us of the many *hoteleras* who have served as the primary operator of the family *ostatu*, and done so with grace and generosity.

Laxalt's account of his mother's role at the French Hotel brings to mind a study by Charlotte Crawford of women's work in an Old World fishing village. Crawford describes the multiple responsibilities that wives assume as their fishermen husbands leave for the five-month cod season.[9] In each of these chronicles, a woman of the village took on full responsibility for her family when her husband was away, and, in many instances, she did not relinquish that role completely upon her husband's return.

Maria Echanis, Leandra Letemendi, Gregoria Sabala, Graciana Elizalde, and Teresa Laxalt are representative of Basque *etxeko andreak* in many ways. Like other *hoteleras*, these transplanted countrywomen mastered their roles out of necessity. Their work involved blending intuitive skills they had learned from their own home situations with new ones they had to adopt in a new land: attending to the birthing, nursing, and nurturing of children while also caring for others; juggling the chores and responsibilities involved in running a successful business enterprise; and adapting to living in the United States.

## THE DAILY WORK OF THE *Hotelera*

Up in the early morning and active until the late evening, a *hotelera* focused on preparing food for breakfast, lunch, and dinner; on organizing cleaning girls and food servers; on coordinating special requests from boarders; on washing and gardening; and on caring for her own children. Although the *hotelera*'s daily routine was subject to unpredictable events and sudden demands, it was also surprisingly consistent throughout the American West. A prototype of a *hotelera*'s daily schedule, based on hundreds of interviews and discussions with *hoteleras*, appears as follows:

| *Time* | *Activity* |
|---|---|
| 5:00–6:00 A.M. | Wake up |
| | Organize kitchen |
| | Make sack lunches for boarders and children |
| | Begin preparation for midday meal |
| 6:00–8:00 | Cook and serve breakfast to family and boarders |
| 8:00–10:00 | Organize and oversee cleaning girls |
| | Set up noon meal |
| | Clean rooms, common areas |
| | Washing |
| | Gardening |
| | Do errands in town—groceries |
| 10:00–12:00 | Set tables |
| | Cooking in earnest for noon meal |
| | Continue with housecleaning details |
| 12:00–2:00 P.M. | Serve noon meal |
| 2:00–4:00 | Errands in town |
| | Clean up after lunch |

| | |
|---|---|
| | Continue unfinished work from morning |
| | Gardening |
| | Sewing |
| | Canning |
| 4:00–6:00 | Oversee children returning from school |
| | Set up evening meal |
| | Cooking |
| 6:00–8:00 | Serve dinner |
| 8:00–10:00 | Clean up |
| | Visiting with friends |
| | Children to bed |
| 8:00–12:00 | "Special Occasions" (Dances, Family Parties) |
| 12:00–2:00 A.M. | Weekend entertaining |
| | Often early breakfast or card crowd |

In *Open Country, Iowa,* Deborah Fink outlined three modes of women's work as found among non-Basque women in the Great Plains.[10] In the first case, women labored on the farm to help sustain the family, perhaps raising crops, milking cows, and preserving food items. In the second, women worked in the home or farm to produce goods—such as woven goods, butter, preserves, or eggs—to exchange for products outside the home. In the third, the women toiled outside the household in order to earn money to help support the household. Basque *hoteleras* did a combination of all three modes of work. During the earliest years and in many locations, they raised crops, hogs, chickens, and cattle for their kitchens; they sewed for their customers and families; and they traded for goods not found in the *ostatuak;* and, finally, they lived with their families in their workplace.

Two recent studies have touched on the role of the *hoteleras*.[11] One suggests that compared with their male counterparts, the *hoteleras* did more than their share of the work and had more rigorous schedules than the men did. Although the majority of the people who were interviewed for these studies were female and thus could be accused of bias for this view, there is certainly good reason to investigate the claim. From the perspective of several children raised in boardinghouses, their mother worked harder than their father. In the case of one former male resident of Los Angeles's Basque town, the women he remembered working in the hotels were virtually slaves, performing every variety of task needed to keep the enterprise going. Daily work hours began around six in the morning and lasted until the last customers were served, with breaks and/or free afternoons granted during lulls in the hotel's busy routine.

Undoubtedly, work for the *etxeko ama*, the serving girls, cooks, and *criadas* (maids or house cleaners) in the hotels was difficult and challenging. A *hotelera* would report differing degrees of difficulty associated with her work at the *ostatu* based on a number of factors: the hotel's popularity, her relationship with her husband, the number of years the *ostatu* had been in business, the hotel's location, and the intensity of local competition. If she remembered that "times were good, we were making a good living then," that usually meant that she was able to hire the requisite number of people to staff her boardinghouse and, thus, was less likely to emphasize the irksome workload. In smaller and less profitable enterprise where the *hotelera* had to shoulder most of the work, however, she was more likely to emphasize her daily toil.

As one would suspect based on what we have seen of life in the *ostatu Euskalduna*, *hoteleras* never reported that work in the boardinghouses was easy or light. When the *hotelero* worked outside the boardinghouse—perhaps in nearby sheep camps on a seasonal basis or in a local enterprise that took him away from the premises on a regular basis—the *hoteleras* were more likely to say that they were often tired, sometimes embittered, and occasionally depressed. Because they carried the primary responsibility for the *ostatu* on their shoulders, these women no doubt had a heavier workload in their boardinghouses than did their husbands. Not surprisingly, *hoteleras* who reported having done more work around the hotel than had their deceased husbands preferred to remain anonymous because they resisted giving the appearance of being disloyal.

Yet there were also women who worked two, three, and four decades alongside their husbands who would refer to "our work" and "our business" rather than differentiating between "his" and "her" work. Much more commonly, *hoteleras* reflected that although the work was hard, these were the best years of their lives. A surprising number stated, "I worked side by side with my husband, and our whole life was in that hotel. We worked hard, we played hard, we had fun."

Based on the available information, it is possible to make distinctions about the division of labor among the husband and wife in the boardinghouse. As mentioned earlier, the *hotelero*'s responsibilities tended to be the barroom, cardroom, *cancha*, and outside employment contacts; the *hotelera*'s were in the kitchen, dining hall, laundry, and rented rooms, as well as tending to the family's needs. An overview of the characteristics, responsibilities, and duties of the *hotelero* and *hotelera* as they have most commonly been reported appears as follows:

| *Hotelero* | *Hotelera* |
| --- | --- |
| Old World–born Basque | New World–born Basque |
| More Basque, less English | Less Basque, more English |
| Ten to fourteen years older | Ten to fourteen years younger |
| Tending bar | Keeping house |
| Stockroom | Buying groceries |
| Organizing *mus* games | Canning and preserving foodstuffs |
| Organizing pelota tourneys | Organizing cooks and staff |
| Keeping family accounts | Overseeing children |
| Overseeing livery and stables | Gardening |
| Repairing or building | Mending and sewing |
| Cleaning after hours | Doing laundry |

Some functions—such as visiting with other *hoteleros* at neighboring *ostatuak*, running errands around town, or accompanying customers to dental or physician's appointments—do not appear in the list, because they seem most often to have been shared by the husband and wife.

Although most Basques who lived and worked in the *ostatuak* freely acknowledge the women's rigorous workload, and studies have supported this notion, one would be hard pressed to prove that their lot was always more difficult than the men's. John Beterbide's sons, for example, remember that their father worked a twelve-hour shift in the local lumber mill every day before returning to the family boardinghouse, eating dinner, tending bar until closing time, and cleaning the premises afterward.[12] In sum, it would be misleading to overstate the comparative difficulty of the workloads of *hoteleros* and *hoteleras* when the *hoteleras* interviewed have given varying assessments of the difficulty of their work at the boardinghouses.

## SERVING GIRLS AND OTHER WORKING WOMEN

Not all women working in the hotels were *hoteleras*, however. A majority of the young Basque women from the Old Country who came to the United States to join neighbors or family members in the boardinghouses had prearranged work in the *ostatuak*. In general, the domestic chores of cleaning, cooking, and serving were their lot.

A large majority of these women met their future husbands while working at the *ostatuak* or while attending dances and social functions there. In fact, of the more than two hundred interviews with Basques I have conducted or consulted, 85 percent of the Basques had met their spouses in the boardinghouses.[13] Such high "marrying in" ratios among first- and second-generation Basques can be explained in part by the common culture and language.

In 1918, for example, Margarita Osa arrived in Boise holding a contract to work as a maid in Boise's Barbero boardinghouse.[14] As was the practice of the day, some of her promised $18 per month was withheld to repay the cost of her transportation from Euskal Herria to Boise. Her daily duties at Barbero's included typical chores, such as housecleaning and laundry. Similarly, the fifteen-year-old Lucy Alboitiz Garatea contracted to work with her aunt and uncle at Boise's Aguirre Hotel, also known as Zapatero's. Both women described suffering bleeding knuckles from cleaning clothes by hand using washboards, sore backs from long hours of work, and "housemaid's knees" from crawling on their hands and knees while polishing floors.[15]

To their credit, both Margarita and Lucy eventually became *hoteleras* in own right. Margarita and her husband Marcelino bought the Plaza Hotel in Burns, Oregon, in 1928 and managed it until 1945, when they sold to Joe and Paulina Lizundia. Four years later, in 1949, the then widowed Lucy Garatea bought the Plaza and went on to manage it for sixteen years. Margarita and Lucy Garatea are just two examples of young Basque women who came to the United States and gradually saved enough of a grubstake with their husbands to buy their own *ostatuak*.

Basque women in other settings besides hotels also worked long, hard hours. Some toiled alongside their husbands on the ranches of the High Desert, where they prepared and served meals to family and ranch hands, cleaned dishes, darned clothing, raised gardens, tended to children, canned vegetables and foodstuffs in the summer, and made *txorizo* and blood sausage in the springtime. On more than a few occasions, Basque women did this work from sheep camp tents: which meant cooking over open fires, baking underground with campfire coals, roasting on spits, and laundering clothes on washboards along riversides.[16] Later, once the family's herds had expanded and their husbands were prospering, these women enjoyed the comparative luxury of two- and three-bedroom ranch houses, but generally they continued to shoulder strenuous daily tasks nonetheless. Basque townswomen also worked extended hours in the laundries and bakeries of San Francisco, Bakersfield, and Stockton.

It should be noted that other authors have suggested that women in Old World Basque society had an elevated status. The anthropological and sociological studies of Teresa del Valle, Jacqueline Urla, and Roslyn Frank suggest that Basque women play a much more important role in family development, financial matters, and societal development than they have been given credit for. In so many words, the New and Old World *andreak* are much more influential than they seem.[17]

Certainly, *Euskaldun andreak* played a greater role in the survival of early Basque communities and families in the American West than Basque-American literature suggests. All too often, such literature focuses on the "lonely Basque shepherd" who roamed the American West with his band of sheep. Although it is true that a majority of Basques who arrived at the turn of the century intended to herd for a few years, save some money, and then return to Euskadi, there were other Basques who did not follow this pattern. Many remained, married girls from villages in their home provinces, and established roots in the Western United States.[18]

The Basque shepherd needed an elaborate support system in order to succeed. The Basque *ostatuak* and the hotel network were critical factors in the newcomer's transition to America.[19] This was especially true during the earliest decades of Basque immigration to the United States, say from 1890 through 1930. But for Basques coming in afterward we witness more of a tendency to settle down. Those young Basque bachelors who did not return to the Basque Country began to find sweethearts, marry, and raise children.

Setting the record straight about the history of Basque women in America is also important for our understanding of Basque-American communities. In some areas, Basque women in key positions have taken on a role that is almost larger than life. For example, in the Bakersfield Basque colony Graciana Elizalde's legacy is enormous.[20] Loved by so many, so kind to so many, she became a matriarchal figure in her community. In other Basque communities, other women have filled similar roles. In Fresno, California, for example, retired restaurateur and *hotelera* Lyda Esain enjoyed a special position of respect and regard because of her sixty years of service to the Basque community. Grace Elizalde and Lyda Esain shared some characteristics with other Basque women mentioned in this chapter. In Ely, Nevada, women such as Gregoria Mariluch, Dora Olareaga, Marie Beltran, and Marianne Goyenetche demonstrated that they were

*Six of Fresno's best-known* hoteleras *(left to right): Juanita Marquant, Maria Ballaz, Asuncion Goni, Benita Garcia, Lyda Esain, and Hilaria Frechou. Courtesy of Juliette Robidart Campos.*

also "wiry and independent" Basque women.[21] More than merely putting in long hours and endless days during the workweek, more than offering invaluable support to their husbands as business partners, more even than running demanding enterprises on their own, they extended themselves to their fellow Basques and made life easier for those around them. After establishing themselves in their communities, each became "the one" that Basque men and women would go to first for help in troubled times. In fact, these *hoteleras* became trusted advisers. Others—particularly local policemen, lawyers, politicians, and other non-Basques seeking information or counsel on Basque-related issues—learned to consult these "Basque senior stateswomen" before making decisions.[22]

### *Hoteleras'* IDENTITY AS WOMEN

To no one's surprise, *hoteleras* in the peak years of 1890 to 1930 do not fit neatly into common stereotypes of women in the American West. Of the three offered by Beverly Stolje, for example, the "refined lady," the "loyal helpmate," and the "bad woman" do not provide useful models for the *etxeko andreak*. If asked, most *hoteleras* would probably identify most closely with the "loyal helpmates" model. Yet this category seems inappropriate when we consider independent and strong women like Teresa Laxalt, Margarita Osa, Lyda Esain, Leandra Letemendi, or Maria Echanis.

In her research on Old World gender identity among Basques, Teresa del Valle has reported that Basque women in ranch, coastal, and urban settings differentiate their roles from those of men along consistent lines. Being a good mother, a clean person, and a hard worker were the three attributes that Basque women in these settings valued most, these three being characteristics supporting "the centrality of the woman within the domestic sphere, of her role as both supporter and mediator. All of this is in perfect agreement with the premise, 'the woman is defined of others.'"[23] If we consider the lives of the *hoteleras* presented in this book with del Valle's commentary in mind, we might conclude that the *etxeko amak* were well prepared for their lives in the *ostatuak*. In their New World settings they were expected to focus on responding to the needs of their customers and families. They served tirelessly and gained strong societal approval and support for doing so.

As ethnic historian Donna Gabaccia has reminded us,

> Immigrant women carried with them not merely Italian or Japanese or German ways, but also the distinctive female traditions found within their native cultures. To become "American," these women invented "ethnic" female identities. Most immigrant women—like most men—creatively blended old and new in doing so."[24]

Like many other immigrant women who came to the United States during the late nineteenth and early twentieth centuries, then, the Basque *hoteleras* were blending the familiar into the new, finding new identities in order to become American.

The *etxeko andreak* we have met in this chapter are ample evidence of the unique role Basque women played in the Basque boardinghouses. Their hospitality, warmth, congeniality, and good cheer earned them well-deserved acclaim, devotion, loyalty, and status within their communities. And although the *hotelero* had a parallel and important function in the *ostatuak*, his role paled in comparison. For it was the *hotelera* who invested twenty-four hours every day in the hotels, and it was she who most influenced the everyday quality of a boarder's stay.

# 12

# Basque Boardinghouses in Other Settings

## BASQUE BUSINESSES IN SOUTH AMERICA

Although California's Basque hotels preceded others in the United States, they were not the first in the Western Hemisphere. Sixteenth-century narratives describe two establishments in South America, one a Bizkaian-owned inn in the mining region of the Peruvian highlands, the other an business owned by a Navarrese and located along the road to Zacatecas, Mexico. Both provided lodging, food, and livery services, and both may have served Basques in what was then a Basque enclave.[1]

In the first half of the nineteenth century, as Basques migrated to Buenos Aires and Montevideo, Uruguay, *ostatuak* were opened to serve the needs of the immigrants from Euskal Herria. For instance, two authorities have referred to the "Basque barrio" in the Río de la Plata region, which was reportedly crowded with Basque-owned bars, hotels, and boardinghouses by 1842. According to Douglass and Bilbao,

> As early as 1842, there was a residential district in Buenos Aires (*Barrio de la Constitución*) that was primarily Basque. This area was filled with the Basque-owned bars, hotels, and boarding houses that served as employment bureaus and way stations for new immigrants,

housing for single men working in the *saladeros*, and places of amusement and relaxation for Basque dairymen and herders in from the pampas.[2]

As in the establishments found in the American West, in the Basque businesses of the barrio Euskara was the vernacular, handball courts and frontons could be found, card players won and lost at *mus*, and dancers knew the *porrusalda* and the *jota*. Author Francisco Grandmontagne recorded the journey of the famous Basque poet and songwriter Jose Maria Iparraguirre to Buenos Aires in 1858. On the day that Iparraguirre arrived, he was met on the docks by a large contingent of Basques who escorted him and his wife to a local *ostatu* operated by Francisco Mendia and his wife.[3]

Given the numbers of Basque settlers in South and Central America during the Spanish colonial period, it is likely that *ostatuak* also appeared in Montevideo, Havana, Caracas, and Mexico City.[4]

Those "Argentine Basques" credited with transplanting large-scale transhumant sheep raising to California's central valleys, although they are not considered the inventors of the techniques, also carried with them a vital social institution that had served them well in South America. In fact, the migratory Basques have established *ostatuak* in most New World locations where they settled in sizeable numbers.

## NORTH ATLANTIC SETTLEMENTS: NOVA SCOTIA, NEWFOUNDLAND, AND LABRADOR

In 1713 the French established the fishing colony of Isle de Royale in Cape Breton, Nova Scotia.[5] Because the settlement was perfectly located for the triangular trade routes between France and her New World colonies, the fortress-town of Louisbourg emerged as one of the busiest ports in the New World during the first half of the eighteenth century. Isle de Royale exported cod far and wide, to the West Indies, the Antilles, Quebec, Acadia, and the American colonies. With prosperity came growth, and with growth, came the fortress designed to be "the Guardian of the St. Lawrence."[6]

As one might suspect, the Basque cod fishermen of Iparralde participated in the development of the colony of Isle de Royale. Today visitors to Louisbourg can view the fort and surrounding townsite painstakingly re-created as it appeared on the eve of the British takeover in 1744, based on archaeology and extensive research into the history of Louisbourg and its people. As one walks along the seaside road approaching the fort's main gate, one encounters a row of cod fishermen's houses, among them the Des Roches Fishing Property.[7] There Madame Jeanne Galbarette lived between 1730 and 1754. Thrice wed, Jeanne married Des Roches, her third and youngest husband, in 1738. At the time, she was sixty-nine and he was twenty-eight. Local historians give an interesting account of the Des Roches property:

> This house, where they lived until her death in 1754, reflects local building usage in its simple log walls and sodded roof, but details such as the overhanging eaves recall the Basque heritage of its owners. Built in 1717, the original house served as an unlicensed tavern for Basque fishermen and sailors. In the fishing season the householder's employees probably took their meals, perhaps their lodgings, here.[8]

The formidable Basque presence in the North Atlantic cod-fishing and whaling industries is further indicated in the work of sixteenth- and seventeenth-century cartographers; Basque place names such as Barrachoa, Tres Irlac, Ferrolgo Amuixco Punta, Etchaire Portu, Oporportu, Portucho Caharra, and Granbayaare were scattered along the Strait of Belle Isle, located between present-day Labrador and Newfoundland.[9] Nonetheless, the Des Roches property at Louisbourg is our solitary example of a possible Basque inn or boardinghouse in the region. Because of the intense trade traffic present in Louisbourg in the early decades of the eighteenth century, then, it is likely that the Galbarette-Des Roches home became an *ostatu* or "home away from home" for numerous French Basque sailors and cod fishermen; further, it is possible that other similar businesses may have existed in what is today Canada's Atlantic Provinces.

The presence of the Basque barrio of Buenos Aires and the Des Roches house in Louisbourg lead one to believe that wherever the migratory Basques have settled, their *ostatuak* have followed. Yet this no longer seems to be the case. Basques arriving in the United States in recent decades no longer choose the boardinghouses as their first residences. Further, there is no evidence to date that the Basques who harvested sugar in Australia or settled in the Philippines, for example, established Basque hotels.

The solitary example of a Basque boardinghouse in an Old World setting is that of Prudencio Clemençot in Liverpool, England.[10] Clemençot traveled to Liverpool first in the 1880s when he was employed by the Bermeo-based Sierra Tinterriva Shipping Company as a marine superintendent.[11] About ten years later, he and his wife, Maria Ignacia, opened their boardinghouse at 41 Hurst Street near Liverpool's Wapping Dock and began arranging transoceanic travel for Basques on the Cunard, White Star, and American Lines. During the fifteen years preceding the outbreak of World War I in Europe, many Bizkaians preferred to go to Liverpool first to arrange for better shipping combinations and accommodations than they could obtain in the ports of Spain and France. And when they were in port, Basque mariners from Bermeo's Larrinaga Lines were also regulars at the Clemençcot's *ostatu*.

Between 1890 and 1915, Liverpool developed a Basque district where Euskara was spoken, where Basque families settled and worked in shipping-related professions, and where Basque children attended the Jesuit-run Saint Francis Xavier School. Most of the Basque mariners residing in Liverpool before and during World War I were sailing under the British flag. In fact, Prudencio Clemençot's father, a chief officer of the Larrinaga's *Esperanza*, was sailing under the Union Jack around 1915 when he and his fellow Basque crew members were lost at sea en route to Galveston, Texas.

The Clemençot *ostatu*'s role as the solitary Old World Basque transit hotel was significant. According to the Consejo Superior de Emigración (emigration records) for example, nearly 8,000 of the 18,547 legal emigrants from Spanish Basque provinces between 1911 and 1915 were Bizkaian, and it seems that a sizeable number of them chose to depart from Liverpool rather than from Bordeaux.[12]

Clemençot's hotel register confirms that many Bizkaian Basques stopped in Liverpool en route to the United States, because Prudencio carefully noted his customers' towns of origin and destinations in the New World. In some instances, Prudencio listed ocean liners by name, train routes in the United States, and the travel fares. Between 1899 and 1907, for example, well over 60 percent of Clemençot's guests were from Bizkaia; slightly over 90 percent were men in their twenties and thirties; and the largest numbers were destined for "Boise City," St. Louis, and Winnemucca.[13] The male-female ratios and average ages of the Basque travel-

Table 12.1 The Clemençot Hotel Register

| Year | Males | Females | Average Age |
|---|---|---|---|
| 1899 | 99 | 11 | 23.8 |
| 1900 | 122 | 13 | 25.3 |
| 1901 | 84 | 10 | 25.3 |
| 1902 | 136 | 10 | 25.4 |
| 1903 | 169 | 11 | 25.5 |
| 1904 | 232 | 27 | 24.5 |
| 1905 | 231 | 20 | 23.3 |
| 1906 | 228 | 36 | 23.3 |
| Total | 1,301 | 138 | 24.5 |

DESTINATIONS FOR GUESTS OF THE CLEMENÇOT

| Place | Number | Place | Number |
|---|---|---|---|
| Baker City | 4 | Massachusetts | 47 |
| Battle Mountain | 12 | Melbourne | 3 |
| Boise City | 189 | Mexico | 6 |
| Boston | 28 | Ogden | 6 |
| Buenos Aires | 3 | Philadelphia | 4 |
| California | 4 | Portland | 3 |
| Colorado Springs | 3 | Reno | 23 |
| Conteros | 7 | Ruchlave | 7 |
| Elko | 51 | Saint Louis | 143 |
| Havana | 8 | San Francisco | 12 |
| Hallowell, M. | 2 | Winnemucca | 116 |
| Kansas | 10 | Virginia | 87 |
| Lovelock, Nevada | 2 | Vermont | 67 |
| Marysville | 3 | | |

*Source:* Clemençot Boarding House Register, Basque Studies Collection, Getchell Library, University of Nevada, Reno.

ers found in the Clemençot register between 1899 and 1906 are listed in table 12.1.

Between 1903 and 1907, Prudencio Clemençot also listed his boarders' destinations in his registry. Overseas destinations and tallies of the number of Basques in transit to specific places were also listed in Prudencio's register, re-created in table 12.1, with the exception of 194 customers for whom no destinations were listed. In some cases, Prudencio entered a state as a destination rather than a city or town, for instance, Virginia, Vermont, and Kansas. Because Ogden was a rail-switching center, one cannot be certain that the six travelers listed as heading there actually remained in Utah or continued on to other destinations. Further, entries such as San Francisco and California might have been combined, and the location of Ruchlave, Hallowell, and Conteros cannot be determined.

Some of the destinations in the Clemençot registry merit further comment. For example, that nearly one third of Clemençot's guests were destined for Boise, Winnemucca, and Reno is consistent with other evidence of Basque settlement patterns during this period. That St. Louis was destined to receive 143 of these "Liverpool Basques," however, seems unlikely. Likewise, the nearly 15 percent of this population that sailed for Virginia, Vermont, and Massachusetts seems uncharacteristically high. Perhaps these were ports of entry for these Basques, who intended to continue west after disembarkation.

In many cases, Prudencio also noted his boarders' hometowns. Ea, Murelaga, Amorebeitia, Elanchove, Marquina, Lequeitio, Bedarona, Rigoitia, Nachitua, Ibarranguelua, and Gernika appeared dozens of times; others, such as Mutriku, Mendaca, Bermeo, Bilbao, Arasbasqui, Murueta, Elanchove, and Múgica, each appear around ten times.[14] The frequency with which these towns were listed suggests that Clemençot's guests were overwhelmingly Bizkaian; only two Gipuzkoan towns were listed. The names of the ships on which the travelers held tickets are also of interest: they included the famous *Lusitania* and the less well known *Elvira, Lorna Santander, Celtic, Saxonia, Cedric, Lucania, Mauretania, Friesland, Carthaganian, Arabic, Baltic*, and others.

Just as the Basque hotels in the American West emerged in response to the needs of the migratory single Basque male, so too did Clemençot's in Liverpool. Whether a North Sea sailor or an Idaho sheepherder, the Basque sojourner had common needs that exceeded room and board. Back in Euskal Herria, however, there neither is nor was any establishment exactly like the *ostatu*.

Prudencio Clemençot's boardinghouse provides us with the solitary example of an *ostatu* located in the Old World. Because I have asserted that the Basque hotels were an American phenomenon, Clemençot's hotel in Liverpool, England, may at first seem to contradict my argument. But since this hotel is the solitary exception among the nearly five hundred *ostatuak* considered in these pages, and since its main function was consistent with those found in critical transit locations in the United States, I would suggest that Clemençot's should be considered to be more a part of the Basque diaspora to the New World than an exception to it. That is, I still believe that the *ostatu* was a New World phenomenon.

As the central and crucial gathering place for groups of American and European Basques in the United States over the past century, the *ostatu* has clearly served as an important social institution. In the first decades of Basque migration to the United States, when young herders arrived unmarried to seek their fortunes and then return to Euskal Herria, the hotels served as the immigrants' job agency, and the *hoteleros* acted as extended family and an assistance league. In fact discussing Basque-American society between 1890 and 1930 without mentioning the hotels and *hoteleros* would be a mistake. For, without question, the *ostatu* was the Basques' major social institution in the United States in those early years. As more and more Basques arrived and began raising their own families, however, the central role of the hotels shifted dramatically. The demise of the hotels is the subject of the following chapter.

# 13

## *Agur Ostatuak*

To speak of Basque hotels in the present tense is anachronistic, for the *ostatuak* of the American West have all but disappeared. In recent decades, we have witnessed the decline of the *ostatuak* and the emergence of the Basque-owned and -operated "tourist hotel." Most often the tendency has been for *hoteleros* to stop offering room and board and make their Basque restaurant the focus of their business, or they might rent rooms without offering board. As opposed to the *ostatuak* we have described, these establishments often employ non-Basques who sometimes don Basque costumes to serve customers. Tourist hotels are also more likely than traditional Basque hotels to decorate their interiors, offer a menu including non-Basque dishes, accept credit cards, and advertise in the local media. Such establishments are a dramatic departure from the authentic *ostatuak*.

In California, the devolution from hotel to restaurant over recent decades has been quite apparent. Of the 88 communities that once hosted Basque boardinghouses in California and Nevada, only 8 towns now contain Basque boardinghouses today; the 9 remaining traditional Basque hotels still in business today in the American West are located in these two states. In Oregon, Washington, Colorado, Arizona, New Mexico, Wyoming, Montana, Utah, New York, and Idaho, none remain.

The last Basque boardinghouse in Idaho stood in the once active Basque community of Shoshone. It was the *ostatu* of Frank and Benita

Oneida, who opened their business in 1917. Nearly fifty years later, their son Pete and daughter-in-law Dollie took over the business in 1968. Dollie explained that the family decided to keep Oneida's open when Benita passed away because their old boarders were still living in the place, "and it's hard to say no."[1] In 1995 they closed the boardinghouse when the final boarder left. This pattern has played out at other boardinghouses as well—the departure of the last long-term boarders has often signalled the death knell of a boardinghouse.

In other locations, Basque *hoteleros*-turned-restaurateurs have attempted to establish what might be called a nouvelle cuisine for Basque restaurants. In San Francisco, for example, Bambi MacDonald attempted to open a New Age version of the Obrero Hotel, where she encouraged a non-Basque bed and breakfast trade and offered Basque cuisine. Despite her attempts, her success was limited and short-lived. In 1992 Bambi sold the Obrero, and although the building still houses a hotel, the Basque-style restaurant closed when MacDonald sold the business. At the other end of town, the Café du Nord, a French Basque restaurant on Market Street, became a late-night music and supper club. With the closing of the Basque Hotel on Romulo Place in 1997, only the Des Alpes on Broadway remains. It continues to offer traditional Basque family-style dining, but its rooms for boarders have not been full for decades.

Similarly, out-of-towners traveling through Mountain Home, Idaho, can stay overnight in the Rose Stone Bed and Breakfast, once Bideganeta's *ostatu*, and potentially not know anything about the edifice's rich and warm heritage as an *ostatu*. Once thriving Madariaga's boardinghouse in Jordan Valley, Oregon, now serves as a popular rest stop for highway travelers passing through town. When it became a restaurant, the Old Basque Inn, it closed its doors to boarders and began serving a limited Basque menu to appeal to a larger non-Basque clientele. Landa's Hogar Hotel in Salt Lake City was renovated and reopened as a fashionable antique shop. In downtown Sacramento, the seventy-year-old Español Hotel was recently sold to non-Basques who retained its name but serve Italian dinners. In Los Angeles, the modest French Basque Lekumberry's Hotel Commercial of the 1920s became a restaurant retaining only French cuisine, and then eventually it became the fashionable Taix Restaurant. Within the past months, *hoteleros* at Chino's Centro Vasco announced that they are searching for a new location for their bar and restaurant business, because their *ostatu* has the unfortunate luck to be located in the middle of a highway expansion project.

Ironically, the first two states to host Basque hotels are the last to retain

*The Winnemucca Hotel as it appears today (above and opposite). Like many of the other boardinghouses discussed herein, the Winnemucca Hotel underwent several expansions. Exterior drawings and plans on page 242 show six different stages of development in the history of the Winnemucca Hotel. Courtesy of the University of Utah Basque Boarding House Project.*

them. In both California and Nevada, only nine *ostatuak* remain, with five in California and four in Nevada. Those that are still open and still have rooms for boarders are listed in table 13.1.

In San Francisco, Boise, Bakersfield, and Fresno, Basque clubhouses and cultural centers have, in some ways, offered a replacement for the old downtown *ostatuak*. In Boise, renovating the Uberuaga boardinghouse, reopening the Anduiza *pala* court (*pala* is a variation of pelota played with a wooden racquet), building the Euzkaldunak clubhouse, and opening the Bar Gernika on the 600 block of Grove Street have resurrected the memory of the town's earlier Basque district. In addition to putting the Boise Basque district on the National Register of Historic Places, some individual Basque hotel owners have also begun this process with their *ostatu*. The fact that the Santa Fe and Basque Hotels of Fresno have been added to the National Register, for example, guarantees that the buildings will be retained as they were constructed. Attempts to conserve them notwithstanding, the Basque hotels are a "thing of the past."

In the 1850s, when those hopeful miners arrived in the Western United States with dreams of wealth and of a triumphant return to South America or Euskal Herria, they did not consciously intend for hotels to be con-

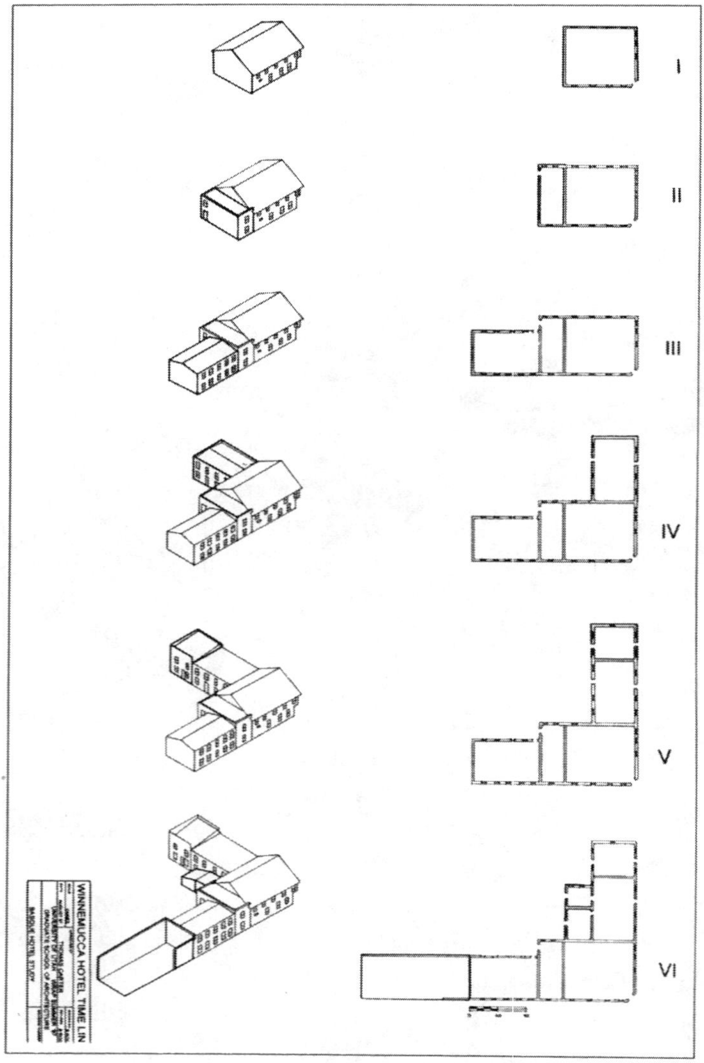


structed nor for there to be a burgeoning sheep industry to support the hotels so well; yet the two became intertwined.

From 1850 through 1890, a few pioneer Basques established way stations along major wagon and railway lines that welcomed travelers and sold them provisions. These early outposts form the first chapter in the history of California's *ostatuak*. By 1890, Basques had arrived in sufficient number to enter the state's booming sheep industry and support the development of Basque boardinghouses catering exclusively to their brothers, sisters, and cousins from Euskal Herria.

Table 13.1 Boardinghouses Still Operating in California and Nevada

| City | Boardinghouse | Year Established |
|---|---|---|
| | CALIFORNIA | |
| Bakersfield | Noriega | 1893 |
| Chino | Centro Vasco | 1940 |
| Fresno | Santa Fe Hotel | 1929 |
| | Basque Hotel | 1935 |
| San Francisco | Des Alpes | 1916 |
| | NEVADA | |
| Elko | Star Hotel | 1910 |
| Winnemucca | Winnemucca Hotel | 1919 |
| Gardnerville-Minden | Overland Hotel | 1908 |
| Reno | Louis' Basque Corner | 1960s |

*Note:* Each of the establishments listed here continues to conduct business in a Basque hotel, serving Basque family-style meals on a daily basis and taking in a few boarders. Since hotels such as the Martin Hotel in Winnemucca and the Woolgrowers' in Los Banos serve meals but no longer take in boarders, they were not included in this table. Note also that although each establishment listed here offers board to Basques, several also rent to non-Basques.

In San Francisco and Los Angeles, clusters of centrally located *ostatuak* opened and led to the formation of California's first two Basque towns. Spin-off hotels from the two centers cropped up next in major Basque settlements in the San Joaquin Valley and northern Nevada. From these sites Basques fanned out even further until all of the eleven states in the American West had boardinghouses. But with the passage of the National Origins Act in 1924 and the Taylor Grazing Act that followed a decade later, the prospects for Basque sheepmen began to dwindle. Also the development of new equipment such as the turbine-powered water pump allowed farmers to plant year-round, thus eliminating their dependence upon local sheepherders and their flocks for the clearing of stubble.

Although the legal importation of herders through the Western Range Association has continued to bring Basques to the United States since the 1940s, their numbers have dwindled in comparison to the years before the quota legislation was enacted.[2] As Basques who had come before the restrictive legislation moved on or passed away, the Basque hotels underwent dramatic transitions. Much less a home away from home, the *ostatuak* became Basque-owned businesses that served Basques but were progressively less dependent upon them.

*A wedding celebration at a Stockton boardinghouse, ca. 1920. Courtesy of the High Desert Museum, Bend, Oregon.*

In fact, one characteristic of Basque hotels has been their remarkable flexibility in adapting to the fluctuations in the sheep industry since the 1850s. Once tiny outposts along rough wagon roads, the hotels evolved into two- and three-story buildings that housed a complicated ethnic institution, providing health care, recreational facilities, employment opportunities, tips for travelers, and potential contacts throughout the Western states. When the Basque clientele became insufficient to support the offering of such diverse amenities, some of the *ostatuak* began to devolve through a gradual process.

The virtual disappearance of the Basque sheepherder in recent decades has been the *ostatuak's* final death knell. Of the 742 herders on Western Range contracts as of December 31, 1976, for example, 58 percent were from Latin America, and only 14 percent were culturally Basque.[3] That less than one sixth of the contract herders were Basque two decades ago illustrates that the ethnic profile of the sheepherders in the West began changing considerably. In the past twenty years the number of Basque herders coming to this country has dwindled to less than a quarter of that figure, to the point where young Basque herders are no longer coming via Western Range contracts. These developments also underscore the poor prospects for the future of Basque hotel keeping in the American West. The once critical *ostatuak* have reached the endangered list and face extinction in the early decades of the twenty-first century.

Throughout this work, I have asserted that the *ostatu* was a major social institution for immigrant Basques. The further suggestion that the *ostatu* has been the Basques' single most important institution in America is a more daring claim. Nonetheless, this assertion rests on the fact that the earliest Basques were single males who arrived without families and depended upon the hotels and other Basques for their daily survival. Also, the *ostatuak* were likely more critical to the Basque immigrant's life than were boardinghouses for other ethnic groups. Basques who emigrated to the Western United States were anything but a cross section of Old World society; they represented a very select group. Among the less educated and least likely to inherit, they were usually illiterate and from the rural-based *baserri* system. The nature of their work in the sheep industry was isolating and tended to promote further alienation from other cultures in the American West. It was not unusual, for example, for it to take a herder eight years to learn to speak English. More than any other group's ethnic boardinghouses the *ostatu* made it possible for the single Old World Basque herder to live life as a transplant in the States, while it supported a great deal of collective solidarity among Basques. In sum, research for this project has led me to conclude that Basques depended upon their boardinghouses more so than did their ethnic counterparts.

Recently, on an early-morning walk through the Noriega Hotel in Bakersfield, I was struck by the sense and size of the hotel. Standing in the midst of the old handball court, with its peeling paint and bird-infested bleachers, I was transported to another, earlier time. The crack of the *pilota* against the side wall and the cheers of fans encouraging their favorite player rang out from the now silent *cancha*. My mind's eye watched my father, then a young *pilotari*, with his broad Bizkaian smile beaming, who had convincingly defeated his opponent. During a later hotel visit I was likewise transported. On a fog-shrouded, sleepy morning in San Francisco, I buzzed the doorbell at Sorhondo's and gained entry through the unmarked doorway. As I ascended the creaking stairway that wrapped around to an upstairs hallway, I was overcome by the rich smells from Amelie's kitchen. So familiar were the aroma and the warmth of the place that for an instant I anticipated my mother rounding the corner that led to the kitchen.

Recently, a granddaughter of the Sabala hotel-keeping family from Nevada offered her reflections about the decline of the hotels in Gardnerville:

> There are those who say like Marcelino, the lone ex-herder who lives upstairs at the Overland, the hotels have outlived their purpose. They are nothing more than glorified, ethnic steak houses. But if you sit quietly, reverently watchful, as the rays of sunlight and warmth filter their way down upon the *mus* table; if you sit sipping a *vermut español* to *jotas Vascas*, C4 on the jukebox, waiting for Elvira to call you to the dining room; if you listen carefully, you'll hear them, feel them, know their collective story.[4]

No history can fully account for human experience, nor can this one fully explain why the *ostatuak* have been so dear to the Amerikanuak. Cherishing a thing of the past, feeling nostalgic for "times gone by," and recalling those who have gone before us perhaps heightens our fondness for things that will not come again. Beyond the longing for the past also lies the truth of Basque-American history: generation after generation of Basques have come to the hotels to discover themselves, relying upon an institution that has been embedded in their culture. Whether in California, Nevada, Montana, Oregon, Idaho, or New York, the *ostatuak* provided the physical setting where a people gathered and shared what and who they thought themselves to be. With a mixture of sadness over their demise and appreciation for all they have given us, we bid them *agur*.

# Epilogue

## *Agur* Lentxo

Lentxo Echanis came to live at our sheep ranch before I was born and remained after I left. As a toddler, I followed him around as he planted, watered, and tended his garden in the early mornings. I loved to listen to him talk of Mutriku, of coming to Amerika, and of his sweet memories and good friends in the hotels. When I was growing up, many Sundays Lentxo, members of my family, and I would pile into our '48 Chevy and head over the hills, past the Chilibolosts' Ranch, to the Centro Vasco in Chino. At the Centro Vasco I stood eye-level to the card tables and watched as my father and uncle tried to take Lentxo and his friend Agustin in several hands of *mus*. And on special occasions, such as the wedding of Agustin's daughter, I remember Lentxo grabbing my teenage hand and leading me to the dance floor, insisting that I join him in the *jota*.

Decades later, as I began considering this project, I realized that Lentxo's eighty-two years in the United States were intricately dependent upon the Basque hotels. Further, I knew that each boardinghouse had its own special individual history and that I could not possibly tell them all in the detail that some might desire. Instead, I decided to tell the stories I have had the pleasure of hearing—from those who lived in the hotels, worked in them, and depended upon them in significant ways.

*The author with John Yturry (left) and Lentxo Echanis in Brea, California, ca. 1988.*

Lentxo's visits to the *ostatuak* were representative of the experiences of thousands of Basques who arrived in the United States between 1890 and 1930 and had to make the transition to the New World. Further, his experiences during his eight-year transition between arriving in New York City and settling in southern California demonstrate the efficiency of the now defunct referral system among boardinghouses. In sum, Lentxo's story is not unique when compared with the immigration experiences of other Amerikanuak, nor was the extent to which he stopped at boardinghouses along his way.

As "homes away from home," the hotels offered conveniences to help Basque newcomers cope with the unfamiliar. As Lentxo summarized it simply: "All I ever had to do when I came to a new place was find a Basque hotel, . . . because there, they all would help you." In the hotels he found jobs, received practical assistance in matters of everyday life, picked up his mail, stored his camp gear and Sunday suit, met his wife, baptized his children, and celebrated special occasions.

A few years ago, Lentxo died at the age of ninety-eight. Well before that time I read him an early draft of this work. As we sat on the porch of the ranch that we had shared for over forty years, I wondered whether he would grant me permission to use his story in this work. At first, he looked at me as if I might have been a bit touched. He simply could not see what the fuss was all about. As we talked, he began to realize that his years in the United States really had paralleled the development of the boardinghouses, and that his experiences were in many ways representative of those of other Basques who had come to America over the course of the preceding century.

Lentxo's final words to me—"Keep up the good work and go get all them *hoteleros*"—indicated that he understood the project I had undertaken and that I had his blessing. Though he and all but a small number of the Basque hotels have gone, to my dear friend and the boardinghouses that brought him along I offer my thanks and fondest regards. *Agur ostatuak . . . agur nere lagun Lentxo. Eskerrik asko.*

# Appendices

## Appendix A

### BASQUE POPULATION IN THE UNITED STATES, 1980 AND 1990

| State | French Basques 1980 | French Basques 1990 | Spanish Basques 1980 | Spanish Basques 1990 |
|---|---|---|---|---|
| Alabama | 36 | 24 | 0 | 44 |
| Alaska | 10 | 37 | 33 | 38 |
| Arizona | 152 | 53 | 199 | 298 |
| Arkansas | 34 | 20 | 0 | 21 |
| California | 3,619 | 3,387 | 3,813 | 3,508 |
| Colorado | 341 | 148 | 168 | 110 |
| Connecticut | 36 | 22 | 64 | 64 |
| Delaware | 18 | 0 | 0 | 7 |
| District of Columbia | 22 | 0 | 12 | 16 |
| Florida | 201 | 117 | 315 | 334 |
| Georgia | 87 | 11 | 59 | 27 |
| Hawaii | 10 | 19 | 4 | 29 |
| Idaho | 221 | 166 | 600 | 353 |
| Illinois | 422 | 49 | 66 | 75 |
| Indiana | 94 | 55 | 48 | 0 |
| Iowa | 260 | 20 | 24 | 8 |
| Kansas | 92 | 10 | 18 | 24 |
| Kentucky | 81 | 11 | 15 | 15 |
| Louisiana | 133 | 73 | 57 | 38 |
| Maine | 22 | 2 | 0 | 21 |
| Maryland | 51 | 60 | 48 | 45 |
| Massachusetts | 34 | 37 | 80 | 73 |
| Michigan | 145 | 7 | 28 | 47 |
| Minnesota | 110 | 24 | 8 | 15 |
| Mississippi | 7 | 4 | 2 | 0 |
| Missouri | 164 | 27 | 18 | 10 |
| Montana | 116 | 66 | 6 | 46 |
| Nebraska | 2,707 | 0 | 6 | 0 |
| Nevada | 371 | 472 | 915 | 766 |
| New Hampshire | 3 | 0 | 0 | 0 |
| New Jersey | 98 | 72 | 134 | 143 |
| New Mexico | 87 | 63 | 83 | 61 |
| New York | 202 | 131 | 508 | 242 |
| North Carolina | 57 | 16 | 48 | 6 |

| Undifferentiated Basques | | Total Basques | |
|---|---|---|---|
| 1980 | 1990 | 1980 | 1990 |
| 46 | 14 | 82 | 82 |
| 62 | 170 | 105 | 245 |
| 749 | 965 | 1,100* | 1,316 |
| 39 | 63 | 73 | 104 |
| 8,098 | 12,227 | 15,530 | 19,122 |
| 446 | 679 | 955 | 937 |
| 120 | 233 | 220 | 319 |
| 3 | 6 | 21 | 13 |
| | | | |
| 29 | 21 | 63 | 37 |
| 343 | 738 | 859 | 1,189 |
| 77 | 90 | 223 | 128 |
| 55 | 121 | 69 | 169 |
| 3,511 | 5,068 | 4,332 | 5,587 |
| 165 | 321 | 654 | 445 |
| 18 | 135 | 160 | 190 |
| 40 | 31 | 324 | 59 |
| 50 | 36 | 160 | 70 |
| 36 | 68 | 132 | 94 |
| 65 | 115 | 255 | 226 |
| 28 | 13 | 50 | 36 |
| 148 | 163 | 247 | 268 |
| 187 | 227 | 301 | 337 |
| 158 | 162 | 331 | 236 |
| 102 | 91 | 220 | 130 |
| 20 | 24 | 29 | 28 |
| 61 | 114 | 243 | 151 |
| 268 | 357 | 390 | 469 |
| 41 | 45 | 2,754† | 45 |
| 2,092 | 3,592 | 3,378 | 4,840 |
| 29 | 53 | 32 | 53 |
| 265 | 319 | 497 | 534 |
| 291 | 378 | 461 | 502 |
| 716 | 927 | 1,426 | 1,300 |
| 31 | 97 | 136 | 119 |

| State | French Basques 1980 | French Basques 1990 | Spanish Basques 1980 | Spanish Basques 1990 |
|---|---|---|---|---|
| North Dakota | 25 | 0 | 0 | 0 |
| Ohio | 207 | 33 | 31 | 15 |
| Oklahoma | 21 | 0 | 5 | 23 |
| Oregon | 369 | 172 | 224 | 298 |
| Pennsylvania | 138 | 23 | 14 | 13 |
| Rhode Island | 5 | 0 | 44 | 0 |
| South Carolina | 25 | 4 | 31 | 14 |
| South Dakota | 50 | 0 | 7 | 8 |
| Tennessee | 34 | 2 | 4 | 14 |
| Texas | 159 | 98 | 170 | 238 |
| Utah | 129 | 148 | 134 | 261 |
| Vermont | 0 | 0 | 0 | 0 |
| Virginia | 168 | 19 | 72 | 59 |
| Washington | 124 | 145 | 306 | 154 |
| West Virginia | 78 | 0 | 5 | 0 |
| Wisconsin | 189 | 8 | 5 | 8 |
| Wyoming | 155 | 146 | 103 | 21 |
| Totals | 11,919 | 6,001 | 8,535 | 7,620 |

*Sources:* U.S. Bureau of the Census, *Ancestry of Population by State*, 1980, 51–56; Douglass, "Counting Basques," 3–7; Douglass, "The Basque Example," 289–96; and Douglass, "Re-counting Basques," 6.

*Notice that the 1990 Census reported eleven states with at least eight hundred Basque residents. When listed in order, they include: California, Idaho, Nevada, Oregon, Washington, Utah, Arizona, New York, Texas, Florida, and Colorado.

†Authorities acknowledge a tallying error for Nebraska's French Basque population in 1980.

| Undifferentiated Basques | | Total Basques | |
|---|---|---|---|
| 1980 | 1990 | 1980 | 1990 |
| 0 | 11 | 25 | 11 |
| 85 | 155 | 323 | 203 |
| 84 | 82 | 110 | 105 |
| 1,660 | 1,787 | 2,253 | 2,257 |
| 68 | 214 | 220 | 250 |
| 40 | 24 | 89 | 24 |
| 14 | 30 | 70 | 48 |
| 5 | 22 | 62 | 3 |
| 16 | 75 | 54 | 94 |
| 558 | 912 | 887 | 1,248 |
| 610 | 1,013 | 873 | 1,422 |
| 28 | 2 | 28 | 2 |
| 112 | 325 | 352 | 403 |
| 704 | 1,471 | 1,134 | 1,770 |
| 23 | 9 | 106 | 9 |
| 49 | 85 | 243 | 101 |
| 241 | 435 | 499 | 602 |
| 22,686‡ | 34,335 | 43,140§ | 47,956 |

‡In 1990 about 72 percent of the subjects self-identified as undifferentiated Basques, as opposed to 52 percent ten years before. These statistics substantiate a trend among American Basques to drop the emphasis on "French versus Spanish" Basque distinctions.

§Scholars have suggested a number of explanations for the apparent overall growth of the Basque American population in recent years. One significant factor is the improved collection and recording procedures used by the U.S. Bureau of the Census. A second important consideration is that ethnic identity, such as Basque, is left to the perception of the subject. That is, some of these respondents may have been born in the Basque region and some could be fourth or fifth generation.

## Appendix B

CHRONOLOGICAL LISTING OF *Ostatuak*

| Date | Name and Location |
|---|---|
| 1856 | Plaza Hotel, San Juan Bautista, California |
| 1863 | Indart Adobe, Sentinella Ranch, California |
| 1866 | Aguirre Hotel, San Francisco, California |
| 1874 | Tres Pinos Hotel, Tres Pinos, California |
| 1878 | Levque's Boarding House, Los Angeles, California |
| 1878 | Oyharzabal's French Hotel, San Juan Capistrano, California |
| 1880 | Yparraguirre's Hotel Vasco, San Francisco, California |
| 1881 | Ballade's or Pyrenees, Los Angeles, California |
| | Harotcavena's, Los Angeles, California |
| | Hotel de France, Los Angeles, California |
| | Hirigoyen's Boarding House, Los Angeles, California |
| 1884 | Iribarne Hotel, Chester, California |
| 1886 | Sartiart's Boarding House, Los Angeles, California |
| | White's Bridge Hotel, White's Bridge, California |
| 1888 | Hotel des Basse Pyrenees, Los Angeles, California |
| 1890s | Idiart Hotel, Firebaugh, California |
| 1890 | Central Hotel (Mouren's), Huron, California |
| | Europa Hotel, San Francisco, California |
| | Hiriart House, Los Angeles, California |
| | Hotel des Basses-Pyrenees, San Francisco, California |
| | Hotel de France, San Francisco, California |
| 1891 | Hotel de Europe, Los Angeles, California |
| 1893 | Arnaudon Hotel, Mendota, California |
| | Buena Vista House, Los Angeles, California |
| | Eskualdun Ostatua, Los Angeles, California |
| | Hotel de Bayonne, Los Angeles, California |
| | Hotel d' Europe, San Diego, California |
| | Hotel Maritonia, Los Angeles, California |
| | *Iberia (Noriega) Hotel, Bakersfield, California |
| | New Lake House, San Jose, California |
| | Ostatua Frantsesa, Bishop, California |
| 1895 | Basses-Pyrenees Hotel, Tehachapi, California |
| | Piute Hotel, Tehachapi, California |
| 1896 | Basko Hotel, Tehachapi, California |
| | European House, Los Angeles, California |
| | Pension Francaise, Los Angeles, California |
| | Savart's Boarding House, San Francisco, California |
| 1897 | Bascongado Hotel, Fresno, California |

| | |
|---|---|
| 1899 | Borderre's French Hotel, Santa Barbara, California |
| | New Pyrenees Hotel, San Francisco, California |
| 1900 | Azcuenaga's Oregon Hotel, Boise, Idaho |
| | French Hotel, Reno, Nevada |
| | Fresno "Sheepcamp" Hotel, Fresno, California |
| | Hotel Cesmat, Tehachapi, California |
| | Pyrenees Hotel, Los Angeles, California |
| | Spanish Hotel and Restaurant, Boise, Idaho |
| 1901 | Hotel des Pyrenees, Fresno, California |
| | Pyrenees Hotel, Bakersfield, California |
| 1903 | Star Rooming House, Boise, Idaho |
| 1904 | Commercial Hotel, Reno, Nevada |
| | Hotel des Alpes (on Pacific), San Francisco, California |
| | Hotel Español, Los Angeles, California |
| 1906 | Español Hotel, Reno, Nevada |
| | Hotel d' Europe, Bakersfield, California |
| | Hotel Indart, Reno, Nevada |
| 1907 | Anchustegui's Basque Hotel, Mountain Home, Idaho |
| | Ascuena's Casa Española, Gooding, Idaho |
| | Basque Hotel (on Hazelton), Stockton, California |
| | Hotel de France, Stockton, California |
| | Hotel de Spanio, Fresno, California |
| | Telescope Hotel, Elko, Nevada |
| | Yrionda's Boarding House, San Francisco, California |
| 1908 | Aguirre's, New York City |
| | Butcher House, Reno, Nevada |
| | Hotel España, San Francisco, California |
| | Hotel Royal, Stockton, California |
| | Hotel Yberico, San Francisco, California |
| | Sabala's Overland Hotel, Elko, Nevada |
| | Yturri-Marquina's "Yellow House," Jordan Valley, Oregon |
| 1909 | Hotel La Bilbaina, Stockton, California |
| | Larrabaster's, Rock Springs, Wyoming |
| | Mayo's Boarding House, Los Angeles, California |
| | Soloaga's Basque Hotel, Shoshone, Idaho |
| 1910s | Agulia's, Marysville, California |
| | Allende's Star Hotel, Park City, Utah |
| | Arrieta's, Battle Mountain, Nevada |
| | Belza's, Marysville, California |
| | Commercial, Battle Mountain, Nevada |
| | Elorriaga's, Jordan Valley, Oregon |
| | Gastenaga's, Paradise Valley, Nevada |
| | Idlewild Hotel, Buffalo, Wyoming |

| | |
|---|---|
| | Jesus's, Flagstaff, Arizona |
| | Juarena's, Cedarville, California |
| | Larre's Boarding House, Winnemucca, Nevada |
| | Madarieta's, Boise, Idaho |
| | Mendiola's, Hailey, Idaho |
| | Mendiola's, Marysville, California |
| | Mendive, Battle Mountain, Nevada |
| | Miles City Hotel, Montana |
| | Occidental Hotel, Buffalo, Wyoming |
| | Paradise Valley Hotel, Paradise Valley, Nevada |
| | Pocatello Hotel, Pocatello, Idaho |
| | Pyrenees French Basque, Ogden, Utah |
| | Star Hotel, Grand Junction, Colorado |
| | Tayo's, Rock Springs, Wyoming |
| | Tehesta's, Marysville, California |
| | Ugarte's Bark Hotel, Marysville, California |
| | Unionville or Evans Exchange Hotel, Unionville, Nevada |
| | Uriz's, Marysville, California |
| | Urquidi's, Crane, Oregon |
| | Viscaino, Ogden, Utah |
| | Yriberri's Boarding House, San Francisco, California |
| 1910 | Beitia's, Shoshone, Idaho |
| | Bengoechea's Mountain Home Hotel, Mountain Home, Idaho |
| | Bermensolo's, Nampa, Idaho |
| | Bicandi's Boarding House, Boise, Idaho |
| | Frechou House, Fresno, California |
| | *Star Hotel, Elko, Nevada |
| 1911 | Arriaga-Unamuno's, Hailey, Idaho |
| | Saracondi's, Boise, Idaho |
| 1912 | Basque Hotel (on Hunter), Stockton, California |
| | Bengochea's Boarding House, Los Angeles, California |
| | Capitol Rooming House, Boise, Idaho |
| | DeLamar Rooming House, Boise, Idaho |
| | Elizalde's-Arralde's, Yakima, Washington |
| | Hotel Basco, Stockton, California |
| | Hotel de France, San Francisco, California |
| | Olasso's Boarding House, Los Angeles, California |
| | Oyamburu, Los Angeles, California |
| | Sempere's Boarding House, Los Angeles, California |
| | Unamuno's Spanish, Vale, Oregon |
| | Urruty's Boarding House, Los Angeles, California |
| | Victoria Hotel, Los Angeles, California |
| 1914 | Anduiza's, Boise, Idaho |

| | |
|---|---|
| | Arrego's, Boise, Idaho |
| | Franco-American Hotel, Tehachapi, California |
| | Lassart Hotel, Los Banos, California |
| | Madariaga's, Jordan Valley, Oregon |
| | Martin's Rooming House, Boise, Idaho |
| | Yriberri's, Reno, Nevada |
| 1915 | Ormachea's/Barbero's, Boise, Idaho |
| 1916 | Hotel des Alpes (on Broadway), San Francisco, California |
| | Hotel Central, Stockton, California |
| | Hotel Español, Stockton, California |
| | Hotel de France, San Francisco, California |
| 1917 | Charcha's, Emmett, Idaho |
| | Egu's Boarding House, Santa Barbara, California |
| | Hotel España, Stockton, California |
| | Mendiola's, Shoshone, Idaho |
| 1918 | Arrego's/Arguinchona's, Boise, Idaho |
| | Arriola's, Boise, Idaho |
| | Bilaustegui's, Boise, Idaho |
| | Oneida's, Shoshone, Idaho |
| | Uberuaga's, Boise, Idaho |
| | Yribar's or Ybar's, Boise, Idaho |
| 1919 | French Hotel, Carson City, Nevada |
| | Retolaza's Cantabarria, Grand Junction, Colorado |
| | Silver State Hotel, Battle Mountain, Nevada |
| | *Winnemucca Hotel, Winnemucca, Nevada |
| 1920s | Abaurrea's Hotel Español, San Francisco, California |
| | Allies Hotel, Price, Utah |
| | Alvarez's, Yakima, Washington |
| | Amistad, Elko, Nevada |
| | Anchordoquy's, Santa Barbara, California |
| | Basabe's Hotel Iriarte, San Francisco, California |
| | Basque House, Guadalupe, California |
| | Busch Hotel, Winnemucca, Nevada |
| | Chachon's, Winslow, Arizona |
| | Cordana's Ely and Plaza Hotels, Ely, Nevada |
| | Elk Hotel, Elko, Nevada |
| | Esain's, Yakima, Washington |
| | Estea's, Oroville, California |
| | Estrella, Marysville, California |
| | French Hotel, Price, Utah |
| | Garretch's Railroad Depot Hotel, Elko, Nevada |
| | Goicoechea's, Gooding, Idaho |
| | Hotel du Midi, San Francisco, California |

Hotel España, Sacramento, California
Hotel España, Santa Barbara, California
Irigaray's Ely Hotel, Ely, Nevada
Mariluch's-Cordana's Spokane Hotel, Ely, Nevada
Mariluch's Currie Ranch Hotel, Currie Ranch, near Ely, Nevada
Martin Hotel, Winnemucca, Nevada
Menchaca's, Hailey, Idaho
Metropole Hotel, Bakersfield, California
Pagoaga's, Shoshone, Idaho
Parma Hotel, Parma, Idaho
Pyrenees Hotel, Alturas, California
Uriarte's Elko Boarding House, Elko, Nevada
Urizar's, Andrews, Oregon
Uruburu's, San Pedro, California
Zabala's, Highland Boy, Utah

1920 Jausoro's Spanish Hotel, Nampa, Idaho
Sabala's, Twin Falls, Idaho
Arregui's, Boise, Idaho
Estrella Hotel, Stockton, California
Letemendi's, Boise, Idaho
Loisate's, Rock Springs, Wyoming

1921 *Overland Hotel, Gardnerville-Minden, Nevada
Ysursa's, Boise, Idaho

1922 Azcuenaga's Jordan Valley Hotel, Jordan Valley, Oregon
Echanis, Ontario, Oregon
Juanita Hotel, Tehachapi, California
Uriaguereca's, Gooding, Idaho

1923 Atiyeh's, Shoshone, Idaho
Hotel Español, Sacramento, California
Jayo's, Boise, Idaho
Pedroarena's or Arena's, Alturas, California

1924 California Hotel, Stockton, California
Inda's Spanish Hotel, Eureka, Nevada
Iribarne's Boarding House, McKittrick, California
Laxague Hotel, Fresno, California
Morning Star Hotel, Fallon, Nevada
Royal Hotel, Stockton, California
Trevino's, Park City, Utah

1925 Bicandi's Boarding House, Emmett, Idaho
Gabica's Metropole, Boise, Idaho
Mingo-Soloaga's, Mullan, Idaho
Selaya's, Twin Falls, Idaho
Urrutia's, Shoshone, Idaho

Woolgrowers Hotel, Los Banos, California
1926 Star Hotel, Burns, Oregon
1927 Alturas Hotel, Reno, Nevada
Landa's Hogar Hotel, Salt Lake City, Utah
Nevada Hotel, Elko, Nevada
Old Toscano Hotel, Reno, Nevada
1929 Berriochoa's, Shoshone, Idaho
Hotel des Pyrenees, Merced, California
Plaza Hotel, Burns, Oregon
*Santa Fe Hotel, Fresno, California
Santa Fe Hotel, Reno, Nevada
Villanueva's Boarding House, Fresno, California
Victoria Hotel, Fresno, California
West Hotel, Elko, Nevada
1930s Alcorta's McDermitt Hotel, McDermitt, Nevada
Ansola's, Shoshone, Idaho
M. Ardans', Buffalo, Wyoming
Arrascada's, Gold Creek, Nevada
Arrascada's, Golconda, Nevada
Dominica Bejino's, Buffalo, Wyoming
Bilbao's, Twin Falls, Idaho
Bilbao's Place, Buffalo, Wyoming
Bilbao-Bengoechea's, Jerome, Idaho
East Fork Hotel, Gardnerville-Minden,Nevada
Ebar's Rooming House, Burns, Oregon
Etcheverry's, Pocatello, Idaho
French Hotel, Gardnerville-Minden, Nevada
Garay's, Yakima, Washington
Grand Hotel, Fallon, Nevada
Grants Hotel, Grants, New Mexico
Mrs. Irigaray's, Buffalo, Wyoming
Itçaina's, Yakima, Washington
Laborde's Eureka Hotel and Cafe, Eureka, Nevada
"La Chata's," Rupert, Idaho
Landa's, Eureka, Nevada
Larraneta's, Burns, Oregon
Lovelock Hotel, Lovelock, Nevada
Orueta's Commercial Hotel, Ely, Nevada
Otasue's Fonda Español, Salt Lake City, Utah
Beltran Paris's Scott Rooms, Ely, Nevada
Puente Hotel, Puente, California
Star Hotel, Golconda, Nevada
1930 Beterbide's Boarding House, Susanville, California

| | |
|---|---|
| | Valley Hotel, Puente, California |
| 1931 | Amestoy Hotel, Bakersfield, California |
| | Tehachapi Hotel, Tehachapi, California |
| 1932 | Altona Hotel, Reno, Nevada |
| 1933 | Campos's Boarding House, Santa Barbara, California |
| 1934 | Astorquia's Rialto Hotel, Hailey, Idaho |
| 1935 | *Basque Hotel, Fresno, California |
| | French Hotel, Stockton, California |
| | Hotel Basque, Stockton, California |
| | Pyrenees Hotel, Stockton, California |
| 1936 | Aldape's Silver State Bar and Hotel, Austin, Nevada |
| | Echevarria's Blue Bird, Boise, Idaho |
| | Eisaguirre's, Grand Junction, Colorado |
| | Inchausti's, Hailey, Idaho |
| | La Coste, Stockton, California |
| | Modern Hotel, Nampa, Idaho |
| | Murelaga's Economy Hotel, Boise, Idaho |
| | Urresti's Eagle, Boise, Idaho |
| 1939 | Bilbao's, Boise, Idaho |
| | Gogenola's, Jerome, Idaho |
| 1940s | Anza's, Montrose, Colorado |
| | Echeverria's, Cascade, Idaho |
| | Gamboa's, Gooding, Idaho |
| | Goñi's, Wellington, Nevada |
| | Olaverria's, Twin Falls, Idaho |
| | Onaindia's, Cascade, Idaho |
| | Sorhondo's Pyrenees, San Francisco, California |
| 1940 | *Centro Vasco, Chino, California |
| | Yturri Hotel, Fresno, California |
| 1941 | Martin Hotel, Reno, Nevada |
| | Ysursa's Valencia Hotel, Boise, Idaho |
| 1943 | Obrero Hotel, San Francisco, California |
| 1945 | Bilbao's Valley Club and Emery Hotel, Cascade, Idaho |
| | Royal Hotel, Mountain Home, Idaho |
| 1947 | Pyrenees Hotel, Gardnerville-Minden, Nevada |
| | St. Francis Hotel, Susanville, California |
| | Sallaberry's-Labarry's Colonnade, Eureka, Nevada |
| 1949 | Basconia, Stockton, California |
| | Woolgrowers' Hotel, Stockton, California |
| 1950s | Imperial Hotel, Park City, Utah |
| | Bengoechea's, Twin Falls, Idaho |
| | Sabala's, Boise, Idaho |
| | Sabala's Del Rio, Boise, Idaho |

| | |
|---|---|
| 1952 | Arruabarrena's Mesa Hotel, Montrose, Colorado |
| 1957 | Carmen Arruti's, Mountain Home, Idaho |
| 1960s | Basque Hotel, San Francisco, California |
| | Errecart's Clifton Hotel, Elko, Nevada |
| | Hotel de France, San Francisco, California |
| | *Louis' Basque Corner, Reno, Nevada |
| | J & T Hotel, Gardnerville-Minden, Nevada |
| 1970s | Uscola's Nuevo Viscaya, Boise, Idaho |

*Note:* This appendix lists chronologically all the Basque hotels discovered during the course of this project. Although some have spanned many decades of business, each is listed by the approximate year when it first appeared. When the exact year of opening was not available, the decade was used instead. A few long-standing hotels may appear more than once if different owners managed the hotels for lengthy amounts of time.

Those hotels marked with an asterisk (*) are Basque-owned establishments that offer room and board today.

## Appendix C

*Ostatuak* AND THEIR OWNERS/OPERATORS
(by State, City/Town, and Approximate Year(s) of Opening)

| Location(s) | Opening Year(s) |
|---|---|
| **ARIZONA** | |
| *Flagstaff* | |
| Jesus's | 1910s |
| *Winslow* | |
| Chachon's | 1920s |
| **CALIFORNIA** | |
| *Alturas* | |
| Pedroarena's or Arena's | 1923 |
| Pyrenees Hotel | 1920s |
| *Bakersfield* | |
| Amestoy Hotel | 1931 |
| Hotel d'Europe | 1906 |
| Iberia (Noriega) Hotel | 1893 |
| Metropole Hotel | 1920s |
| Pyrenees Hotel | 1901 |
| *Bishop* | |
| Ostatua Frantsesa | 1893 |
| *Cedarville* | |
| Juarena's | 1910s |
| *Chester* | |
| Iribarne's Chester Hotel | 1884 |
| *Chino* | |
| Centro Vasco | 1940 |
| *Firebaugh* | |
| Idiart Hotel | 1890s |
| *Fresno* | |
| Bascongado Hotel | 1897 |
| Basque Hotel | 1929 |

| | |
|---|---|
| Frechou House | 1910 |
| Fresno ("Sheepcamp") Hotel | 1900 |
| Hotel des Pyrenees | 1901 |
| Hotel de Spanio | 1907 |
| Laxague Hotel | 1924 |
| Santa Fe Hotel | 1926 |
| Victoria Hotel | 1929 |
| Villanueva's Boarding House | 1929 |
| Yturri Hotel | 1940 |

### Guadalupe

| | |
|---|---|
| Basque House | 1920s |

### Huron

| | |
|---|---|
| Mouren's Central Hotel | 1890 |

### La Puente

| | |
|---|---|
| Puente Hotel | 1930s |
| Valley Hotel | 1930 |

### Los Angeles

| | |
|---|---|
| Ballade's or Pyrenees | 1881 |
| Bengochea's Boarding House | 1920 |
| Buena Vista House | 1893 |
| Eskualdun Ostatua or Pension Francaise | 1893 |
| European House | 1896 |
| Harotcavena's Boarding House | 1881 |
| Hiriart House | 1900 |
| Hirigoyen's Boarding House | 1881 |
| Hotel des Basse Pyrenees | 1888 |
| Hotel de Bayonne | 1893 |
| Hotel Español | 1904 |
| Hotel de Europe | 1891 |
| Hotel de France | 1881 |
| Hotel Maritonia | 1893 |
| Levque's Boarding House | 1878 |
| Mayo's Boarding House | 1909 |
| Olasso's Boarding House | 1912 |
| Oyamburu | 1912 |
| Pension Francaise | 1896 |
| Pyrenees Hotel | 1900 |
| Sartiart's Boarding House | 1886 |

| | |
|---|---|
| Sempere's Boarding House | 1912 |
| Urruty's Boarding House | 1912 |
| Victoria Hotel | 1912 |

Los Banos

| | |
|---|---|
| Lassart Hotel | 1914 |
| Woolgrowers Hotel | 1925 |

McKittrick

| | |
|---|---|
| Iribarne's Boarding House | 1924 |

Marysville

| | |
|---|---|
| Agulia's | 1910s |
| Belza's | 1910s |
| Estrella | 1920s |
| Mendiola's | 1910s |
| Tehesta's | 1910s |
| Ugarte's Bark Hotel | 1910s |
| Uriz's | 1910s |

Mendota

| | |
|---|---|
| Arnaudon Hotel | 1893 |

Merced

| | |
|---|---|
| Hotel des Pyrenees | 1939 |

Oroville

| | |
|---|---|
| Estea's | 1920s |

Sacramento

| | |
|---|---|
| Hotel España | 1920s |
| Hotel Español | 1923 |

San Diego

| | |
|---|---|
| Hotel d' Europe | 1893 |

San Francisco

| | |
|---|---|
| Abaurrea's Hotel Español | 1920s |
| Aguirre Hotel | 1866 |
| Basabe's Hotel Iriarte | 1920s |
| Basque Hotel | 1960s |
| Europa Hotel | 1899 |
| Hotel des Alpes (on Pacific) | 1904 |

| | |
|---|---|
| Hotel des Alpes (on Broadway) | 1916 |
| Hotel des Basse-Pyrenees | 1890 |
| Hotel España | 1908 |
| Hotel de France | 1890 |
| Hotel de France | 1912 |
| Hotel de France | 1916 |
| Hotel de France | 1960s |
| Hotel du Midi | 1920s |
| Hotel Yberico | 1908 |
| New Pyrenees Hotel | 1899 |
| Obrero Hotel | 1943 |
| Savart's Boarding House | 1896 |
| Sorhondo's Pyrenees | 1940s |
| Yparraguirre's Hotel Vasco | 1888 |
| Yriberri's Boarding House | 1910s |
| Yrionda's Boarding House | 1907 |

San Jose

| | |
|---|---|
| New Lake House | 1893 |

San Juan Bautista

| | |
|---|---|
| Plaza Hotel | 1856 |

San Juan Capistrano

| | |
|---|---|
| Oyharzabal's French Hotel | 1878 |

San Pedro

| | |
|---|---|
| Uruburu's | 1920s |

Santa Barbara

| | |
|---|---|
| Anchordoquy's Boarding House | 1920s |
| Borderre's French Hotel | 1899 |
| Campos's Boarding House | 1933 |
| Egu's Boarding House | 1917 |
| Hotel España | 1920s |

Sentinella Ranch

| | |
|---|---|
| Indart Adobe | 1863 |

Stockton

| | |
|---|---|
| Basconia Hotel | 1949 |
| Basque Hotel (Hazelton) | 1907 |
| Basque Hotel (Hunter) | 1912 |

| | |
|---|---|
| California Hotel | 1924 |
| Estrella Hotel | 1921 |
| French Hotel | 1935 |
| Hotel Basco | 1912 |
| Hotel Basque | 1935 |
| Hotel La Bilbaina | 1909 |
| Hotel Central | 1916 |
| Hotel España | 1917 |
| Hotel Español | 1916 |
| Hotel de France | 1907 |
| Hotel Royal | 1908 |
| La Coste | 1936 |
| Pyrenees Hotel | 1935 |
| Royal Hotel | 1924 |
| Woolgrowers Hotel | 1949 |

Susanville

| | |
|---|---|
| Beterbide's Boarding House | 1930 |
| St. Francis Hotel | 1947 |

Tehachapi

| | |
|---|---|
| Basko Hotel | 1896 |
| Basses-Pyrenees Hotel | 1895 |
| Franco-American Hotel | 1914 |
| Hotel Cesmat | 1900 |
| Juanita Hotel | 1922 |
| Piute Hotel | 1895 |
| Tehachapi Hotel | 1931 |

Tres Pinos

| | |
|---|---|
| Tres Pinos Hotel | 1874 |

White's Bridge

| | |
|---|---|
| White's Bridge Hotel | 1886 |

COLORADO

Grand Junction

| | |
|---|---|
| Eisaguirre's | 1936 |
| Retolaza's Cantabarria | 1919 |
| Star Hotel | 1910s |

### Montrose

| | |
|---|---|
| Anza's | 1940s |
| Arruabarrena's Mesa Hotel | 1952 |

## IDAHO

### Boise

| | |
|---|---|
| Anduiza's | 1914 |
| Arrego's | 1914 |
| Arrego/Arguinchona's | 1918 |
| Arregui's | 1921 |
| Arriola's | 1918 |
| Azcuenaga's Oregon Hotel | 1900 |
| Bicandi's Boarding House | 1910 |
| Bilaustegui's | 1918 |
| Bilbao's | 1939 |
| Capitol Rooming House | 1912 |
| DeLamar Rooming House | 1912 |
| Echevarria's Blue Bird | 1936 |
| Gabica's Metropole | 1925 |
| Jayo's | 1923 |
| Letemendi's | 1921 |
| Madarieta's | 1910s |
| Martin's Rooming House | 1914 |
| Murelaga's Economy Hotel | 1936 |
| Ormachea's/Barbero's | 1915 |
| Sabala's | 1950 |
| Sabala's Del Rio | 1950 |
| Saracondi's | 1911 |
| Spanish Hotel and Restaurant | 1900 |
| Star Rooming House | 1903 |
| Uberuaga's | 1918 |
| Urresti's Eagle | 1936 |
| Uscola's Nuevo Viscaya | 1970s |
| Yribar's, Ybar's | 1918 |
| Ysursa's Modern Hotel | 1921 |
| Ysursa's Valencia Hotel | 1941 |

### Caldwell

| | |
|---|---|
| Caldwell Hotel | unknown |

Cascade

| | |
|---|---|
| Bilbao's Valley Clu and Emery Hotel | 1945 |
| Echeverria's | 1940s |
| Onaindia's | 1940s |

Emmett

| | |
|---|---|
| Bicandi's Boarding House | 1925 |
| Charcha's | 1917 |

Gooding

| | |
|---|---|
| Ascuena's Casa Española | 1907 |
| Gamboa's | 1940s |
| Goicoechea's | 1920s |
| Uriaguereca's | 1922 |

Hailey

| | |
|---|---|
| Arriaga-Unamuno's | 1911 |
| Astorquia's Rialto Hotel | 1934 |
| Inchausti's | 1936 |
| Menchaca's | 1920s |
| Mendiola's | 1910s |

Jerome

| | |
|---|---|
| Bilbao-Bengoechea's | 1930s |
| Gogenola's | 1939 |

MacKay

| | |
|---|---|
| Urresti's | 1930s |

Mountain Home

| | |
|---|---|
| Anchustegui's Basque Hotel | 1907 |
| Carmen Arruti's | 1957 |
| Bengoechea's Mountain Home Hotel | 1910 |
| Royal Hotel | 1945 |

Mullan

| | |
|---|---|
| Mingo-Soloaga's | 1925 |

Nampa

| | |
|---|---|
| Bermensolo's | 1910 |

| | |
|---|---|
| Jausoro's Spanish Hotel | 1920 |
| Modern Hotel | 1936 |

Parma

| | |
|---|---|
| Parma Hotel | 1920s |

Pocatello

| | |
|---|---|
| Etcheverry's | 1930s |
| Pocatello Hotel | 1910s |

Rupert

| | |
|---|---|
| "La Chata's" | 1930s |

Shoshone

| | |
|---|---|
| Ansola's | 1930s |
| Atiyeh's | 1923 |
| Beitia's | 1910 |
| Berriochoa's | 1929 |
| Mendiola's | 1917 |
| Oneida's | 1918 |
| Pagoaga's | 1920s |
| Soloaga's Basque Hotel | 1909 |
| Urrutia's | 1925 |

Twin Falls

| | |
|---|---|
| Bengoechea's | 1950 |
| Bilbao's | 1930s |
| Olaverria's | 1940s |
| Sabala's | 1920 |
| Selaya's | 1925 |

MONTANA

Miles City

| | |
|---|---|
| Miles City Hotel | 1910s |

NEVADA

Austin

| | |
|---|---|
| Aldape's Silver State Bar and Hotel | 1936 |

Battle Mountain

| | |
|---|---|
| Arrieta's | 1910s |

| | |
|---|---|
| Commercial | 1910s |
| Mendive | 1910s |
| Silver State Hotel | 1919 |

Carson City

| | |
|---|---|
| French Hotel | 1910s |

Currie Ranch

| | |
|---|---|
| Mariluch's Currie Ranch Hotel, outside of Ely | 1920s |

Elko

| | |
|---|---|
| Amistad | 1920s |
| Arrascada's | 1920s |
| Errecart's Clifton Hotel | 1960s |
| Garretch's Railroad Depot Hotel | 1920s |
| Nevada Hotel | 1927 |
| Sabala's Overland Hotel | 1908 |
| Star Hotel | 1910 |
| Telescope Hotel | 1907 |
| Uriarte's Elko Boarding House | 1920s |
| West Hotel | 1929 |

Ely

| | |
|---|---|
| Beltran Paris's Scott Rooms | 1930s |
| Cordana's Ely and Plaza Hotels | 1920s |
| Irigaray's Ely Hotel | 1920s |
| Mariluch/Cordana's Spokane Hotel | 1920s |
| Orueta's Commercial Hotel | 1930s |

Eureka

| | |
|---|---|
| Inda's Spanish Hotel | 1924 |
| Laborde's Eureka Hotel | 1930s |
| Landa's | 1930s |
| Sallaberry-Labarry's Colonnade | 1947 |

Fallon

| | |
|---|---|
| Grand Hotel | 1930s |
| Morning Star Hotel | 1924 |

### Gardnerville-Minden

| | |
|---|---|
| East Fork Hotel | 1930s |
| French Hotel | 1930s |
| J & T Hotel | 1960 |
| Overland Hotel | 1921 |
| Pyrenees Hotel | 1947 |

### Golconda

| | |
|---|---|
| Arrascada's | 1930s |
| Star Hotel | 1930s |

### Gold Creek

| | |
|---|---|
| Arrascada's | 1930s |

### Jack Creek

| | |
|---|---|
| Jack Creek Hotel | 1900 |

### Lovelock

| | |
|---|---|
| Lovelock Hotel | 1930s |

### McDermitt

| | |
|---|---|
| Alcorta's McDermitt Hotel | 1930s |

### Paradise Valley

| | |
|---|---|
| Bridge Street Hotel | 1910s |
| Gastenaga's | 1910 |
| Paradise Valley Hotel | 1900s |

### Reno

| | |
|---|---|
| Altona Hotel | 1932 |
| Alturas Hotel | 1927 |
| Butcher House | 1912 |
| Colonial Hotel Español | 1911 |
| Commercial Hotel | 1904 |
| Español Hotel | 1906 |
| French Hotel | 1900 |
| Hotel Indart | 1906 |
| Louis' Basque Corner | 1960s |
| Martin Hotel | 1941 |
| Old Toscano Hotel | 1927 |
| Santa Fe Hotel | 1929 |
| Yriberri's | 1914 |

### Unionville

| | |
|---|---|
| Unionville or Evans Exchange Hotel | 1910s |

### Wellington

| | |
|---|---|
| Goñi's Hotel | 1940s |

### Winnemucca

| | |
|---|---|
| Busch Hotel | 1920s |
| Larre's Boarding House | 1910s |
| Martin Hotel | 1920s |
| Winnemucca Hotel | 1919 |

## NEW MEXICO

### Grants

| | |
|---|---|
| Grants Hotel | 1930s |

## NEW YORK

### New York City

| | |
|---|---|
| Aguirre's | 1908 |

## OREGON

### Andrews

| | |
|---|---|
| Urizar's | 1920s |

### Burns

| | |
|---|---|
| Ebar's Rooming House | 1930s |
| Larraneta's | 1930s |
| Plaza Hotel | 1929 |
| Star Hotel | 1926 |

### Crane

| | |
|---|---|
| Urquidi's | 1910s |

### Jordan Valley

| | |
|---|---|
| Azcuenaga's Jordan Valley Hotel | 1922 |
| Elorriaga's | 1910s |
| Madariaga's | 1914 |
| Yturri-Marquina's "Yellow House" | 1908 |

### Ontario

| | |
|---|---|
| Echanis | 1922 |

### Vale

| | |
|---|---|
| Unamuno's Spanish | 1912 |

## UTAH

### Highland Boy

| | |
|---|---|
| Zabala's | 1920s |

### Ogden

| | |
|---|---|
| Pyrenees French Basque | 1910s |
| Viscaino | 1910s |

### Park City

| | |
|---|---|
| Allende's Star Hotel | 1910s |
| Imperial Hotel | 1950s |
| Trevino's | 1924 |

### Price

| | |
|---|---|
| Allies Hotel | 1920s |
| French Hotel | 1920s |

### Salt Lake City

| | |
|---|---|
| Landa's Hogar Hotel | 1927 |
| Otasue's Fonda Español | 1930s |

## WASHINGTON

### Yakima

| | |
|---|---|
| Alvarez's | 1920s |
| Elizalde's-Arralde's | 1912 |
| Esain's | 1920s |
| Garay's | 1930s |
| Itçaina's | 1930s |

## WYOMING

### Buffalo

| | |
|---|---|
| M. Ardans' | 1930s |
| Dominica Bejino's | 1930s |
| Bilbao's Place | 1930s |

| | |
|---|---|
| Idlewild Hotel | 1910s |
| Mrs. Irigaray's | 1930s |
| Occidental Hotel | 1917 |

Rock Springs

| | |
|---|---|
| Larrabaster's | 1909 |
| Loisate's | 1921 |
| Tayo's | 1910s |

# Notes

## PROLOGUE. LENTXO: COMING TO AMERIKA, BASQUE-STYLE

1. Brief definitions and explanations of foreign terms used in this text, such as *hoteleros* (hotelkeepers), can be found in the Glossary.

2. William A. Douglass and Jon Bilbao, *Amerikanuak: Basques in the New World* (Reno: University of Nevada Press, 1975), 151, 160. Like so many scholarly efforts dealing with Basque American topics since the publication of *Amerikanuak*, this text is greatly indebted to authors William A. Douglass and Jon Bilbao for their landmark history of the Basque diaspora in the New World.

3. After decades of using Spanish and English in the American West, Lentxo mixed descriptions of his early years in Spanish, Gipuzkoan Basque, and English. Please refer to the map of the seven Basque provinces in Chapter 1 (Figure 1.1) for the locations of Gipuzkoa and Mutriku.

4. Lorenzo (Lentxo) Echanis, interview with author, Brea, California, February 16, 1984. Oral History Collection, University of North Texas, Denton, Texas. All quoted and non-quoted material on Lentxo is taken from either the North Texas interview or a series of subsequent interviews with the author on April 28, May 30, June 3, and October 8 of 1987; January 22 and July 5 of 1988; February 6, 1989; December 20, 1991; January 4 and 6 of 1992; and July 2 and November 5 of 1993 in Brea, California. In addition, the original draft of this chapter was reviewed and approved by Lentxo in 1993.

5. Lentxo remembered the ship's name as the *La Turena*, though this name seems unlikely since it was a French ocean liner. Another French ship cited by several High Desert Basques who traveled the same route as Lentxo was *La Touraine*.

6. Emilia Doyaga, "History of *Euzko-Extea* of New York," in *First International Basque Conference in North America*, ed. Society of Basque Studies in America (Bilbao: La Gran Enciclopedia Vasca, 1982), 132–40; Douglass and Bilbao, *Amerikanuak*, 374. Many of the boardinghouses mentioned in this chapter, such as Aguirre's, will be discussed in further detail throughout this book.

7. Echanis interviews; Olive Groefsema, *Elmore County: Its Historical Gleanings* (Boise: Caxton Press, 1949); Jack Beardwood, "Mountain Home Is Typical of Basque Colonies," Boise *Capitol News*, June 26, 1937, 3–4; and Lucia Osa, letter to author, Gooding, Idaho, Fall 1988, Echeverria Collection, Fresno, California.

8. Note the appearance of *Euskara* rather than *Euskera* (both meaning "Basque language"). Where spelling or dialectical differences occur in direct quotations, the

author has chosen the dialectical spellings. For the narrative, the author has selected the universal Basque spelling or Euskara Batua version.

9. In one interview, Lentxo stated that Boise had eleven boardinghouses in 1919. He could recall the informal names of four: Zapatera's, Barbero's, Antonio's, and Anduiza's (with a fronton). J. Patrick Bieter's recent article states that "there were more than a score," and Paquita Garatea counted twelve in her thesis. J. Patrick Bieter, "Letemendi's Boarding House: A Basque Cultural Institution in Idaho," *Idaho Yesterdays* 37 (Spring 1993): 2; and Paquita Lucia Garatea, "*Burns'eko Etxekoandreak*: Basque Women Boarding House Keepers of Burns, Oregon" (master's thesis, Portland State University, 1990), 34.

10. Lucy Alboitiz Garatea, interview with author, Boise, Idaho, March 22, 1989; and *Boise and Ada County Directory*, 1914 and 1918–1919 (Salt Lake City: R. L. Polk and Company, 1914 and 1918).

11. Lentxo used the expression "Boise Bascos" in his later years while living in California. The term *Bascos*, however, is rarely used to this day by Idaho's Basque population, since it reminds them of when *Bascos* was used as a pejorative by the local press in the 1930s.

12. Lentxo consistently referred to this establishment as Urquidi's, although in other sources the surname also appears as Uriquiris.

13. Lentxo mentioned "Chino's" on numerous occasions. Joaquin "Chino" Berdugo and Pete French opened the Star in 1917, and it went on for decades in Burns, Oregon. Garatea, "*Burns'eko*," 36.

14. Chris Moore, "Echanis Boardinghouse Has Been Activity Center Through the Years," *Ontario, Oregon, Daily Argus Observer*, February 15, 1974, 10.

15. Lorenzo Echanis, Jr., interview with author, Ontario, Oregon, March 23, 1989.

16. A. René Martin, letter to the North Central Nevada Historical Society, Winnemucca, Nevada, July 14, 1980. Holbert-Osa Oral History Collection, Basque Studies Collection, Getchell Library, University of Nevada, Reno.

17. In the 1980s Gretchen Holbert and Mateo Osa interviewed dozens of Nevada's *hoteleros*. Tapes of these interviews are housed at the University of Nevada Basque Studies Collection. Holbert-Osa Oral History Collection, Winnemucca File, Basque Studies Collection, Getchell Library, University of Nevada Library, Reno, Nevada. The hotel is still Basque owned, with the bar still standing as it did in 1922. Early owners of the hotel were David Giroux, John Ezparza, Jose Incera, Frank Escabel, Steve Martinez, and Angel Mendiola. Miguel Olano and Claudio Yzaguirre purchased the hotel in 1965, and Miguel continues there today.

18. Dominic Sorcabal, interview with author, Huntington Beach, California, May 1, 1987; L. A. Mur, letter to the author, February 1989, Echeverria Collection; and Karen J. Weitz, "Aliso Street Historical Report for the City of Los Angeles," State of California, Office of Environmental Planning, Department of Transportation, Sacramento, California, January 1980. Occasionally people I interviewed referred to a cluster of downtown Basque boardinghouses and businesses as a "Basque town," so I have used this term throughout the text.

19. Basques often refer to handball and/or jai alai using the general term *pilota* (Basque for "ball") or *pelota* (Spanish for "ball"). *Pilota* is preferred throughout this book, except in quotations.

20. The exact location and formal name of this *ostatu* remains a mystery. Lentxo and Anthony Ondaro remembered Ines clearly, but neither could recall a formal name for the boardinghouse or Ines's surname. Anthony Ondaro interview with Sonia Eagle Diaz, Brea, California, October 14, 1971, Oral History Collection, California State University at Fullerton.

21. Ibid.

22. Moore, "Echanis Boardinghouse," 10; and Anthony Yturri, interview with author, Ontario, Oregon, March 23, 1989.

### CHAPTER ONE. FROM *Euskal Herria* TO THE NEW WORLD

1. William A. Douglass, "The Basques," *Harvard Encyclopedia of American Ethnic Groups*, ed. Stephen Thernstrom (Cambridge, Mass.: Harvard University Press, 1980), 173. For a discussion of Euskara today and its historical development, see Teresa del Valle, *Korrika: Basque Ritual for Ethnic Identity* (Reno: University of Nevada Press, 1994), 4–9; and Alan R. King and Begotxu Olaizola Elordi, *Colloquial Basque: A Complete Language Course* (London: Routledge Press, 1996).

2. For additional information on physical and serological evidence related to Basques, see the "Articles" section of the Bibliography.

3. William A. Douglass, "Re-counting Basques," *Basque Studies Program Newsletter* 47 (April 1993): 7.

4. Lynne Fereday, "Descriptive Study of the Integration and Assimilation of Basques in Boise, Idaho," in *The Basques—A Preservation of a Culture* (Boise: Fereday Memorial, 1971); Carol Pagliarulo, "Basques in Stockton: A Study of Assimilation" (master's thesis, College of the Pacific, Stockton, 1948); and Joseph Gaiser, "The Basques of Jordan Valley" (Ph.D. diss., University of Southern California, 1944) are three examples.

5. Morton E. Levine, "The Basques," *Natural History* 76 (April 1967): 50.

6. Linda White, "Feminism and Lexicography: Dealing with Sexist Language in a Bilingual Dictionary," *Frontiers* 10, no. 3 (1989): 61–64.

7. The two-volume *Basque-English, English-Basque Dictionary* (Reno: University of Nevada Press, 1989), by Gorka Aulestia and Linda White, features a useful discussion of Basque language and linguistics in its introduction.

8. White, "Feminism and Lexicography," 62.

9. Davydd Greenwood, "Continuity and Change: Spanish Basque Ethnicity as a Historical Process," in *Ethnic Conflict in the Western World*, ed. Milton J. Esman (Ithaca: Cornell University Press, 1977), 81–102.

10. Ibid., 87–92; and Rachel Bard, *Navarra: The Durable Kingdom* (Reno: University of Nevada Press, 1982), 85–91.

11. Gregorio Monreal, "Annotations Regarding Basque Traditional Political Thought in the Sixteenth Century," in *Basque Politics: A Case Study in Ethnic Na-*

*tionalism*, ed. William A. Douglass (Reno: University of Nevada Press and Basque Studies Program, 1985), 21–22.

12. James A. Tuck and Robert Grenier, "A 16th-Century Basque Whaling Station in Labrador," *Scientific American* 245 (November 1981): 180–88; James A. Tuck and Robert Grenier, *Red Bay, Labrador: World Whaling Capital, 1550–1600* (St. John's, Newfoundland: Atlantic Archaeology, Ltd., 1989), 16–23; Brian Fagan, "The Basques of Red Bay," *Archaeology* 46 (September–October 1993): 44–51; Selma H. Barkham, "The Basques: Filling a Gap in Our History between Jacques Cartier and Champlain," *Canadian Geographical Journal* 96 (February–March 1978): 8–19; James A. Tuck, "Discovery in Labrador: A 16th Century Basque Whaling Port and Its Sunken Fleet," *National Geographic* 168 (July 1985): 50–57; Carl O. Sauer, *Northern Mists* (Berkeley: University of California Press, 1968), 62–76; Rodney Gallop, *A Book of the Basques* (1930; reprint, Reno: University of Nevada Press, 1970), 268–81; M. Ciriquian-Gaizlarro, *Los Vascos en la pesca de la ballena* (San Sebastián: Bilblioteca Vascongadas de los Amigos del País, 1961); and Jeronima Echeverria, "A Pilgrimage to Red Bay, Summer Home of Basque Whaling Fleets Centuries Ago," *Journal of the Society of Basque Studies in America* 14 (1994): 49–57.

13. Douglass and Bilbao, *Amerikanuak*, 49–53, 67–69; and J. H. Elliott, "Economic and Social Foundations of the New Spain," in *Imperial Spain, 1469–1716* (New York: St. Martin's Press, 1963), 108–23.

14. John Lynch, *Spain Under the Hapsburgs*, vol. 1, *Empire and Absolutism, 1516–1598* (New York: Oxford University Press, 1964), 165.

15. Surnames are highly recognizable among Basques. Names such as *etxea berria* (new house) appear frequently and *Iturriberrigorrigoikoerrotakoetxea* (new red fountain near the upper mill spring) is said to be the longest. The definitive listing of Basque surnames has been compiled by Luís Michelena, *Apellidos Vascos* (San Sebastián: Editorial Txertoa, 1973).

16. William A. Douglass, "Rural Exodus in Two Spanish Basque Villages: A Cultural Explanation," *American Anthropologist* 73 (October 1971): 1100–14; and Douglass, *Echalar and Murélaga: Opportunity and Rural Depopulation in Two Spanish Basque Villages* (New York: St. Martin's Press, 1975).

17. Of the European-born Basques interviewed in this project, about 90 percent stated that the "nothing to inherit" factor was the major impetus for them to immigrate.

18. Marianne Heiberg, "Inside the Moral Community: Politics in a Basque Village," in Douglass, ed., *Basque Politics: A Case Study in Ethnic Nationalism*, 285–308.

19. Alfred W. Crosby, Jr., *The Columbian Exchange: Biological and Cultural Consequences of 1492* (Westport, Conn.: Greenwood Press, 1972), 165–205; and Michael W. Flinn, *The European Demographic System, 1500–1820* (Baltimore: Johns Hopkins University Press, 1981), 65–101.

20. Douglass and Bilbao, *Amerikanuak*, 124.

21. Ibid., 129.

22. Julio Caro Baroja, *Los Vascos: una etnología* (San Sebastián: Biblioteca Vascongada de los Amigos del País, 1949). For a colorful supplement to Caro Baroja, see Gallop, "The Basque House," in *A Book of the Basques*, 203–14.

23. William A. Douglass, "Serving Girls and Sheepherders: Emigration and Continuity in a Spanish Basque Village," in *The Changing Faces of Rural Spain*, ed. Joseph B. Aceves and William A. Douglass (New York: John Wiley and Sons, 1976), 45–46.

24. Fermín Leizaola, "Aspects of Pastoral and Nomadic Life in the Basque Country," in *Primera semana internacional de antropología Vasca*, ed. José Luís Goti Iturriaga (Bilbao: La Gran Enciclopedia Vasca, 1971), 533–50; and Sandra Ott, *The Circle of Mountains: A Basque Sheepherding Community* (Oxford: Clarendon Press, 1981).

25. Richard Lane, "The Cultural Ecology of Sheep Nomadism: Northeastern Nevada, 1870–1972" (Ph.D. diss., Yale University, 1974); William A. Douglass and Richard Lane, *Basque Sheepherders of the American West: A Photographic Documentary* (Reno: University of Nevada Press, 1985); and Robert Laxalt, "Basque Sheepherders, Lonely Sentinels of the American West," *National Geographic* 129 (June 1966): 870–88.

26. Ott, *The Circle of Mountains*.

27. Ibid., 213.

28. The introductory chapters of Caro Baroja's *Los Vascos* includes detailed layouts of Basque towns and villages.

29. Gallop, *A Book of the Basques*, 230; Teresa B. Urquidi, "An Historical Relationship between *Pelote* and the Church in Old World Basque Society," in *Proceedings of the First International Basque Conference in North America*, ed. Society of Basque Studies in America (Bilbao: Gran Enciclopedia Vasca, 1985), 106–18; and Fernando Maria Mugica, "The Basques in Sport," in ed. Goti, *Primera semana internacional*, 515–26.

30. In *Bat, Ball and Bishop* (New York: Rockport Press, 1947), Robert Henderson presented the idea that the cloistered courtyards of the fifteenth and sixteenth centuries—where the clergy played handball while it was publicly outlawed—were the forerunners of the modern indoor jai alai and *pilota* courts.

31. Early Basque settlements in other parts of the Americas and references to their boardinghouses are the subject of chapter 11.

### CHAPTER TWO. FROM THE MOTHER LODE TO THE GREAT BASIN

1. Ralph J. Roske, *Everyman's Eden: A History of California* (New York: Macmillan Company, 1968), 250.

2. Douglass and Bilbao, *Amerikanuak*, 209. It should also be noted that the southwestern United States, namely Arizona and New Mexico, experienced some early Basque settlement during the sixteenth and seventeenth centuries as well. For more on this topic, see Donald T. Garate, "Basque Names, Nobility, and Ethnicity

on the Spanish Frontier," *Colonial Latin American Historical Review* 2 (winter 1993): 77–104.

3. Douglass and Bilbao, *Amerikanuak*, 418–20. This listing is based on Santiago de Zarautz's "Pasajeros salidos de Valparaíso para California, años 1849–1852," manuscript, Basque Studies Collection, Getchell Library, University of Nevada, Reno.

4. Carol Hovey, "The Spanish Ranch," *Journal of Basque Studies* 5 (1984): 87.

5. Walker A. Tompkins, ed., *Tompson and West's History of Santa Barbara and Ventura Counties* (Berkeley: Howell-North, 1961), 241–42.

6. Douglass and Bilbao, *Amerikanuak*, 210–12. The information obtained from these biographical sketches in county and local histories represents only fourteen Basques, and therefore it reflects the experiences of a limited portion of the Basque American population.

7. Roske, *Everyman's Eden*, 258.

8. E. N. Wentworth and C. W. Towne, *Shepherd's Empire* (Norman: University of Oklahoma Press, 1945), 166; and Robert Glass Cleland, *Cattle on a Thousand Hills: Southern California, 1850–1880* (San Marino, Calif.: Huntington Library, 1964), 140–42.

9. Douglass and Bilbao, *Amerikanuak*, 225–30 and 421–24.

10. Ibid., 218–33.

11. *Cajon de Santa Ana Sheep Licenses, 1868–1870*. Orange County Registrar, Santa Ana, California; and *Inyo County Sheep License Book, 1896–1897*. Inyo County Registrar, Independence, California. *Amerikanuak* Papers, Basque Studies Collection, Getchell Library, University of Nevada Reno.

12. James J. Ayers, *Transactions of the California State Agricultural Society, 1883* (Sacramento: State of California Printing, 1884), 204.

13. Craig Campbell, "The Basque-American Ethnic Area: Geographical Perspectives on Migration, Population, and Settlement," *Journal of Basque Studies* 6 (1985): 83–89. See figure 2 for a reproduction of Campbell's map of immigration flow patterns from 1850 through 1930.

14. Lane, "Cultural Ecology of Sheep Nomadism," 44.

15. New data will tell us about the numbers of Basques settling from 1920 to the present as well as the settlement and movement of second-, third-, and fourth-generation Basques.

16. Iban Bilbao and Chantal de Equilaz, *Diáspora Vasca*, vol. 1, *Vascos llegados al puerto de Nueva York, 1897–1902* (Vitoria: Diputación Floral de Álava, Consejo de Cultura, Sección Bibliografía y Diáspora Vascas, 1981). In this study researchers scanned passenger lists for Basque surnames from ships departing France and Spain between 1897 and 1902. National immigration records, for example, place Basques with other French and Spanish citizens, thus making the researcher's task more challenging.

17. Marie Pierre Arrizabalaga, "A Statistical Study of Basque Immigration into California, Nevada, Idaho and Wyoming between 1900 and 1910" (master's thesis, University of Nevada, Reno, 1986).

18. Ibid., 40.

19. Ibid., 53 and 54.

20. Frank Araujo, "Basque Cultural Ecology and Echinoccocosis in California" (Ph.D. diss., University of California, Davis, 1974), 112.

21. Douglass and Bilbao, *Amerikanuak*, 302.

22. Arrizabalaga, "Statistical Study," 58.

23. Ibid., 129–32.

24. Edward P. Hutchinson, *Legislative History of American Immigration Policy, 1798–1965* (Philadelphia: University of Pennsylvania Press, 1981), 484.

25. United States Department of the Interior, *Taylor Grazing Act: Explanation of the Law and Text of the Act* (Washington D.C.: Government Printing Office, 1934), 1–2.

26. U.S. House of Representatives, *Hearings Before the Committee on Public Lands*, HR 2835 and HR 6462, June 7–9, 1933 (Washington D.C.: Government Printing Office, 1933), 14.

27. Roske, *Everyman's Eden*, 246.

28. "Nevada's Danger," *Carson Morning Appeal* (Carson City, Nevada), May 4, 1898, 3. Two additional studies of Basques in American literature are Wilbur S. Shepperson, *Restless Strangers: Nevada's Immigrants and Their Interpreters* (Reno: University of Nevada Press, 1970); and Richard W. Etulain, "The Basques in Western American Literature," in *Anglo-American Contributions to Basque Studies: Essays in Honor of Jon Bilbao*, ed. William A. Douglass, Richard W. Etulain, and William H. Jacobsen, Jr. (Reno: Desert Research Institute Publications on the Social Sciences, 1977), 7–18.

29. Richard W. Etulain, "Basques of the American West: Some Problems for the Historian," in *Basques of the Pacific Northwest*, ed. Richard W. Etulain (Pocatello: Idaho State University Press, 1991), 86–90.

30. Felix Urizar, Letter to the editor, Burns *Times-Herald*, November 16, 1937. As cited in *Talking on Paper: An Anthology of Oregon Letters and Diaries*, ed. Shannon Applegate and Terence O'Donnell (Corvallis, Oreg.: Oregon State University Press, 1994), 270–71.

31. Douglass and Bilbao, *Amerikanuak*, 369, 394; and Shepperson, *Restless Strangers*, 187–89, provide several examples.

32. Chapter 9 contains detailed information on Stockton's Basque boardinghouses.

33. Steve Ybarrola, letter to the author, April 8, 1987. Ybarrola Papers, Central College, Pella, Iowa.

34. For more on McCarran's biography and senatorial activities, see Jerome E. Edwards, *Pat McCarran: Political Boss of Nevada* (Reno: University of Nevada Press, 1982).

35. S1 165-Public Law 587 granted special quota visas to a maximum of 250 alien shepherds per year. *Congressional Quarterly Almanac*, 81st Congress, 2nd Session (Washington, D.C.: Congressional Quarterly News Features, 1950), 6: 218–19.

36. Hutchinson, *Legislative History*, 490.

37. HR 5678-Public Law 414, *Congressional Quarterly Almanac*, 82nd Congress, 2d sess. (Washington, D.C.: Congressional Quarterly News Features, 1952), 8: 154–60.

38. Pierre Salinger, "Senator Lehman Protests Bills," *New York Times*, 21 June 1956. Newspaper coverage of the "Sheepherders' Laws" was generally sympathetic to the need for more herders. Christie Peters's article in the *New York Times*, 9 January 1955; Pierre Salinger's article in the *Wall Street Journal*, 29 November 1960; and C. M. Cianfarra's article in the *New York Times*, 21 August 1954, are examples of more favorable viewpoints.

39. Allura Nason Ruiz, "The Basques—Sheepmen of the West" (master's thesis, University of Nevada, Reno, 1964), 51.

40. Douglass and Bilbao, *Amerikanuak*, 306.

41. Grant McCall, "Basque Americans and a Sequential Theory of Migration and Adaptation" (master's thesis, San Francisco State University, 1968), 46.

42. United States Department of Commerce, Bureau of the Census, *Ancestry of the Population by State*: 1980 (Washington, D.C.: Government Printing Office, 1983), 51–56; William A. Douglass, "Counting Basques: The U.S. Census," *Basque Studies Program Newsletter* 28 (November 1983): 3–7; William A. Douglass, "Recounting Basques," *Basque Studies Program Newsletter* 47 (April 1993): 6; and William A. Douglass, "Ethnic Categorization in the 1980 U.S. Census: The Basque Example," *Government Publications Review* 12 (1985): 289–96. Appendix A contains a summary of the 1980 and 1990 census results.

43. Campbell, "Basque-American Ethnic Area," 96–97. See figure 4 for a reproduction of Basque geographical zones within the United States, with southwestern Idaho reflecting the strongest "core" region.

## CHAPTER THREE. *Ostatu Amerikanuak:* THE BASQUE-AMERICAN BOARDINGHOUSE

1. Lentxo Echanis, interview by author, Brea, Calif., 8 October 1987.

2. Paul Groth, *Living Downtown: The History of Residential Hotels in the United States* (Berkeley: University of California, 1994), 107.

3. Ibid., 163.

4. Douglass and Bilbao, *Amerikanuak*, 375.

5. U.S. Bureau of the Census. *Sixth Census*, 1850.

6. George C. Pipkin, *Pete Aguerreberry: Death Valley Prospector and Gold Miner* (Trona, Calif.: Murchison Publications, 1982).

7. Arrizabalaga, "Statistical Study," 11.

8. Sheldon Davis, "Stockton's Citizens from the Pyrenees Mountains," *Stockton Record*, 22 May 1917.

9. Raymond Uruburu, interview by author, Wonder Valley, Calif., 10 February 1994.

10. Arrizabalaga, "Statistical Study," 126.

11. Ibid., 66. See also chapter 5.

12. Richard W. Etulain, "Basque Beginnings in the Pacific Northwest," *Idaho Yesterdays* 18 (spring 1974): 26–32.

13. For a map showing towns that have been home to Basque boardinghouses, see figures 5, 6, 14, 15, and 17. Appendices B and C contain chronological and geographical listings of all boardinghouses included in this study. For a listing of those boardinghouses that remain today, see table 13.1.

14. Douglas G. Hale, "Quasi-Groups and Boundary Maintenance in a Basque Hotel," (student paper, National Science Field Foundation, 1969). Basque Studies Collection, Getchell Library, University of Nevada Reno.

15. Beltran Paris and William Douglass, *Beltran: Basque Sheepman of the American West* (Reno: University of Nevada Press, 1979), 21.

16. Doyaga, "*Eusko Etxea*," 132–41.

17. Bob Iturralde, "Agur, Hogar, Agur," *Boise, Idaho, Voice of the Basques*, April 1977, 6; and Nancy Zubiri, *A Travel Guide to Basque America* (Reno: University of Nevada Press, 1998), 468.

18. Commentary about vacationing in these hotels can be found in Paris and Douglass, *Beltran*; in personal interviews with Stockton's Pete Iroz; and Dollie Iberlin's *The Basque Web: A Story about the Basque People of Buffalo, Wyoming* (Buffalo, Wyo.: Buffalo Bulletin, 1981).

19. Douglass and Bilbao, *Amerikanuak*, 371–84.

20. Pagliarulo, "Basques in Stockton," 54.

21. Catherine Inda Goyenetche, interview by author, San Francisco, Calif., 13 May 1987.

22. Douglass and Bilbao, *Amerikanuak*, 377.

23. "Echanis Boarding House Has Been Basque Activity Center," *Daily Argus Observer*, 15 February 1974.

24. Gretchen Holbert, interview by author, Gardnerville, Nev., 20 May 1987. *Urtekoak*, literally translated, means "of the same year." In this instance, the term signified Basque couples who met while honeymooning at the same boardinghouses and thereafter became long-term friends.

25. Noriega's Hotel in Bakersfield had such a "parlor room" through the 1920s, which boarders currently use as a televison room.

26. Gretchen Holbert, "Elko's Overland Hotel," *Northeastern Nevada Historical Society Quarterly* 5 (winter 1975): 15.

27. Zubiri, *A Travel Guide to Basque America*, 398.

28. Elena Elizalde Arralde, interview by author, Yakima, Wash., 24 July 1990.

29. Sarah Baker Munro, "Basque Folklore in Southeastern Oregon," *Oregon Historical Quarterly* 76 (June 1975): 162–63.

30. Zubiri, *A Travel Guide to Basque America*, 469.

31. Garatea, "*Burns'eko*," 52–53.

32. Ibid.

33. Serafina Uberuaga Mendiguren, interview by author, Ontario, Oreg., 23 March 1989.

34. The "perfect couple" concept is presented in DeCroos, *Long Journey*, 44–47; Douglass, "Home Is a Hotel: Nevada's Basque Establishments," *Nevada Magazine* 39 (spring 1979): 23; and Douglass and Bilbao, *Amerikanuak*, 379.

35. Jean DeCroos, *The Long Journey: Social Integration and Ethnicity Maintenance Among Urban Basques in the San Francisco Bay Region* (Reno: Associated Faculty Press and Basque Studies Program, 1983), 45.

36. Table 9.1, for example, demonstrates that only three Stockton hotels lasted for over fifteen years. Of those, the Alustizas at the California Hotel and the Artozquis at the Hotel Central exceeded twenty years of ownership.

37. Louise Amestoy Maitia, interview by author, Bakersfield, Calif., 2 April 1987.

38. Garatea, "*Burns'eko*," 57–58.

39. Elena Celayeta Talbott, interview by author, Los Banos, Calif., 8 May 1987.

40. Tables 5.1, 5.2, and 5.5 and figure 8 in chapter 5 note this phenomenon.

41. For more specific information on all the picnics and festivals, send for a calendar from the North American Basque Organization, Inc., 1101 Court, Elko, NV 89801, or send an E-mail to bobech@isat.com.

42. L. S. Cressman and Anthony Yturri, "The Basques in Oregón," *Commonwealth Review* 20 (1938), 370.

43. Beltran Paris and William A. Douglass, *Beltran*, 64.

44. Catherine Inda Goyenetche and Bambi MacDonald, interviews by author, San Francisco, Calif., 13 May 1987.

45. Elena Celayeta Talbott, interview by author, 10 March 1987.

## CHAPTER FOUR. THE EARLIEST HOTELS

1. "Basque Beginnings in California," Talbott Papers, Private Collection, Los Banos, California.

2. Joseph Arburua, "Rancho Panocha de San Juan y los Carrizalitos," manuscript, 1970, 10, Basque Studies Collection, Getchell Library, University of Nevada, Reno.

3. Isaac L. Mylar, *Early Days at the Mission San Juan Bautista* (Watsonville, Calif.: Valley Publishers and San Juan Historical Society, 1970), 52–55, 131–35.

4. Tony Taix, interview by Ralph L. Milliken, San Juan Bautista, Calif., 5 March 1937, Ralph Milliken Papers, Milliken Museum, Los Banos, California.

5. Mylar, *Early Days*, 131–32.

6. Mrs. L. Castle, interview by Ralph Milliken, San Juan Bautista, Calif., 17 April 1938, Ralph Milliken Papers.

7. "Basque Beginnings in California," Talbott Papers.

8. C. C. Zanetta, interview by Ralph Milliken, San Juan Bautista, Calif., 5 January 1936, Ralph Milliken Papers.

9. The census of 1870 listed the value of Zanetta's building at $6,000. This was considerably higher than the value of other buildings in the community. U.S. Bureau of the Census, *Population Schedules of the Eighth Census of the United States*, 1870, National Archives Microfilm Publications, M593-74, 34–35.

10. "History of San Juan Bautista, Panoche, Los Banos," Talbott Papers. The partners were known locally as "Juan Primo" (Iribarri), "Juan Chico" (Indart), and "Juan Grande" (Etcheverry).

11. Joseph Arburua, "Rancho Panocha," 10.

12. Ibid., 19. Arrivallaga, Ayoigar, and Gastimbide are probably misspellings.

13. U.S. Bureau of the Census. *Eighth Census*, 1870, National Archives, M593-74, 34–35. Table 4.2 summarizes the 1870 census information for nine of the Plaza's employees.

14. U.S. Bureau of the Census, *Population Schedules of the Seventh Census of the United States*, 1860, National Archives Microfilm Publications, M653-060, 62.

15. San Joaquin County Marriage Records, 1850–1865, Stockton, California, Talbott Papers.

16. Mrs. M. Indart, interview by Ralph Milliken, San Juan Bautista, Calif., 5 February 1933, Ralph Milliken Papers.

17. "History of San Juan Bautista," Talbott Papers.

18. Y. P. Villegas, "Gold Mountains," *Hollister Free Lance*, 7 May 1947.

19. Mrs. M. Indart, interview by Ralph Milliken.

20. Arburua, "Rancho Panocha," 28–30.

21. "Basque Beginnings," Talbott Papers.

22. Rockwell D. Hunt, *California and Californians*, vol. 3 (Chicago: Lewis Publishing Company, 1932), 121.

23. Ibid.; and Arburua, "Rancho Panocha," 16.

24. "History of San Juan Bautista," Talbott Papers, 4. The same Aurrecochea appeared in the Plaza Hotel registers.

25. Hunt, *California and Californians*, vol. 3, 122.

26. Ibid.; and Arburua, "Rancho Panocha," 16–17.

27. Arburua, "Rancho Panocha," 16–17.

28. These examples refer to Aguirre's in San Francisco; to Letemendi's in Boise (which apparently never had a formal name); and to the Noriega Hotel in Bakersfield. Numerous other examples exist.

29. Anne B. Fisher, *The Salinas: Upside-Down River* (New York: Farrar and Rinehart, 1945), 208–33.

30. Ibid., 211.

31. Arburua, "Rancho Panocha," 17. In Arburua's text the surname appears as Labayon; and the hometown as Areso, although neither can be substantiated. In Rockwell Hunt's *California and Californians* the surname appears as Lebayon. The probable correct spelling is *Labayen*.

32. Fisher, *The Salinas*, 212.

33. Douglass and Bilbao, *Amerikanuak*, 377.

34. Elena Celayeta Talbott, interview, 8 May 1987.

35. Hunt, *California and Californians*, 122.

36. Mr. L. Larios, interview by Ralph Milliken, Hollister, Calif., not dated. Ralph Milliken Papers.

37. Fannie Yturriarte McCullough, interview by Elena Talbott, Hollister, Calif., 25 September 1972. Talbott Papers.

38. Merced *Express*, 2 February 1884, 3, Ralph Milliken Papers.

39. "Basque Presence," Talbott Papers. Such early claims cannot be fully substantiated, but *ostatuak* did appear in the communities of Firebaugh, Mendota, Huron, Fresno, Bakersfield, and Stockton, California, by the mid-1890s. Jeronima Echeverria, "*California-ko ostatuak*: A History of California's Basque Hotels" (Ph.D. diss., University of North Texas, Denton, 1988), 134–68.

40. Sanborn Fire Insurance Maps, San Juan Capistrano, June 1929, Map A. Map Collection, California State University, Northridge.

41. U.S. Department of the Interior, National Register of Historic Places Inventory Nomination Form, p. 2, Oyharzabal's French Hotel File, City Hall, San Juan Capistrano, California.

42. Ibid., 3; Samuel Armor, *History of Orange County, California* (Los Angeles: Historic Record Company, 1921), 1964; Brad Bonhall, "History in the Making: Basque Compiles His Culture's Contributions to San Juan Capistrano," *Los Angeles Times*, 6 February 1994, Orange County Section; and Pamela Hallan, *Dos Cientos Años in San Juan Capistrano* (San Juan Capistrano: Layman Publishing Company, 1975), 33. Sources disagree on the opening date of the French Hotel: Armor claimed 1778, and County Records give the date as 1880.

43. Orange County Deeds of Record, August 1891, Book 14: 387, Santa Ana, California.

44. All citations from Clifton Johnson and his observations can be found in U.S. Department of the Interior, National Register of Historic Places, Inventory Nomination Form, pp. 4–5, Oyharzabal's French Hotel File, San Juan Capistrano Historical Society, San Juan Capistrano, California.

45. Doris Drummond, "Learn Your History on Foot," *San Clemente Sun Post*, 2 August 1978; and Hallan, *Dos Cientos Años*, 33.

46. The census of 1880 assigns the two men these occupations. By 1880 the forty-three-year-old Salaberri and his wife Catalina had one infant daughter, Juanita. Also living at the adobe was Domingo, thirty-three; a cook named Teresa Yorba; and a carpenter/laborer, Juan Laralde. U.S. Bureau of the Census, *Population Schedules of the Ninth Census of the United States*, 1880, National Archives Microfilm Publications, T9-0066, 26.

47. Carmen Oyharzabal, interviewer unlisted, n.d. Oyharzabal's French Hotel File, San Juan Capistrano Historical Society, San Juan Capistrano, California.

48. Armor, *History of Orange County*, 1644; and Maurice H. Newmark and Marco R. Newmark, ed., *Sixty Years in Southern California, 1853–1913: Containing Reminiscences of Harris Newmark*, 4th ed. (Los Angeles: Zeitlin and Ver Brugge, 1970), 549.

49. The unlikely name William in this instance was probably adopted after arrival in the United States.

50. More likely spellings are G. Etchevarren and D. Gaztambide.

51. U.S. Bureau of the Census, *Ninth Census, 1880*, National Archives, T9-0067, 9–10.

52. Ibid., 13–14. Surnames appear as recorded by the census taker, but a few were most likely misspelled, such as Erasmuspe and Ybarl, which were more likely *Erramuspe* and *Ybar*.

53. Orange County Index, 1889–1908, Santa Ana, California.

54. *Orange County Deeds of Record*, Book 99: 121, Santa Ana, California.

55. Armor, *History of Orange County*, 1644.

56. U.S. Department of the Interior, National Register of Historic Places Inventory Nomination Form, p. 5.

57. Ibid., 5–6.

## CHAPTER FIVE. LOS ANGELES AND SAN FRANCISCO: TWO EARLY BASQUE TOWNS

1. Arrizabalaga, "Statistical Study," 36–38.

2. Ward, Ritchie, and J. McQuinn, ed., *The First Los Angeles City and County Directory, 1872* (Los Angeles: Ward and Ritchie Press, 1963). This reproduction of the city's earliest directory contains a ten-page listing of residents, nine of whom are Basques.

3. Aaron Smith, ed., *Los Angeles City Directory, 1878* (Los Angeles: Mirror Printing, 1878), 69. Although Levque (probably spelled L'éveque) is a French surname, the relatively high number (fifteen) of French Basque surnames listed at the residence in the 1878 directory suggests that Levque may have been culturally Basque.

4. *Los Angeles City and County Directory, 1881–1882* (Los Angeles: Southern California Directory Company, 1882), 22; Arrizabalga, "Statistical Study," 61.

5. *Los Angeles City and County Directory, 1881–1882*, 27.

6. Etcheverria correspondence, Paquette Papers, Private Collection, Sonora, California.

7. Ibid., 79. See figure 7 for a map of Los Angeles's early Basque town.

8. Ibid., 73. Spellings of Harotcavena's name vary widely in the directories. The correct spelling was probably Harotçarena.

9. For a listing of all Basque hotels and boardinghouses found in Los Angeles directories between 1872 and 1890, see table 5.1. Hotels and boardinghouses listed in table 5.1 also correspond to figure 7.

10. Weitz, "Aliso Street Historical Report," 12; and *Los Angeles City Directory*, 375. Apestegui was probably spelled *Apeztegui*.

11. Ibid.; and *Los Angeles City and County Directory, 1886–1887* (Los Angeles: A. A. Bynum and Company, 1886), 217.

12. *Los Angeles Directory, 1886–1887*, 12; and Ferdinand Loyer and Charles

Beaudreau, *Le Guide Francais de Los Angeles et du sud de la Californie* (Los Angeles: Loyer and Beaudreau, 1932), 29–35.

13. *Los Angeles Directory, 1886–1887*, 220, 215.

14. *Los Angeles City and County Directory, 1887–1888* (Los Angeles: A. A. Bynon and Company, 1888), 55.

15. Ibid., 217, 220.

16. Ibid., 215.

17. Weitz, "Aliso Street Historical Report," p. 20, and Maps 8 and 14; and Sanborn Fire Insurance Maps, Los Angeles, California, 1883–1887, California State University at Northridge Map Collection. See figure 8 for a composite map of the Hotel de France and neighboring Pyrenees.

18. Tables 5.1, 5.2, and 5.4 and figures 7 and 9 in this chapter document this phenomenon.

19. Weitz, "Aliso Street Historical Report," 13.

20. Maurice H. Newmark and Marco R. Newmark, *Sixty Years in Southern California, 1853–1913: Containing Reminiscences of Harris Newmark*, 4th ed. (Los Angeles: Zeitlin and Ver Brugge, 1970), 459.

21. Douglass and Bilbao, *Amerikanuak*, 336; and Weitz, "Aliso Street Historical Report," 13.

22. *Los Angeles City and County Directory, 1883–1884* (Los Angeles: Los Angeles Directory Company, 1883), 12.

23. Sofia Martina Landa, interview by author, Brea, Calif., 22 September 1975.

24. Douglass and Bilbao, *Amerikanuak*, 336–37.

25. Only a few copies of the two newspapers remain; they can be found at the Los Angeles Public Library. Some editions include mention of even more remote Basque colonies, such as Van Horn, Texas, and Oklahoma City, Oklahoma.

26. *California'ko Eskual Herria*, December (*Abendoaren*) 30, 1893, Lib. 2, no. 9, 3–4, Los Angeles Public Library.

27. Sonia Eagle, "Work and Play among the Basques of Southern California" (Ph.D. diss., Purdue University, 1979), 75.

28. Weitz, "Aliso Street Historical Report," 14.

29. Arrizabalaga, "Statistical Survey," 61.

30. Ibid., 62.

31. Ibid., 66.

32. Dominic Sorcabal, interview by author, Huntington Beach, Calif., 1 May 1987.

33. See figure 9 for a reproduction of Sorcabal's hand-drawn map of the hotels he remembered in Los Angeles's Basque town between 1900 and 1920.

34. *Los Angeles City Directory, 1912* (Los Angeles: Los Angeles Directory Company, 1912), 1050.

35. Landa, interview, 22 September 1975. The marriage license was discovered in Sofia Landa's personal papers.

36. Sorcabal, interview, 1 May 1987.

37. Ibid.

38. Ibid.

39. For a complete listing of *ostatuak* in chronological order and by geographical location, please see Appendices B and C, respectively.

40. *Langley's San Francisco Directory*, 1890 (San Francisco: G. B. Wilbur, 1890), 661. See table 5.5 for San Francisco's hotels as of 1866–1906, and consult Appendices B and C for a listing of other San Francisco Basque hotels from 1906 to the present.

41. Although the New Pyrenees and Europa Hotels did not appear in city directories from 1895 through 1905, they are included in table 5.5.

42. Elvira Yparraguirre Root, interview by author, San Francisco, Calif., 14, 15 May 1987.

43. Photograph of Yparraguirre's Basque Hotel in Talbott Papers.

44. *San Francisco Directory*, 1905 (San Francisco: H. S. Crocker and Company, 1905), 1981.

45. Root, interview, 14, 15 May 1987; and Frank Bailey Millard, *The History of the San Francisco Bay Region* (San Francisco: American Historical Society, Inc., 1924), 280–81.

46. *California'ko Eskual Herria*, December (*Abendoaren*), 30 1893, Lib. 2, no. 9, 3–4.

47. Arrizabalaga, "Statistical Study," 66.

48. Ibid., 68.

49. Warren A. Beck and Ynez D. Haase, *Historical Atlas of California* (Norman: University of Oklahoma Press, 1974), 80.

50. *San Francisco Directory*, 1907 (San Francisco: H. S. Crocker Company, 1907), 1715. Proper spelling may have been Yriondo.

51. *San Francisco Directory*, 1908 (San Francisco: H. S. Crocker Company, 1908), 905, 1888.

52. *World Almanac and Encyclopedia*, 1908 (New York: Press Publishing, 1908), 637; and Arrizabalaga, "A Statistical Study," 67.

53. *San Francisco Directory*, 1912 (San Francisco: H. S. Crocker Company, 1912), 862; and *San Francisco Directory*, 1916 (San Francisco: H. S. Crocker Company, 1916), 834. Directories between 1910 and 1918 fail to include the proprietor's names.

54. *San Francisco Directory* 1912, 1065.

55. Grace R. Lugea, interview by author, San Francisco, Calif., 13 May 1987.

56. The Lugeas also operated the Hotel de Spanio from 1907 to 1917 in Fresno, California. Paul E. Vandor, *History of Fresno County, California, with Biographical Sketches* (Los Angeles: Historic Record Company, 1919), 2559.

57. Maria Ballaz, interview by author, Fresno, Calif., 7 May 1987; Root, interview, 15 May 1987.

58. Ibid.; and Honoria Juvney, *History of Sonoma County, California* (San Francisco: S. J. Clarke Publishing Company, 1926), 382.

59. Pete Iroz, interview by author, Stockton, Calif., 11 June 1987.

60. Ibid.; and *San Francisco Directory, 1930* (San Francisco: R. L. Polk and Company, 1930), 957.

61. It is likely that she was referring to the Hotel España. Ballaz, interview by author, May 7, 1987.

62. Elena Etcheverry and Dominica Arambel, interviews by author, Los Banos, Calif., 17 May 1987; *San Francisco Directory, 1930*, 681. The proper spelling may have been *Olague*.

63. Iroz, interview, 11 June 1987; and Talbott, interview, 26 February 1987.

64. Ibid.

65. Ibid., and *Crocker-Langley San Francisco City Directory, 1930* (San Francisco: R. L. Polk and Company, 1930), 681.

66. Letter to War Price and Rationing Board from Jean and Marie Cazahous, San Francisco File, *Amerikanuak* Papers, Basque Studies Collection, Getchell Library, University of Nevada, Reno. Though calf's head is not a particularly typical Basque dish, it was a favorite among Des Alpes regulars.

67. The Des Alpes is the only San Francisco *ostatu* continuing to offer room and board to Basques and serving evening meals to the public.

68. Ganesh and Ana Iriartborde, interview by author, San Francisco, Calif., 15 May 1987.

69. Ciriaco Iturri, interview by author, San Francisco, Calif., 15 May 1987; and *Voice of the Basques*, June 1975, 3.

70. Merrill Schindler, "Calories Don't Count in a Basque Boardinghouse," *Los Angeles Times*, 15 July 1979, Calendar Section, 104.

71. Goyenetche, interview, 13 May 1987; and *San Francisco Directory, 1960* (San Francisco: R. L. Polk and Company, 1960), 374, 685, and 1096.

72. *San Francisco Directory, 1964–1965* (San Francisco: R. L. Polk and Company, 1965), 446.

73. *Voice of the Basques*, June 1975, 3.

74. Goyenetche, interview by author, 13 May 1987.

75. *Voice of the Basques*, September 1975, 3.

76. Bambi MacDonald, interview, 13 May 1987.

77. Marie Walker, "San Francisco's Obrero," *Air California Magazine*, June 1980, 66.

78. Jean Emile Idiart, interview by author, San Francisco, Calif., 14 May 1987.

79. Ibid.; and *Voice of the Basques*, June 1975, 3.

80. Francisco Oroz, interview by author, San Rafael, Calif., 14 May 1987.

81. Lindsay Fenley, "Ex-Basque Boy Buys Le Chalet Basque," San Rafael *Independent*, 17 December 1986, 6.

82. Francisco Oroz, interview, 14 May 1987.

83. Goyenetche, interview, 13 May 1987.

84. Grace Iribarren, interview by author, San Francisco, Calif., 14 May 1987.

85. DeCroos, *The Long Journey*, 46–47. The other three areas hosting Basque cafés and bars were the Richmond, Sunset, and Marina districts of San Francisco.

86. Iriartborde, interview, 15 May 1987.

87. Jean Francis Decroos, *The Long Journey*, 42–43.

88. Another pre-quake *ostatu*, the New Lake House, operated in San Jose in the 1890s and was advertised in *California'ko Eskual Herria*, December (Abendoaren) 30, 1893. And much has been written about the numerous *hoteleros* who left Los Angeles to establish new businesses in Tehachapi, Bakersfield, Santa Barbara, and Fresno, California. Echeverria, "*California-ko Ostatuak.*"

## CHAPTER SIX. SOUTHERN CALIFORNIA'S SPIN-OFF HOTELS: THE LEGACY OF LOS ANGELES'S EARLY BASQUE TOWN

1. Mary Grace Paquette, *Basques to Bakersfield* (Bakersfield, Calif.: Kern County Historical, 1982), 81.

2. Arrizabalaga, "Statistical Study," 70.

3. Ibid., 42–72.

4. Ibid., 70–71.

5. James M. Guinn, *History of the State of California and Biographical Record of the San Joaquin Valley* (Chicago: Chapman Publishing Company, 1905), 1571.

6. Ibid.; Paquette, *Basques to Bakersfield*, 15; and Deeds of Record Book, Kern County, July 31, 1893, Bakersfield, California.

7. *California'ko Eskual Herria* contained an advertisement for an "*Ostatu Frantsesa*" (French Basque Hotel) in Bishop Creek, California, in 1895. The Hotel Fletcher, as it was called, was located directly east of Bakersfield, over the Sierra Nevadas, and would have been a likely stopover for Bakersfield and Tehachapi sheepmen summering their flocks. Whether it was a Basque hotel or a hotel that catered to Basques is unknown, but it seems appropriate to consider it part of Bakersfield's early period. *California'ko Eskual Herria*, December (*Abendoaren*) 15, 1895, Lib. 4, no. 16, 3.

8. Paquette, *Basques to Bakersfield*, 87.

9. *Bakersfield and Kern City Directory*, 1899 (Fresno: Marks, Weston, and Cooper, 1899), 45.

10. Ibid.

11. Frank Amestoy, interview by author, Bakersfield, Calif., 2 April 1987.

12. Louise Amestoy Maitia, interview, 2 April 1987.

13. Janice Elizalde, interview by author, Bakersfield, Calif., 1 April 1987.

14. Louise Amestoy Maitia, interview, 2 April 1987.

15. *Los Angeles City Directory* 1891 (Los Angeles: W. H. L. Corran, 1891), 753.

16. Ibid.; Mariana Etcheverria, personal correspondence; and Paquette Papers, Private Collection, Sonora, California. Refer to tables 4.1 and 4.2 in chapter 4.

17. Wallace W. Morgan, *History of Kern County, California, with Biographical Sketches* (Los Angeles: Historic Record Company, 1914), 1335.

18. Paquette, *Basques to Bakersfield*, 87.

19. Ibid.; Morgan, *History of Kern*, 1335; and Thelma B. Miller, *History of Kern County, California* (Chicago: S. J. Clarke Publishing Company, 1929), 309.

20. John Allen Stafford, "Basque Ethnohistory in Kern County, California" (master's thesis, Sacramento State University, 1971), 22; and Morgan, *History of Kern*, 1214–15.

21. Frank Amestoy, interview, 2 April 1987.

22. Ibid.

23. Paquette, *Basques to Bakersfield*, 88.

24. Ibid.

25. Louise Amestoy Maitia, interview, 2 April 1987. Douglass and Bilbao mention at least eight such loans in *Amerikanuak*, 235.

26. Louise Amestoy Maitia, interview, 2 April 1987.

27. John Yturry, interview by author, Brea, Calif., 28 April 1987.

28. Frank Amestoy, interview, 2 April 1987.

29. Ibid.

30. Janice Elizalde, interview, 1 April 1987.

31. Frank Amestoy, interview, 2 April 1987.

32. Louise Amestoy Maitia, interview, 2 April 1987.

33. Paquette, *Basques to Bakersfield*, 92.

34. *Bakersfield City Directory*, 1930 (Los Angeles: R. L. Polk and Company, 1930), 279; *Bakersfield City Directory* 1935 (Los Angeles: R. L. Polk and Company, 1935), 266; and *Bakersfield City Directory*, 1940 (Los Angeles: R. L. Polk and Company, 1940), 279.

35. Paquette, *Basques to Bakersfield*, 57.

36. Ibid., 89. The source gives the spelling as *Anhaux*, but the *English-Basque Dictionary*, vol. 2, by Gorka Aulestia and Linda White (Reno: University of Nevada Press, 1990) spells the place *Anhauze* and locates it in lower Navarra. It is probably the same village.

37. Paquette, *Basques to Bakersfield*, 90; and Janice Elizalde, interview, 1 April 1987.

38. Mayie Maitia, interview by author, Bakersfield, Calif., 2 April 1987.

39. Ibid.

40. *Bakersfield and Kern City Directory*, 1902–1903 (Bakersfield, Calif.: W. A. Cannady, 1903), 120.

41. Frank Maitia Sr., interview by author, Bakersfield, Calif., 1 April 1987.

42. Ibid.

43. A clippings file in Bakersfield's Public Library included stories on the quake and its aftershocks. *Los Angeles Times*, 23 August 1952, and *Denver Post*, 23 August 1952.

44. "Rites for Basque Hotel Keeper, Restauranteur Set," *Bakersfield Californian*, 16 April 1974, 11:5–6.

45. "Biggest, Best Basque Eatery Rising on Union: Maitia's New Basque Restaurant," *Bakersfield Californian*, 21 October 1979, E1:1–6 and E2:1–3; and "Basques Celebrate at Maitia's House," July 11, 1980, D2:3–6.

46. "Basque Restaurant Fulfills His Dreams," *Bakersfield Californian*, 26 June 1983, F1:1–3.

47. Morgan, *History of Kern County*, 89.

48. Ibid.

49. *California'ko Eskual Herria*, July (*Uztailaren*) 15, 1893, Lib. 1, no. 1: 2.

50. *California'ko Eskual Herria*, December (*Abendoaren*) 30, 1893, Lib. 2, no. 9: 3–4.

51. Paquette, *Basques to Bakersfield*, 48.

52. Morgan, *History of Kern County*, 1350.

53. Paquette, *Basques to Bakersfield*, 53.

54. Morgan, *History of Kern County*, 1351.

55. Ibid.

56. *California'ko Eskual Herria*, May (*Maiatza*) 15, 1897, Lib. 2, no. 37: 2.

57. Paquette, *Basques to Bakersfield*, 53, 55–56.

58. Morgan, *History of Kern County*, 1351. Jean Pierre's niece Lyda later married Felix Esain and became a successful hotelkeeper in her own right at the Basque Hotel in Fresno, California. On Martinto see Paquette, *Basques to Bakersfield*, 92; and Lyda Martinto Esain, interview by author, Fresno, Calif., 18 February 1987.

59. Ibid., 53–56.

60. *Memorial and Biographical History of the Counties of Fresno, Tulare, and Kern, California* (Chicago: Lewis Publishing Company, 1892), 325.

61. *Tehachapi Tomahawk*, April 18, 1903, Paquette Papers, Private Collection, Sonora, California.

62. *Index Atlas of Kern County, California, 1901* (Bakersfield, Calif.: Randell-Denne, 1901), 58–59. Pages 24 and 25 of the Kern County index also contain town maps of Kern City, or early Bakersfield. The Iberia (Noriega's) was the only Bakersfield hotel located on the maps.

63. Paquette, *Basques to Bakersfield*, 57–58.

64. "Tehachapi Devastated," *Bakersfield Californian*, 21 July 1952, 1, 17–18, 21, and 31.

65. Paquette, *Basques to Bakersfield*, 94.

66. Sodie Arbios, *Memories of My Life: An Oral History of a California Sheepman* (Stockton, Calif.: Techni-Graphics, 1980), 243.

67. Iribarne Contract, Paquette Papers, Private Collection, Sonora, California.

68. Douglass and Bilbao, *Amerikanuak*, 235. Los Angeles still reported a substantial 330,350 head and Monterrey 126,644 head in the 1870s. Numbers in Kern, Merced, San Joaquin, Sonoma, Tulare and Stanislaus Counties, on the other hand, were growing, and each county had between 117,000 and 180,000 sheep.

69. Ibid.

70. Major transhumant sheep trails from 1865 through 1905 are charted in Warren A. Beck and Ynez D. Haase, *Historical Atlas of California* (Norman: University of Oklahoma Press, 1974), 73.

71. Beck and Haase, *Historical Atlas*, 69; and Arbios, *Memories of My Life*, 22–25.

72. Ibid., 93. Today Fresno County continues to lead the state in agricultural output.

73. Charles W. Clough and William B. Secrest, Jr., *Fresno County—The Pioneer Years: From the Beginnings to 1900* (Fresno: Panorama West Books, 1984), 44.

74. Ibid.

75. All three towns were once on major train transportation routes and are much smaller than Fresno today. They can be found in north-to-south line about 50 miles east of Fresno. Also note that the development of early Basque hotels occurred in the "west side" of the San Joaquin Valley, presumably due to sheep transhumance.

76. *Fresno City and County Directory, 1898* (Fresno: C. T. Cearley, 1898), 234; and Clough and Secrest, *Fresno County*, 255.

77. Thelma Miller, "Valley Homes of *Paisanos*," *Fresno Bee*, 1 February 1943.

78. Ibid.

79. Ibid., 256; Fresno County Naturalization Records (June 8, 1896, Fresno County Courthouse, Fresno, California) show that Arripe became a citizen around the time he was working with Arnaudon (Amerikanuak Papers, Basque Studies Collection, Getchell Library, University of Nevada, Reno).

80. Paul E. Vandor, *History of Fresno County, California, with Biographical Sketches* (Los Angeles: Historic Record Company, 1919), 1927.

81. Ibid.

82. *Fresno Daily Evening Expositor*, 6 May 1896, 2. Cited in Clough and Secrest, *Fresno County*, 256.

83. Ibid.

84. Ibid. The article originally appeared in the *Tulare Register*, 1888. Cited in Clough and Secrest, *Fresno County*, 262.

85. Ibid., 262.

86. "Mouren Farm Company of Huron," *Fresno Bee*, 28 August 1981, C4.

87. Douglass and Bilbao, *Amerikanuak*, 376,

88. Clough and Secrest, *History of Fresno*, 310.

89. Arrizabalaga, "A Statistical Study," 70.

90. Ibid., 72.

91. *Fresno City and County Directory*, 1900 (Fresno: Hedges, 1900), 51. Actually this directory locates the Bascongado at 1223 G, but all subsequent directories indicate that 1228 G was the hotel address.

92. Juanita Iribarren Marquand, interview by author, Fresno, Calif., 11 June 1987.

93. Ibid.; and Hilaria Frechou, interview by author, Fresno, Calif., 7 May 1987.

94. Vandor, *History of Fresno County*, 1585.

95. *Fresno City and County Directory*, 1901 (Fresno: F. M. Husted, 1901), 75; and *Fresno City Directory*, 1904 (Fresno: F. M. Husted and Company, 1904), 79, 163, and 167.

96. *Fresno City and County Directory*, 1910 (Fresno: Polk-Husted, 1910), 174.

97. Talbott, interview, 10 March 1987.

98. Arbios, *Memories of My Life*, 77.

99. Paquette, *Basques to Bakersfield*, 61.

100. Vandor, *History of Fresno County*, 2514.

101. *Fresno City and County Directory, 1922* (Fresno: Polk-Husted, 1922); there are no page numbers in the directory.

102. Vandor, *History of Fresno County*, 1901.

103. *Fresno City and County Directory, 1901* (Fresno: F. M. Husted, 1901), 75 and 120.

104. Vandor, *History of Fresno County*, 1901.

105. *Fresno City and County Directory, 1908–1909* (Fresno: Polk-Husted, 1909), 153.

106. Frechou, interview, 7 May 1987.

107. Sanborn Fire Insurance Maps, Fresno, California, 1915 and 1933, volume 1, map 30. Fresno County Library, Fresno, California. The first directory listing of the Frechous' gas station was in 1933 but the last citation for the Frechou House appeared in 1920. The station may have been constructed in the mid-1920s.

108. Vandor, *History of Fresno County*, 2559.

109. *Fresno City and County Directory, 1925* (Fresno: Polk-Husted, 1925), 228.

110. Ballaz, interview, 7 May 1987. Unless otherwise indicated, the following description of the Victoria is also from Maria Ballaz; L. Schuster, "My Basque Friend . . . Tom Ballaz," *The Fresnopolitan*, July 1956, 31–34; and "Vitoria Hotel, Noted for Its Basque Food, Closes," *Fresno Bee*, 18 May 1962.

111. *Fresno City and County Directory, 1929* (Fresno: Polk-Husted, 1929), 445.

112. Esain, interview, 18 February 1987.

113. Asuncion Curutchet Goñi, interview by author, Clovis, Calif., 7 May 1987; and *Fresno City and County Directory, 1929*, 241; and *Fresno City and County Directory, 1933* (Fresno: Polk-Husted, 1933), 194.

114. Vandor, *History of Fresno County*, 2576.

115. Sanborn Fire Insurance Maps, Fresno, California, 1933, vol. 1, Map W, 71. Fresno County Library, Fresno, California.

116. "Basque Hotel Closes and Reopens," *Fresno Bee*, 1 February 1980.

117. Paquette, *Basques to Bakersfield*, 35.

118. Some people I spoke with even described two neighboring hotels; others infer that the two occupied the same building during different periods.

119. Asuncion Curutchet Goñi, interview, 7 May 1987.

120. *Fresno City and County Directory, 1933*, 135.

121. *Fresno City and County Directory, 1937* (Fresno: R. L. Polk, 1937), 197; *Fresno City and County Directory, 1958* (Fresno: Polk-Husted, 1958), 588; and *Fresno City and County Directory, 1962* (Fresno: Polk-Husted, 1962), 704.

122. "Paul Yturri, 57, Hotel Man, Dies," *Fresno Bee*, 8 August 1950, 1B.

123. Mrs. Albert Lassart, interview by author, Los Banos, Calif., 26 February 1987.

124. Ibid.

125. Mrs. Barcelona, interview by Ralph Milliken, Los Banos, Calif., 1945,

Talbott Papers, Los Banos, California. In recent decades the hotel business was sold to non-Basques and became the Colonnade Hotel. Downstairs the Woolgrowers' Restaurant and Bar still serves Basque cuisine.

126. Talbott, interview, 26 February 1987.

127. Michel Iturbide, interview by author, Los Banos, Calif., 26 February 1987.

128. Pat McNally, "Family Style Basque Restaurants," *Merced Sun Star*, 10 October 1980, 5.

129. *Polk's Merced, Madera and Chowchilla California Directory, 1928–1929* (San Francisco: R. L. Polk, 1928), 68.

130. Mary Jean Elgart Uhalde, interview by author, Madera, Calif., 23 April 1987.

131. Angie Goñi Anaut, interview by author, Merced, Calif., 30 January 1987, 17 February 1987

132. Paquette, *Basques to Bakersfield*, 71.

133. Bernard Borderre, interview by Patricia G. Cleek, Santa Barbara, Calif., 6 December 1983, Borderre Hotel File, Santa Barbara Historical Society, Santa Barbara, California.

134. Borderre Hotel File, Santa Barbara Historical Society, Santa Barbara, California.

135. Deed of Records, County of Santa Barbara, 68: 64, Borderre Hotel File, Santa Barbara Historical Society, Santa Barbara, California.

136. Paquette, *Basques to Bakersfield*, 71.

137. Photographs from the Borderre Hotel File, Santa Barbara Historical Society, Santa Barbara, California.

138. Sanborn Fire Insurance Maps, Santa Barbara, 1898, Map 13, Borderre Hotel File, Santa Barbara Historical Society.

139. *Santa Barbara City and County Directory, 1909–1910* (Santa Barbara: Santa Barbara Directory Company, 1910), 60 and 53.

140. Borderre Hotel File, Santa Barbara Historical Society, Santa Barbara, California.

141. Blanche Amorena Johnson, interview by author, Santa Barbara, Calif., 5 June 1987.

142. Dominica Borderre, interview by Mary Paquette. Noted in *Basques to Bakersfield*, 72.

143. Borderre Hotel File, Santa Barbara Historical Society, Santa Barbara, California; and Walter Tompkins, *Thomas Storke: California Editor* (Santa Barbara: Pacific Coast Publications, 1968), 55.

144. Spanish for "drinks beneath the law" or bootlegging. Jose Campos, interview by author, Santa Barbara, Calif., 4 June 1987.

145. Blanch Amorena Johnson, interview, 5 June 1987.

146. Jose Campos, interview by author, Santa Barbara, Calif., 4 June 1987.

147. "Where Cowboys and Basques Eat," *Sunset Magazine*, November 1985, 56–57.

148. *California'ko Eskual Herria*, December (*Abendoaren*) 30, 1893, Lib. 2, no. 9:3–4.

149. For the San Diego City and County Directories consulted, see the "Directory" section in the Bibliograpy. *Monteith's Directory of San Diego and Vicinity, 1889–1890* (San Diego: J. C. Monteith, 1890); *Directory of San Diego City, Coronado, and National City, 1892–1893* (San Diego: Olmstead and Bynon, 1893); *San Diego City and County Directory, 1895, 1897, 1899–1900, and 1910* (San Diego: Olmstead and Bynon, 1895; Olmstead, 1897; Baker Brothers, 1900; San Diego Directory Company, 1903; and San Diego Directory Company, 1910).

150. This situation is even more curious because San Diego's neighbor to the south, Tijuana, Mexico, has been home to a couple of hotels, a Basque colony, and a jai alai court, which has primarily employed Basque *pelotariak*.

151. These interviews are part of the "Early Basques in Orange County" Series, Oral History Collection, California State University, Fullerton.

152. Eagle, "Work and Play Among the Basques," 107. These Basque citrus-ranching families were Yturry, Erramuspe, Bastanchury, Oyharzabal, Sansinena, Yriarte, Dunhart, Erreca, Lacougue, Ondaro, Echeto, Lorea, and Oxandaboure.

153. John Yturry, interview, 28 April 1987.

154. Eagle, "Work and Play Among the Basques," 164.

155. David Echeverria, interview by author, Brea, Calif., 29 March 1980.

156. Eagle, "Work and Play Among the Basques," 165.

157. Juliette Robidart Campos, interview by author, Caruthers, Calif., 23 April 1987.

158. Melanie Sallaberry, interview by author, Chino, Calif., 30 April 1987.

159. Monique Berterretche, interview by author, Chino, Calif., 30 April 1987.

160. Nancy Harding, "Basques Leave Pyrenees for Rolling Hills of Chino," *Santa Ana Register*, 9 March 1980, A3.

161. Melanie Sallaberry, interview, 30 April 1987.

162. Monique Berterretche, interview, 30 April 1987.

163. Lorenzo Echanis, John Yturry, and Francisca Echeverria, interview by author, Brea, Calif., 3 June 1987.

## CHAPTER SEVEN. THE GOLDEN YEARS IN THE GREAT BASIN AND BEYOND

1. The Centro Vasco in Chino, California, could possibly be considered an exception, because it opened in 1940 a few miles from La Puente, a town whose earliest *ostatuak* preceded this date.

2. Please refer to figure 5. In later years, Basques also worked in many other occupations, particularly in ranching, dairy work, and in orchards.

3. Douglass and Bilbao, *Amerikanuak*, 250–52.

4. Ben Hazeltine, Charles Salisbury, and Harry Taylor, "They Came for Range and Left a Heritage," *Western Livestock Journal* (August 1961): 99–109; and Clel

Georgetta, "Sheep in Nevada," *Nevada Historical Society Quarterly* 8, no. 2 (summer 1965): 28.

5. Shepperson, *Restless Strangers*, 14.

6. Douglas and Bilbao, *Amerikanuak*, 250–58.

7. Robert G. Boyd, *Amerikanuak!: Basques in the High Desert* (Bend, Oreg.: High Desert Museum, 1995), 24–25.

8. As quoted by Robert Laxalt, *Nevada: A Bicentennial History* (Reno: University of Nevada Press, 1991), 15–16.

9. Edna B. Patterson, Louise A. Ulph, and Victor Goodwin, *Nevada's Northeast Frontier* (Reno: University of Nevada Press and the Northeastern Nevada Historical Society, 1991), 298–300. In fact, Basques ran a store and an *ostatu* in Jack Creek around the turn of the century. It was located about twelve miles from Altube's Spanish Ranch headquarters.

10. Boyd, *Basques in the High Desert*, 25.

11. Arrizabalaga, "Statistical Study," 130.

12. The comparable increase in California's Basque population for the same decade was 8.4 times.

13. Arrizabalaga, "Statistical Study," 72; and William A. Douglass, "The Basques of Nevada," *Nevada: Official Bicentennial Book* (Las Vegas: Nevada Publications, 1976), 56.

14. Ibid., table 5.2.17, 86. Given the growth patterns of the boardinghouses in other Basque communities, it is plausible that a few more *hoteleros* may have existed in 1900, and that the census takers may have missed a few or overlooked them.

15. The extensive Oral History project conducted by Gretchen Holbert retrieved and recorded valuable information on Nevada's *ostatuak*, emphasizing what life was like in them and how they served Nevada's Basque communities rather than focusing on dates and the duration of ownership at each town site. See table 7.1 for mention of hotels not directly discussed in the narrative. For example, Goni's in Wellington, Arrascada's and the Star in Golconda, the Grand and Morning Star in Fallon, the Lovelock in Lovelock, the Evans in Unionville. Table 7.2 contains a composite listing of hotels mentioned in these works.

16. Barbara and Myrick Land, *A Short History of Reno* (Reno: University of Reno Press, 1995), 13–17.

17. Silen, *Historia de Vascongados de los Estados Unidos* (New York: Los Novedades, 1917), 145. *Reno City Directory*, 1904 (Reno: Haley and Darley, 1904), 44.

18. *Reno City Directory* 1900 (Reno: *Daily Nevada State Journal*, 1900), 45.

19. A. Rene Martin, letter to Gretchen Holbert, July 14, 1980, Holbert-Osa Oral History Collection, Basque Studies Collection, Getchell Library, University of Nevada, Reno.

20. Oral accounts, Holbert-Osa Collection.

21. Such comments can be found in Gretchen Holbert's interviews with Irlene Arbeloa, Lenore Holbert Sabala, Augustine Sabala, and Lenore Sabala Holbert, Holbert-Osa Oral History Collection; and Zubiri, *A Travel Guide to Basque America*,

60–62. One source places the location of one such home at the corner of Park and East Fourth Street. *Reno City Directory 1911–1912* (Reno: Reno City Publishing Company, 1912), 44.

22. Jai Aldi 1990 Commission, *Jai Aldi '90 Program*, 93; and Holbert-Osa Oral History Collection.

23. Douglass and Bilbao, *Amerikanuak*, 242.

24. The boardinghouses of Idaho, Oregon, and Washington will be discussed more fully in chapter 8.

25. Jai Aldi 1990 Commission, *Jai Aldi '90 Program*, 110. Although there have been other Basque-owned businesses in Winnemucca—including mention of an early boardinghouse operated by the J. Larre family and Basques staying at the Busch Hotel—only the Martin and Winnemucca Hotels have served as the area's Basque *ostatuak*.

26. See the illustration in chapter 13 for drawings of Winnemucca's six stages of construction.

27. A. Rene Martin, letter to Gretchen Holbert, July 14, 1980, Holbert-Osa Oral History Collection, Basque Studies Collection, Getchell Library, University of Nevada, Reno.

28. Margaret Sermons Purser, "Community and Material Culture in Nineteenth Century Paradise Valley, Nevada," (Ph.D. diss., University of California, Berkeley, 1987), 102, 109–11.

29. We know that Antonio and Leandra Letemendi left Paradise Valley in 1907 with the intent to open a boardinghouse in Boise, which they did. It is possible that the Letemendis began hotel keeping on a small scale at the Paradise Valley residence as well, although we have no evidence to substantiate the claim.

30. Initial settlement of Elko began in December of 1868, when the Central Pacific Railway reached the site and began laying out lots for the future town. It is possible that Basques settled in and opened boardinghouses in Elko during the last decades of the nineteenth century, but to date there is no such record. Patterson et al., *Nevada's Northeast Frontier*, 175.

31. Laxalt, *Nevada: A Bicentennial History*, 13.

32. Patterson et al., *Nevada's Northeast Frontier*, 541–61.

33. Gretchen Holbert, "Elko's Overland Hotel."

34. Patterson et al., *Nevada's Northeast Frontier*, 300. See table 7.3 for a listing of Elko's boardinghouses.

35. Unhappy with hotel life, Francisco and Julianna sold their portion of the partnership and returned to country life, establishing their Goicoechea Home Ranch 65 miles north of Elko in 1912.

36. Linda White, "Mathilde Jauregui: Symbol of the Basque Woman in the West," *Basque Studies Program Newsletter* 45 (April 1992): 11.

37. Patterson et al., *Nevada's Northeast Frontier*, 304.

38. Jai Aldi 1990 Commission, *Jai Aldi '90 Program*, 79.

39. Zubiri, *A Travel Guide to Basque America*, 319.

40. Examples of Basque bachelors owning and operating boardinghouses for an extended period are extremely rare. Chapters 3, 10, and 11 provide further discussion of *hoteleros* and hotel keeping.

41. Gretchen Holbert-Osa, "The Overland: The Last Basque Hotel," in *Essays in Basque Social Anthropology and History*, ed. William A. Douglass, Basque Studies Program Occasional Paper Series, No. 4 (Reno: Basque Studies Program, 1989), 317.

42. Robert Laxalt, interview by Mateo Osa, Carson City, Nev., 31 March 1988, Holbert-Osa Oral History Collection, Basque Studies Collection, Getchell Library, University of Nevada, Reno.

43. Robert Laxalt, *The Basque Hotel* (Reno: University of Nevada Press, 1989).

44. Patterson et al., *Nevada's Northeast Frontier*, 646.

45. Zubiri, A *Travel Guide to Basque America*, 345–46. The Holbert-Osa tapes also mention a French Hotel in Eureka and a hotel named Martin's. The latter was probably the Spanish Hotel operated by Martin Inda, and the former may have been an earlier establishment.

46. *California'ko Eskual Herria*, August 24, 1895, 2.

47. Personal Correspondence File, Irene Echeverria Aja, January 31, 1989.

48. Douglass and Bilbao, *Amerikanuak*, 78–79; and Garate, "Basque Names," 81.

49. William A. Douglass, "On the Naming of Arizona," *Names: The Journal of the American Name Society* 27 (December 1979): 221–23.

50. *California'ko Eskual Herria*, April 7, 1894, Lib. 2, no. 23, 2.

51. Douglass and Bilbao, *Amerikanuak*, 244–45; Donald Brown, "Emmett Elizondo: Sheepman Extraordinary," *Letter* (spring–summer, 1980): 5–10; and Walker D. Wyman and John D. Hart, "The Legend of Charlie Glass," *Colorado Magazine* 46 (1969): 40–54.

52. Douglass and Bilbao, *Amerikanuak*, 373.

53. Bob Iturralde, "Agur, Hogar, Agur."

54. Raimundo Urrutia Personal Papers, Idaho State Historical Library, Boise, Idaho. Although Urrutia's papers refer to the establishment as Fonda Español, it could also have been the Fonda Española.

55. *California'ko Eskual Herria*, July 29, 1893, Lib. 1, no. 3, 2.

56. Iberlin, *The Basque Web*, 12.

57. Ibid., 103–7.

58. Arrizabalaga, "Statistical Study." 102–4.

59. Personal Correspondence File, Lorraine Kuhn Williams, December 14, 1988; Iberlin, *Basque Web*, 30 and 98; Dollie Iberlin and David Romtvedt, ed., *Buffalotarrak: An Anthology of the Basque People of Buffalo, Wyoming* (Buffalo, Wyo.: Red Hills Publications, 1995), 27; and Zubiri, A *Travel Guide to Basque America*, 495–97.

60. Zubiri, A *Travel Guide to Basque America*, 484.

61. *California'ko Eskual Herria*, 7, Lib. 5, no. 23, 2, November 10, 1894; Lib. 3, no. 11, and February 6, 189.

62. Ibid., August 18 and 25, 1894.

1. Leonard J. Arrington, *History of Idaho*, vol. 1 (Moscow: University of Idaho Press and Idaho State Historical Society, 1994), 183–87.

2. Douglass and Bilbao, *Amerikanuak*, 242; and Munro, "Basque Folklore in Southeastern Oregon."

3. *Boise City Directory, 1891* (Boise City, Idaho: Leadbetter and Waterbeek Publishers, 1891), 5. It is likely, however, that not all Basques in Boise were included in the directory.

4. Arrizabalaga, "Statistical Study," 90. In 1910, 961 of 999 Idaho Basques were Spanish Basques, and in both 1900 and 1910 over 90 percent of Idaho's Basque population had been born in Euskal Herria. Julio Bilbao, "Basque Names in Early Idaho," *Idaho Yesterdays* 15 (summer 1971): 26–29.

5. J. Patrick Bieter, "Letemendi's Boarding House: A Basque Cultural Institution in Idaho," *Idaho Yesterdays* 37, no. 1 (spring 1993): 5.

6. *Boise City Directory, 1891*, 73.

7. Bilbao, "Basque Names in Early Idaho," 28.

8. *Boise City, Nampa, and Caldwell Directory 1893* (Salt Lake City: Western Publishing Company, 1893); *Boise City Directory 1899* (Boise: Statesman Printing, 1899); *Farr and Smith's 1901–02 Boise City and Ada County Directory* (Boise: Statesman Printing, 1901); *Polk's Boise City Directory, 1902–03* (Salt Lake City: R. L. Polk, 1902).

9. Zubiri, "A Travel Guide to Basque America," 337.

10. Jay Uberuaga Hormaechea, interview by author, Boise, Idaho, 5 September 1993.

11. Ibid.

12. "Basques in Boise," *Oasis Magazine*, November 1977, 5.

13. Bieter, "Letemendi's Boarding House," 5.

14. Ibid., 6.

15. Patrick Bieter, "Folklore of the Boise Basques," *Western Folklore* 24 (1965): 264.

16. Bradford Sax, "Sons of the Pyrenees in the Northwest," *Travel Magazine*, September 1942, 14.

17. Louise Shadduck, *Andy Little: Idaho's Sheep King* (Caldwell, Idaho: Caxton Printers, 1990), 152.

18. Ibid.

19. Barbero was the nickname of an early operator of the Modern Rooming House at 613 West Idaho. Hormaechea, interview, 5 September 1993.

20. Jai Aldi 1990 Commission, "City of the Basques," *1990 Jai Aldi Program*, 64; and Hormaechea, interview, 5 September 1993.

21. Ibid.; and Patterson et al., *Nevada's Northeast Frontier*, 299. Because one source cites 1907 as Mateo's date of arrival in Winnemucca and the other cites 1905 as the date of his arrival in Boise, one can speculate that one record is in error.

Because Mateo worked in northern Nevada, it seems likely that the Arreguis arrived in Boise closer to 1915 than 1905.

22. Lucy Alboitiz Garatea, interview by author, Boise, Idaho, 22 March 1989.

23. Jai Aldi 1990 Commission, *Jai Aldi '90 Program*, 105.

24. Ibid., 109.

25. Personal correspondence File, Lucia Uriaguereca Osa, December 12, 1988.

26. Ibid.

27. Zubiri, *A Travel Guide to Basque America*, 412–16.

28. Jack Beardwood, "Mountain Home Is Typical of Idaho Basque Colonies," *Boise Capitol News*, 26 June 1937.

29. Groefsema, *Elmore County*, 230.

30. Patterson et al., *Nevada's Northeast Frontier*, 299.

31. Groefsema, *Elmore County*, 108.

32. Ibid., 99; Jimmy Jausoro, interview by Steve Siporin, Boise, Idaho, 12 August 1982, Oral History Collection, Idaho Historical Library, Boise, Idaho.

33. Floyd Acarrequi, "Jordan Valley, the Home of the Basques." *Voice of the Basques*, November 1976, 8–9; Anthony Yturry, interview by author, Ontario, Oreg., 23 March 1989; Helen Marquina Smith, interview by author, Ontario, Oreg., 23 March 1989; and "Basques Tell History, Culture to Local Historical Society Members," *Voice of the Basques*, May 5, 1976.

34. John Croner, "Independent Basque Sheepmen Brought Unique Lifestyles," *Daily Argus Observer*, June 5, 1983. Though Croner uses the name Uriquiri, local Basques have referred to the sheepman as Urquidi.

35. Garatea, "*Burns'eko*," 36–40; Marcelino Osa, interview by author, Burns, Oreg., 23 March 1989; Garatea, interview, 22 March 1989; and Personal Correspondence File, Ana Andueza, 2 January 1989, 20 February 1989.

36. Garatea, "*Burns'eko*," 37.

37. Margarita Aramaio Osa, interview by Paquita Garatea, Burns, Oreg., 30 April 1989.

38. The spelling of *Ebar* in this case is unusual and could have been changed from the more likely *Eibar* or *Ybar* at an earlier date. See Garatea, "Burns'eko," 37.

39. Arralde, interview, 24 July 1990.

## CHAPTER NINE. STOCKTON'S BASQUE TOWN AND NORTHERN CALIFORNIA *Ostatuak*

1. *City and County Directory of San Joaquin, Stanislaus, Merced, and Tuolumne, 1881* (San Francisco: L. M. McKenny and Company, 1881), 57–58.

2. Ibid., 61.

3. Ibid., 57; and *Stockton City Directory*, 1905 (San Francisco: L. M. McKenney and Company, 1905), 30.

4. Steve Ybarrola, a native of Stockton, compiled an exhaustive list of hotels in Stockton's Basque town and shared it generously with the author (Ybarrola papers,

Central College, Pella, Iowa). Pete Iroz and Jon Domench, two people I interviewed who lived in the neighborhood for years, assisted him. Ybarrola's list has been checked against directory information and the memory of other Basques and modified only slightly. See table 9.1 for a summary of Stockton *ostatuak* from 1907 through 1970 and figure 18 for a map of Stockton's Basque town.

5. George H. Tinkham, *History of San Joaquin County* (Los Angeles: Historical Record Company, 1923), 1404; and Tom McKay, "Last Pioneer of San Joaquin Valley Sheep Ranchers Reviews 56 Years' Progress," *Stockton Record*, 7 May 1949.

6. Elena Celayeta Talbott, interview, 26 February 1987.

7. *History of Stockton Fire Department* (Stockton: Atwood Printing, 1908), 104.

8. Ibid. The mixture of Spanish, French, and Basque terms in this quotation is noteworthy.

9. Pagliarulo, "Basques in Stockton," 59.

10. Ibid.

11. *Stockton Record*, 5 April 1917, Talbott Papers, Los Banos, California; Iroz, interview, 11 June 1987; and Sanborn Fire Insurance Maps, Stockton, California, 1917, vol. 1, maps 74 and 82, California State University, Northridge Map Collection. Fire insurance maps give details for one court adjacent to the Royal and a second at the Español. Although the other two are not shown on Sanborn maps, they were probably there as reported.

12. Peter Iroz, interview by author, Stockton, Calif., 11 June 1987.

13. Works Progress Administration, "History of Stockton and San Joaquin County," (unpublished manuscript, Stockton Public Library, 1938), 88.

14. Ibid.

15. Refer to table 9.2 for years of operation. Ernie La Coste, Personal Correspondence File, December 14, 1988.

16. Compiled from author's research and from the Ybarrola papers.

17. Pagliarulo, "Basques in Stockton."

18. Ibid., 63.

19. Ibid., 59.

20. Many *ostatuak* discussed in earlier chapters emerged during the 1890 to 1930 watershed as well.

21. Arrizabalaga, "A Statistical Study," 69.

22. Ibid., 70.

23. *California'ko Eskual Herria*, December (*Abendoaren*) 30, 1893, 4.

24. This is the same Goñi family that moved to Merced and purchased the Pyrenees Hotel there in 1929.

25. Angie Goñi Anaut, interview by author, 30 January 1987.

26. Boyd, *High Desert*, 25, 26.

27. William and Albert Beterbide, interview by author, Susanville, Calif., 21 May 1987.

28. Jane Goñi, interview by author, Susanville, Calif., 21 May 1987.

29. Personal correspondence file, Dolores Juarena Young, January 1989, Prairie City, Oregon.

30. Steve Mendive, "The Basques in Marysville and Northern California," (senior paper, 1980, University of Nevada, Reno), Basque Studies Collection, Getchell Library, University of Nevada, Reno; Victor Uriz, interview by author, Marysville, Calif., 5 April 1990; and Helen C. Hollander, Personal Correspondence File, December 1988. *Luthio* may also be spelled *Lucio*.

31. Personal correspondence file, Richard Ramos, Portola Valley, California, February 1990.

32. Iroz, interview, 11 June 1987. According to Iroz, the two Sacramento *ostatuak* were called the Hotel España and the Hotel Español.

33. Stephen Magagnini, "An Outpost with an Oldtime Accent," *Sacramento Bee*, 10 February 1989, 5. Although occasional mention of other Sacramento *ostatuak* can be found, references to them remain incomplete. It is likely that earlier Sacramento *ostatuak* existed, but only two in the 1920s have been recorded to date.

34. Arthur McEwen. "Basques 'Invade' Fort Ord," *Monterey Peninsula Herald*, 8 April 1961, Peninsula Life Section, 1–4.

## CHAPTER TEN. INSIDE THE *Ostatu Euskalduna*

1. Doyaga, "History of *Eusko-Extea*," 131–41; William A. Douglass, "Home Is a Hotel," 22–23; and Douglass and Bilbao, *Amerikanuak*, 374.

2. Literally translated, "mother of the house" or "father of the house."

3. Holbert, "Elko's Overland Hotel," 18.

4. Holbert-Osa, "The Overland," 322.

5. Douglas G. Hale, "Quasi-Groups and Boundary Maintenance in a Basque Hotel," (student paper, National Science Field Foundation, 1969), 5. Basque Studies Collection, Getchell Library, University of Nevada, Reno.

6. Mary Grace Paquette, *Lest We Forget: The History of the French in Kern County* (Bakersfield, Calif.: Kern County Historical Society, 1978), 135–42.

7. *California'ko Eskual Herria*, July (*Uztailaren*) 15, 1893, 2.

8. Frank Maitia Sr., interview, 1 April 1987.

9. Two sources, one an oral history of Joe Mosconi and the other a paper written by Debi Del Papa, are available on the relationship between Basques and Italians in Reno and Bakersfield. Basque Studies Collection, Getchell Library, University of Nevada Library, Reno.

10. Verses in the lefthand column are in the original Basque and English, while verses on the right were translated from Basque to Spanish and English by Josu Bijuesca, "No. 52: Un *bertsopapera* norteamericano," Symposium on Basques in the U.S.A., University of California, Santa Barbara, April 7, 1995.

11. Zubiri, *A Travel Guide to Basque America*, 424–25.

12. Ibid., 414–15.

13. Iberlin, *Basque Web*, 83.

14. Jose Elgorriaga, interview by author, Fresno, Calif., 26 April 1987.

1. Croner, "Independent Basque," *Argus*, 5 June 1983.

2. Ibid.

3. Josephine Echanis Keim, quoted in Croner, "Independent Basque."

4. Bieter, "Letemendi's Boarding House," 6–7.

5. Holbert, "Elko's Overland," 14.

6. Goyenetche, interview, 13 May 1987.

7. Robert Laxalt, *Sweet Promised Land* (New York: Harper Brothers, 1957); *The Basque Hotel* (Reno: University of Nevada Press, 1989); and *Child of the Holy Ghost* (Reno: University of Nevada Press, 1992).

8. Monique Urza, *The Deep Blue Memory* (Reno: University of Nevada Press, 1993), 11.

9. Charlotte Crawford, "The Position of Women in a Basque Fishing Community," in Douglass, Etulain, and Jacobsen, ed., *Anglo-American Contributions to Basque Studies*, 145–52.

10. Deborah Fink, *Open Country, Iowa: Rural Women, Tradition, and Change* (Albany: State University of New York Press, 1986), 3.

11. Paquita Garatea's master's thesis (1990) dealt with the women of the Burns boardinghouses. And, finally, Nancy Zubiri's *A Travel Guide to Basque America* includes commentary from a number of *hoteleras* in the American West.

12. William and Albert Beterbide, interviews, 21 May 1987.

13. For further discussion, see Echeverria, "*California'ko ostatuak*," 186–203.

14. Garatea, "*Burn'seko*," 34–36.

15. Ibid.; and Garatea, interview, 22 March 1989.

16. Talbott, interview, 10 March 1987; and Arbios, *Memories of My Life*, 20–33.

17. Teresa del Valle, "The Current Status," in Douglass, ed., *Essays in Basque Social Anthropology and History*, 129–48; Jacqueline Urla, "Reinventing Basque Society: Cultural Difference and the Quest for Modernity, 1918–1936," in Douglass, ed., *Essays in Basque Social Anthropology and History*, 149–76; and Roslyn M. Frank, "The Religious Role of Women in Basque Culture," in Douglass, Etulain, and Jacobsen, ed., *Anglo-American Contributions to Basque Studies: Essays in Honor of Jon Bilbao*, 153–60.

18. Iban Bilbao and Chantal de Equilaz, *Diáspora Vasca*, vol. 1, *Vascos llegados al puerto de Nueva York, 1897–1902* (Vitoria: Diputación Floral de Álava, Consejo de Cultura, Sección Bibliografía y Diáspora Vascas, 1981); and Arrizabalaga, "Statistical Study."

19. Echeverria, "*California'ko ostatuak*," 186–204.

20. Paquette, *Basques to Bakersfield*, 89; Janice Elizalde, interview, 1 April 1987; and Mayie Maitia, interview, 2 April 1987.

21. Zubiri, "*A Travel Guide to Basque America*, 338–40.

22. It should be noted that a few Basque men have also enjoyed such regard in the American West. In *Amerikanuak*, for example, Douglass and Bilbao refer to John Archabal of Boise, Jose Bengoechea of Mountain Home, Jean Esponda of

Buffalo, Wyoming, and Guy Saval of northeastern Nevada as "King" or "Father" of the Basques in their respective areas (Douglass and Bilbao, *Amerikanuak*, 386).

23. Teresa del Valle, "The Current Status of the Anthropology of Women: Models and Paradigms," in Douglass, ed., *Essays in Basque Social Anthropology and History*, 141. See also del Valle's *Mujer Vasca: Imagen y realidad* (Barcelona: Editorial Anthropos, 1985); and *Korrika: Basque Ritual for Ethnic Identity* (Reno: University of Nevada Press, 1994).

24. Donna Gabaccia, *From the Other Side: Women, Gender, and Immigrant Life in the United States, 1820–1990* (Bloomington: Indiana University Press, 1994), xi.

## CHAPTER TWELVE. BASQUE BOARDINGHOUSES IN OTHER SETTINGS

1. Information provided by Joxe Mallea-Olaetxe.

2. Douglass and Bilbao, *Amerikanuak*, 160.

3. Francisco Grandmontagne, *Los immigrantes prósperos* (Madrid, 1933).

4. Early Basque participation in the Cuban sugar industry, *alto comercio* ventures, paper mills, and the clergy are cited in Ignacio Galbís, "Basques in Cuba: The Republican Years," in Society of Basques Studies in America, ed., *Proceedings of the First International Basque Conference in North America*, 143–53. Colonization of Mexico City is well documented in Joxe Mallea-Olaexte's doctoral disseration on Bishop Juan Zumarraga, in which the bishop is credited with being the first Patriarch of Mexico City's Basque Colony between 1535 and 1548. Mexico's early Basque colonies are also discussed in Lorin Gaardner's "Preliminary Comments on the Basque Colony of Mexico City," in Douglass, Etulain, and Jacobsen, ed., *Anglo-American Contributions to Basque Studies*, 59–69.

5. B. A. Balcom, *The Cod Fishery of Isle Royale, 1713–58* (Ottawa, Ontario: National Historic Parks Canada, 1984), 1–5.

6. A. J. B. Johnson, *Louisbourg: The Phoenix Fortress* (Halifax, Nova Scotia: Nimbus Publishing Company, 1990), 1–10.

7. Christopher Moore, *Fortress of Louisbourg* (Louisbourg: College of Cape Breton Press, 1981), 8–10.

8. Ibid., 9.

9. Selma Huxley Barkham, *The Basque Coast of Newfoundland* (Plum Point, Newfoundland: The Great Northern Pennisula Development Corporation, 1989), 25. *Barrachoa* was probably *Barratxoa*, or "little sand bar" in English; *Tres Irlac* would mean "three islands"; *Ferrolgo Amuixco Punta* translates as "Old Ferrole Harbor"; *Etchaire Portu* means "port with a group of houses"; *Oporportu* means "vacation port"; *Portucho Caharra* translates as "old port"; and *Granbayarre* is a mixture of French and Basque and means "large bay."

10. Doroteo Vicente Elordieta y Clemençot, letter to the author, January 31, 1989 and June 18, 1989, Georgetown Royalty, Prince Edward Island, Canada.

11. Doroteo Vicente Elordieta y Clemençot, letter to William A. Douglass, undated, Georgetown Royalty, Prince Edward Island, Canada. Basque Studies Collection, Getchell Library, University of Nevada, Reno.

12. Douglass and Bilbao, *Amerikanuak*, 129.

13. Statistics in this section were tabulated from notations in the Clemençot Hotel Register, Basque Studies Collection, Getchell Library, University of Nevada, Reno. Compilations were performed by graduate student Mr. Jesse Mendez.

14. It is likely that Mutriku and Arasbasqui were misspelled in the hotel ledgers. The former was probably Mutriko and the latter Arbatzegi, formerly written Arbacegui.

## CHAPTER THIRTEEN. *Agur Ostatuak*

1. Zubiri, *A Travel Guide to Basque America*, 413.

2. William Douglass, "The Vanishing Basque Sheepherder," *American West* 17 (July–August 1980): 30–31, 59–61, contains a detailed review of post-quota legislation. Between 1942 and 1961, for example, only 383 Basques were granted stays in the United States under the Sheepherder Bills.

3. Ibid., 61. Of the 433 Latin Americans, 271 were Peruvians, 161 Mexicans, and one was Colombian.

4. Holbert-Osa, "The Overland," 322.

# *Glossary of Terms*

For unfamiliar terms used in the definitions below, look for entries elsewhere in the glossary, or consult the index for text references. Italicized entries are Basque words, unless otherwise indicated in the definitions.

*agur*. goodbye or farewell
*aita*. father
*ama*. mother
Amerikanuak. Basques in the United States or Basque Americans
Araba. Basque region in Spain
*aurresku*. a typical Basque folk dance

Basco(s). informal English and Spanish word for "Basque(s)"
*baserri(ak)*. farmstead(s), home, and/or property
*baserritar(rak)*. dweller(s) of the *baserri*
Bizkaia. Basque region in Spain

*California'ko Eskual Herria*. newspaper title, meaning "California Basque Land" or "Basques of California"
*cancha*. Spanish word for "handball" or "jai alai court"

*département*. French word for "prefecture"

*Escualdun Gazeta*. newspaper title, meaning "Basque Gazette"
*eskerrik asko*. many thanks
*etxeko aita*. house father or father of the house
*etxeko ama*. house mother or mother of the house
*etxeko andre(ak)*. woman (women) of the house
Euskadi/Euzkadi. Basque Country in Spain, which includes the Autonomous Basque Community of Araba, Bizkaia, Gipuzkoa, and Navarre
*Euskalduna(k)*. speaker(s) or "holders" of the Basque language; term also means "Basques"
Euskal Herria. popular and historical name for the land of the Basques, which includes the seven regions of Araba, Bizkaia, Gipuzkoa, Lapurdi, Nafarroa Beherea, Navarre, and Zuberoa

Euskara/Euskera. the Basque language, including Euskara Batua
Euskara Batua. unified Basque language, with Bizkaian and Gipuzkoan spellings

*fors*. French word for the sixteenth-century legal charters between Basques and the French Crown
fronton. handball or jai alai court
*fueros*. Spanish word for the sixteenth-century legal charters between the Basques and the Crown

Gipuzkoa. Basque region in Spain
Gipuzkoan/Gipuzkoano(s). Basque(s) from Gipuzkoa

*hotelero(s)*. Spanish word for "Basque hotel owner(s)/hotelkeeper(s)"

Iparralde. Northern (upper) region of the Basque Country in France, which includes the regions of Lapurdi, Nafarroa Beherea, and Zuberoa

jai alai. ball game played with wicker; the word literally means "happy festival"
*jota*. dance

*kaletar(rak)*. Old World Basque(s) who live in towns and cities

Lapurdi. Basque region in France
*lehenbiziko atia*. the first neighbor in Old World Basque setting

*mendi beltza*. name of the Echanis *baserri* in Mutriku, literally meaning "black or dark mountain"
*mus*. Basque card game
Mutriku. village in Gipuzkoa

Nafarroa Beherea. Basque region in France
Navarre/Nafarroa. Basque region in Spain
North American Basque Organization (NABO). a federation of Basque organizations in the United States and western hemisphere

*ostatu(ak)*. Basque hotel(s) or boardinghouse(s)
*ostatu Eskualduna*. Basque hotel or boardinghouse

País Vasco. Spanish term for the "Basque Country" or regions
*pala*. a variation of *pilota* played with a wodden racket on a typical handball court
Pays Basque. French term for the "Basque Country" or regions
*pilota/pelota*. handball
*pilotari(ak)*. handball or jai alai player(s)
*porrusalda*. a lively Basque dance or rhythm

*saladero(s)*. Spanish term for "worker(s)" in a meat-salting plant

*txorizo*. sausage

*xistera*. the basketlike extension worn on the hand for playing jai alai

Zuberoa. Basque region in France

# Bibliography

BOOKS


Alegria, Henry. *75 Years of Memoirs*. Caldwell, Idaho: Caxton Press, 1981.

Applegate, Shannon, and Terrence O'Donnell, ed. *Talking on Paper: An Anthology of Oregon Letters and Diaries*. Corvallis, Oreg.: Oregon State University Press, 1994.

Arbios, Sodie. *Memories of My Life: An Oral History of a California Sheepman*. Stockton, Calif.: Techni-Graphics Printing, 1980.

Archdeacon, Thomas J. *Becoming American: An Ethnic History*. New York: Free Press, 1983.

Arciniegas, Germán. *America in Europe: A History of the New World in Reverse*. Translated by R. Victoriana Arana. New York: Harcourt Brace, 1986.

Armitage, Susan, and Elizabeth Jameson, ed. *The Women's West*. Norman: University of Oklahoma Press, 1987.

Armor, Samuel. *History of Orange County, California*. Los Angeles: Historic Record Company, 1921.

Arrington, Leonard J. *The History of Idaho*. 2 vols. Moscow: University of Idaho Press, 1994.

Aulestia, Gorka. *Improvisational Poetry from the Basque Country*. Reno: University of Nevada Press, 1995.

Austin, Mary. *The Flock*. New York: Houghton, Mifflin and Company, 1906.

Ayers, James J. *Transactions of the California State Agricultural Society, 1883*. Sacramento: State of California Printing, 1884.

Balcom, B. A. *The Cod Fishery of Isle Royale, 1713–1758*. Ottawa, Ontario: National Historic Parks Canada, 1984.

Bancroft, Hubert H. *The Works of Hubert Howe Bancroft*. Vol. 34 of *California Pastoral* and vol. 35 of *California Inter Pocula*. San Francisco: History Company Publishers, 1888.

Barahona, Renato. *Vizcaya on the Eve of Carlism: Politics and Society, 1800–1833*. Reno: University of Nevada Press, 1989.

Bard, Rachel. *Navarra: The Durable Kingdom*. Reno: University of Nevada Press, 1982.

Barkham, Selma Huxley. *The Basque Coast of Newfoundland*. Plum Point, Newfoundland: The Great Northern Peninsula Development Corporation, 1989.

Baroja, Pio. *El País Vasco*. 2d ed. Madrid: Ediciones Destino, 1961.
Barthel, Manfred. *The Jesuits: History and Legend of the Society of Jesus*. Translated by Mark Howsen. New York: William Morrow, 1984.
Becker, Carl L., and Leo Gershey. 4th ed. *Survey of European History*. Boston: Houghton Mifflin, 1969.
Bilbao, Iban, and Chantal de Equilaz. *Diáspora Vasca*, vol. 1, *Vascos llegados al puerto de Nueva York, 1897–1902*. Vitoria: Diputación Floral de Álava, Consejo de Cultura, Sección Bibliografía y Diáspora Vascas, 1981.
Bilbao, Jon. *Los Vascos en Cuba, 1492–1511*. Buenos Aires: Editorial Vasca Akin, 1958.
Botkin, M. P., Ray A. Field, and C. LeRoy Johnson. *Sheep and Wool: Science, Production, and Management*. Englewood Cliffs, N.J.: Prentice-Hall, 1988.
Boyd, Robert G. *Amerikanuak! Basques in the High Desert*. Bend, Oreg.: High Desert Museum, 1995.
Boyd, William C. *Genetics and Races of Man: An Introduction to Modern Physical Anthropology*. Boston: Little, Brown, 1950.
Browning, Peter, ed. *John Muir: In His Own Words*. Lafayette, Calif.: Great West Books, 1988.
Brusen, Bernice. *Basques from the Pyrenees to the Rockies*. Portland, Oreg.: Dynagraphics Printing, 1985.
Buckbee, Edna Bryan. *The Saga of Old Tuolumne*. New York: Press of the Pioneers, 1935.
Caro Baroja, Julio. *Los Vascos: una etnología*. San Sebastián: Biblioteca Vascongada de los Amigos del País, 1949.
Carr, Raymond. *Spain: 1808–1975*. Oxford: Clarendon Press, 1982.
Castillo Puche, and José Luís. *Oro blanco*. Madrid: Ediciones CID, 1963.
Ciriquian-Gaizlarro, M. *Los Vascos en la pesca de la ballena*. San Sebastián: Biblioteca Vascongadas de los Amigos del País, 1961.
Clark, Robert P. *The Basques: The Franco Years and Beyond*. Reno: University of Nevada Press, 1979.
———. *The Basque Insurgents: ETA, 1952–1980*. Madison: University of Wisconsin Press, 1984.
Clavería Arza, Carlos. *Leyendas de Vasconia*. Pamplona: Editorial Gómez, Colección Ipar, 1974.
Cleland, Robert Glass. *Cattle on a Thousand Hills: Southern California, 1850–1880*. San Marino, Calif.: Huntington Library, 1964.
Clough, Charles W., and William B. Secrest, Jr. *Fresno County: The Pioneer Years from the Beginnings to 1900*. Fresno, Calif.: Panorama West Books, 1984.
Cloverdale, John F. *The Basque Phase of Spain's First Carlist War*. Princeton, N.J.: Princeton University Press, 1984.
Collins, Roger. *The Basques*. New York: Basil Blackwell, Ltd., 1986.
Crosby, Alfred W., Jr. *The Columbian Exchange: Biological and Cultural Consequences of 1492*. Westport, Conn.: Greenwood Press, 1972.

Crow, John A. *The Root and the Flower*. New York: Coward McCann, 1963.

Davis, R. Trevor. *The Golden Century of Spain, 1501–1621*. 4th ed. New York: Harper and Row, 1961.

DeCroos, Jean Francis. *The Long Journey: Social Integration and Ethnicity Among Urban Basques in the San Francisco Bay Region*. Reno: Associated Faculty Press and Basque Studies Program, 1983.

de Ugalde, Martín, ed. *El libro blanco del Euskera*. Bilbao: Euskalzaindia, Real Academia de la Lengua Vasca, 1977.

del Valle, Teresa. *Korrika: Basque Ritual for Ethnic Identity*. Reno: University of Nevada Press, 1994.

———. *Mujer vasca, Imagen y realidad*. Barcelona: Editorial Anthropos, 1985.

Douglass, William A., ed. *Basque Politics: A Case Study in Ethnic Nationalism*. Reno: University of Nevada Press and Basque Studies Program, 1985.

———. *Death in Murélaga: Funerary Ritual in a Spanish Basque Village*. Seattle: University of Washington Press, 1969.

———. *Echalar and Murélaga: Opportunity and Rural Depopulation in Two Spanish Basque Villages*. New York: St. Martin's Press, 1975.

———, ed. *Essays in Basque Social Anthropology and History*. Basque Studies Occasional Paper Series, no. 4. Reno, 1989.

Douglass, William A., and Joseph B. Aceves, eds. *The Changing Faces of Rural Spain*. New York: John Wiley and Sons, 1976.

Douglass, William A., and Jon Bilbao. *Amerikanuak: Basques in the New World*. Reno: University of Nevada Press, 1975.

Douglass, William A., Richard W. Etulain, and William H. Jacobsen, Jr., eds. *Anglo-American Contributions to Basque Studies: Essays in Honor of Jon Bilbao*. Reno: Desert Research Institute Publications on the Social Sciences, 1977.

Douglass, William A., and Richard H. Lane. *Basque Sheepherders of the American West: A Photographic Documentary*. Reno: University of Nevada Press, 1985.

Edwards, Jerome E. *Pat McCarran: Political Boss of Nevada*. Reno: University of Nevada Press, 1982.

Eiguren, Joseph. *Kashpar*. Caldwell, Idaho: Caxton Press, 1988.

Elliott, J. H. *Imperial Spain, 1469–1716*. New York: St. Martin's Press, 1963.

Etulain, Richard W., ed. *Basques of the Pacific Northwest*. Pocatello, Idaho: Idaho State University Press, 1991.

Fedden, Katherine. *The Basque Country*. London: A. & C. Black, Ltd., 1921.

Fisher, Anne B. *The Salinas: Upside-Down River*. New York: Farrar and Rinehart, 1945.

Flinn, Michael W. *The European Demographic System, 1500–1820*. Baltimore: The Johns Hopkins University Press, 1981.

Friis, Leo. *Orange County Through Four Centuries*. Santa Ana, Calif.: Pioneer Press, 1965.

Gabaccia, Donna. *From the Other Side: Women, Gender, and Immigrant Life in the United States, 1820–1990*. Bloomington: Indiana University Press, 1994.

Gabbett, John Raymond. *History of Riverside City and County*. Riverside: Record Publishing Company, 1935.

Gachiteguy, Adrien. *Les Basques dan l'ouest Americain*. Bordeaux: Edición Ezkita, 1955.

Gallop, Rodney. *A Book of the Basques*. London: Macmillan, 1930; reprint, Reno: University of Nevada Press, 1970.

Goti Iturriaga, José Luís, ed. *Primera semana internacional de antropología Vasca*. Bilbao: La Gran Enciclopedia Vasca, 1971.

Goyeneche, Eugene. *Le Pays Basque: Soule, Labourd and Basse Navarre*. Pau: Societe d'Editions Regionales et de Diffusión, 1979.

Greenleaf, Richard. *Zumárraga and His Family Letters to Viscaya, 1536–1548*. Washington, D.C.: Academy of America Franciscan History, 1979.

Groefsema, Olive. *Elmore County: Its Historical Gleanings*. Boise: Caxton Press, 1949.

Groth, Paul. *Living Downtown: The History of Residential Hotels in the United States*. Berkeley: University of California Press, 1994.

Guinn, James M. *History of the State of California and Biographical Record of the San Joaquin Valley*. Chicago: Chapman Publishing Company, 1905.

Hallan, Pamela. *Dos Cientos Años in San Juan Capistrano*. San Juan Capistrano, Calif.: Layman Publishing Company, 1975.

Handlin, Oscar., ed. *Immigration as a Factor in American History*. Englewood Cliffs, N.J.: Prentice-Hall, 1959.

———. *The Uprooted*. Boston: Little, Brown, 1951.

Hanley, Mike, and Ellis Lucia. *Owyhee Trails: The West's Forgotten Corner*. Caldwell, Idaho: Caxton Press, 1988.

Hansen, Marcus Lee. *The Atlantic Migration, 1607–1860*. Cambridge, Mass.: Harvard University Press, 1940.

———. *The Immigrant in American History*. Edited by Arthur H. Schlesinger. Cambridge, Mass.: Harvard University Press, 1942.

Henderson, Robert. *Bat, Ball, and Bishop*. New York: Rockport Press, 1947.

Hennigson, Gustav. *The Witches' Advocate: Basque Witchcraft and the Spanish Inquisition, 1609–1614*. Reno: University of Nevada Press, 1980.

Higham, John. *Strangers in the Land*. New Brunswick, N.J.: Rutgers University Press, 1955.

*History of Stockton Fire Department*. Stockton: Atwood Printing, 1908.

Holmes, Elmer Wallace. *History of Riverside County, California*. Los Angeles: Historical Record Company, 1912.

Hunt, Rockwell D. *California and Californians*. Vol. 3. Chicago: Lewis Publishing Company, 1932.

Hutchinson, Edward P. *Legislative History of American Immigration Policy, 1798–1965*. Philadelphia: University of Pennsylvania Press, 1981.

Iberlin, Dollie. *The Basque Web: A Story about the Basque People of Buffalo, Wyoming*. Buffalo, Wyo.: Buffalo Bulletin, 1981.

Iberlin, Dollie, and David Romtvedt, eds. *Buffalotarrak: An Anthology of the Basque People of Buffalo, Wyoming*. Buffalo, Wyo.: Red Hills Publications, 1995.

Irigaray, Louis, and Theodore Taylor. *A Shepherd Watches, A Shepherd Sings*. Garden City, N.Y.: Doubleday and Company, 1977.

Jackman, Jarrell C. *Felipe de Goicoechea: Santa Barbara Presidio Comandante*. Santa Barbara, Calif.: Ansom Luman Press, 1993.

Jackson, Gabriel. *The Making of Medieval Spain*. New York: Harcourt Brace and Jovanovich, 1972.

Jacob, James E. *Hills of Conflict: Basque Nationalism in France*. Reno: University of Nevada Press, 1994.

Jai Aldi 1990 Commission. *Jai Aldi '90: International Basque Cultural Festival Program Booklet*. Boise, Idaho: Idaho Centennial 1990.

Johnson, A. J. B. *Louisbourg: The Phoenix Fortress*. Halifax, Nova Scotia: Nimbus Publishing Company, 1990.

Juvney, Honoria. *History of Sonoma County, California*. San Francisco: S. J. Clarke Publishing Company, 1926.

Land, Barbara, and Myrick Land. *A Short History of Reno*. Reno: University of Nevada Press, 1995.

Larrea, M. A., and Rafael M. Mieg. *Introduction to the History of the Basque Country*. Translated by Michael G. Fast. Madrid: Ediciones Beramar, 1985.

Lasagabaster, Jesus Maria, ed. *Contemporary Basque Fiction: An Anthology*. Reno: University of Nevada Press, 1990.

Laxalt, Robert. *The Basque Hotel*. Reno: University of Nevada Press, 1989.

———. *Child of the Holy Ghost*. Reno: University of Nevada Press, 1992.

———. *The Governor's Mansion*. Reno: University of Nevada Press, 1994.

———. *In a Hundred Graves*. Reno: University of Nevada Press, 1972.

———. *Nevada: A Bicentennial History*. New York: William Norton and Company, 1977.

———. *Sweet Promised Land*. New York: Harper Brothers, 1957; reprint, Reno: University of Nevada, 1986.

Legarreta, Dorothy. *The Guernica Generation: Basque Refugee Children of the Spanish Civil War*. Reno: University of Nevada Press, 1984.

Lenski, Gerald. *The Religious Factor*. Garden City, N.Y.: Doubleday and Company, 1961.

Loyer, Ferdinand, and Charles Beaudreau. *Le Guide Français de Los Angeles et du sud de la Californie*. Los Angeles: Loyer and Beaudreau, 1932.

Lynch, John. *Spain Under the Hapsburgs*. Vol. 1, *Empire and Absolutism, 1516–1598*. New York: Oxford University Press, 1964.

McGowan, Joseph A. *History of Sacramento Valley*. New York: Lewis Publishing Company, 1939.

McGregor, Alexander Campbell. *Counting Sheep: From Open Range to Agribusiness on the Columbia Plateau*. Seattle: University of Washington Press, 1982.

McGrew, Clarence A. *City of San Diego and San Diego County*. Chicago: American Historical Society, 1922.

McGroarty, John Stephen. *California of the South: A History*. Los Angeles: S. J. Clarke Publishing, 1935.

Malone, Michael P., ed. *Historians and the American West*. Lincoln: University of Nebraska Press, 1983.
Mayeur, Jean-Marie, and Madeliene Reberioux. *The Third Republic from Its Origin to the Great War, 1871–1914*. Translated by J. R. Foster. New York: Cambridge University Press, 1973.
*Memorial and Biographical History of the Counties of Fresno, Tulare, and Kern, California*. Chicago: Lewis Publishing Company, 1892.
Michelena, Luís. *Apellidos Vascos*. San Sebastián: Editorial Txertoa, 1973.
Millard, Frank Bailey. *The History of San Francisco Bay Region*. San Francisco: American Historical Society, Inc., 1924.
Miller, Thelma B. *History of Kern County, California*. Chicago: S. J. Clarke Publishing Company, 1929.
Miller, Townsend. *The Castles and the Crown*. New York: Coward-McCann, 1963.
Monteiro, Mariana. *Legends and Popular Tales of the Basque People*. 1887. Reprint, New York: Benjamin Bloom, 1971.
Moore, Christopher. *Fortress of Louisbourg*. Louisbourg, Cape Breton, Nova Scotia: College of Cape Breton Press, 1981.
Morgan, Wallace M. *History of Kern County, California, with Biographical Sketches*. Los Angeles: Historic Record Company, 1914.
Mourant, A. E. *The ABO Blood Groups*. Springfield, Ill.: Charles Thomas, 1958.
———. *Blood Relations: Blood Groups and Anthropology*. London: Oxford University Press, 1983.
Moynihan, Daniel P., and Nathan Glazer. *Beyond the Melting Pot*. Cambridge, Mass.: Massachusetts Institute of Technology Press, 1963.
Mylar, Isaac L. *Early Days at the Mission San Juan Bautista*. Watsonville, Calif.: Valley Publishers and San Juan Historical Society, 1970.
Newmark, Maurice H., and Marco R. Newmark. *Sixty Years in Southern California, 1853–1913: Containing Reminiscences of Harris Newmark*. 4th ed. Los Angeles: Zeitlin and Ver Brugge, 1970.
Novak, Michael. *The Rise of the Unmeltable Ethnic*. New York: Macmillan Company, 1972.
Ortega y Gasset, José, ed. *Del espíritu de los Vascos*. Bilbao: Publicaciones de Editorial Vasca, 1920.
Ossa Echaburu, Rafael. *Pastores y pelotaris Vascos en U.S.A.* Bilbao: Ediciones de la Caja de Ahorros Vizcaína, 1963.
Ott, Sandra. *Circle of Mountains: A Basque Sheepherding Community*. Oxford: Clarendon Press, 1981.
Paquette, Mary Grace. *Basques to Bakersfield*. Bakersfield, Calif.: Kern Historical Society, 1982.
———. *Lest We Forget: The History of the French in Kern County*. Bakersfield, Calif.: Kern County Historical Society, 1978.
Paris, Beltran, and William A. Douglass. *Beltran: Basque Sheepman of the American West*. Reno: University of Nevada Press, 1979.

Patterson, Edna B., and Louise A. Beebe. *Halleck Country: The Story of the Land and Its People*. Helen Marye Thomas Memorial Series, no. 4. Reno: University of Nevada Press, 1982.

Patterson, Edna B., Louise A. Ulph, and Victor Goodwin. *Nevada's Northeast Frontier*. Reno: University of Nevada Press and the Northeastern Nevada Historical Society, 1991.

Payne, Stanley G. *Basque Nationalism*. Reno: University of Nevada Press, 1975.

Phillips, Michael James. *History of Santa Barbara County, California*. Chicago: S. J. Clarke Publishing, 1927.

Pipkin, Don, and Chris Brewer. *Bakersfield and Kern, California*. Bakersfield, Calif.: Brewer-Pipkin Publications, 1986.

Pipkin, George G. *Pete Aguerreberry: Death Valley Prospector and Gold Miner*. Trona, Calif.: Murchison Publications, 1982.

Pitt, Leonard. *The Decline of the Californios*. Berkeley: University of California Press, 1966.

Pleasants, J. E. *History of Orange County, California*. Los Angeles: Finnell and Sons, 1931.

Robinson, W. W. *The Old Spanish and Mexican Ranchos of Orange County*. Los Angeles: Title Insurance and Trust Company, 1954.

Roske, Ralph J. *Everyman's Eden: A History of California*. New York: Macmillan Company, 1968.

Sahlins, Peter. *Boundaries: The Making of France and Spain in the Pyrenees*. Berkeley: University of California Press, 1989.

Sauer, Carl O. *Northern Mists*. Berkeley: University of California Press, 1968.

Shattuck, Louise. *Andy Little: Idaho Sheep King*. Caldwell, Idaho: Caxton Press, 1990.

Shepperson, Wilbur S., ed. *East of Eden, West of Zion: Essays on Nevada*. Reno: University of Nevada Press, 1989.

———. *Restless Strangers: Nevada's Immigrants and Their Interpreters*. Reno: University of Nevada Press, 1970.

Silen, Sol. *La historia de Vascongadas de los Estados Unidos*. New York: Los Novedades, 1917.

Simpson, Peter K. *The Community of Cattlemen: A Social History of the Cattle Industry in Southeastern Oregon, 1869–1912*. Moscow, Idaho: University of Idaho Press, 1987.

Society of Basque Studies in America, ed. *Proceedings of the First International Basque Conference in North America*. Bilbao: La Gran Enciclopedia Vasca, 1985.

Sowell, Thomas. *Ethnic America*. New York: Basic Books, Inc., 1981.

Swanner, Charles P. *Santa Ana: A Narrative of Yesterday, 1870–1910*. Claremont: Saunder Press, 1953.

Talbert, Thomas. *Historical Volume and Reference Works of Southern California*. Whittier: Historical Publishers, 1963.

Thomas, Hugh. *The Spanish Civil War*. New York: Harper and Row, 1977.
Tinkham, George H. *History of San Joaquin County*. Los Angeles: Historic Record Company, 1923.
Tompkins, Walter A. *Santa Barbara: Past and Present*. Santa Barbara, Calif.: Tecolete Books, 1975.
———. *Thomas Storke: California Editor*. Santa Barbara, Calif.: Pacific Coast Publications, 1968.
———, ed. *Thompson and West's History of Santa Barbara and Ventura Counties*. Berkeley: Howell-North, 1961.
Tuck, James A., and Robert Grenier. *Red Bay, Labrador: World Whaling Capital, 1550–1600*. St John's, Newfoundland: Atlantic Archaeology Ltd., 1989.
United States Farm Land Company. *The Chowchilla Ranch*. San Francisco: Sunset Publishing House, 1913.
Urza, Carmelo. *Solitude: Art and Symbolism in the National Basque Monument*. Reno: University of Nevada Press, 1993.
Urza, Monique. *The Deep Blue Memory*. Reno: University of Nevada Press, 1993.
Vandor, Paul E. *History of Fresno County, California, with Biographical Sketches*. Los Angeles: Historic Record Company, 1919.
Veyrin, Philippe. *Les Basques de Labourd, de Soule et de Basse Navarre, leur historie et leur traditions*. Bayonne: Museé Basque, 1942.
Weinberg, Roy D. *Eligibility for Entry to the United States of America*. Dobbs Ferry, N.Y.: Oceana Publications, 1967.
Wentworth, E. N. *America's Sheep Trails*. Ames, Iowa: Iowa College Press, 1948.
Wentworth, E. N., and C. W. Towne. *Shepherd's Empire*. Norman: University of Oklahoma Press, 1945.
Wright, Gordon. *Rural Life in France: The Peasants in the Twentieth Century*. Stanford, Calif.: Stanford University Press, 1964.
Ziesing, Grace H. *Archeological Investigations of the Vasco Adobe Site, CA-CCO-470H, for the Los Vaqueros Project, Alamenda and Contra Costa Counties, California*. Rohnert Park, Calif.: Anthropological Studies Center, Sonoma State University Academic Foundation, 1997.
Zubiri, Nancy. *A Travel Guide to Basque America: Families, Feasts, and Festivals*. Reno: University of Nevada Press, 1998.
Zubizarreta, Trisha Clausen. *Chorizo, Beans, and Other Things: A Poetic Look at the Basque Culture*. Boise, Idaho: Lagun Txiki Press, 1987.
Zumalde, Iñaki. *Pedro Altube y los pastores en los Estados Unidos*. San Sebastián: Real Sociedad Bascongada, 1980.

## ARTICLES

Alberdi, F., A. C. Alison, B. S. Blumberg, Elizabeth W. Ikin, and A. C. Mourant. "Blood Groups of the Spanish Basques." *Journal of the Royal Anthropological Institute* 87 (July–December 1957): 217–21.
Barandiarán, José Miguel. "Features of Popular Basque Mentality." In *Primera*

*semana internacional de antropología Vasca*, edited by José Luís Goti Iturriaga, 87–102.

Barkham, Selma H. "The Basques: Filling a Gap in Our History Between Jacques Cartier and Champlain." *Canadian Geographical Journal* 96 (February–March 1978): 8–19.

———. "Guipuzcoan Shipping in 1571 with Particular Reference to the Decline of the Transatlantic Fishing Industry." In *Anglo-American Contributions to Basque Studies*, edited by William A. Douglass, Richard W. Etulain, and William H. Jacobsen, Jr., 73–82.

Bieter, J. Patrick. "Folklore of the Boise Basques." *Western Folklore* 24 (1965): 262–66.

———. "Letemendi's Boarding House: A Basque Cultural Institution in Idaho." *Idaho Yesterdays* 37 (spring 1993): 2–9.

———. "Reluctant Shepherds: The Basques in Idaho." *Idaho Yesterdays* (summer 1957): 11–17.

Bilbao, Jon. "Basques in the Philippine Islands," *Basque Studies Program Newsletter* 20 (July 1979): 5–6.

Bilbao, Julio. "Basque Names in Early Idaho." *Idaho Yesterdays* 15 (summer 1971): 26–29.

Bloom, Leonard. "Settlement of Basques in New England." *Basque Studies Program Newsletter* 15 (November 1976): 1–3.

Boyd, William, and Lyle G. Boyd. "New Data on Blood Groups and Other Inherited Factors in Europe and Egypt." *American Journal of Physical Anthropology* 28 (1937–1938): 49–70.

Breton, Raymond. "Institutional Completeness of Ethnic Communities and Personal Relations of Immigrants." *American Journal of Sociology* 70 (September 1964):193–205.

Brown, Donald. "Emmett Elizondo: Sheepman Extraordinary." *Letter* (spring–summer 1980): 5–10.

Burchell, Robert A. "Opportunity and the Frontier: Wealth-Holding in Twenty-Six Northern California Counties, 1848–1880." *Western Historical Quarterly* 18 (April 1987): 177–96.

Campbell, Craig. "The Basque-American Ethnic Area: Geographical Perspectives on Migration, Population, and Settlement." *Journal of Basque Studies* 6 (1985): 83–104.

Caro Baroja, Julio. "Psychological, Social, and Legal Problems of Witchcraft in the Basque Country." In *Primera semana internacional de antropología Vasca*, edited by José Luís Goti Iturriaga, 61–86.

Chalmers, J. N., Elizabeth W. Ikin, and A. E. Mourant. "The ABO, MN and Rh Blood Groups of the Basque People." *American Journal of Physical Anthropology* 7 (December 1949): 529–44.

Crawford, Charlotte. "The Position of Women in a Basque Fishing Community." In *Anglo-American Contributions to Basque Studies*, edited by William A. Douglass, Richard W. Etulain, and William H. Jacobsen, Jr., 145–52.

Cressman, L. S., and Anthony Yturri. "The Basques in Oregon." *Commonwealth Review* 20 (March 1938): 367–80.

Daniel, Glyn. "Megalithic Monuments." *Scientific American* 243 (July 1980): 78–90.

del Valle, Teresa. "The Current Status of the Anthropology of Women: Models and Paradigms." In *Essays in Basque Social Anthropology and History*, edited William A. Douglass, 129–48.

Douglass, William A. "The Basques." *Basque Studies Program Newsletter* 1 (November 1968): 5–6.

———. "The Basques." In *Harvard Encyclopedia of American Ethnic Groups*, edited by Stephan Thernstrom, 173–78. Cambridge, Mass.: Harvard University Press, 1980.

———. "Basque Identity: Past Perspectives and Future Prospects." Symposium on Basque Language and Culture, Jai Aldi '90, Boise, Idaho, June 1990.

———. "Basques in Australia." *Basque Studies Program Newsletter* 18 (March 1978): 4–6.

———. "The Basques in Nevada." In *Nevada: Official Bicentennial Book*, edited by Stanley Payne, 430–31. Vegas: Nevada Publications, 1976.

———. "The Basques of the American West." *Nevada Historical Quarterly* 13, no. 4 (1970): 12–25.

———. "Borderland Influences in a Navarrese Village." In *Anglo-American Contributions to Basque Studies: Essays in Honor of Jon Bilbao*, edited William A. Douglass, Richard W. Etulain, and William H. Jacobsen, Jr., 135–44.

———. "Counting Basques: The U. S. Census." *Basque Studies Program Newsletter* 28 (November 1983): 3–7.

———. "Ethnic Categorization in the 1980 United States Census: The Basque Example." *Government Publications Review* 12 (1985): 289–96.

———. "Home Is a Hotel: Nevada's Basque Establishments." *Nevada Magazine* 39 (spring 1979): 22–23.

———. "In the Mirror: Reflections on the Origins of the Basque Studies Program" and "Through a Looking Glass or Becoming the Datum." Twenty-fifth Anniversary of the Basque Studies Program, Reno, Nevada, 29 April and 1 May 1992.

———. "Lonely Lives under the Big Sky." *Natural History* (March 1973): 28–29.

———. "On the Naming of Arizona." *Names: The Journal of the American Name Society* 27 (December 1979): 217–34.

———. "Re-counting Basques." *Basque Studies Program Newsletter* 47 (April 1993): 5–8.

———. "Rural Exodus in Two Spanish Basque Villages: A Cultural Explanation." *American Anthropologist* 73 (October 1971): 1100–14.

———. "Serving Girls and Sheepherders: Emigration and Continuity in a Spanish Basque Village." In *The Changing Faces of Rural Spain*, edited by Joseph Aceves and William A. Douglass, 45–61. New York: John Wiley and Sons, 1976.

———. "The Vanishing Basque Sheepherder." *American West* 17 (July/August 1980): 30–31, 59–61.

Doyaga, Emilia. "The History of Eusko-Extea of New York." In *Proceedings of the First International Basque Conference in North America*, edited by the Society of Basque Studies in America, 131–41. Bilbao: La Gran Enciclopedia Vasca, 1982.

Echeverria, Jeronima. "Basque 'Tramp Herders' on Forbidden Ground: Early Grazing Controversies in California's National Reserves." *Locus: An Historical Journal of Regional Perspectives* 4 (fall 1991): 41–58.

———. "California's Basque Hotels and Their *Hoteleros*." In *Essays in Basque Social Anthropology and History*, edited by William A. Douglass, 297–316.

———. "*Euskaldun andreak*: Basque Women as Hard Workers, *Hoteleras*, and Matriarchs." *Writing the Range: Race, Class, and Gender in the Women's West*, edited by Sue Armitage and Elizabeth Jamison. Norman: University of Oklahoma Press, 1997.

———. "Lorenzo Echanis: Coming to Amerika, Basque-Style." *Journal of the Society of Basque Studies in America* 9 (1989): 83–90.

———. "Old World *Bertsolaris* to Basque-American Sages: A Tradition of Storytelling." *Journal of the Society of Basque Studies in America* 11 and 12 (1991–1992): 1–6.

———. "Ole Man Landa's Place: Reflections on Southern California Sheep-Raising." *Journal of the Society of Basque Studies* 10 (1990): 47–56.

———. "A Pilgrimage to Red Bay, Summer Home of Basque Whaling Fleets Centuries Ago." *Journal of the Society of Basque Studies* 14 (1994): 49–57.

———. "Were the Basques Uprooted?" *Journal of the Society of Basque Studies* 7 (1986): 63–74.

Edlefson, John. "Enclavement Among Southwest Idaho Basques." *Social Forces* 29 (December 1950): 155–58.

Etulain, Richard W. "Basque Beginnings in the Pacific Northwest." *Idaho Yesterdays* 18 (spring 1974): 26–32.

———. "Basques in Western North American Literature." In *Anglo-American Contributions to Basque Studies*, edited by William A. Douglass, Richard W. Etulain, and William H. Jacobsen, Jr. 7–18.

———. "Basques of the American West: Some Problems for the Historian." In *Basques of the Pacific Northwest*, edited by Richard W. Etulain, 86–90.

———. "Basques of Yakima, Washington." *Basque Studies Program Newsletter* 10 (May 1974): 8.

———. "Shifting Interpretations of Western Cultural History." In *Historians and the American West*, edited by Michael P. Malone, 414–33. Lincoln: University of Nebraska, 1983.

Fagan, Brian. "The Basques of Red Bay." *Archaeology* 46 (September–October 1993): 44–51.

Fallows, James. "Immigration: How It's Affecting Us." *Atlantic* (November 1983): 45–108.

Fereday, Lynne. "Descriptive Study of the Integration and Assimilation of Basques in Boise, Idaho." In *The Basques—A Preservation of a Culture*. Boise: Fereday Memorial, 1971.

Frank, Roslyn M. "The Religious Role of the Woman in Basque Culture." In *Anglo-American Contributions to Basque Studies*, edited by William A. Douglass, Richarad W. Etulain, and William H. Jacobsen, Jr., 153–60.

Gaardner, Lorin. "Preliminary Comments on the Basque Colony in Mexico City." In *Anglo-American Contributions to Basque Studies*, edited by William A. Douglass, Richard W. Etulain, and William H. Jacobsen, Jr., 59–69.

Galbís, Ignacio. "Basques in Cuba: The Republican Years." In *Proceedings of the First International Basque Conference in North America*, edited by Society of Basque Studies, 143–53.

Garate, Donald T. "Basque Names, Nobility, and Ethnicity on the Spanish Frontier." *Colonial Latin American Historical Review* 2 (winter 1993): 77–104.

Georgetta, Clel. "Sheep in Nevada." *Nevada Historical Society Quarterly* 8, no. 2 (summer 1965): 26–32.

Goti Iturriaga, José Luís. "Blood Groups in Our Population." In *Primera semana internacional de antropología Vasca*, edited by José Luís Goti Iturriaga, 35–60.

Grandmontagne, Francisco. *Los immigrantes prósperos*. Madrid: M. Aguilar, 1933.

Greenwood, Davydd. "Continuity in Change: Spanish Basque Ethnicity as a Historical Process." In *Ethnic Conflict in the Western World*, edited by Milton J. Esman, 81–102. Ithaca: Cornell University Press, 1977.

———. "Tourism as an Agent of Change: A Spanish Basque Case." *Ethnology* 11 (January 1972): 80–91.

Handlin, Oscar. "Immigration in American Life: A Reappraisal." In *Immigration in American History*, edited by Henry Steele Commager, 8–25. Minneapolis: University of Minnesota Press, 1961,

Hansen, Marcus Lee. "The Third Generation." In *Children of the Uprooted*, edited by Oscar Handlin, 43–46. Englewood Cliffs, N.J.: Prentice-Hall, 1959.

———. "The Third Generation in America." *Commentary* 14 (November 1952): 492–500.

Harkness, Ione B. "Basque Settlement in Oregon." *Oregon Historical Quarterly* 34 (December 1933): 273–75.

Hazeltine, Ben, Charles Salisbury, and Harry Taylor. "They Came for Range and Left a Heritage." *Western Livestock Journal* (August 1961): 99–109.

Heiberg, Marianne. "Inside the Moral Community: Politics in a Basque Village." In *Basque Politics*, edited by William A. Douglass, 285–308.

Higham, John. "Immigration." In *Comparative Approach to American History*, edited by C. Vann Woodward, 91–105. New York: Basic Books, 1968.

Holbert, Gretchen. "Elko's Overland Hotel." *Northeastern Nevada Historical Society Quarterly* 5 (winter 1975): 13–20.

Holbert-Osa, Gretchen. "The Overland: The Last Basque Hotel." In *Essays in Basque Social Anthropology and History*, edited by William A. Douglass, 317–23.

Hovey, Carol. "The Spanish Ranch." *Journal of Basque Studies* 5 (1984): 84–101.

Hunbelle, Danielle. "The Basques—The Anthropologist's Most Baffling Case." *Realitiés* 192: 78–83.

Jacob, James E. "Ethnic Identity and the Crisis of Separation of Church and State: The Case of the Basques of France, 1870–1914." *Journal of Church and State* 24 (spring 1982): 303–20.

———. "The French Revolution and the Basques of France." In *Basque Politics*, edited by William A. Douglass, 51–102.

Jones, Maldwyn. "Oscar Handlin." In *Pastmasters*, edited by Marcus Cunliffe and Robin W. Winks, 239–77. New York: Harper and Row, 1969.

Lane, Richard. "Basque Tree Carvings." *Northeastern Nevada Historical Society Quarterly* 1 (winter 1971): 1–7.

———. "Trouble in the Sweet Promised Land: Basques in Early Twentieth-Century Northeastern Nevada. In *Anglo-American Contributions to Basque Studies*, edited by William A. Douglass, Richard W. Etulain, and William H. Jacobsen, Jr., 33–42.

Larrea, M. A., and Rafael M. Mieg. "La Diputación Géneral del Señorio de Viscaya, 1841–1866." *Journal of Basque Studies* 6 (summer 1985): 8–20.

Larronde, Suzanne. "The Basque Who Won the West." *Modern Maturity* (September 1982): 32–36.

Laxalt, Robert. "Basque Sheepherders: Lonely Sentinels of the American West." *National Geographic* 129 (June 1966): 870–88.

———. "Land of Ancient Basques." *National Geographic* 134 (August 1968): 240–77.

———. "The Other Nevada." *National Geographic* 145 (June 1974): 733–61.

———. "The Sheepmen." *Nevada Magazine* 2 (1977): 22–25.

Lazerwitz, Bernard, and Louis Rowitz. "The Three Generations Hypothesis." *American Journal of Sociology* 69 (June 1964): 529–38.

Leizaola, Fermín. "Aspects of Pastoral and Nomadic Life in the Basque Country." In *Primera semana internacional de antropología Vasca*, edited by José Luís Goti Iturriaga, 533–50.

Levine, Morton E. "The Basques." *Natural History* 76 (April 1967): 45–50.

Link, Diane. "The American Basques." *Literature of Ethnic Minorities* (spring 1974): 70–76.

Luebke, Frederick C. "Ethnic Minorities in the American West." In *Historians and the American West*, edited by Michael P. Malone, 387–413. Lincoln: University of Nebraska, 1983.

Magee, Molly. "A Day on the Mountain with the Basque Buckaroos." *Nevada Highways and Parks* 26 (Fall 1966): 4–9, 50–51.

Mercier, Laurie. "Idaho's Basque Americans." In *Idaho's Ethnic Heritage*, vol. 2., edited by Laurie Mercier, Carole Simon- Smolonski. Washington, D.C.: U.S. Department of Interior, 1990.

Michelena, Luís. "Language and Culture." In *Primera semana internacional de antropología Vasca*, edited by José Luís Goti Iturriaga, 305–39.

Monreal, Gregorio. "Annotations Regarding Basque Traditional Political Thought in the Sixteenth Century." In *Basque Politics*, edited by William A. Douglass, 19–50.

Mougeon, Raymond, and François Mougeon. "Basque Language Survival in Rural Communities from the *Pays Basque*, France." In *Anglo-American Contributions to Basque Studies*, edited by William A. Douglass, Richard W. Etulain, and William H. Jacobsen, Jr., 97–117.

Moulinier, Jacques. "The Rh Factor in Southwestern France: An Examination of the Basque and Bearnais Populations." *American Journal of Physical Anthropology* 7 (December 1949): 595–98.

Mourant, A. E. "Blood Groups of the Basques." *Nature* (October 1947): 505–6.

Moya, Jesus. "Blood Groups of the Kell and Duffy Systems in Basques." In *Primera semana internacional de antropología Vasca*, edited by José Luís Goti Iturriaga, 551–62.

Mugica, Fernando Maria. "The Basques in Sport." In *Primera semana internacional de antropología Vasca*, edited by José Luís Goti Iturriaga, 515–26.

Munro, Sarah Baker. "Basque Folklore in Southeastern Oregon." *Oregon Historical Quarterly* 76 (June 1975): 153–86.

Myers, Sandra L. "Women in the West." In *Historians and the American West*, edited by Michael P., 369–86. Malone. Lincoln: University of Nebraska.

Nelson, Barney. "Sheepherders in the Sierra." *Range: Cowboy Caretakers on America's Outback* (fall 1993): 13–15.

Nolan, John E. "Life in the Land of the Basques." *National Geographic* 105 (February 1954): 147–86.

Norris, Monty. "Chef's Special." *Friends Magazine* 36 (October 1979): 26–28.

Payne, Stanley G. "Carlism—Basque or 'Spanish' Traditionalism?" In *Anglo-American Contributions to Basque Studies*, edited by William A. Douglass, Richard W. Etulain, and William H. Jacobsen, Jr., 119–26.

Reade, John. "The Basques in North America." *Royal Canadian Society Proceedings and Transactions* 6 :21–36.

Reid, Alistair. "Letters from *Euzkadi*." *The New Yorker* 37: 171–93.

Roberts, D. F., E. Coope, and B. Kerr. "Dermatoglyphic Variation among the Spanish Basques." *Man* 11 (December 1976): 492–504.

Rothman, David. "*The Uprooted:* Thirty Years Later." *Reviews in American History* 10 (September 1982): 311–19.

Sax, Bradford. "Sons of the Pyrenees in the Northwest." *Travel Magazine*, September 1942, 10–15.

Shepperson, Wilbur. "An Essay on *Amerikanuak*." *Nevada Historical Society Quarterly* 14 (summer 1976): 139–44.

Strauss, Lawrence Guy, Geoffrey A. Clark, Jesus Altuna, and Jesus A. Ortea. "Ice-Age Subsistence in Northern Spain." *Scientific American* 242 (June 1980): 142–52.

Subramanian, Sribala. "The Story in Our Genes." *Time*, January 16, 1995, 54–55.

Tuck, James A. "Discovery in Labrador: A 16th-Century Basque Whaling Port and Its Sunken Fleet." *National Geographic* 168 (July 1985): 50–57.

Tuck, James A., and Robert Grenier. "A 16th-Century Whaling Station in Labrador." *Scientific American* 245 (November 1981): 180–88.

Turner, Fredrick. "Triumph of the 'Bascos.'" *Country Journal* 8 (August 1986): 62–68.

Urla, Jacqueline. "Reinventing Basque Society: Cultural Difference and the Quest for Modernity 1918–1936." In *Essays in Basque Social Anthropology and History*, edited by William A. Douglass, 149–76.

Urquidi, Teresa B. "An Historical Relationship between *Pelote* and the Church in Old World Basque Society." In *Proceedings of the First International Basque Conference in North America*, edited by Society of Basques Studies, 106–18.

Van Der Heide, H. M., Willy Magnee, J. J. Nan Loghem, and L. Souchard. "Blood Group Distribution in Basques." *American Journal of Human Genetics* 3 (1951): 356–61.

Walker, Marie. "San Francisco's Obrero." *Air California Magazine* (June 1980): 66–67.

Weber, Heidi. "The Mining Town Boarding House: A Surrogate Family for the Immigrant." *Pennsylvania Ethnic Studies Newsletter* (winter 1985).

"Where Cowboys and Basques Eat." *Sunset Magazine* (November 1985): 56–57.

White, Linda. "Euskaldun, Euskaldon't: Should Basque Americans Learn Euskara?" *Journal of the Society of Basque Studies in America* 15 (1995): 16–32.

———. "Female Bertsolaris: Not the Customary Thing." *Journal of the Society of Basque Studies in America* 14 (1994): 1–16.

———. "Feminism and Lexicography: Dealing with Sexist Language in a Bilingual Dictionary." *Frontiers* 10, no. 3 (1989): 61–64.

———. "Mathilde Jauregui: Symbol of Basque Woman in the West." *Basque-Studies Program Newsletter* 45 (April 1992): 11.

Worster, Donald. "New West, True West: Interpreting the Region's History." *Western Historical Quarterly* 18 (April 1987): 141–56.

Wyman, Walker D., and John D. Hart. "The Legend of Charlie Glass." *Colorado Magazine* 46 (1969): 40–54.

## SPECIAL COLLECTIONS

Amerikanuak Papers. Basque Studies Collection, Getchell Library, University of Nevada, Reno, Nev.

Borderre Hotel File. Santa Barbara Historical Society. Santa Barbara, Calif.

Correspondence Files with Former *Hoteleros*. Echeverria Collection. Fresno, Calif.

"Early Basques in Orange County." Oral History Interviews. California State University, Fullerton, Calif.
Holbert-Osa Oral History Interviews. Basque Studies Collection, Getchell Library, University of Nevada, Reno, Nev.
Ralph L. Milliken Papers. Milliken Museum. Los Banos, California.
Oyharzabal's French Hotel File. San Juan Capistrano Historical Society. San Juan Capistrano, Calif.
Mary Grace Paquette Papers. Private Collection. Sonora, Calif.
Elena Celayeta Talbott Papers. Private Collection. Los Banos, Calif.
Raimundo Urrutia Personal Papers. Idaho State Historical Library. Boise, Idaho.
*Voice of the Basques* Newspapers. Publications from January 1975 through December 1977. Boise, Idaho.
Steve Ybarrola Papers. Private Collection. Pella, Iowa.

## INTERVIEWS

Aldape, Elisa Gandolfo. Interview by Gretchen Holbert. Austin, Nev. 27 July 1986. Holbert-Osa Oral History Collection.
Anaut, Angie Goñi. Interview by author. Merced, Calif., 23 and 30 January 1987, and 17 February 1987.
Amestoy, Frank. Interview by author. Bakersfield, Calif., 2 April 1987.
Arambel, Dominica. Interview by author. Los Banos, Calif., 17 May 1987.
Arboloa, Irene, Lucy Giglierri, and Marie Arla. Interview by Gretchen Holbert. Reno, Nev., 14 May 1984. Holbert-Osa Oral History Collection.
Arguinchona, Laura, Rosie Dick, and Carmen Solasabal. Interview by author. Boise, Idaho, 22 March 1989.
Arralde, Elena Elizalde. Interview by author. Yakima, Wash., 24 July 1990.
Arriet, Josephine Manville. Interview by author. Fresno, Calif., 5 June 1987.
Arroues, Jean Pierre and Leonie Sarrail. Interview by Esther Cramer. Fullerton, Calif., 25 May 1966. Oral History Collection, California State University, Fullerton.
Arroues, Marcelina. Interview by Steve Guttman. Fullerton, Calif., 29 June 1970. Oral History Collection, California State University, Fullerton.
Ballaz, Maria. Interview by author. Fresno, Calif., 7 May 1987.
Berterretche, Monique. Interview by author. Chino, Calif., 30 April 1987.
Beterbide, William and Albert. Interview by author. Susanville, Calif., 21 May 1987.
Bordegaray, Ernie. Interview by author. Bakersfield, Calif., 31 March 1987.
Borderre, Bernard. Interview by Patricia G. Cleek. Santa Barbara, Calif., 6 December 1983. Borderre Hotel File, Santa Barbara Historical Society.
Buck, Susan C. Interview by author. Bakersfield, Calif., 31 March 1987.
Campos, Jose. Interview by author. Santa Barbara, Calif., 4 June 1987.
Campos, Juliette Robidart. Interview by author. Caruthers, Calif., 23 April 1987.

Echanis, Lentxo (Lorenzo). Interview by author. Brea, Calif., 16 February 1984. North Texas State Oral History Collection. Follow-up interviews on 28 April, 30 May, 3 June, 8 October, 1987; 22 January, 5 July, 1988; 6 February, 1989; 30 December, 1991; 4, 6 January 1992; and 2 July, 5 November 1993 in Brea, Calif.
Echanis, Lorenzo, Jr. Interview by author. Ontario, Oreg., 23 March 1989.
Echanis, Lorenzo, John Yturry, and Francisca Echeverria. Interview by author. Brea, Calif., 28 April, 30 May, 3 June, 8 October, 20 October 1987.
Echegaray, Pete. Interview by author. Merced, Calif., 7 February 1987.
Echeverria, David. Interview by author. Brea, Calif., 20 August 1975, 29 March 1980.
Echeverria, Francisca. Interview by author. Orange, Calif., 30 May 1987.
Elgorriaga, Jose. Interview by author. Fresno, Calif., 26 April 1987.
Elizalde, Janice. Interview by author. Bakersfield, Calif., 1 April 1987.
Elu, Marie. Interview by author. San Francisco, Calif., 13 May 1987.
Esain, Lyda Martinto. Interview by author. Fresno, Calif., 18 February, 24 April 1987.
Etcheverry, Elena. Interview by author. Los Banos, Calif., 17 May 1987.
Etcheverry, Odette. Interview by author. San Francisco, Calif., 15 May 1987.
Fernandez, Father Francis. Interview by author. Fort Worth, Tex., spring 1985. North Texas State Oral History Collection.
Frechou, Hilaria. Interview by author. Fresno, Calif., 7 May 1987.
Garatea, Lucy Alboitiz. Interview by author. Boise, Idaho, 22 March 1989.
Goni, Asunción Curutchet. Interview by author. Clovis, Calif., 7 May 1987.
Goñi, Jane. Interview by author. Susanville, Calif., 21 May 1987.
Goyenetche, Catherine Inda. Interview by author. San Francisco, Calif., 13 May 1987.
Holbert, Gretchen. Interview by author. Gardnerville, Nev., 20 May 1987.
Hoover, Jay. Interview by Millicent Purcell and Joe Wilson. Boise, Idaho, 1 July 1978. Idaho State Historical Library Oral History Collectio, Boise, Idaho.
Hormaechea, Jay Uberuaga. Interviews by author. Boise, Idaho, 22 March 1989, 14 June 1990, 5 September 1993.
Idiart, Jean Emile. Interview by author. San Francisco, Calif., 14 May 1987.
Inchauspe, Paul and Grace. Interview by Sylvia Arden. Pioneers of Lander County Oral History Project, fall 1994.
Iriartborde, Ganesh and Ana. Interview by author. San Francisco, Calif., 15 May 1987.
Iribarren, Grace. Interview by author. San Francisco, Calif., 14 May 1987.
Iroz, Pete. Interview by author. Stockton, Calif., 11 June 1987.
Iturbide, Michel. Interview by author. Los Banos, Calif., 26 February 1987.
Iturri, Ciriaco. Interview by author. San Francisco, Calif., 15 May 1987.
Jausoro, Jimmy. Interview by Steve Siporin. Boise, Idaho, 12 August 1982. Idaho Historical Library Oral History Collection.
Johnson, Blanche Amorena. Interview by author. Santa Barbara, Calif., 2 April, 5 June 1987.

Landa, Sofia Martiṇa. Interview by author. Brea, Calif., 25 August, 22 September 1975.
Lassart, Mrs. Albert. Interview by author. Los Banos, Calif., 26 February 1987.
Laxalt, Robert. Interview by Mateo Osa. Carson City, Nev., 31 March 1988. Holbert-Osa Oral History Collection.
Lugea, Grace R. Interview by author. San Francisco, Calif., 13 May 1987.
MacDonald, Bambi. Interview by author. San Francisco, Calif., 13 May 1987.
Maitia, Frank, Sr. Interview by author. Bakersfield, Calif., 1 April 1987.
Maitia, Louise Amestoy. Interview by author. Bakersfield, Calif., 2 April 1987.
Maitia, Mayie. Interview by author. Bakersfield, Calif., 2 April 1987.
Marquand, Juanita Iribarren. Interview by author. Fresno, Calif., 11 June 1987.
Mendiguren, Serafina Uberuaga. Interview by author. Ontario, Oreg., 23 March 1989.
Mendiguren, Serafina Uberuaga. Interview by Lois M. Palmgren. Boise, Idaho, 3 February 1982. Idaho State Historical Library Oral History Collection, Boise, Idaho.
Mujica, Mary Louise. Interview by author. Chino, Calif., 15 February 1984. North Texas State Oral History Collection.
Ondaro, Anthony. Interview by Sonia Eagle Diaz. Brea, Calif., 14 October 1971. Oral History Collection, California State University, Fullerton, Calif.
Oroz, Francisco. Interview by author. San Rafael, Calif., 14 May 1987.
Osa, Marcelino Aramaio. Interview by author. Burns, Oreg., 23 March 1989.
Osa, Margarita. Interview by Paquita Garatea. Burns, Oreg., 30 April 1989.
Oxandaboure, Benoit and Frank. Interview by Andrea Thies. Fullerton, Calif., 18 November 1971. Oral History Collection, California State University, Fullerton, Calif.
Oxandaboure, Frank. Interview by Andrea Thies. Fullerton, Calif., 22 October 1981. Oral History Collection, California State University, Fullerton, Calif.
Oxarart, Joseph Bertrand. Interview by Esther Cramer. La Habra, Calif., 22 October 1964. Oral History Collection, California State University, Fullerton, Calif.
Oyharcabal, Malvina. Interview by author. Greenbrae, Calif., 14 May 1987.
Paquette, Mary Grace. Interview by author. Sonora, Calif., 10 June 1987.
"Pushulu" and "Ambrosio." Interview by author. Chino, Calif., 30 April 1987.
Root, Elvira Yparraguirre. Interview by author. San Francisco, Calif., 14, 15 May 1987.
Sabala, Lenore Holbert. Interview by Gretchen Holbert-Osa. Elko, Nev., 1 August 1987. Holbert-Osa Oral History Collection.
Sallaberry, Melanie. Interview by author. Chino, Calif., 30 April 1987.
Sese, Steve. Interview by author. Merced, Calif., 2 March 1987.
Shobe, Augustine Sabala, and Lenore Sabala Holbert. Interview by Gretchen Holbert. Elko, Nev., 1–4 April 1986. Holbert-Osa Oral History Collection.
Smith, Helen Marquina. Interview by author. Ontario, Oreg., 23 March 1989.
Sorcabal, Dominic. Interview by author. Huntington Beach, Calif., 1 May 1987.
Sorhondo, Amelie. Interview by author. San Francisco, Calif., 13 May 1987.

Talbott, Elena Celayeta. Interview by author. Los Banos, Calif., 26 January, 26 February, 10 March, 8, 17 May 1987.

Tremewan, Anna. Interview by Gretchen Holbert. Elko, Nev., 6 August 1987. Holbert-Osa Oral History Collection.

Uhalde, Mary Jean Elgart. Interview by author. Madera, Calif., 23 April 1987.

Uberuaga, Phillip and Marie. Interview by Susan Bertram, Boise, Idaho, 17 January 1986. Idaho State Historical Library Oral History Collection, Boise, Idaho.

Uriz, Victor. Interview by author. Marysville, Calif., 5 April 1990.

Uruburu, Raymond. Interview by author. Wonder Valley, Calif., 10 February 1994.

Yriarte, John and Patricio. Interview by Adolph Flores. Brea, Calif., 3 July 1982. Oral History Collection, California State University, Fullerton, Calif.

Yturri, Anthony. Interview by author. Ontario, Oreg., 23 March 1989.

Yturri, Anthony. Interview by Oregon Historical Society. 19 November 1990. Jordan Valley File, Oregon Historical Library, Portland, Oreg.

Yturri, Ciriaco. Interview by author. San Francisco, Calif., 13 May 1987.

Yturry, John. Interview by author. Brea, Calif., 16 February 1984, 28 April 1987. North Texas State Oral History Collection.

## GOVERNMENT DOCUMENTS

Kern County *Deeds of Records Book*. Bakersfield, Calif., 1850–1952.

Los Angeles City *Deeds of Record*. Los Angeles, Calif., 1896–1920.

Orange County *Deeds of Record Book*. Santa Ana, Calif., 1899–1910.

State of California. *Genealogical Research in the California State Archives*. Sacramento: California Office of State Printing, 1969.

*United States Code*. 1976 edition, vol. 2, Title 8, "Aliens and Nationality." Washington, D.C.: Government Printing Office, 1977.

U.S. Bureau of the Census. State of California. *Population Schedules of the Sixth Census of the United States*, 1850. Washington, D.C.: National Archives Publication.

U.S. Bureau of the Census. State of California. *Population Schedules of the Seventh Census of the United States*, 1860. Washington, D.C.: National Archives Publication.

U.S. Bureau of the Census. State of California. *Population Schedules of the Eighth Census of the United States*, 1870. Washington, D.C.: National Archives Publications.

U.S. Bureau of the Census. State of California. *Population Schedules of the Ninth Census of the United States*, 1880. Washington, D.C.: National Archives Publications.

U.S. Bureau of the Census. State of California. *Population Schedules of the Thirteenth Census of the United States*, 1910. Washington, D.C.: National Archives Publications.

U.S. Congress. *Congressional Quarterly Almanac*. 81st–83rd Congresses. Washington, D.C.: Congressional Quarterly News Features, 1950–1954.

U.S. Department of Commerce. Bureau of the Census. *Ancestry of Population by State: 1980*. Washington, D.C.: Government Printing Office, 1983.

U.S. Department of the Interior. *Taylor Grazing Act: Explanation of the Law and Text of the Act*. Washington, D.C.: Government Printing Office, 1934.

U.S. House of Representatives. *Hearings Before the Committee on Public Lands*. Washington, D.C.: Government Printing Office, 1933.

Weitz, Karen J. State of California. "Aliso Street Historical Report for the City of Los Angeles," Office of Environmental Planning, Department of Transportation, Sacramento, California, January 1980.

## MAPS, ATLASES, DICTIONARIES

Allen, James Paul, and Eugene James Turner. "Basque Ancestry." In *We the People: An Atlas of American Ethnic Groups*. New York: Macmillan Publishing Company, 1988.

Aulestia, Gorka, and Linda White. *English-Basque Dictionary*. Vol. 2. Reno: University of Nevada Press, 1990.

Bancroft, H. H. *Maps of California and Nevada, 1868*. San Francisco: H. H. Bancroft and Company, 1868.

Beck, Warren A., and Ynez D. Haase. *Historical Atlas of California*. Norman: University of Oklahoma Press, 1974.

*Index Atlas of Kern County, California, 1901*. Bakersfield: Randell-Denne, 1901.

Sanborn Fire Insurance Maps, Fresno, Calif., 1915 and 1933. Fresno Public Library. Sanborn Fire Insurance Maps, Los Angeles, 1883–1887, and 1894. California State University at Northridge Map Collection.

Sanborn Fire Insurance Maps, Reno, 1918 and 1920. Special Collections, Getchell Library, University of Nevada, Reno.

Sanborn Fire Insurance Maps, San Francisco, Calif., 1899. California State University at Northridge Map Collection.

Sanborn Fire Insurance Maps, San Juan Capistrano, Calif., 1888 and 1929. California State University at Northridge Map Collection.

Sanborn Fire Insurance Map, Santa Barbara, Calif., 1892 and 1898. Santa Barbara Historical Society.

Sanborn Fire Insurance Map. Stockton, Calif., 1917. California State University at Northridge Map Collection.

Sanborn-Perris Maps, Santa Ana, Calif., 1895. Santa Ana Public Library.

*World Almanac and Encyclopedia, 1908*. New York: Press Publishing, 1908.

## DIRECTORIES

*Bakersfield and Kern City Directory, 1899*. Fresno: Marks, Weston and Cooper, 1899.

*Bakersfield and Kern City Directory, 1900*. Bakersfield: M. Cohen Publishing, 1900.

*Bakersfield and Kern City Directory, 1902–1903*. Bakersfield: W. A. Cannady, 1903.

*Bakersfield and Kern City Directory, 1904–1905*. Bakersfield: A. P. Skinner, 1905.

*Bakersfield and Kern City Directory, 1907–1908*. Oakland: Polk-Husted, 1908.

*Bakersfield City Directory, 1910, 1911, 1920*. Oakland: Polk-Husted, 1910, 1911, and 1920.

*Bakersfield City Directory, 1930*. Los Angeles: R. L. Polk and Company, 1930.

*Bakersfield City Directory, 1935, 1940*. Los Angeles: R. L. Polk and Company, 1935 and 1940.

*Boise and Ada County Directory, 1914, 1918–19, 1921, 1923, 1925, 1929, 1932–33, 1936–37, 1939–40, 1945, 1956, and 1962*. Salt Lake City: R. L. Polk and Company, 1914, 1918, 1921, 1923, 1925, 1929, 1932, 1936, 1939, 1945, 1956, and 1962.

*Boise City Directory, 1891*. Boise City, Idaho: Leadbetter and Walterbeek Publishers, 1891.

*Boise City Directory, 1899*. Boise: Statesman Printing Company, 1899.

*Boise City, Nampa, and Caldwell Directory, 1893*. Salt Lake City, Utah: Western Publishing Company, 1893.

*City and County Directory of San Joaquin, Stanislaus, Merced, and Toulumne, 1881*. San Francisco: L. M. McKenney and Company, 1881.

*Crocker-Langley San Francisco Directory, 1930, 1945–1946, 1960, 1964–65*. San Francisco: R. L. Polk and Company, 1930, 1946, 1960, and 1965.

*Directory of San Diego City, Coronado, and National City, 1892–1893*. San Diego: Olmstead and Bynon, 1893.

*Farr and Smith's 1901–2 Boise City and Ada County Directory*. Boise: Statesman Printing Company, 1901.

*The First Los Angeles City and County Directory, 1872*. Los Angeles: Ward and Ritchie Press, 1963.

*Fresno City Directory, 1903*. Fresno: Cannady and Company, 1903.

*Fresno City Directory, 1904*. Fresno: F. M. Husted and Company, 1904.

*Fresno City and County Directory, 1896*. Fresno: A. R. Denbar, 1896.

*Fresno City and County Directory, 1898*. Fresno: C. T. Corley, 1898.

*Fresno City and County Directory, 1900*. Fresno: Hodges, 1900.

*Fresno City and County Directory, 1901*. Fresno: F. M. Husted, 1901.

*Fresno City and County Directory, 1905*. Fresno: Fresno Directory Company, 1905.

*Fresno City and County Directory, 1906*. San Francisco: Crocker-Langley, 1906.

*Fresno City and County Directory, 1907*. Fresno: Polk-Husted, 1907.

*Fresno City and County Directory, 1908–1909*. Fresno: Polk-Husted, 1909.

*Fresno City and County Directory, 1910, 1911, 1912, 1913, 1914, 1915, 1916, 1917, 1918, 1919*. Fresno: Polk-Husted, 1910 through 1919.

*Fresno City and County Directory, 1920, 1921, 1922*. Fresno: Polk-Husted, 1920, 1921, and 1922.

*Fresno City and County Directory*, 1924, 1925, 1929, 1933, 1934, 1937, 1938, 1942, 1955, 1958, 1962. Fresno: Polk-Husted, 1924, 1925, 1929, 1933, 1934, 1937, 1938, 1942, 1955, 1958, and 1962.

*Fresno County Directory*, 1881–1882. Fresno: Fresno Republican, 1882.

*Fresno County Directory*, 1892–1893. Fresno: A. R. Denbar, 1893.

*Fresno County Business Directory*, 1894. Fresno: Polk-Husted, 1894.

*Langley's San Francisco Directory*, 1890, 1891, 1892, 1893, 1894. San Francisco: G. B. Wilbur, 1890, 1891, 1892, 1893, and 1894.

*Langley's San Francisco Directory and Gazette Supplement*, 1895. San Francisco: J. B. Painter, 1895.

*Los Angeles Business City Directory*, 1900, 1901. Los Angeles: Modern, 1900 and 1901.

*Los Angeles City and County Directory*, 1881–1882. Los Angeles: Southern California Directory Company, 1882.

*Los Angeles City and County Directory*, 1883–1884. Los Angeles: Los Angeles Directory Company, 1883.

*Los Angeles City and County Directory*, 1886–1887. Los Angeles: A. A. Bynon, 1886.

*Los Angeles City and County Directory*, 1887–1888. Los Angeles: A. A. Bynon, 1888.

*Los Angeles City Directory*, 1878. Los Angeles: Mirror Printing, 1878.

*Los Angeles City Directory*, 1879–1880. Los Angeles: Star Publishing, 1879.

*Los Angeles City Directory*, 1888, 1890, 1891, 1892. Los Angeles: W. H. L. Corran, 1888, 1890, 1891, and 1892.

*Los Angeles City Directory*, 1895, 1896. Los Angeles: G. W. Maxwell, 1895 and 1896.

*Los Angeles City Directory*, 1898. Los Angeles: Los Angeles Directory Company, 1898.

*Los Angeles City Directory*, 1903, 1904, 1905, 1909, 1912, 1917. Los Angeles: Los Angeles Directory and Company, 1903, 1904, 1905, 1909, 1912, and 1917.

*Los Angeles City Directory and Guide*, 1899. Los Angeles: Los Angeles Directory Company, 1899.

*Maxwell's Directory and Gazeteer*, 1894. Los Angeles: G. W. Maxwell, 1894.

*Monteith's Directory of San Diego and Vicinity*, 1889–1890. San Diego: J. C. Monteith, 1890.

*Polk's Boise City Directory*, 1902–3. Salt Lake City, Utah: R. L. Polk, 1902.

*Polk's Canyon, Gem, Washington, and Payette County Directories*, 1925. Seattle: R. L. Polk, 1925.

*Polk's Canyon, Gem, Washington, and Payette County Directories*, 1931–32. Colorado Springs, Colo.: R. L. Polk, 1932.

*Polk's Canyon, Gem, Washington, and Payette County Directories*, 1931–32. Salt Lake City, Utah: R. L. Polk, 1937.

*Polk's Merced, Madera, and Chowchilla, California Directory*, 1928–1929. San Francisco: R. L. Polk, 1928.

*Polk's Reno City, Washoe County, and Carson City Directory, 1920–1921, 1925–1926, 1929–1930, 1935, 1940, 1944, and 1950*. San Francisco: R. L. Polk, 1921, 1926, 1930, 1935, 1940, 1944, and 1950.

*Reardon's Fresno Directory, 1888–1889*. Fresno: E. P. Reardon, 1889.

*Reno City and Sparks, Nevada, Directory, 1900–1901*. Reno: *Daily Nevada State Journal*, 1901.

*Reno City and Sparks, Nevada, Directory, 1904*. Reno: Haley and Durley, 1904.

*Reno City and Sparks, Nevada, Directory, 1906*. Reno: Barndollar Durley, 1906.

*Reno and Sparks Directory with Carson City, Gardnerville, Minden, Virginia City, and Fallon, Nevada, 1912*. Reno: Reno City Directory Publishing Company, 1912.

*San Diego City and County Directory, 1887–1888*. San Diego: D. K. Donne, 1888.

*San Diego City and County Directory, 1895*. San Diego: Olmstead and Bynon,1895.

*San Diego City and County Directory, 1897*. San Diego: Olmstead, 1897.

*San Diego City and County, 1899–1900*. San Diego: Baker Brothers, 1900.

*San Diego City and County Directory, 1903, 1910*. San Diego: San Diego Directory Company, 1903 and 1910.

*San Francisco Directory, 1896, 1897, 1898, 1899, 1900, 1901, 1903, 1904, 1905, 1907, 1908, 1909, 1910, 1912, 1916, 1918, 1921*. San Francisco: H. S. Crocker, 1896, 1897, 1898, 1899, 1900, 1901, 1903, 1904, 1905, 1907, 1908, 1909, 1910, 1912, 1916, 1918, and 1921.

*Santa Barbara City and County Directory, 1909–1910*. Santa Barbara: Santa Barbara Directory Company, 1910.

*Slater's Directory of Fresno, 1891*. Fresno: J. L. Slater, 1891.

*Stockton City and County Directory, 1884–1885*. San Francisco: L. M. McKenney, 1884.

*Stockton City Directory, 1905*. San Francisco: L. M. McKenney and Company, 1905.

*Stockton City Directory, 1907, 1908, 1918*. Stockton: Polk-Husted, 1907, 1908, and 1918.

## UNPUBLISHED MATERIALS

Araujo, Frank. "Basque Cultural Ecology and Echinoccocosis in California." Ph.D. diss., University of California, Davis, 1974.

Arburua, Joseph. "Rancho Panocha de San Juan y los Carrizalitos." Family history, Reno Basque Studies Collection, Getchell Library, University of Nevada, Reno, 1970.

Arrizabalaga, Marie Pierre. "A Statistical Study of Basque Immigration into California, Nevada, Idaho and Wyoming Between 1900 and 1910." Master's thesis, University of Nevada, Reno, 1986.

Baker, Sarah. "Basque-American Folklore in Eastern Oregon." Master's thesis, University of California, Berkeley, 1972.

Baksh, Teresa Urquidi. "*Jai Alai* of the Basques." Master's thesis, San Diego State University, 1979.

Belaustegi, J. "My Grandfather Belaustegui." Class Project, Holbert-Osa Oral History Collection.

Bijuesca, Josu. "*No. 52: Un bertsopapera norteamericano*." Paper presentation, Symposium on Basques in the U.S.A., University of California, Santa Barbara, April 7, 1995.

Blaud, Henry. "The Basques." Master's thesis, College of the Pacific, Stockton, California, 1957.

Bousenard, Christine. "Basque Emigration to California and Nevada since 1960." Ph.D diss., University of Pau, France, 1976.

Castelli, Joseph. "Basques in the Western United States: A Functional Approach to Determination or Cultural Presence in the Geographic Landscape." Ph.D diss., University of Colorado, Boulder, 1972.

Dunn, Louise. "The Salt Lake City Basque Community: Atypical in the American West." Master's thesis, University of Utah, 1972.

Eagle, Sonia Jacqueline. "Work and Play Among the Basques in Southern California." Ph.D. diss., Purdue University, 1979.

Echeverria, Jeronima. "*Amerikanuak eta Asmoak*: New World Basques and Immigration Theories." Master's thesis, University of North Texas, 1984.

———. "*California-ko Ostatuak*: A History of California's Basque Hotels." Ph.D. diss., University of North Texas, Denton, 1988.

Edlefson, John. "A Sociological Study of the Basques of Southwest Idaho." Ph.D. diss., Washington State College, 1948.

Etulain, Richard W. "Basques in the American West: Some Problems for the Historian." Paper presented at Idaho Historical Conference, Boise, Idaho, March 1974.

Frye, Leland Tom. "Social Organization, Social Functions, and Social Interaction in a Basque Hotel (*Host'atua*)." Student paper, University of California, Berkeley, 1961. Basque Studies Collection.

Gaiser, Joseph. "The Basques of the Jordan Valley Area." Ph.D. diss., University of Southern California, 1944.

Garatea, Paquita Lucia. "*Burns'eko Etxekoandreak*: Basque Women Boarding House Keepers of Burns, Oregon." Master's thesis, Portland State University, 1990.

Hale, Douglas G. "Quasi-Groups and Boundary Maintenance in a Basque Hotel." Student Paper, National Science Field Foundation, 1969. Basque Studies Collection, University of Nevada, Reno.

Hayden, Kathleen. "The Boardinghouse of Santa Guisasola Bilbao." Student paper, Idaho Historical Library. Boise, Idaho.

Lane, Richard. "The Cultural Ecology of Sheep Nomadism: Northeastern Nevada, 1870–1973." Ph.D. diss., Yale University, 1974.

McCall, Grant. "Basque Americans and a Sequential Theory of Migration and Adaptation." Master's thesis, San Francisco State University, 1968.

———. "Bibliography of Materials Relating to Basque Americans." Bibliographic compilation, University of Nevada Basque Studies Library, Reno.

McCullough, Sister Flavia. "The Basques in the Northwest." Master's thesis, University of Portland, 1945.

Mallea-Olaetxe, Jose. "Juan Zumarraga, Bishop of Mexico, and the Basques: The Ethnic Connection." Ph.D. diss., University of Nevada, Reno, 1988.

Mendive, Steve. "The Basques in Marysville and Northern California." Senior paper, Basque Studies Collection, Getchell Library, University of Nevada, Reno, 1980.

Michalski, Thomas A. "A Social History of Yugoslav Immigrants in Tonopah and White Pine County, Nevada, 1860–1920." Ph.D. diss., New York State University, Buffalo, 1983.

Pagliarulo, Carol. "Basques in Stockton: A Study of Assimilation." Master's thesis, College of the Pacific, Stockton, California, 1948.

Purser, Margaret Sermons. "Community and Material Culture in Nineteenth Century Paradise Valley, Nevada." Ph.D. diss., University of California, Berkeley, 1987.

Ruiz, Allura Nason. "The Basques—Sheepmen of the West." Master's thesis, University of Nevada, Reno, 1964.

Sather, Clifford. "Marriage Patterns Among the Basques of Shosone, Idaho." Senior research paper, Reed College, Portland, Oregon, 1961.

Smith, Carrie, and Michael Baldrica. "Basqueing in the Sun: Research and Interpretation of Basque Sites on the East Side of the Tahoe National Forest." Paper presented at the Society for California Archeology Annual Meeting, 1993.

Stafford, John Allen. "Basque Ethnohistory in Kern County, California." Master's thesis, Sacramento State University, California, 1971.

Urla, Jacqueline. "Being Basque, Speaking Basque: The Politics of Language and Identity in the Basque Country." Ph.D. diss., University of California, Berkeley, 1987.

Urquidi, Richard. "History of Mountain Home Basques." Master's thesis, Boise State University, 1980.

White, Linda. "*Euskara*: A Heritage in Transition." Symposium on Basque Language and Culture: Past Perspectives and Future Prospects, Jai Aldi '90, Boise, Idaho, June 1990.

Wilcox, Mary Stevenson. "A Historical Study of the Basque Race with Special Reference to the United States." Master's thesis, University of Utah, 1939.

Works Progress Administration. "History of Stockton and San Joaquin County." Stockton Public Library, 1938.

Zucci, John E. "Italians in Toronto: Development of National Identity, 1875–1935." Ph.D. diss., University of Toronto, 1984.

## NEWSPAPERS

Bakersfield *Daily Californian*, 2 January–31 December 1895; 18 April–22 May 1900; 4 January–30 June 1905; and 1 January–30 April 1910. Advertising Sections.

"Basque Girls Meet for Their 43rd Year." *Idaho Statesman*, 27 27, 1980.
"Basque Herder Import Plan Hits Snag." *Fresno Bee*, 31 August 1952.
"Basque Hotel Closes and Reopens." *Fresno Bee*, 1 February 1980.
"Basque Restaurant Fulfills His Dreams." *Bakersfield Californian*, 26 June 1983.
Beardwood, Jack. "Mountain Home Is Typical of Basque Colonies." *Boise Capitol News*, 26 June 1937.
"Biggest, Best Basque Eatery Rising on Union." *Bakersfield Californian*, 21 October 1979.
Bonhall, Brad. "History in the Making: Basque Compiles His Culture's Contributions to San Juan Capistrano." *Los Angeles Times*, 6 February 1994.
*California'ko Eskual Herria*. Los Angeles, California, 15 July 1893–15 August 1897.
"Carlos Berriochoa, Senior: Family Patriarch Recalls Sheep Days." *Lincoln County Journal*, 10 May 1979.
Cianfarra, C. M. "Congress Passes Bill Admitting 385 Spanish Sheepherders." *New York Times*, 21 August 1954.
"Congressional Action Is Asked to Aid Sheepmen." *Fresno Bee*. 23 July 1954.
Croner, Chris. "Independent Basque Sheepmen Brought Unique Lifestyles." *Daily Argus Observer*, 5 June 1983.
Davis, Sheldon. "Stockton's Citizens from the Pyrenees Mountains." *Stockton Record*, 22 May 1917.
"Daguerre Descendents Compile History." *El Paso Herald Post*, 9 January 1974.
Drummond, Doris. "Learn Your History on Foot." *San Clemente Sun Post*, 2 August 1978.
Earthquake Clippings File, Bakersfield Public Library, 1952.
Ensunsa, David. "Services Celebrate the Resurrection: Easter Brought New Life to Basques 93 Years Ago." *Idaho Statesman*, 19 April 1987.
"Family Style Basque Restaurants." *Merced Sun-Star*, 10 October 1980.
Fenley, Lindsay. "Ex-Basque Boy Buys Le Chalet Basque." *San Rafael Independent*, 17 December 1986.
"First Basque Museum Opens in Boise." *Idaho Statesman*, 24 March 1989.
Harding, Nancy. "Basques Leave Pyrenees for Rolling Hills of Chino." *Santa Ana Register*, 15 March 1980.
Hellinger, Charles. "House Passes Senate Bill to Cancel Deportation." *New York Times*, 19 August 1954.
———. "The Long Sheep Trail Through California." *San Francisco Chronicle*, 3 July 1966.
Iturralde, Bob. "Agur Hogar Agur." *Voice of the Basques*, April 1977, 6–7.
"Labor Division Okehs Entry of 200 Sheepherders." *Fresno Bee*, 17 September 1954.
*Laurac Bat, Revista de la Sociedad Vascongada de Montevideo y Buenos Aires*, 29 November 1879–15 January 1886. Getchell Library, University of Nevada, Reno.

McEwen, Arthur. "Basques 'Invade' Fort Ord." Monterrey *Peninsula Herald*, 8 April 1961.
McKay, Tom. "Last of Pioneer San Joaquin Valley Sheep Ranchers Reviews 56 Years' Progress." *Stockton Record*, 7 May 1949.
McMillan, Doug. "Living History: Winnemucca's Basque Hotels." *Reno Gazette-Journal*, 5 March 1978.
MacNally, Pat. "Family Style Basque Restaurants." *Merced Sun Star*, 10 October 1980.
Magagnini, Stephen. "An Outpost with an Oldtime Accent." *Sacramento Bee*, 10 February 1989.
Markham, James. "For Basques, After 40 Years, Day of Truth Is Almost at Hand." *New York Times*, 5 April 1977.
Miller, Thelma. "Valley Homes of the *Paisanos*." *Fresno Bee*, 1 February 1943.
"More Herders Are Okayed." *Fresno Bee*, 5 February 1952.
Moore, Chris. "Echanis Boardinghouse Has Been Activity Center Through the Years." *Ontario, Oregon Daily Argus Observer*, 15 February 1974.
"Mouren Farming Company of Huron." *Fresno Bee*, 28 September 1981.
"Nevada's Danger." *Carson City, Nevada, Carson Morning Appeal*, 4 May 1898.
"Paul Yturri, 57, Hotel Man, Dies." *Fresno Bee*, 8 August 1950.
Pendergast, Curtis. "Mystery Race of Europe." *Fresno Bee*, 6 February 1938.
Peters, Christie. "Ranchers to Urge Bringing in More Basque Sheepherders." *New York Times*, 9 January 1955.
"Portrait of a Resident." *Idaho Statesman*, 18 May 1989.
"Reverend Bernardo Arregui." *The Boise Catholic Monthly*. Basque File, Idaho State Historical Library. Boise, Idaho.
"Rites for Basque Hotel Keeper, Restauranteur Set." *Bakersfield Californian*, 16 April 1974.
Salinger, Pierre. "Senator Lehman Protests Bills." *New York Times*, 21 June 1956.
———. "Spanish Shepherds Ease Labor Shortage." *Wall Street Journal*, 29 November 1960.
"San Juan Library Finds New Funds." *Laguna Beach News Post*, 17 August 1977.
Schindler, Merrill. "Calories Don't Count in a Basque Boardinghouse." *Los Angeles Times*, 15 July 1979.
Schuster, L. "My Friend . . . Tom Ballaz." *The Fresnopolitan*. July 1956.
Schwartz, Stephanie. "Historic Hotel Changes Hands." *San Francisco Chronicle*, 1 March 1993.
Steele, Judy M. "Basque Museum Plans Fundraiser for Expansion." *Idaho Statesman*, 26 September 1989.
Taylor, Ron. "House Committee Backs Bill to Admit 385 Basque Sheepherders." *New York Times*, 6 August 1954.
"Tehachapi Devastated." *Bakersfield Californian*, 21 July 21 1952.
"Truman Signs Basque Entry Bill." *Fresno Bee*, 28 March 1951.
Urzaiz, Jaime de. "The Guernica 'Myth.'" *Washington Post*, 1 May 1967.

"Victoria Hotel, Noted for Its Basque Food, Closes." *Fresno Bee*, 18 May 1962.
Villegas, Y. P. "Gold Mountains." *Hollister Free Lance*, 7 May 1947.
*Voice of the Basques*. Boise, Idaho, vol. 1, no. 7–vol. 3, no. 9 (June 1975–August 1977).
"Yturri, Hotel Man, Dies." Fresno *Bee*, 8 August 1950.

# Index

Page numbers in italics refer to illustrations and tables